The School Superintendency

New Responsibilities, New Leadership

M. Scott Norton
Arizona State University

L. Dean Webb
Arizona State University

Larry L. Dlugosh
University of Nebraska-Lincoln

Ward Sybouts
University of Nebraska-Lincoln

Allyn and Bacon
Boston • London • Toronto • Sydney • Tokyo • Singapore

This textbook is dedicated to the following individuals, who have made lifelong contributions to education and have served as teachers, administrators, and mentors in a distinguished manner in leadership roles as school superintendents:

Dr. Timothy J. Dyer, who served as superintendent of schools in the Wayne-Westland Community Schools, Michigan, and the Phoenix Union High School District, Arizona.

Dr. Walter M. Ostenberg, who served as superintendent of schools in the Eureka School District, Kansas, the Coffeyville School District, Kansas, and the Salina School District, Kansas.

Dr. John C. Prasch, who served as superintendent of schools in the Racine School District, Wisconsin, and the Lincoln School District, Nebraska.

Senior Editor: Ray Short
Editorial Assistant: Christine Svitila
Production Administrator: Rob Lawson
Cover Administrator: Suzanne Harbison
Manufacturing Buyer: Aloka Rathnam
Editorial-Production Service: Electronic Publishing Services Inc.

Copyright © 1996 by Allyn & Bacon
A Simon & Schuster Company
Needham Heights, Massachusetts 02194

Library of Congress Cataloging-in-Publication Data
Norton, M. Scott.
 The school superintendency / M. Scott Norton . . . [et al.].
   p.   cm.
 Includes bibliographical references and index.
 ISBN 0-205-15933-8
 1. School superintendents—United States. 2. School superintendents—United States—History. I. Title.
LB2831.72.N67   1996
371.2'011'0973—dc20
                                                                                95-34819
                                                                                CIP

Printed in the United States of America

10 9 8 7 6 5 4 3 2 1   99 98 97 96 95

Contents

Preface

A recent publication reporting findings concerning the American school superintendency noted that school superintendents hold some of the most challenging, yet satisfying, positions in American society. The report goes on to state that these school executives have become "the lightning rods" for every social and economic problem facing our nation. There is little question that American schools are inextricably related to American society and the issues and problems encountered by that society. This book assumes the position that the human element largely determines the ultimate effectiveness and success of the school organization. The extent to which all school personnel perform competently in their positions sets the foundation for the accomplishment of program outcomes. We submit that the leadership of the school superintendent is crucial for providing the climate and conditions needed for realizing human potential. The book focuses on the school superintendent as an individual and as an educational leader: the superintendent's philosophy, personal competency, and obligations as a school and community leader.

The book is organized into three major parts. Part I centers on the challenges facing the school superintendency today and in the future. The historical evolution of the position of the school superintendent reveals its challenges to become established and in many respects to survive. Major issues facing the American school and the school superintendent such as financing education, educational reform movements, and role relationships pointedly reveal the complexity and conflicts that surround this leadership role.

Many forces weigh heavily on the school superintendency and directly affect the superintendent's behavior. School board and community relationships, the increasing need for futuristic planning strategies, governance policy, and legal considerations all shape the work of the school superintendent. These factors are examined in depth in Part II.

Part III focuses on the dimensions of specific responsibility of the school superintendent. The complexity and comprehensiveness of the role of superintendent are further revealed in the examination of work responsibilities in the areas of fiscal management, planning of educational facilities, curriculum and instruction, work with employee groups, human resources administration, the student personnel program, and relationships with the school district and the many school publics.

The book is written for three primary groups. The intent at the outset was to create a work that would be of great benefit to those graduate students who were preparing for careers in educational administration, especially for careers as school superintendents. The book will be beneficial to those institutions and instructors preparing students for careers in educational administration. Since such preparation programs must provide insight into the nature of the work of school leaders and help develop the knowledge and skills needed in such positions, we believe that a book emphasizing these factors will be welcomed by instructors in such programs. Additionally, we believe that the book will serve practicing school administrators well; those persons in other administrative roles who are looking forward to the challenges of the superintendency as well as those superintendents presently in practice. Other individuals such as school board members and professional educators will find the book to be a useful resource as well.

We wish to express our appreciation to many people who contributed to the publication of this book. We would like to thank our reviewers Larry W. Hughes, Evelyn J. Lynn, and Roland C. Haun. Special appreciation is expressed to L. Kay Hartwell-Hunnicutt, Ph.D., J.D., who served as a contributing author for Chapter 9, "The Superintendency and the Law." Dr. Hartwell-Hunnicutt serves as Professor of Educational Administration at Arizona State University and as a practicing attorney in the state of Arizona. Her legal knowledge coupled with her several years of experience in educational administration provided a significant and relevant chapter for the book. Appreciation also is expressed to Donna Larson of Arizona State University, for her services in preparing the manuscripts. Finally, we wish to give special thanks to Ray Short, Christine Shaw, and Christine Svitile of Allyn & Bacon for their support and assistance in the completion of this project.

M. Scott Norton
L. Dean Webb
Larry L. Dlugosh
Ward Sybouts

Chapter 1

Historical Perspectives

The position of school superintendent is a product of growth and necessity. It
was fashioned; it was not born. It unraveled; it was not conceived.
                                                                    —R. E. WILSON[1]

The position of superintendent of schools in the United States did not have its origins in a pronouncement of a board of education or the creative mind of some board member. Rather, it is a position that evolved as the schools of this country evolved. Our purpose is to focus on the position of superintendent of schools and to review its history while to the extent possible not ignoring the context in which it evolved. In so doing we will trace the evolution of the position from its origins as the school inspector; through its first formal years, during which the superintendent functioned largely as schoolmaster; and into the second half of the nineteenth century, during which the superintendent gained additional duties and responsibilities and the position came to more closely resemble that we know today. We then continue our historical coverage into the twentieth century, discussing the impact of the theories of scientific management, democratic administration, and the human relations movement on the practice of school administration. Finally, in the last two sections of the chapter we explore the changes in the role of the superintendent in the last half of the twentieth century, as well as changes in the problems and challenges they face.

Administering the Schools in Colonial America and the Early Republic

In colonial America the schools were managed directly by the general public at the town or district meeting. What leadership there was came from the church or from wealthy or

1

prominent laymen who were interested in education or were influenced by the church. The association between the schools and the church was natural: the masters of the schools were often ministers of the church or subject to its close supervision.[2]

The School Committee

As the towns grew in size and the business of the town, including that of administering the schools, became more complex, it became common practice for the town meeting to authorize the selectmen, or councilmen, to manage the schools. As the population continued to grow, these selectmen, in turn, formed special school committees to help them with their tasks. These committeemen visited the schools, saw to it that means were provided to pay the teachers and supply slates and books, and saw that there was a place for the school to meet.[3]

In time it was realized that the committee formed to help the selectmen was really better qualified to manage the schools than the selectmen, and that the logical next step should be taken of annually electing regular committees to manage the schools.[4] In fact, the same year that the U.S. Constitution was ratified, the Massachusetts Law of 1789, "An Act to Provide for the Instruction of Youth, and for the Promotion of Good Education," became not only the first law to recognize the school district, but the first law to give legal recognition to the school committee as an organization for the administration and supervision of the schools. From this time on, school committees were appointed in most towns, and the authority of selectmen and ministers gradually declined.[5]

The School Visitor

Among the duties and responsibilities of the school committee was the selection and certification of teachers, supervision of instruction, textbook selection, facilities management, the examination of pupils, and school visitations. The practice of school visitations was considered an important supervisory task in the colonial and early republic periods:

> the schools were frequently visited by the ministers, if they were not teachers, "for the purpose of examining the pupils in their catechism and their other religious instruction." . . . Gradually the duty fell upon the selectmen and later on the regular school committee. . . . But it was natural that one member of a school committee might have more ability than others in visiting the schools and . . . might have been delegated to represent the other members in such visitations.[6]

Thus, there emerged the position of "school visitor" or "school inspector." In 1829 Delaware became the first state to appoint a county official whose sole duty was school visitation and supervision. This is the origin of the office of the county school superintendent. The county superintendent became very important in rural and isolated areas, where he was given not only the responsibility to visit and supervise the schools, but also to keep official records, select, certify, and assign teachers, and to arbitrate county and district boundary disputes.[7]

School Boards Grow and Operate by Subcommittees

As the population and school attendance increased, and cities grew in size and number, the number of schools to be visited increased, as did their problems. In an effort to handle their many duties and responsibilities, the school committees, or what may appropriately now be called boards of education, divided themselves into special standing subcommittees each responsible for a particular aspect of the administration and supervision of the schools. A dozen such committees was common; and at one time Chicago reportedly had 79 subcommittees, and Cincinnati 74. Cubberley credits the subcommittee form of school board organization with being the first phase in the separation of the legislative and executive functions of school governance and control.[8]

In order to staff so many subcommittees, the size of the board necessarily grew. Boards also grew in size because in the cities members of the board were elected by ward and on the basis of party issues. According to Gilland, the view that each ward of the city or school district needed explicit and separate representation on the board of education was the major reason for the large size they attained.[9]

In the cities the large number of committees frequently frustrated the accomplishment of even conventional matters.[10] For example, a 1847 report of a Boston school committee said that there was no one:

- whose duty it is to find the best and most economical plans for schoolhouses, their ventilation and warming, and their apparatus, and furniture.
- to look out for the best teacher, when a vacancy occurs. . . .
- to find out what is the most successful teaching in all the schools, and to point it out for the benefit of all. . . .
- whose special duty it is to see whether the best course of studies is pursued, or to suggest improvement from the experience of the best schools elsewhere.
- to oversee the organization of new schools.
- to say what libraries should be in the schools, for teachers or pupils.
- to exercise the complete supervision of the schools which is needed, or to examine them as thoroughly as they require.[11]

It was situations such as this that led the Boston school committee, as had occurred elsewhere, to recognize the need for the appointment of an executive officer to perform the functions it could not. Thus emerged the superintendent of schools.

First Superintendents

Buffalo, New York is most often credited with having appointed the first superintendent of schools in 1837. In actuality this person was a lay person who served for no salary and basically was assigned the duties of the school inspector then common in New York state. He resigned after a few months and was succeeded by a man who received a salary of $75 per year. In 1839, Louisville and several other cities in Kentucky appointed "agents of public schools" who were paid small salaries. The next year St. Louis also named a superintendent of schools but paid him no salary. However, that same year, Providence, Rhode Island named Nathan Bishop as full-time superintendent with a beginning salary of $1,250 per year, a handsome salary in those times. He served as superintendent in Providence until 1851, when he became the first superintendent of schools in Boston.[12]

Obstacles to Adoption

Many other school boards also called for the establishment of the superintendency, often 10 or 20 years before it was actually created.[13] In fact, while the first superintendent was appointed in 1837, 30 years later only 30 American cities had appointed superintendents (see Table 1–1). There were several obstacles to the appointment of superintendents. The dependence of most school boards on the city council was one major obstacle. Sometimes the city council refused to approve the school board's request to appoint, and other times it simply failed to act on the request.[14] Other factors and conditions opposing the establishment of the superintendency were (a) teachers and principals feared a loss of control; (b) the board feared a loss of power (and the opportunity to dispense favors); (c) the public's and board's fear of "one man control"; (d) a lack of trained men for the position; (e) the absence of legal authority for the position; (f) the belief the position (and expense) was unnecessary; (g) satisfaction with the schools as they were; and (h) a general resistance to change.[15]

From School Master to School Executive

The early superintendents served mostly as representatives or assistants to the board of education. Most boards continued to view themselves as executive as well as legislative bodies and were reluctant to delegate their executive functions. The work of the board continued to operate through the subcommittee arrangement, and the superintendent was expected to supplement, not supplant, them. Gilland analyzed the duties and responsibilities of 26 of the first city superintendents and found the greatest number were related to instruction and the least to finance (see Table 1–2). The duties most frequently mentioned were the making of an annual report and supervision and visitation of the schools. The limited assignment of financial responsibilities resulted, in part, because "many board members were businessmen and considered themselves more competent than the superintendent in matters of business administration."[16] Of the 26 cities whose regulations were analyzed by Gilland, only three had designated the superintendent as the executive officer of the board of education.

Gradually, during the second half of the nineteenth century, as a result of a variety of factors, the superintendent–school board relationship began to change. First, as boards of education gained more experience with the superintendency, and as superintendents themselves gained experience and confidence, the administrative organizations were altered. That is, the appointment of the superintendent and the delegation of certain duties and responsibilities to him[17] allowed the number of committees to be reduced. And, as the number of committees was reduced and as the superintendent proved his competence, even more duties were delegated to him and the number of committees reduced even further.

A second factor contributing to the change in superintendent–board relations was the change in how school board members were elected: as the size of the board was reduced, its members came to be elected from the city at large rather than from each ward. The two major responsibilities gained by the superintendent from this reorganization were the full

TABLE 1–1   The First City Superintendents of Schools in the United States, 1837–1890

City	Year of Appointment (and reappointment if temporarily abolished)	Population as of nearest census at time of appointment (and reappointment)
1. Buffalo	1837	18,213
2. Louisville	1837	21,210
3. Providence	1839	23,171
4. St. Louis	1839	16,469
5. Springfield	1840	10,985
	(1865)	15,199
6. Philadelphia	1840	93,665
	(1883)	847,424
7. New Orleans	1841	102,193
8. Rochester	1841	20,191
9. Columbus	1847	17,882
10. Brooklyn	1848	96,838
11. Memphis	1848	8,841
12. Baltimore	1849	169,054
13. Cincinnati	1850	115,435
14. Boston	1851	136,881
15. Jersey City	1851	6,856
16. New York	1851	515,574
17. San Francisco	1851	34,776
18. Nashville	1852	10,165
19. Cleveland	1853	17,034
20. Newark	1853	38,894
21. Los Angeles	1853	1,610
22. Chicago	1854	29,963
23. Detroit	1855	21,109
	(1863)	(45,649)
24. Indianapolis	1855	8,091
25. Worcester	1856	24,960
26. Minneapolis	1858	2,564
27. Milwaukee	1859	45,246
28. New Haven	1860	39,267
29. Savannah	1866	28,235
30. Kansas City	1867	32,260
31. Pittsburgh	1868	86,076
32. Washington, D.C.	1869	109,199
33. Richmond	1869	51,058
34. Wilmington	1870	30,841
35. Atlanta	1871	21,789
36. Denver	1871	4,759
37. Omaha	1872	16,083
38. Houston	1873	9,382
39. Portland	1873	8,293
40. Seattle	1882	3,533
41. Dallas	1888	80,067
42. Salt Lake City	1890	44,843

SOURCES: Thomas M. Gilland, *The Origins and Development of the Powers and Duties of the City-School Superintendent* (Chicago: University of Chicago Press, 1935), p. 15, and Theodore Lee Rheller, *The Development of the City Superintendency* (Philadelphia: Theodore Lee Rheller, 1935), pp. 81–82.

TABLE 1–2   Duties and Responsibilities of Early Superintendents

Responsibilities	Percent of Cities
1. Responsibilities to the board of education	
Act under direction of the board	42.3
Act as executive officer of board	11.5
Act as secretary of board	11.5
Attend meetings of board	42.3
Enforce regulations of board	46.1
Accept additional duties from board	19.2
Give advice to board	42.3
2. Responsibilities to board committees	
Aid committee meetings when requested	23.0
Attend committee meetings when requested	19.2
3. Responsibilities for financial administration	
Make quarterly financial report	7.7
Recommend financial measures	11.5
Execute contracts for work, materials, or leases	3.8
Assist in audit of school accounts	3.8
Make bills for contingent expenses	3.8
Keep an expense account for each school	3.8
4. Responsibilities for school plant	
Give aid in planning new buildings	14.4
Notify board or committee when repairs are needed	23.0
Superintend schools, schoolhouses and apparatus	34.6
Issue proposals for furnishing fuel	7.7
Prohibit use of school buildings for other purposes	3.8
5. Responsibilities for reporting	
Make an annual report	77.0
Make a quarterly report	38.5
Make a monthly report	30.8
Make additional reports on request of board	27.0
6. Responsibilities for teaching staff	
Assist in examining applicants for teaching positions	43.2
Hold teachers' meetings	50.0
Fill temporary vacancies	30.8

right to be called the executive officer of the board and the privilege of nominating teachers—a privilege previously exercised by members of the board in return for personal or political favors.[18] Lastly, many of the school boards who had a dependent relationship with city councils were able to gain separation from the city government and were awarded many of the basic powers and duties they have today. The board began to operate as a legislative body rather than both a legislative and an executive body; the executive functions were delegated to the superintendent, who came to be officially designated as the executive officer of the board of education. Operating in this new role, he assumed more responsibility for business management, finance, and school facilities.

Responsibilities	Percent of Cities
Report inefficient teachers to board	34.6
Assist in establishing a normal class or school	15.4
Recommend teachers for election	11.5
7. Responsibilities for distribution	
Supervise the schools	96.2
Visit all schools	84.6
Guard classification of pupils	46.1
Aid teachers in discipline	61.5
Provide books for indigent pupils	11.5
8. Responsibilities for pupil personnel	
Assist in or conduct examinations for promotion	57.7
Make promotions	30.8
Determine form of records for pupils	38.6
Keep attendance register of all pupils	7.7
Ascertain number of children not in school	30.8
Suspend children for violation of rules of school	27.0
Transfer pupils from one district to another	11.5
Admit pupils to school	11.5
9. Responsibilities for conducting office	
Keep daily office hours	30.8
Devote full time to the office	30.8
Communicate directions to teachers and pupils	7.7
Have discretionary power where there are no rules	15.4
Keep record of proceedings open to board	15.4
Study local school system	11.5
Study other school systems	50.0
10. Responsibilities for high schools	
Take charge of high school	7.7
Teach in high school	3.8
Visit the high school	3.8

SOURCE: Thomas McDowell Gilland, *The Origin and Development of the Power and Duties of the City-School Superintendent* (Chicago: The University of Chicago Press, 1935), pp. 73–74.

The Profession Is Established

As the duties and responsibilities of the superintendent grew, along with their numbers, they corresponded with each other, sharing ideas and practices.[19] Increasingly they saw themselves as a unique profession. And in 1865 those in attendance at the meeting of the National Teachers Association in Harrisburg, Pennsylvania decided to form an organization that would be limited in membership to those involved in educational supervision. The new organization, calling itself the National Association of School Superintendents, held its first meeting in Washington, D.C., in February 1866. In 1870 this organization joined with the American Normal School Association and the National Teachers Association to form the National Education Association (NEA) and became the Department of Superintendence of the NEA, the predecessor of the American Association of School Administrators (AASA).

The Era of Scientific Management

The topics and papers presented at the annual meeting of the Department of Superintendence during the late nineteenth century "indicate the efforts of superintendents to utilize the machinery of their organization to accomplish a common goal: namely (to) acquire enough power to be effective as an executive."[20] Their goal to become more effective was spurred on by the reform crusade of the early 1900s and the criticism that the schools (indeed all public institutions) were not being operated effectively and efficiently. The criticism of the schools reached new heights with a series of articles in the *Saturday Evening Post* and *Ladies Home Journal* that extended the mounting criticism over a two-year period, 1911–1913. Articles such as "Our Medieval High School—Should We Educate Children for the Twelfth or the Twentieth Century?" "The Case of Seventeen Million Children—Is Our Public School System Proving an Utter Failure?" and "Are We Living in b.c. or a.d.?" claimed that the schools were inefficient, ineffective, and a shame to America.[21]

As business and industry grew in size and importance in the last decades of the nineteenth century, the values and beliefs of their leaders held great sway. These businessmen often dominated the downsized boards of education and brought with them the language and ideology of corporate America. They increasingly urged that business principles be applied to the operation of the schools.

In this atmosphere, superintendents attempted to apply the "science" of management to the educational enterprise. The concept of *scientific management* had been brought to prominence by Frederick W. Taylor, an engineer at Bethlehem Steel. Basically, scientific management involved:

- The identification of tasks. Scientific methods should be used by managers to discover the most effective ways to perform minute aspects of every task.
- The setting of controlled conditions and specified equipment for completing each task. The procedures for doing the task and the time specifications for completion must be stated and enforced.
- An incentive system that rewarded efficiency and high production. Merit pay and job incentives were essential in the compensation process; "punishment" or personal loss in case of failure also was to be considered.
- Planning work and controlling its accomplishment were the responsibilities of management. Workers were to be hired to carry out the plans under close supervision.[22]

Beginning in 1911, the meetings of the Department of Superintendence evidenced the attention given by superintendents to the application of scientific management to public education. At the 1912 meeting, one entire session was devoted to "The Determining of School Efficiency." At the 1913 meeting of the Department, Frank E. Spaulding, superintendent of Newton, Massachusetts, delivered an address entitled "The Application of the

Principles of Scientific Management," in which he described how he had applied the principles of scientific management to the Newton system, specifically how cost accounting had been used to determine the cost of various educational units, the "educational value" of a subject, and to establish standards for implementing cost cutting measures. Six of the thirteen resolutions adopted at the meeting reflected the growing influence of the efficiency/scientific management movement.[23]

Franklin Bobbitt, Instructor of Educational Administration at the University of Chicago, was one of the first to attempt to make direct application of Taylor's principles to the schools. According to Bobbitt:

> In an organization, the directive and supervisory members must clearly define the ends towards which the organization strives. They must coordinate the labors of all so as to attain the end. They must find the best methods of work, and they must enforce the use of these methods on the part of the workers. They must determine the qualifications necessary for the workers and see that each rises to the standard qualifications, if it is possible; and when impossible, see that he is separated from the organization.[24]

Ellwood P. Cubberley, Dean of the School of Education at Stanford, advocated the creation of efficiency bureaus or departments patterned directly or indirectly after Taylor's "planning departments." He was also an advocate of the establishment of the position of educational efficiency expert.[25]

Superintendents embraced the notion of efficiency departments and efficiency experts in the hope they could solve problems in education as they had purportedly done in business and industry. Superintendents also "made frequent analogy to the business community in order to reinforce their identity with it" and to gain a share "in the new breed of scientific business managers."[26] The influence of the efficiency movement was also evidenced in the emphasis given teacher selection and evaluation, supervision, job analysis, cost accounting, and the introduction of merit pay and incentive plans.

Another very visible manifestation of the movement was the school survey. Hundreds of school surveys were conducted between the 1911 and 1925 covering every aspect of the school operation. The school year 1915–16 marked the high point for the school survey, when no less than 76 surveys were under way simultaneously.[27] Lastly, the application of scientific management tended to promote the centralized, hierarchial bureaucratic structures still in place in some districts today.

The Professional Preparation of Superintendents

A 1899 survey of big city superintendents found that 58 percent held a bachelor's degree, 14 percent a master's degree, 13 percent a doctorate, 9 percent a normal school degree, and 4 percent held no degree.[28] At the same time, little formal training existed for school administrators: only 12 out of 25 of the major institutions of higher education offered courses dealing primarily with educational administration.[29] And those courses offered focused mostly on the reminiscences of successful superintendents and philosophical works, while the textbooks written by the founding fathers of the superintendency (e.g., Ellwood Cubberley, George Strayer, and Frank Spaulding) were basically compendiums of "best practices."[30] By 1914, however, coursework began to change. Courses became more numerous and specialized, and the influence of the efficiency movement was visible in course titles, which included such terms as efficient or efficiency and words related to financial–mechanical problems and organization and administration of the staff.[31]

In 1923 the Department of Superintendence recommended the following educational preparation for the superintendent:

(1) Graduation from a standard college, the courses in which should result in (a) breadth of information, (b) intensive specialization in at least one field of study, (c) general and fundamental courses in the science of education, (d) general and fundamental courses in economics and sociology.

(2) From one to three years of specialized professional graduate work designed especially for the technical training of school administrators. This work should include such courses or such lines of work as State and city school administration, principles of supervision, educational psychology, history and philosophy of education, general and educational sociology, economics, finance, and other such courses as bear directly upon the work of a city superintendent. This graduate work should give them through direct instruction, observation, supervised practice, participation in surveys or organized apprenticeship, a mastery of the actual technique of administering school systems or various sizes.[32]

In the same year that this training was being proposed by the Department of Superintendence, it described the desirable qualifications of a superintendent of schools for "one of our great cities" as being that detailed in Figure 1–1.

Not only was the training of school administrators becoming more specialized and extended, so was their overall level of educational attainment. A 1923 survey of city superintendents by the Department of Superintendence found that the median time spent in college was in excess of four years. The study attributed this to the fact that most superintendents entered the profession from the high school principalship, where college graduation was a standard prerequisite for the position. The study also found that the level of educational attainment of the superintendent increased with the size of the city.[33]

One force driving the professional training of superintendents was the growing certification movement. In 1921, 23 states required that teachers be certified and 14 issued certificates for administrators and supervisors.[34] By 1932 the later had increased to 32 states, with 10 others at the point of having developed special requirements, if not special certificates.[35] The certification requirements for administrators normally required that they hold a teaching certificate, have had teaching experience, and have completed a minimum of 15 hours of collegiate work in school administration.[36]

Democratic Administration and the Human Relations Movement

The years leading up to and following the 1929 crash of the stock market brought a change in the image and role expectation of the superintendent. One of the most visible ways in which the role of superintendents was changing was in the powers and duties they performed. Table 1–3 compares the initiatory, executing, and approval functions of superintendents in 1923 and 1933. Personnel matters between 1923 and 1933 became

Personal

A dominating personality—a leader of men.

A man of good moral character and religious belief.

A good speaker.

A man of strong constitution and good health, industrious, persevering, courageous, and with a high sense of personal honor, clean in person and in mind, temperate in act and speech, knowing when to speak and when to keep silent; honest and square, tactful and diplomatic.

A man of forty to fifty years of age.

A man who is animated by ideals of service and who is kindly and sympathetic towards his assistants.

A man who, when the needs of the schools demand it, knows how to fight and to fight hard.

Professional

A graduate of a reputable college.

A graduate student of school administration or a professor of administration in one of the leading graduate schools of education.

An important contributor to publications of scientific societies or to educational periodicals upon contemporary problems, of consequence to the administration of city schools.

A man who is recognized among superintendents of city schools as one of the ablest and most successful of their group.

Experience

A man who in his earlier years was a teacher and a principal of an elementary school, who later became a superintendent in a small city which employed only one executive officer, and who now holds or has within the past two years held the superintendency in a city school system in which there are one or more other department heads such as business manger, superintendent of buildings, etc., and in which there is a wide variety of schools represented, such as vocational schools, special classes for gifted and sub-normal children, etc.

A man who is fully up-to-date in matters pertaining to supervision of instruction.

A man who has had uniformly conspicuous success in each of these classes of positions and especially in those cities where conditions made success difficult to attain.

FIGURE 1–1   Desirable Qualifications for a City Superintendent: 1923

SOURCE: National Education Association (NEA), Department of Superintendence, First yearbook, *The Status of the Superintendent* (Washington, D.C.: NEA, 1923), pp. 7–8.

increasingly important to the superintendent, and routine and specialized administrative functions became of lesser importance. Another noticeable difference is that while the initiatory function of "supervision of classroom instruction" moved from twelfth place in 1923 to eighth place in 1933, the executing function, "supervision of instruction," went from first place in 1923 to eighth place in 1933.

As the Great Depression deepened, the public not only became disillusioned with business, but with the image of the business executive model of leadership of the public schools. Throughout the economic crisis of the 1930s, and as democracy was being threatened abroad, the schools were increasingly being advanced as the "safeguards of democracy," a place where the democratic tradition should be preserved, transmitted, and modeled. A corollary of this argument was that a more democratic style of administration should be practiced in the schools—one that provided for greater teacher participation in educational policy making. For example, at the 1937 convention of the Department of Superintendence, John Dewey urged that every teacher be given "some regular organic way in which he can, directly or through representatives chosen, participate in the formulation of the controlling aims, methods, and materials of the school of which he is a part."[37] And the

TABLE 1–3   Functions of the Superintendent: 1923 and 1933

Function	Rank in 1923	Rank in 1933
Initiatory Functions:		
Appointment of teachers	1	1
Appointment of principals	2	3
Determination of new policies	3	9
Dismissal of teachers and principals	4	5
Determination of subjects in curriculum	5	2
Selection of instruction supplies	6	7
Selection of textbooks	7	10
Transfer of teachers and principals	8	4
Preparation of the budget	9	15
Determination of the content of subjects	10	11
Selection of noneducational supplies	11	13
Supervision of classroom instruction	12	8
Execution Functions:		
Supervision of instruction	1	8
Determination of content of subjects	2	7
Determination of subjects of curriculum	3	2
Selection of instructional supplies	4	3
Transfer of teachers and principals	5	1
Making of routine rules	6	4
Selection of textbooks	7	5
Enforcement of attendance laws	8	14
Selection of noneducational supplies	9	9
Appointment of teachers	10	6
Appointment of principals	11	11
Direction of medical inspection	12	12
Approval Functions:		
Purchase and sale of buildings and grounds	1	28
Preparation of plans	2	23
Appointment of janitors	3	18
Construction of buildings	4	24
Preparation of budget	5	26
Taking census	6	12
Maintenance and repairs	7	20
Appointment of attendance officers	8	22
Direction of medical inspection	9	8
Rent of buildings and grounds	10	32

SOURCE: National Education Association (NEA), Department of Superintendence, *Educational Leadership: Progress and Possibilities* (Washington, D.C.: NEA, 1933), pp. 141–142.

next year, the American Association of School Administrators urged educators to "exemplify in the relations both between teachers and pupils and between administrators and teachers, the essential spirit of democracy."[38]

Not only was teacher participation being advocated by some administrators, it was being demanded by teachers' organizations. The increase in the membership and activities of teachers' groups had brought a change in relations between teachers and administrators. This change represented a movement of power from administrators to the teachers and thus brought democratic administration closer to realization.[39]

The second major criticism of scientific management was that it had been detrimental to relationships between administrators and teachers, and between teachers and students. Yet this situation was not significantly improved by the initial attempts at democratic administration, nor did they change the basic role or functioning of the superintendent. The superintendent was still considered the head of the hierarchial organization of the schools, the final authority for the maintenance of all systems within the organization, and the dispenser of rewards and punishments. In most districts personnel policies were developed by boards of education with the advice of the superintendent, with or without the consent of the teachers.[40]

By the end of World War II, however, students and practitioners of school administration had begun to realize that superintendents would not become democratic leaders just because it was advocated in the professional literature or resolved by professional associations, or by simply providing for some teacher participation in decision making. What was required was a knowledge of principles and techniques of what had come to be known as *human relations*.[41]

By the early 1950s the human relations movement was having an impact on educational administration. Research studies documented in school administration, as they had in business administration, the important role of human interactions to the success of operations in both the work place and the board room. Special conferences and seminars offering human relations training in such topics as skills development in working with groups were widely offered. The professional literature was also replete with articles both discussing the need for and offering guidance on improving human relations in school systems.

For example, the January 1954 issue of *Nations Schools* featured a "Human Relations Portfolio," which included nine articles, each of which underscored the importance of human relations to the superintendent. According to the author of the first article, 90 percent of the time of the school administrator is spent working with people, not things, and "studies of reasons for failure in school administration clearly show that it usually results from the inability of the administrator to work with people."[42] Another author went so far as to declare that educational administration "is much more specifically dependent upon good human relations than is the administration of an industry or business."[43]

The bottom line of all these discussions was the contention that the superintendent needed to be a human relations expert possessed of the necessary knowledge and skills to work effectively with groups and individuals. Thus, by the end of the decade the term *democratic administrator* became used not only to describe a superintendent who was involving the staff in decision making, but one who practiced good human relations skills and was seen as "a means of bringing about effective co-operative activity to achieve the purposes of an enterprise."[44]

The Application of Behavioral Science Theory to the Practice of School Administration

While the human relations movement was still under way, other educational administrators were turning their attention to the application of behavioral science theory to educational administration. Behavioral scientists view organizations as having an institutional dimension and a human dimension that are in constant interaction. The effect of this interaction on human behavior and the achievement of the organization's goals is the subject of human relations research. By the late 1950s and early 1960s, the work of behavioral scientists such as Barnard, Getzels, Argyris, McGregor, Halpin, Herzberg, and Parsons was making inroads in the study and practice of educational administration. Employee morale and teacher motivation were the primary topics of investigation and concern. The interest of superintendents in behavioral science theory was based, in part, on the anticipation that its application would enable them to predict how members of the organization would respond to changes in policy and procedures and to more accurately predict or explain certain events.

Improving the Professional Status of the Superintendent

Another major motivation for superintendents in emphasizing the application of theory to practice was that in so doing they reinforced the proposal that there was a science of administration and that as a practitioner of this science they were entitled to increased professional status. Superintendents' concern for their professional status is attested to by the number of resolutions passed by the American Association of School Administrators in the years 1960–1973 relating to "professional status."[45] And indeed, the qualifications of those entering the superintendency had improved both as a result of improved preparation programs and state certification requirements that required higher levels of professional preparation. For example, between 1939 and 1955 the number of states requiring some graduate work more than doubled (from 19 to 41),[46] and between 1957 and 1966 the number of states requiring six or more years of professional preparation increased from 2 to 24.[47] The trend toward higher levels of educational preparation for superintendents is documented by the data in Table 1–4.

One of the major efforts of the AASA to improve preparation programs for superintendents was the 1949 formation, in cooperation with the Council of Chief State School Officers and the National Conference of County and Rural Area Superintendents, and with the financial support of the Kellog Foundation, of the Cooperative Program in Education Administration (CPEA). The CPEA established centers at a number of major universities to study school administration and to provide on-the-job education to school administrators at every level. In addition, the Kellog Center at Columbia University established the University Council of Educational Administration, a consortium of doctoral granting institutions of higher education that publishes professional journals and training materials in educational administration and conducts seminars and conferences where professors are introduced to new knowledge and challenged to explore solutions to new problems.[48]

TABLE 1–4   Highest Degree Held by Superintendents: 1923–1992

Highest Degree Held	Percentage of Respondents Holding Degree in Report Year					
	1923	1933	1951	1971	1982	1992
No College Degree	12.8	3.8	0.2	0.3	0	na
Bachelor's Degree	51.9	36.2	5.5	2.1	0.9	0.8
Master's Degree	32.0	56.7	78.7	55.1	44.3	37.9
Specialist/6th Year				13.4	14.9	15.8
Doctorate	2.9	3.0	14.0	22.7	32.5	36.0
Post Doctorate				6.5	7.0	8.4
Other	0.4	0.3	1.6	na	0.4	1.2

The Role of the Superintendent 1954–1982:
Issues and Challenges

Without question, one of the greatest social changes of the twentieth century was the desegregation of the schools that began with the U.S. Supreme Court decision in *Brown v. Board of Education* in 1954. The following quarter century was one of great social tension as the concepts of equal opportunity and civil rights were tested in society and applied to the schools. The spillover of this tension to the schools "led to a superintendency much different from the one that existed during the quiet years of the 1950."[49]

In 1954 the superintendent was viewed as "Mr. Education" in the community—the final mediator of conflicts and interpreter of both community and professional expectations for the proper education of children.[50] In the years after 1954, however, as the schools increasingly served as instruments of social policy, the public became more vocal, and the lay and professional leadership of the schools became focal points of controversy. The response of many school boards was to assume a greater leadership role in the formulation of policy. Citizens, too, demanded greater involvement in both policy making and the operation of the schools. As the most visible figure representing the school system, the superintendent was no longer deferred to as the educational expert, but became the target of criticism. State and federal mandates encroached on the school systems' authority. And to make matters worse, not only was there an "encroachment into the authority of the superintendency by a more involved citizenry and school board," but growing teacher unionization "created a superintendency where leaders found themselves in continuous defensive postures, both personally and on behalf of their districts."[51]

Goldhammer's comparison of the role of the superintendent in 1974 with that in 1954 provides these insights:

> The superintendent is still the executive officer of the school board. . . . His position now sets him apart, however, and he represents neither the local administrative spokesman for the educational profession nor the chief representative of the school board and the diverse community groups that are impressed upon it. . . . His office is a focal point for all groups desiring to make impacts upon policy and program. He is now the figurehead of an agency that diverse groups seek to control or, at least, manipulate toward their own ends, and he is one of the key figures who must be manipulated.
>
> . . . [By] 1974 his authority was curtailed and limited by new exigencies and commitments. Rather than developing recommendations for policies within the school district, he had to interpret social policy established by other agencies to which the school district had, to some extent, to conform.
>
> The superintendent of schools was no longer an independent executive, exercising the authority of his position on the basis of his professional judgment, training, experience, and wisdom. He was, rather, a coordinator of influential groups and the orchestrator of diverse interests and demands made upon the schools.
>
> As the result of his changed role as executive, the superintendent now manages by negotiation and bargaining. He is no longer the father figure dispensing largess among dependents. He is an administrator who negotiates and interprets actions and needs in terms of contractual agreements made with various groups

within the organization. The superintendent has assumed a middle management position in which he has less opportunity to be self-directing and must spend more time in reactive rather than proactive activities.[52]

A 1970 survey of superintendents asked them to identify the most important issues and challenges facing them in their district, as well as which of them would cause them to leave the superintendency if they were to intensify. The results as presented in Tables 1–5 and 1–6.

The issue of financing the schools was ranked as the most significant issue by superintendents of all three district size groups. The pressure for education innovations, "demands for new ways of teaching or operating programs," was second in priority for superintendents in the larger districts, and fourth for superintendents in the smallest districts.

Interestingly, the ranking of the top six problems that would cause the superintendent to leave the position as reported in Table 1–6 does not follow the ranking given by superintendents to these same issues of their importance. Increasing attacks on superintendents, which ranked only fifteenth in order of general significance, was named as the factor most likely to cause superintendents to leave the field. And somewhat unexpectedly, in spite of the highly publicized attacks on administrators in large districts, these superintendents rated this problem as less significant than superintendents in the smallest districts, who listed it as the number one factor most likely to cause them to leave the field. The reverse

TABLE 1–5 Superintendents' Ranking of Issues and Challenges Facing the Superintendency: 1971

Type of Issue or Challenge	National Rank	District Size 25,000+	District Size 24,999–3,000	District Size 2,999–300
Financing schools	1	1	1	1
Demands for new ways of teaching or operating	2	2	2	4
Greater visibility of the superintendent	3	6.5	5	2
Changes in values and norms	4	5	3.5	5
Staff relations, strikes, sanctions, or other forms of teacher militancy	5	3.5	3.5	6
Growing federal involvement	6	9	6	7
Reorganization of small districts	7	18	15	2
Assessment of outcomes	8	6.5	8	9
Caliber of persons assigned to or removed from local boards of education	9	8	9	9
Caliber of responsibilities assigned to or removed from local boards of education	10	13	10	10
Social cultural issues such as race relations, integration, segregation	11	3.5	7	12
Rapidly increasing enrollments	12	17	13	11
Changing priorities in the curriculum	13	11	11	13
Use of drugs in the schools	14	12	12	15
Increasing attacks on the superintendent	15	15.5	17	14
Growing pressure for public support of nonpublic schools	16	14	16	16
Student activism	17	10	14	17
Decentralization of large districts	18	15.5	18	18

SOURCE: Stephen J. Knezevich (Ed.), *The American School Superintendent* (Washington, D.C.: American Association of School Administrators, 1971), Table 53, p. 58.

TABLE 1–6   Issues Likely to Cause Superintendents to Leave the Field if They Intensify: 1971

Issue	National Rank	District Size		
		25,000+	24,999–3,000	2,999–300
Attacks on superintendents	1	4	3	1
Teacher negotiations and strikes	2	3	1	1
Low caliber of board members	3	2	2	3
Inadequate school finance	4	7	6	4
Student unrest	5	5	5	5
Social-cultural ferment	6	1	4	6

SOURCE: Stephen J. Knezevich (Ed.), *The American School Superintendent* (Washington, D.C.: American Association of School Administrators, 1971), Table 53, p. 59.

was true in regard to sociocultural ferment. When superintendents were asked a decade later to rank the issues and challenges they faced in order of significance, beyond ranking financing the schools as the number one issue, little similarity existed (see Table 1–7).

Unlike the dissimilarity of issues and challenges between the 1971 and 1982 reports, there was surprising similarity between the two reported data in regard to the issues that would cause the superintendent to leave the superintendency, should they intensify. Four out of the top five issues named in the 1982 report were the same as those named in 1971 (see Table 1–8).

The high rankings given "administrator/board relations" and "caliber of persons assigned to or removed from local boards of education" in the 1982 survey were a reflection of the serious tensions between boards and superintendents that existed in many dis-

TABLE 1–7   Superintendents' Ranking of Issues and Challenges Facing the Superintendency: 1982

Issue/Challenge	Rank
Financing schools	1
Planning and goal setting	2
Assessing educational outcomes	3
Accountability/credibility	4
Staff and administrator evaluation	5
Administrator/board relations	6
Special education/Public Law 94-142	7
Obtaining timely and accurate information	8
Negotiations and strikes	9
Rapidly increasing/decreasing enrollments	10
Greater visibility of the superintendent	11
Personal time management	12
Parent apathy and irresponsibility about their own children—including child abuse	13
Compliance with state and federal recordkeeping requirements	14
Student discipline	15
Staff recruitment/selection	16
Changes in values and behavioral norms	17
Use of drugs and alcohol in the schools	18

SOURCE: Luvern L. Cunningham and Joseph T. Hentges, *The American School Superintendency 1982, A Summary Report* (Arlington, Va.: American Association of School Administrators, 1982), Table 19, p. 38.

TABLE 1–8   Issues Likely to Cause Superintendents to Leave the Field if They Intensify: 1982

Issue	Rank
Issues such as negotiations, strikes, and other forms of teacher militancy	1
Caliber of persons assigned to or removed from local boards of education	2
Administrator/board relations	3
Increasing attacks upon the superintendent	4
Financing the schools	5
No issue significant enough to cause one to leave	6
Consolidation of small districts	7
Social-cultural issues such as race relations, segregation, integration	8
Parent apathy and irresponsibility about their own children, including child abuse	9
Rapidly increasing/decreasing enrollments	10

SOURCE: Luvern L. Cunningham and Joseph T. Hentges, *The American School Superintendency 1982, A Summary Report* (Arlington, Va.: American Association of School Administrators, 1982), pp. 42–43.

tricts in the late 1970s and early 1980s. The rankings given "negotiations, strikes, and other forms of teacher militancy" also reflect that the superintendency had increasingly become a high-conflict position. While it is true, as Cuban reminds us, that "Conflict is the DNA of the superintendency. It was present from the beginning,"[53] the 1982 report described the then current relationships to be "deteriorating."[54] The explanations for this condition, the authors contend, reside in the times:

> In these times of declining enrollments and inflation, there is a high prospect for conflict to occur, even when the climate is filled with good intentions. The most persuasive and difficult-to-solve problem is school finance. . . . In addition, collective bargaining places increasing stress and strain on local school districts.[55]

As the authors note, the highest ranked issues and challenges in the 1982 report "are consistent with society's demand for higher and more favorable institutional performance. They reflect society's call for prudence, efficiency and stewardship in times of declining resources . . . [and] our incredible battle with inflation."[56]

The Challenges of Reform in the 1980s and 1990s

The 1980s brought no end to the conflict surrounding the position of the superintendency. It was increasingly a position that demanded that the incumbent reject the myth of it being an apolitical position and acknowledge (and master) its political nature. In *The School Superintendent: Living with Conflict,* Blumberg declares:

> The very fabric of the schooling function in American society, because of the nature of that society, is essentially political . . . [and] being a superintendent inevitably involves the manipulation and exercise of organizational power. This is essentially a political activity, as are, or course, the mobilization of community support and the management of conflict. . . .

The image of the superintendency as being "totally immersed in politics," then, is an apt if broad metaphor for the position.[57]

Perhaps the major challenge faced by superintendents in the 1980s and early 1990s was responding to the myriad of reform reports and initiatives that began with the publication of *A Nation at Risk* in 1983. In the first wave of reform, a diverse group of educational, civic, and corporate interests concerned over lower levels of achievement and lower skills of graduates, and the resultant effect on our nation's economic competitiveness, pressured state policymakers to enact reforms addressed at the curriculum, graduation requirements, and the testing of students and teachers. Most of these top-down mandates came from the state with no increase in funding. As a result, many superintendents resisted demands made by their legislatures.[58]

The second wave of school reform (1986–1992) was directed at the local level and focused on teachers, parents, and principals. Site-based management, teacher empowerment, and parental choice became topics of importance. A growing disenchantment with bureaucratic forms of school management was voiced. Centralized school governance and control was seen as a source of inefficiency and as an impediment to the creativity needed to bring about change at the local school level. And administrators in general, and superintendents, as the chief administrator, in particular, were seen as part of the problem rather than part of the solution.[59]

While it is too early to determine the full impact of the reform movement on the position of the superintendency, the 1992 AASA study of superintendents asserted that it has had the effect of eroding the authority and policy-making leadership of the superintendent:

> The 1980s era of school reform, dominated by state and federal initiatives, created a backseat role for superintendents and school boards, thus putting a damper on successful results. The emergence in 1990 of "choice" movements across the country, as well as advocacy for more control at the local level by principals, parents, teachers, and students themselves, have brought additional challenges to superintendents' authority and policymaking leadership.[60]

When superintendents in the 1992 study were asked to rank the issues and challenges they faced, 5 of the top 10 ranked issues/challenges were new to the top 10 from 1982, and 3 had not appeared on the 1982 list at all (see Table 1–9). However, finance continued to be the dominant issue facing superintendents, and the pressures for increased accountability, along with the assessment and testing required, remained strong as evidenced by the high ranking given these issues. And as already noted, administrator–board relations remained an issue, as did the challenge to provide special education services.

More dramatic differences between the responses of superintendents in 1982 and 1992 are found in regard to the question of what issues if not corrected would be most likely to cause them to leave the field (see Table 1–10). Financial matters was the leading reason given by superintendents in the 1992 study; it had been ranked fifth in the 1982 study. On the other hand, attacks on the superintendent, which ranked fourth in the 1982 study, is not even listed in the 1992 study, and teacher negotiations and strikes, ranked number one in 1982, had significantly declined in importance to eleventh.

TABLE 1–9   Superintendents' Ranking of Issues and Challenges Facing the Superintendency: 1992

Issue/Challenge	Rank
Financing schools	1
Assessment and testing	2
Accountability/credibility	3
Changing priorities in curriculum	4
Changing societal values	5
Administrator/board relations	6
New teaching demands	7
Compliance with mandates	8
Parent apathy and irresponsibility	9
Special education/Public Law 94-142	10
Obtaining timely and accurate information	11
Staff recruiting/selection	12
Developing and funding at-risk programs	13
Strategic planning	14
Personal time management	15
Staff and administrator evaluation	16
Providing early childhood education	17
Community involvement	18
Use of drugs and alcohol in the schools	19
Caliber of board persons	20

Source: Thomas E. Glass, *The 1992 Study of the American School Superintendency* (Arlington, Va.: AASA, 1992), Table 5.23, p. 45.

Perhaps not surprisingly, however, the one set of issues common to the two reports were those that represented relationships with the board: lack of community (including board) support was ranked second among the reasons that would make superintendents leave the field in 1992, frustrated with board was ranked eighth, and planning/participation twelfth.

TABLE 1–10   Issues Likely to Cause Superintendents to Leave the Field if Not Corrected: 1992

Issue	Rank
Financial matters	1
Lack of community support	2
Lack of control	3
Nonproductive staff	4
Impression I make	5
Relations/support of local power structure	6
Individual or group reactions	7
Frustrated with board	8
Tasks undone/problems unsolved	9
Whether I made the right decision	10
Relations with unions	11
Planning/participation in board meetings	12

Source: Thomas E. Glass, *The 1992 Study of the American School Superintendency* (Arlington, Va.: American Association of School Administrators, 1992), Table 5.28, p. 50.

In the next chapter the challenges and issues the superintendent faces in trying to establish a leadership role in school reform are explored, along with those associated with the various proposals for alternative governance structures. The superintendent in the 1990s not only faces the challenges associated with responding to demands for reform, but those associated with what appears to be increased tensions with the school board. As will be discussed more fully in the following chapter, school boards are becoming more assertive in their leadership role and in their involvement in the administrative functions of the school district.

Summary

Initially, schools were administered by the town council, then by a school committee elected for that purpose. The position of superintendent grew out of the position of school visitor or school inspector: that person on the school committee chargedwith performing regular school visitations and important supervisory tasks. As the schools grew and the work of the board increased, many boards felt a need to appoint an administrative officer to perform the functions it could not, and the first superintendents were appointed. These first superintendents had little executive power and were charged primarily with the overseeing of instruction. As the nineteenth century progressed, however, as superintendents proved their competence and as the size and organization of school boards changed, the superintendent gained more and more responsibility and authority and came to function as the true executive officer of the board.

The first part of the twentieth century saw many superintendents respond to the pressures for the schools to become more efficient and effective by adopting the techniques of scientific management. It also saw the training of superintendents become more specialized and extended. The stock market crash brought the model of the business leader into disfavor, and the concepts implicit in democratic administration and the human relations movement gained favor. At the same time, the work of behavioral scientists was having an impact on the study and practice of educational administration.

The second half of the twentieth century has seen the role of the superintendent undergo considerable change. No longer is the superintendent looked up to as the expert on schools in the community. Rather, he or she is often the target of criticism and at the center of controversy, forced to become the defender of policy and the implementor of state and federal mandates, and the orchestrator of diverse interests seeking to influence the schools. Conflicts with the board are common, as are the financial pressures under which superintendents operate. Superintendents in the 1980s and 1990s have faced the challenges brought on by the reform movement. Many of the proposals that have grown out of this movement (e.g., site-based management, teacher empowerment, and parental choice) have brought additional challenges to the superintendent's authority and leadership. In the next chapter we will discuss the issues and challenges facing superintendents as they enter the twenty-first century.

Discussion Questions

1. Distinguish between the superintendent of schools functioning as a schoolmaster and the superintendent of schools functioning as the executive officer of the board of education.

2. How do the desirable qualifications for a superintendent in 1923 differ from those that would be considered desirable today?

3. What principles of scientific management are still practiced in school systems today? Which are being advocated?

Case Study

The case study approach became popular in the study of school administration in the 1950s, at about the same time the junior high school was becoming an established part of the educational system. The following case is based on a case study presented in the literature of the period.[61]

CASE 1.1   The Superintendent Gets His Way: Leadership by Manipulation?

Sam Howell, superintendent of Bridgeport School District, was convinced that a junior high school should be established in the community but knew that the board of education was opposed to the idea. Mr. Howell was new on the job, and so he waited several months before he even mentioned junior high school. During these months he worked on building an effective relationship with the board.

After several months Superintendent Howell found, or began to make, the opportunity, after board meetings and at other times, to mention the spread of junior high schools in this country. He also presented board members with some articles about junior high schools. And in reporting on his attendance at professional meetings, he had further opportunity to mention junior high schools by referring to addresses about their advantages.

Finally the time came to make a recommendation about a junior high school. However, rather than recommend that a decision be made about the establishment of a junior high school, Mr. Howell recommended that the board give careful consideration to the advantages of junior high schools. Along with the recommendation he presented data on the growth of the junior high school movement and a summary of the arguments for such an organization. The board accepted his recommendation and appointed a subcommittee to study the issue and present a recommendation. In the end, the subcommittee recommended the establishment of a junior high school and the full board voted approval.

Questions

1.   What type of leadership is being exercised by the superintendent in this case?
2.   How does the indirect approach differ from manipulation?
3.   What are the relative merits of the direct and the indirect approaches?

Inbasket Exercise

A. DAVID KNIGHT & ASSOCIATES
6201 ASH, SUITE 108
UNIVERSITY HEIGHTS, MO

November 15, 1994

Dear Superintendent Adams;

As you are of course aware, A. David Knight & Associates specializes in the development and evaluation of personnel systems. Our clients include public and private organizations a representing a wide range of interests. As you also are aware, we have entered into a contract with the Board of Education of University Heights School District to perform an evaluation of the district personnel classification system and district personnel policies and to suggest any needed revisions, additions, or deletions.

One of the first steps in this process is to review existing job descriptions and to perform a job analysis. Our review of existing personnel documents suggests that there is no written job description for the position of Superintendent (as well for a several other adminstrative and classified positions. Therefore we are asking that you prepare a job description for the position that you now occupy, namely, the superintendency. In so doing please remember that a job description is to describe the job, not the person holding it, and that its ultimate purpose is to provide the basis for recruiting and selecting candidates and evaluating job performance. The uniform format that we are asking be followed in preparing the job descriptions is as follows:

1. Job title
2. Job summary
3. Job functions
4. Required qualifications, including education, experience, and license or any specific physical requirements
5. Person(s) to whom responsible and the extent of supervision received
6. Position in the organizational structure
7. Relationship to other positions
8. Conditions of employment (e.g., hours of work, salary/wage scale, fringe benefits, etc.)

After all existing and new job descriptions have been reviewed and suggested revisions will be made to the board of education who ultimately is responsible for their approval.

I am aware of the many demands on your time but I know that you are aware of the importance of this activity and will give it your fullest attention. If there are any questions I can answer or any way that I can assist in the preparation of the job description, please do no hesitate to call. Thank you in advance for your cooperation.

Sincerely,

A. David Knight

A. David Knight

Having been given the above responsibility, prepare a job description for the position of Superintendent of Schools.

Notes

1. R. E. Wilson, *The Modern School Superintendent* (New York: Harper and Brothers, 1960), p. 2.

2. National Education Association (NEA), Department of Superintendence, Eleventh yearbook, *Educational Leadership: Progress and Possibilities* (Washington, D.C.: NEA, 1933).

3. Wilson, *The Modern School Superintendent.*

4. NEA, Eleventh yearbook, p. 27.

5. Ibid.

6. Ibid., pp. 30–31.

7. Emery Stoops and M. L. Rafferty Jr., *Practices and Trends in School Administration* (Boston: Ginn, 1961).

8. Ellwood P. Cubberley, *Public School Administration* (Boston: Houghton Mifflin, 1929).

9. Thomas M. Gilland, *The Origins and Development of the Powers and Duties of the City-School Superintendent* (Chicago: University of Chicago Press, 1935).

10. Ibid.

11. *Annual Reports, School Committee, 1847* (Boston, 1847), pp. 117–121, as cited in Theodore Lee Rheller, *The Development of the City Superintendency* (Philadelphia: Theodore Lee Rheller, 1935), pp. 39–40.

12. NEA, Eleventh yearbook.

13. Harold Stewart Young, *In Pursuit of a Profession: A Historical Analysis of the Concept of "Professionalization" for the American Public School Superintendency, 1865–1973,* Doctoral dissertation, The Pennsylvania State University, 1976.

14. American Association of School Administrators (AASA), Thirtieth yearbook, *The American School Superintendency* (Washington, D.C.: AASA, 1952).

15. Young, *In Pursuit of a Profession.*

16. Ibid., p. 105.

17. The male pronoun is used in the chapter until such time as females began entering the profession.

18. Gilland, *The Origins and Development of the Powers and Duties of the City-School Superintendent.*

19. Daniel E. Griffiths, *The School Superintendent* (New York: Center for Applied Research in Education, 1966).

20. Young, *In Pursuit of a Profession,* p. 157.

21. Raymond E. Callahan, *Education and the Cult of Efficiency* (Chicago: University of Chicago Press, 1962).

22. L. Dean Webb, Paul A. Montello, and M. Scott Norton, *Human Resources Administration: Personnel Issues and Needs in Education,* 2nd ed. (New York: Merrill, an imprint of Macmillian College Publishing, 1994), p. 5.

23. Young, *In Pursuit of a Profession;* Callahan, *Education and the Cult of Efficiency.*

24. J. Franklin Bobbitt, "The Supervision of City Schools: Part I. Some General Principles of Management Applied to Problems of City School Systems" in *Twelfth Yearbook of the National Society for the Study of Education* (Chicago: University of Chicago Press, 1913), pp. 7–8.

25. Young, *In Pursuit of a Profession.*

26. Walter H. Drost, "Educational Administration: History," *Encyclopedia of Education* (New York: Macmillian, 1971), p. 69.

27. Ibid.

28. David B. Tyack, "Pilgrim's Progress: Towards a Social History of the School Superintendency, 1860–1960," *History of Education Quarterly,* 12 (fall 1972): pp. 257–300.

29. Young, *In Pursuit of a Profession.*

30. Tyack, "Pilgrim's Progress"; Thomas E. Glass, *The 1992 Study of the American School Superintendency: America's Education Leaders in a Time of Reform* (Arlington, Va.: American Association of School Administrators, 1992).

31. Callahan, *Education and the Cult of Efficiency.*

32. National Education Association (NEA), Department of Superintendence, First yearbook, *The Status of the Superintendent* (Washington, D.C.: NEA, 1923), p. 17.

33. Ibid.

34. Enid Larson, "Administration as a Profession," *School Executives Magazine,* 48 (March 1929): p. 292.

35. NEA, Eleventh yearbook. (See n. 2.)

36. Callahan, *Education and the Cult of Efficiency.*

37. John Dewey, "Democracy and Educational Administration," *Proceedings of the Department of Superintendence of the National Education Association* (Washington, D.C.: National Education Association, 1937), pp. 52–53.

38. "Resolutions," 1938, p. 198, cited by Young, *In Pursuit of a Profession.*

39. Griffiths, *The School Superintendent.*

40. Keith Goldhammer, "Roles of the American School Superintendent, 1954–1974," in Luvern L. Cunningham, Walter G. Hack, Raphael O. Nystrand, *Educational Administration: The Developing Decades* (Berkeley, Calif.: McCutchan, 1977), p. 157.

41. Young, *In Pursuit of a Profession.*

42. Frederick C. McLaughlin, "Different Kind of Statesmanship," *Nations Schools,* 23 (January 1954): p. 47.

43. A. L. Winsor, "Exemplify Democracy at Work," *Nations Schools,* 23 (January 1954): p. 47.

44. American Association of School Administrators (AASA), 1955 Yearbook, *Staff Relations in School Administration* (Washington, D.C.: AASA, 1955), p. 10.

45. Young, *In Pursuit of a Profession.*

46. H. Thomas James, "Educational Administration: A Forty Year Perspective," paper presented at the Annual Meeting of the American Educational Research Association, Los Angeles, April 1981.

47. Young, *In Pursuit of a Profession.*

48. Griffiths, *The School Superintendent.*

49. Glass, *1992 Study,* p. 3.

50. Goldhammer, "American School Superintendent, 1954–1974."

51. Glass, *1992 Study,* p. 3.

52. Goldhammer, "American School Superintendent, 1954–1974," pp. 158–160.

53. Larry Cuban, "Conflict and Leadership in the Superintendency," *Phi Delta Kappan,* 67 (September 1985): p. 28.

54. Luvern L. Cunningham and Joseph T. Hentges, *The America School Superintendency 1982, A Summary Report* (Arlington, Va.: American Association of School Administrators, 1982), p. 60.

55. Ibid.

56. Ibid., p. 63.

57. Arthur Blumberg, *The School Superintendent: Living in Conflict* (New York: Teachers College Press, 1985), pp. 46, 48.

58. Glass, *1992 Study.*

59. Joseph Murphy, "The 'Maytag Man' of School Reform," *School Administrator,* 2(48) (February 1991), pp. 32–33.

60. Glass, *1992 Study,* p. 4.

61. Daniel E. Griffiths, *Human Relations in School Administration* (New York: Appleton-Century-Crofts, 1956), p. 332.

Chapter *2*

Issues and Problems Facing the Superintendent

At the close of the previous chapter we presented a profile of the superintendency during the first part of the 1990s and a discussion of the problems they faced. As the superintendency approaches the twenty-first century, many of these issues and challenges remain; some have become even more difficult and complex, and new ones have emerged. In this chapter the most significant and persistent issues and challenges facing the superintendent in the latter half of the 1990s are examined. Most of these issues and challenges seem likely to continue into the twenty-first century. Discussion will focus on several broad areas of concern: inadequate financing; the superintendent's leadership role in school reform and improvement; alternative governance structures; superintendent–school board relations; the changing demographics of students, teachers, and administrators; violence and crime in the schools; and pressures from special interest groups. Greater attention is given to many of these topics in subsequent chapters of the text.

Inadequate Financing

As was noted in the previous chapter, over the last several decades, superintendents have identified finance (or the lack thereof) as the number one problem they face. They are not alone in their perception; school boards also perceive inadequate financing as the leading problem facing the schools,[1] and parents of public school children see only lack of discipline as a bigger problem.[2] The plight of the public schools has been highlighted by a Michigan school district closing its schools a month early because of a lack of funds, a California school district declaring bankruptcy, and the nation's third largest school system, Chicago, delaying the opening of schools because of a budget shortfall.[3]

The financial distress of schools has been exacerbated by the continuing demands for new programs and by state mandates that often come with no provision for funding. In particular, many of the demands of the reform movement, specifically those related to higher student achievement, higher graduation requirements, and better trained teachers, while not without costs, rarely received additional support. Added to these demands have been the pressures to stay abreast of current technology and to meet the special needs of the ever more diverse student population. And on top of the programmatic concerns come the serious problems many districts face with the need to replace deteriorating and sometimes unsafe buildings.

At the same time that increased demands are being placed on already beleaguered public school budgets, "taxpayers and property owners are more reluctant than ever to pay more taxes when they are bombarded with news reports about how badly the public schools are performing and how little our students are learning."[4] Yet they have been asked to do just that: the weak economy of the 1980s and early 1990s brought a shift of financial responsibility from the state to the local school district. As noted in Table 2–1, between 1985–86 and 1991–92, the state's share of the funding of public education dropped from 49.4 percent to 46.4 percent, forcing the local share to increase from 43.9 percent to 47.0 percent. As a result, since 1985 local taxes have risen faster than either state or federal taxes, rising at a rate greater than both inflation and the growth of personal income.[5]

In response to the increase in local taxation, in states ranging from Michigan to New Jersey to Oregon, voters have rejected ballot referendums designed to increase funding for education, and efforts to enact tax and spending limitations have reached levels not seen since the days of Proposition 13. Ever since Michigan voted to eliminate the use of the local property tax to fund education there has been a ground swell of copycat legislation and constitutional amendments in other states.[6]

However, the fiscal ability of states to reduce property taxes is less today than in the 1970s. When Proposition 13 was passed in 1973, many states began receiving federal revenue sharing dollars and thus had a "free" revenue source they could use to cut property taxes. Other states that did not have sales or income taxes enacted these taxes, while others raised their historically low rates, and thereby generated new revenues to replace the local property tax. Unfortunately, in most states, these revenue options are no longer available. And to make matters worse, in a number of states spending limitations have been enacted or proposed. In this climate, where both tax and spending limitations are growing in popularity, the prospect for any growth in education revenues is indeed tenuous.[7]

Currently about 20 states are involved in litigation or legislative review that could change the way the schools are funded.[8] In many of these cases, concern has shifted from issues of fiscal disparities to issues of adequacy and student performance: the extent to which districts can provide the learning experiences that produce students who have the kind of skills needed for the information and knowledge producing economy of the next century. Examined are things like the number of students per computer, the number of books, the depth and breadth of the curriculum, and teacher qualifications. Ultimately this scrutiny will lead to even greater attention being focused on student outcomes and better methods of assessing student performance.[9]

The issues surrounding the financing of education are not likely to disappear in the next decade. Pressures for market-driven solutions (e.g., parental choice, vouchers, charter schools, and performance contracting) will continue as will accountability demands and the enactment of new accountability systems. In fact, according to experts in school finance, accountability, or the linking of dollars to results in student achievement, will dominate the future of school finance and be a major concern of school administrators.[10]

TABLE 2–1 Revenues for Public Elementary and Secondary Schools, by Source of Funds: 1919–20 to 1991–92

School year	In thousands				Percentage distribution			
	Total	Federal	State	Local (including intermediate)	Total	Federal	State	Local (including intermediate)
1919–20	$ 970,121	$ 2,475	$ 160,085	$ 807,561	100.0	0.3	16.5	83.2
1929–30	2,088,557	7,334	353,670	1,727,553	100.0	0.4	16.9	82.7
1939–40	2,260,527	39,810	684,354	1,536,363	100.0	1.8	30.3	68.0
1941–42	2,416,580	34,305	759,993	1,622,281	100.0	1.4	31.4	67.1
1943–44	2,604,322	35,886	859,183	1,709,253	100.0	1.4	33.0	65.6
1945–46	3,059,845	41,378	1,062,057	1,956,409	100.0	1.4	34.7	63.9
1947–48	4,311,534	120,270	1,676,362	2,514,902	100.0	2.8	38.9	58.3
1949–50	5,437,044	155,848	2,165,689	3,115,507	100.0	2.9	39.8	57.3
1951–52	6,423,816	227,711	2,478,596	3,717,507	100.0	3.5	38.6	57.9
1953–54	7,866,852	355,237	2,944,103	4,567,512	100.0	4.5	37.4	58.1
1955–56	9,686,677	441,442	3,828,886	5,416,350	100.0	4.6	39.5	55.9
1957–58	12,181,513	486,484	4,800,368	6,894,661	100.0	4.0	39.4	56.6
1959–60	14,746,618	651,639	5,768,047	8,326,932	100.0	4.4	39.1	56.5
1961–62	17,527,707	760,975	6,789,190	9,977,542	100.0	4.3	38.7	56.9
1963–64	20,544,182	896,956	8,078,014	11,569,213	100.0	4.4	39.3	56.3
1965–66	25,356,858	1,996,954	9,920,219	13,439,686	100.0	7.9	39.1	53.0
1967–68	31,903,064	2,806,469	12,275,536	16,821,063	100.0	8.8	38.5	52.7
1969–70	40,266,923	3,219,557	16,062,776	20,984,589	100.0	8.0	39.9	52.1
1970–71	44,511,292	3,753,461	17,409,086	23,348,745	100.0	8.4	39.1	52.5
1971–72	50,003,645	4,467,969	19,133,256	26,402,420	100.0	8.9	38.3	52.8
1972–73	52,117,930	4,525,000	20,843,520	26,749,412	100.0	8.7	40.0	51.3
1973–74	58,230,892	4,930,351	24,113,409	29,187,132	100.0	8.5	41.4	50.1
1974–75	64,445,239	5,811,595	27,211,116	31,422,528	100.0	9.0	42.2	48.8
1975–76	71,206,073	6,318,345	31,776,101	33,111,627	100.0	8.9	44.6	46.5
1976–77	75,322,532	6,629,498	32,688,903	36,004,134	100.0	8.8	43.4	47.8
1977–78	81,443,160	7,694,194	35,013,266	38,735,700	100.0	9.4	43.0	47.6
1978–79	87,994,143	8,600,116	40,132,136	39,261,891	100.0	9.8	45.6	44.6
1979–80	96,881,165	9,503,537	45,348,814	42,028,813	100.0	9.8	46.8	43.4
1980–81	105,949,087	9,768,262	50,182,659	45,998,166	100.0	9.2	47.4	43.4
1981–82	110,191,257	8,186,466	52,436,435	49,568,356	100.0	7.4	47.6	45.0
1982–83	117,497,502	8,339,990	56,282,157	52,875,354	100.0	7.1	47.9	45.0
1983–84	126,055,419	8,576,547	60,232,981	57,245,892	100.0	6.8	47.8	45.4
1984–85	137,294,678	9,105,569	67,168,684	61,020,425	100.0	6.6	48.9	44.4
1985–86	149,127,779	9,975,622	73,619,575	65,532,582	100.0	6.7	49.4	43.9
1986–87	158,523,693	10,146,013	78,830,437	69,547,243	100.0	6.4	49.7	43.9
1987–88	169,561,974	10,716,687	84,004,415	74,840,873	100.0	6.3	49.5	44.1
1988–89	192,016,374	11,902,001	91,768,911	88,345,462	100.0	6.2	47.8	46.0
1989–90	207,752,932	12,700,784	98,238,633	96,813,516	100.0	6.1	47.3	46.6
1990–91	223,340,537	13,776,066	105,324,533	104,239,939	100.0	6.2	47.2	46.7
1991–92	234,485,729	15,493,330	108,792,779	110,199,621	100.0	6.6	46.4	47.0

SOURCE: U.S. Department of Education, National Center for Education Statistics, *Digest of Education Statistics* 1994 (Washington, D.C.: U.S. Department of Education 1994), Table 157.

And taxation issues will in all probability become even more serious as the aging population demands that "local property taxes go on the chopping block."[11] A very real question facing superintendents in the twenty-first century is the extent to which the existing system of publicly supported schools resembles those they have participated in much of their lives.

The Superintendent's Leadership Role in School Reform

By and large, educators, including superintendents, have not been key players in the education reform efforts that have engulfed education since the publication of the highly critical *A Nation at Risk* in 1983. In fact, as Harvard's Jerome Murphy notes, the school superintendent has been the "forgotten player in the game of school reform."[12] However, superintendents realize that they can no longer afford to be forgotten. For they know, and a growing number of researchers and policymakers are coming to understand, that "widespread improvements in schools are unlikely to be realized unless superintendents are more substantially involved in the reform agenda."[13]

The critical importance of leadership in organizational reform is widely accepted outside of public education. From the Harvard Business School to the U.S. military, the importance of leadership to organizational success is stressed. Entire industries have been developed to train leaders, and organizations spend millions of dollars each year to develop leaders.[14] As Louis Gerstner, CEO of IBM, and his co-authors write in *Reinventing Education:*

> Leaders are especially critical to organizations that must adapt and change. Without a leader who can articulate a new mission, an organization will plow straight ahead, a creature of habit. Without a leader who can organize and motivate others to pursue a new strategy, an organization will follow its traditional modes of operation, or pursue the private agendas of its members or employees. Without leaders, organizations will do the same thing tomorrow that they did today.[15]

It has been suggested that one reason the reform movement has not focused on the superintendent is that, in general, the movement brought a disenchantment with bureaucratic, centralized forms of school management, of which the superintendent was the chief representative. Such forms of governance were viewed as being not only inefficient, but as obstacles to the creativity needed to bring about significant change.[16] Yet one positive outcome of the criticisms about school governance is that they have provided the major impetus for the shift from the management focus of the 1970s and 1980s to an emphasis in the 1990s on transformational leadership[17]—the type of leadership that has been positively associated with bringing about change in business and elsewhere.

Sarason, in his book *The Predictable Failure of Educational Reform,* suggests that a major reason for the failure of many of the reform initiatives is that they require an alteration of the existing power relationships in schools.[18] The traditional power relationships that have existed between school board members and the superintendent, between teachers and administrators, between teachers and students, and between educators and parents must give way to ones providing increased opportunities for shared decision making. Transformational leadership is intended to do just that—it empowers those involved in the decision-making process and helps them recognize what needs to be done to reach a desired outcome.[19] While it does involve risk taking on the part of the superintendent, it does not in any way lessen the superintendent's significance; in fact, a higher level of leadership ability is demanded of the transformational leader than the traditional transactional leader, who relies on his or her ability to control the distribution of incentives.[20] The difference between the transactional and transformational superintendent is described by Mitchell and Tucker this way:

> Transactional superintendents seek indirect control through attention to the design of district organizational structures. They give careful thought to how organizational structures serve to facilitate or impede the work of the school staff. Transformational superintendents think quite differently. They give primary attention to the staffs rather than the structures.
>
> Transactional superintendents, concerned with structures, concentrate on defining job functions and on developing district policies and procedures. They believe that if they succeed in improving organizational operations, school instructional improvement will follow. They concentrate on creating and stabilizing district programs. They have a high sensitivity to hierarchy and standardization of practices.
>
> Transformational superintendents, concerned with staff skills and beliefs, direct their efforts to building and strengthening organizational norms and attitudes. They strive to establish common meaning systems, believing that quality education will arise when professional staff agree about educational goals and the most effective strategies for their attainment.[21]

Because transformational superintendents see themselves as more responsible for transforming the goals of the organization and the aspirations of participants than for implementing existing programs, they are oriented to carry out the kinds of structural changes mandated by the various restructuring initiatives. If superintendents do not assume this new role for themselves—the role of transformational leader—they will not let go of enough power to permit the development of responsibilities and leadership abilities needed to make shared decision making function smoothly.[22] Corporate America in embracing TQM (Total Quality Management) has recognized that shared decision making enhances performance.[23] The challenge for superintendents is to claim and assert a leadership role in the monumental task of reform and restructuring that still lies ahead for most school districts. The "reform agenda is not going to come superintendents; they will need to take a much more active stance to ensure they don't watch schools change from the sidelines."[24] The topic of organizational culture and change is discussed fully in Chapter 4.

Alternative Governance Structures

Several of the more sweeping proposals to emerge from the reform movement call for major changes in the way schools are organized and administered and in how educational services are delivered. Some proposals involve a restructuring of the existing delivery system, while others propose the delivery of education outside the existing structure. And as noted in the preceding section, many require an alteration of existing power and authority relationships within the system.

Site-based Management

Among the more popular of the proposals for restructuring the existing system is decentralization, or site-based management. As discussed in detail in Chapter 10, site-based management (SBM) is a strategy to improve education by transferring significant authority and responsibility for decision making from the central office to the individual school site. Superintendents have an important role to play in site-based management. For, as Jerome Murphy points out, the paradox of decentralization, and in particular SBM, is that it depends greatly on the existence of centralization. It requires strong central action from the superintendent's office. According to Murphy, a critical role for superintendents under SBM is promoting the good of the whole:

> It is important to promote the vitality of individual schools, but it is equally important to promote the common good of the school district. . . . They will need to do this in order to overcome the by-products of decentralization which can include fragmentation, loss of cohesion, inequality, and the inevitable foul-ups that go along with the exercise of discretion. In promoting the common good, superintendents need to rely less on heavy handed rules and regulations and more on what has been called the "institutionalization of precarious values."
>
> The "institutionalization of precarious values" means that superintendents need to identify and articulate the core values which inspired their organizational goals. . . . The core values will serve to promote unity as opposed to fragmentation.[25]

Murphy's advice is supported by the experience of superintendents who have been involved in SBM. According to Irwin Blumer, superintendent of Newton (Massachusetts) Public Schools, the superintendent is a system attempting to implement SBM "should develop a process that ensures that these values are implemented through shared ownership in the values."[26] And this is a process that takes time. You cannot mandate acceptance of core values. The superintendent must communicate the vision of the district in a way that makes people want to become involved in creating the culture in which the core values can grow and mature.[27]

In addition to his or her critical role of promoting the whole, the superintendent also plays an important role in creating the dynamic for change and in establishing and maintaining the "political space" needed for experimentation and the inevitable, unintended mistakes that accompany experimentation.[28] And last but certainly not least, the superintendent must model shared decision making and promote the development of leadership at the individual schools and throughout the system.

Promoting the whole—developing core values—promoting ownership in shared values—creating the dynamic for change—maintaining political space—modeling shared decision making—promoting the development of leadership: these are the challenges that face superintendents involved in site-based management. While formidable, they are ones that only the superintendent is in the position to meet.

Privatization

While site-based management maintains the delivery of education within the existing organizational structure, the various privatization proposals would have the government removed, to a greater or lesser extent, from the business of providing education. Privatization options range along a continuum from school–business partnerships to the contracting with a for-profit organization for the entire operation of the school system. As is discussed in greater detail in Chapter 10, school–business partnerships have greatly expanded in number and scope. In one of the more recent and publicized ventures, Walt Disney Company and the Osceola County (Florida) schools are jointly building a pre-K–12 school as part of the Disney Celebration Learning Center, which will also house a "Teaching Academy" offering professional development programs for educators from Florida and the nation.[29]

Charter Schools

Also growing in popularity is the notion of charter schools. Since Minnesota passed the first charter school law in 1991, 10 other states have enacted similar legislation, and it is being considered in a number of others. The concept has been given support by the Goals 2000: Educate America Act, which includes a provision that would allow federal funds to go to charter schools. Charter schools are seen as a way to increase accountability, to give greater autonomy to individual schools, and as a "compromise between limiting school choice to public schools and implementing voucher programs."[30]

Charter schools are publicly supported schools that are established upon the issuance of a charter (i.e., contract) from the local school board, state, or other entity (the Michigan law allows community colleges and universities to issue charters). The charter may be given to the faculty of an existing or proposed school, a group of parents, an institution of higher education, or any other group of individuals sharing similar interests and views about education. For example, in Massachusetts 3 of the first 15 charters issued went to partnerships that included the Edison Project as a co-applicant with the Horace Mann Foundation for a school in Boston and as a co-applicant with coalitions of educators, politicians, and business officials to set up schools in Lowell and Worcester. Another charter went to Boston University to establish a residential high school for homeless youth.[31]

In most states, if an existing public school proposes to become a charter school the law requires that at least half of the teachers of the school approve the application. State laws also declare that charter schools cannot be home schools and that they be nonsectarian and nondiscriminatory. Other than these requirements, few state rules are mandated.[32] Charter schools typically establish their own governing boards that function much the same as a board of trustees at a private school, and the principal runs the school on a day-to-day basis. The school is allowed to expend funds without intervention from the state or local school district. However, the charter is subject to nonrenewal if the performance standards of the contract are not met.[33]

Performance Contracting for Specialized Services

In the middle of the privatization continuum are arrangements whereby private contractors are used to provide selected school district services. Private contractors have long been used to provide services such as food services, custodial work, and transportation. In fact, 40 of the nation's 100 largest school bus fleets are operated by private contractors.[34] Performance contracting with private companies to deliver parts of the instructional program is also not a new phenomenon. Several such experiments were begun in the 1970s. More recently such arrangements have increased as more and more providers are entering the arena. For example, Sylvan Learning Systems has contracted with the Baltimore school system to improve math and reading skills to 800 Chapter 1 students and to tutor eleventh and twelfth graders reading below grade level in Washington, D.C. Berlitz Language Schools delivers foreign language instruction to public school students in 15 states, and Ombudsman Educational Services delivers special education services to more than 100 districts in 5 states. Among the other national providers of specialized instructional services are Huntington Learning Centers, Britannica Learning Centers, Kaplan Educational Centers, and Kumon Educational Institute.[35]

In one of the more unusual contracts, the school board of Minneapolis hired a private contractor, Public Strategies Group, Inc. (PSG) to administer the school district. PSG's president, Peter Hutchinson, will serve as superintendent. PSG will be paid only if it achieves the performance objectives detailed in the contract. Because any savings or profit will remain with the district, some do not consider this action privatization.[36] Nonetheless, this is an unprecedented move that could have a significant impact on the superintendency.

Performance Contracting for the Operation
of Entire Schools or School Districts

At the far right of the privatization continuum is the contracting with private enterprise for the operation of the entire school or school system. As an example, in addition to their involvement with the charter schools in Massachusetts, the for-profit Edison Project has been awarded a contract to operate two elementary schools in Wichita, Kansas. And in an unprecedented move, the Hartford, Connecticut, school districts contracted with Education Alternatives Incorporated (EAI) to run every facet of the 25,000-student district's operation. EAI also has been contracted to run nine schools in Baltimore as well as to provide services to two others. The district is also currently negotiating with the Hyde Foundation, which operates a private school for troubled youth in Bath, Maine, to take over the operation of another school. The Hyde Foundation also currently operates the Hyde School of Leadership, a public school for ninth and tenth graders in New Haven, Connecticut. Other for-profit companies such as Alternative Public Schools Incorporated, a Nashville-based firm, and Houston's Performance Schools Corporation are also seeking contracts to take over the management of select public schools.

The teachers' unions have been strongly opposed to turning over the entire operation of schools to private contractors and have been instrumental in having negotiations between several schools districts and EAI suspended. While they openly decry privatization as a threat to democratically run public schools, they also fear a cut in jobs and wages. However, many school boards and superintendents find the prospect appealing, primarily for economic reasons. One of EAI's major selling points is its willingness to make up-front investments in computers, facilities, and staff development that districts would otherwise not be able to afford.[37] In Wichita, the Edison Project promised to invest between $1.5 and $3 million in each of the schools it had contracted to operate.[38] And if the private contractor will guarantee that its payment, which is the same or less than the average per pupil cost in the district, will depend on students attaining specified performance standards, school boards often feel they have little to risk.[39]

The major issue and challenge for superintendents under these and other privatization arrangements is to clarify their role. Are they serve as the enforcer of the contract? Or since the contract is between the board and the private contractor, is enforcement the sole responsibility of the board? How is success to be measured? To what extent is the superintendent's responsibility for the individual school or service affected by the contract? Would involvement by the superintendent be seen as either an attempt to undermine or as a conflict of interest? What is the superintendent's relationship with the private contractor? John Golle, CEO of Education Alternatives, Inc., answers the latter question as follows:

> The school district's superintendent remains the chief executive officer of the schools and works with the private management firm to meet the goals set forth by the board. . . .
> The management company offers to provide additional financial incentives to the superintendent for meeting the performance goals set forth in the contract. If approved by the school board, a bonus, stock options, or stock itself become possible additional perquisites for the entrepreneurial superintendent of schools in cases where the management company manages the entire district.[40]

But what does this mean? Is the superintendent to become the new class of American entrepreneurs?

As previously stated, encouragement for privatization has been provided by the increase in charter school legislation and the federal Goals 2000: Educate America Act, which allows school districts to spend federal funds to experiment with privatization. In addition, a growing number of states have passed laws that provide for the state to take over financially or academically troubled schools. And in at least one of these states, Maryland, the law provides that the school may be entrusted to a private contractor. Recognizing that the movement toward privatization is likely to continue, public school superintendents face the challenge of defining and establishing their appropriate role in what could be a number of hybrid alternative governance structures.

Superintendent and School Board Relations

From the day the office of the superintendent was created until today, there has been a strained relationship between the school board that makes policy and the superintendent who implements it.[41] This tension appears to become accentuated during periods of reform and as the problems faced by the district become more numerous and seemingly unsolvable—a description of the circumstances many school districts find themselves in today. In fact, a number of survey findings, expert analyses, and opinions of superintendents, board members, and others all indicate that while by and large the board–superintendent relationship remains solid, tensions have increased in recent years.[42]

Nothing undermines the productive operation of a school district faster or absolutely than a poor working relationship between the school board and the superintendent.[43] When there is an intense or protracted conflict between the school board and the superintendent, programs suffer, morale is weakened, political factions form, and the district's effectiveness and stability is at risk.[44] And it is precisely because they know the negative consequences of a poor relationship with the school board that superintendents consider establishing and maintaining a positive, productive relationship with the board to be one of the foremost challenges they face. They know, as school board members are reminded in the *American School Board Journal,* that the school board–superintendent relationship "does more to determine the quality of education in your school system than any other single factor."[45]

Role Conflicts

Most superintendents seem pretty clear in their perception of the major source of conflict with the school board: the attempt of school boards to micromanage and become inappropriately involved in administration rather than limiting their role to policy formation. As noted in the previous chapter, in the 1992 AASA study of the superintendency, superintendents perceived the extent to which board members understand and fulfill their appropriate role as the second most serious problem board members face. A Twentieth Century Fund report issued the same year as the AASA report agreed that in many districts school boards have become obstacles to effective change because of their tendency to micromanage and become "immersed in the day-to-day administration" of the schools.[46]

The area where superintendents perceive school boards most want to micromanage is personnel.[47] For some board members, the desire to be involved in personnel decisions stems from an effort to get political supporters or friends or family hired. For others it is because hiring and firing represents power.[48] And for yet others it may simply be a desire to be involved in what are perhaps the most important decisions an organization makes: a number of superintendents have noted that the "new breed" of board members of today are more educated than any in history, often are political activists, and want to be active and involved.[49] Regardless of their intentions, both school boards and superintendents agree that personnel decisions are a major source of their disagreement.

School board members are equally clear that problems with the superintendent come as a result of superintendents attempting to exercise too much control and thinking they should not be questioned or challenged by the school board: superintendents fail to recognize that board members are obligated to represent and respond to those who elected them.[50] Board members today feel a responsibility as well as a pressure to play more active leadership roles. And while this may be a "sign of the times," some superintendents feel it is an invasion of their prerogatives as superintendent.[51] Clearly, resolving the conflict in roles and understanding and practicing shared decision making are major challenges for the superintendent of today and the foreseeable future.

Recognizing the need for clearly defined roles and responsibilities for both the school board and the superintendent, the National School Boards Association (NSBA) and the American Association of School Administrators (AASA) have recently developed and disseminated a publication called *Roles and Relationships . . . School Boards and Superintendents,* designed to meet the need. The joint NSBA/AASA statement is presented in Figure 2–1.

Communication

While open communication is crucial to resolving school board–superintendent role conflicts, communication (or the lack thereof) seems to be a major source of conflict between superintendents and school boards. In fact, several studies of school board–superintendent relationships have found that school board members consider communication problems to be the single biggest cause of conflict between the two parties. Often the failure to communicate results from superintendents not devoting enough time to it. Glass's study of Illinois superintendents found that almost three-fourths of the superintendents spent two hours or less each week in direct contact with board members outside of board meetings.[52]

FIGURE 2–1   Joint NSBA/AASA Statement on Roles and Responsibilities of School Boards and Superintendents

School boards

School boards, the NSBA/AASA statement says, have these specific responsibilities:

• To make clear that the board's primary role is the establishment of policy in furtherance of its function of governance as the epitome of the American institution of representative governance of public elementary and secondary education in our free democracy.

• To work with the superintendent and the community to develop a vision for the schools.

• To establish a structure and crate an environment that will help the school system achieve its vision.

• To develop academic standards based on high expectations and an assessment system to measure academic performance toward the achievement of such standards, so that the school board can be accountable to the people of the community.

• To formulate strategies to help students who are not performing up to standards to attain their maximum potentials.

• To engage in advocacy on behalf of students and their schools and promote the benefits of a public education system to the community.

• To support the superintendent in all decisions that conform to board policy, other decisions made by the board, or recognized professional standards.

• To hold the superintendent responsible and accountable for the administration of the schools through regular, constructive, written and oral evaluations of an ongoing effort and should be linked to goals established by the board with the advice and counsel of the superintendent.

• To provide the superintendent with a comprehensive employment contract.

• To provide fair and adequate compensation that will attract and retain excellent people in all circumstances.

• To give the superintendent the benefit of individual board members' expertise, familiarity with the local school system, and community interests.

• To hold all board meetings with the superintendent or a designee present.

• To consult with the superintendent on all matters, as they arise, that concern the school system, and on which the board may take action.

• To develop a plan for board-superintendent communications.

• To channel communications with school employees through the superintendent, especially if any action is suggested, and to refer all applications, complaints, and other communications, oral or written, first to the superintendent. Doing so ensures that such communications can be processed in a coordinated fashion that is responsive to students and patrons.

• To take action on matters only after hearing the recommendation of the superintendent.

• To include in board policies a specific policy on the effective management of complaints against district personnel.

• To provide the superintendent with administrative assistance, especially in the area of monitoring teaching and learning.

• To exercise continued oversight of all education programs.

• To work closely, where appropriate, with other governmental agencies and bodies.

• To collaborate with other school boards through state and national school boards associations to let state legislators, members of Congress, and all other appropriate state and federal officials know of local concerns and issues.

• To mandate and provide resources for high-quality board and professional development programs using qualified trainers that will enable school leaders to have the knowledge and skills needed to provide excellent policy leadership for the school system. In some cases, boards and superintendents should engage in joint training.

• To provide for self-evaluation of the board's own effectiveness in meeting its stated goals and performing its role in public school governance.

• To establish a periodic review of all school board policies for current relevance and necessity to ensure students' needs are being appropriately served.

• To work to ensure that the district has the necessary funds and that a balance is maintained between needs and resources in the distribution of available monies.

• To delegate to the superintendent responsibilities for all administrative functions, except those specifically reserved to the board's presiding officer through board policy. Those reserved areas include establishing a regular time for the superintendent and the ladder of the school board to meet for discussion of school board policy matters and joint preparation of each meeting agenda, conducting board meetings and certain public hearings, approving the agenda and minutes of board meetings, and engaging in other activities related to serving as the presiding officer of the board.

• To ensure board members understand that, under law, the school board acts as a board and that individual board members have no independent authority.

Superintendents

In keeping with this division of effort, NSBA and AASA say, superintendents have the following specific responsibilities:

• To serve as the school board's chief executive officer and preeminent educational adviser in all efforts of the board to fulfill its school system governance role.

• To serve as the primary educational leader for the school system and chief administrative officer of the entire school district professional and support staff, including staff members assigned to provide support service to the board.

• To serve as a catalyst for the school system's administrative leadership team in proposing and implementing policy changes.

• To propose and institution a process for long-range and strategic planning that will engage the board and the community in positioning the school district for success in ensuring years.

• To keep all board members informed about school operations and programs.

• To interpret the needs of the school system to the board.

• To present policy options along with specific recommendations to the board when circumstances require the board to adopt new policies or review existing policies.

• To develop and inform the board of administrative procedures needed to implement board policy.

• To develop a sound program of school/community relations in concert with the board.

• To oversee management of the district's day-to-day operations.

• To develop a description for the board of what constitutes effective leadership and management of public schools, taking into account that effective leadership and management are the result of effective governance and effective administration combined.

• To develop and carry out a plan for keeping the total professional and support staff informed about the mission, goals, and strategies of the school system and about the important roles all staff members play in realizing them.

• To ensure that professional development opportunities are available to all school system employees.

• To collaborate with other administrators through national and state professional associations to inform state legislators, members of Congress, and all other appropriate state and federal officials of local concerns and issues.

• To ensure that the school system provides equal opportunity for all students.

• To evaluate personnel performance in harmony with district policy and keep the board informed about such evaluations.

• To provide all board members with complete background information and a recommendation for school board action on each agenda item well in advance of each board meeting.

• To develop and implement a continuing plan for working with the news media. —*The Editors*

SOURCE: "NSBA and AASA Sketch Your Roles," *The American School Board Journal,* 181 (June, 1994), pp. 20–21. Reprinted with permission, from *The American School Board Journal* (June 1994). Copyright 1994, the National School Boards Association. All rights reserved.

Other times, communication problems seems to be more the result of commission rather than omission. Among the complaints that board members cite that fall into this category are that the superintendent would not keep the board informed of what was going on in the district; wanted things his or her way or no way; would not take suggestions or advice; got mad if challenged or disagreed with; and tried to intimidate.[53] Another common complaint was that the superintendent withheld information or would not give clear answers. One board president reported that the superintendent "could talk for 30 to 40 minutes and then the board would have to ask him if that was a yes or a no."[54]

Increased Politicization of Board Members

Increasing tensions between boards and superintendents may also be related to school board members becoming more politicized. As Art Gosting, superintendent in Arlington, Virginia, noted: "They have to be more responsive to pressure groups, who are harder and harder to fend off. . . . Sometimes they have to take up issues with the superintendent for their own survival."[55] Pressures come not only from community groups but from employee unions. As Ed Whigham, the former superintendent of Dade County, Florida observed: "Unions increasingly have taken the position that school employee representatives should bypass administrative staff and negotiate directly with boards, who make the final decisions. . . . This has pushed boards deeper into an area traditionally reserved for management.[56]

The increased politicization of board members, the increased criticism of schools, and the growth of special interest groups has also resulted in an increase in single-issue board members. The single-issue board member is one who was elected on a single issue (which could be a geographic area) and remains preoccupied with that issue. A survey by the National School Boards Association found that "the most serious impediments to stable relationships between the school board and the superintendent occur when a single board member advocates an agenda on behalf of his/her constituency that is in conflict with school board goals."[57] Dealing with the single-issue board member can be problematic not only for the superintendent but for the entire board and can interfere with the governance process. Very often the single-issue board member is a member of, or supported by, a special interest group and in the representation of the interests of that group, or in their preoccupation with the single issue, they fail to recognize that they are to represent the interests of all the children in the community and to be equally concerned with all matters affecting their education.

School districts operate best when there is a strong and positive relationship between the school board and the superintendent. As pressures to accomplish major school reform and restructuring continue throughout the 1990s, attention is increasingly being turned to the role of school boards and superintendents in reenergizing public education.[58] In fact, some have gone so far as to declare that there is a "moral and political mandate . . . for improving the relationships between boards and superintendents."[59] Chapter 6 discuss the matter of school board and superintendent relationships in detail.

The Changing Demographics of Students, Teachers, and Administrators

In the 1992 AASA study of the superintendent, changing demographics was identified as the fourth most important issue or challenge facing superintendents. As the following discussion documents, the predicted demographic changes related to students, teachers, and administrators indicates this is likely to remain a major issue for years to come. For example, in 1993–94, for the ninth straight year, the "baby echo boom" of the 1980s combined with immigration from Latin America and Asia to produce an increase in enrollments in the nation's public schools (see Table 2–2). Public school enrollments increased to 43.5 million, up from 42.5 million in the previous year, while private school enrollments increased by almost 100,000, from 5.4 million to 5.5 million. Enrollment increases were greatest in the states of California, Florida, Georgia, Maryland, New Jersey, New York, Ohio, Pennsylvania, Texas, and Washington, each of which experienced enrollment growths of more than 20,000 students from the previous year.

The enrollment increases of the past decade are expected to continue into the next century. The Department of Education's National Center for Education Statistics predicts that total public and private school enrollments will reach 51.8 million in 1996, surpassing the previous peak of 51.3 million attained in 1971. Enrollments are projected to increase further to 55.7 million by the year 2004, an increase of 14 percent from 1993.

Not only the student population is growing and predicted to continue to grow: so is the minority student enrollment. The percentage of Hispanic students in the public schools increased from 8.0 to 12.3 percent between the school years 1980–81 and 1991–92, while the percentage of Asian-American and Pacific Islander students rose from 1.9 to 3.5 percent over the same period. Smaller increases were evidenced for the black and American Indian/Alaskan Native students populations, which grew from 16.1 to 16.5 percent and from 0.8 to 1.0 percent, respectively. The U.S. Department of Education predicts that by the year 2020 almost half the students in our nation's schools will be minorities.[60] In some states this situation has already occurred. In California, Hawaii, Mississippi, New Mexico, and Texas, minority students constitute a majority of the school age population.

A major factor contributing to the increase in the student population, particularly the minority population, is immigration. Immigration accounts for one-third of the annual increase in the U.S. population. The impact of immigration on many school districts, large and small alike, has been staggering. Immigrant children are often non– or limited–English speakers. Thus, in a large part the result of immigration, while overall school enrollments increased 4 percent from 1986 to 1991, the number of limited English proficient students rose by 50 percent.[61] One of the most visible examples of the cost of immigration can be seen in the Dade County, Florida school system, where one-fourth of its student population is foreign-born. Dade County estimates that in 1993 it expended $311 million in operating expenses for its foreign-born students, only $10.8 million of which was provided by the federal government. The district also estimates that the cost of housing these students will be $282 million.[62] And for many districts, like Dade County, the problem is not only one of instructional space, but finding enough bilingual teachers for the array of languages spoken by the immigrant children.

As the student population grows, so does the need for school personnel. Unfortunately, the critical issue for superintendents is that the projections regarding the availability of teaching and administrative staff required to meet the needs of the burgeoning and changing student population is not positive. The need for teachers is expected to increase at an annual rate of 1.7 percent from 1993 to 1997, then 1.0 percent from 1998 to 2004. This means that by the year 1998 a total of 3.1 million classroom teachers would be needed, and by 2004 this would increase to 3.3 million,[63] producing a demand for 130,000–135,000 new teachers per year over much of this period.[64]

This demand will result in a shortage of teachers, which will be greater in some areas and in some disciplines than others. Florida, one of the many states with projected enrollment increases, expects to have 10,000 public school vacancies per year until the year

TABLE 2–2   Elementary and Secondary School Enrollments: 1869–70 to Fall 2004 (in thousands)

Year	Total	Public Schools			Private Schools		
		Total	K–8	9–12	Total	K–8	9–12
1869–70	—	6,872	6,792	80	—	—	—
1879–80	—	9,868	9,757	110	—	—	—
1889–90	14,334	12,723	12,520	203	1,611	1,516	95
1899–1900	16,855	15,503	14,984	519	1,352	1,241	111
1909–10	19,372	17,814	16,899	915	1,558	1,441	117
1919–20	23,278	21,578	19,378	2,200	1,699	1,486	214
1929–30	28,329	25,678	21,279	4,399	2,651	2,310	341
1939–40	28,045	25,434	18,832	6,601	2,611	2,153	458
1949–50	28,492	25,111	19,387	5,725	3,380	2,708	672
Fall 1959	40,857	35,182	26,911	8,271	5,675	4,640	1,035
Fall 1964	47,716	41,416	30,025	11,391	6,300	5,000	1,300
Fall 1965	48,473	42,173	30,563	11,610	6,300	4,900	1,400
Fall 1966	49,239	43,039	31,145	11,894	6,200	4,800	1,400
Fall 1967	49,891	43,891	31,641	12,250	6,000	4,600	1,400
Fall 1968	50,744	44,944	32,226	12,718	5,600	4,400	1,400
Fall 1969	51,050	45,550	32,513	13,037	5,500	4,200	1,300
Fall 1970	51,267	45,894	32,558	13,336	5,363	4,052	1,311
Fall 1971	51,271	46,071	32,318	13,753	5,200	3,900	1,300
Fall 1972	50,726	45,726	31,879	13,846	5,000	3,700	1,300
Fall 1973	50,444	45,444	31,401	14,044	5,000	3,700	1,300
Fall 1974	50,073	45,073	30,971	14,103	5,000	3,700	1,300
Fall 1975	49,819	44,819	30,515	14,304	5,000	3,700	1,300
Fall 1976	49,478	44,311	29,997	14,314	5,167	3,825	1,342
Fall 1977	48,717	43,577	29,375	14,203	5,140	3,797	1,343
Fall 1978	47,637	42,551	28,483	14,088	5,086	3,732	1,353

2010. And even in California, where budget problems have forced districts to increase class size and cut back on hiring replacements for teachers who leave or retire, there is currently, and is projected to continue to be, a strong demand for bilingual and special education teachers. These same teachers are in demand in almost all states, as are teachers who are members of minority groups.[65]

There is projected to be a shortage of not only teachers, but also of administrators. About one-half of the nation's superintendents are over the age of 50[66] and will retire by the year 2000.[67] The "graying of administrators" is no less a occurrence among principals, the customary source of new applicants for the superintendency.[68] Superintendents, then, are faced with not only the challenge of finding qualified personnel for the classrooms, but with finding qualified personnel to fill their own ranks.

Violence and Crime in the Schools

Goal 7 of the Goals 2000: Educate America Act states that "By the Year 2000, every school will be free of drugs, firearms, alcohol and violence and will offer a disciplined environ-

Year	Total	Public Schools			Private Schools		
		Total	K–8	9–12	Total	K–8	9–12
Fall 1979	46,651	41,651	28,034	13,616	5,000	3,700	1,300
Fall 1980	46,208	40,877	27,647	13,231	5,331	3,992	1,339
Fall 1981	45,544	40,044	27,280	12,764	5,500	4,100	1,400
Fall 1982	45,166	39,566	27,161	12,405	5,600	4,200	1,400
Fall 1983	44,967	39,252	26,981	12,271	5,715	4,315	1,400
Fall 1984	44,908	39,208	26,905	12,304	5,700	4,300	1,400
Fall 1985	44,979	39,422	27,034	12,388	5,557	4,195	1,362
Fall 1986	45,205	39,753	27,420	12,333	5,452	4,116	1,336
Fall 1987	45,488	40,008	27,933	12,076	5,479	4,232	1,247
Fall 1988	45,430	40,189	28,501	11,687	5,241	4,036	1,206
Fall 1989	45,898	40,543	29,152	11,390	5,355	4,162	1,193
Fall 1990	46,448	41,217	29,878	11,338	5,232	4,095	1,137
Fall 1991	47,246	42,047	30,506	11,541	5,199	4,074	1,125
Fall 1992	48,109	42,735	30,997	11,738	5,375	4,212	1,163
Fall 1993	48,824	43,353	31,374	11,979	5,471	4,280	1,191
Fall 1994	49,819	44,254	31,837	12,417	5,565	4,333	1,232
Fall 1995	50,709	45,049	32,275	12,774	5,660	4,393	1,267
Fall 1996	51,762	45,988	32,841	13,147	5,774	4,470	1,304
Fall 1997	52,714	46,835	33,395	13,440	5,879	4,545	1,333
Fall 1998	53,382	47,430	33,798	13,632	5,952	4,600	1,352
Fall 1999	53,942	47,927	34,145	13,782	6,015	4,648	1,367
Fall 2000	54,412	48,345	34,441	13,904	6,067	4,688	1,379
Fall 2001	54,816	48,705	34,670	14,035	6,111	4,719	1,392
Fall 2002	55,162	49,014	34,846	14,168	6,148	4,743	1,405
Fall 2003	55,459	49,280	34,955	14,325	6,179	4,758	1,421
Fall 2004	55,706	49,506	34,923	14,583	6,200	4,753	1,446

SOURCE: U.S. Department of Education, National Center for Education Statistics, *Digest of Education Statistics* (Washington, D.C.: U.S. Department of Education, 1993), p. 12.

ment conducive to learning." Few superintendents in this country believe that this goal can be met unless there is a dramatic reversal in the tide of violence and crime that is sweeping our nation, including its schools. In fact, the level of violence in the nation's schools has led some educators to ask public officials to declare a "state of emergency" to deal with the problem.[69] Deeply troubled by the "corrosive and debilitating" violence in society that has spilled over into the schools, Secretary of Education Riley joined President Clinton and other national educational and political leaders in supporting the Safe Schools Act and other legislation aimed at crime prevention and intervention in and around the schools.[70]

The magnitude of the problem of school violence has been documented by numerous surveys and reports, as well as on the front pages of the newspapers and on prime time news. The U.S. Justice Department's National Crime Survey estimates 3 million thefts and violent crimes occur on school property each year, or 16,000 per day, and that teenagers are more than twice as likely to be the victims of violent crime as any other group.[71] In fact, the Metropolitan Life survey of *Violence in America's Public Schools* found that one-fourth of America's public school students have been the victim of an act of violence in or around school.[72] The situation is even more serious in urban areas. A Justice Department study of 10 inner-city schools found that 45 percent of the students had been threatened with a gun or shot at while on the way to or from school and 10 percent had been stabbed.[73] According to Pepperdine University's National School Safety Center, many of today's students

> face daily decisions regarding high risk situations. . . . Plotting a hallway route becomes a matter of survival. Attending class depends upon the presence or absence of weapons carriers. To use or not to use the restroom replaces the decision to memorize or not to memorize Hamlet's soliloquy.[74]

Not only students, but school board members and school personnel are also reporting an increase in school violence. In a recent report by the National School Boards Association (NSBA), 82 percent of the districts surveyed reported an increase in violence in the past five years, with student-on-student violence being reported as the most frequent form of violence.[75] In a similar survey of principals and superintendents, 46 percent of the respondents said that they were dealing with more acts of violence than five years previously, and 66 percent predicted school violence to increase in the next two years. Perhaps most disturbing, they also reported that more violence is infiltrating middle and elementary schools compared with five years earlier: one in five elementary principals and one in four middle school principals reported an increase in incidents involving guns at school. Also worrisome is that alcohol problems and alcohol-related incidents are increasingly affecting elementary schools. In addition, the problem of violence and gang-related incidents was reported to be greatest in urban school districts and in schools with a majority black or racially mixed student body.[76]

School District Responses

In response to the growing culture of violence, school districts across the country have been forced to take additional security measures. For example, a growing number of school districts are spending millions of dollars to hire their own police force. And a number of districts in California and elsewhere have adopted a "zero tolerance" policy requiring that any student who brings a weapon to school or commits a violent act is automatically remanded to the control of the police and sent to Juvenile Hall and detained there until he or she can see a judge. Since this policy was adopted in 1993 in San Diego, the number of violent crimes in or around the San Diego district has decreased by 33 percent.[77]

While not hiring its own police force, in a smaller school district outside Pittsburgh (Monroeville), the superintendent issued metal detecting "wands" to building administrators and hired a plainclothes security officer to park in a red pickup truck outside the high school to report to the office by radio anyone entering the school grounds who might create a problem. And in areas where the infiltration of gangs is a major concern, school officials are working with the police to identify and prohibit the wearing of gang-related colors and clothing symbols, such as baseball caps worn backward, sagging shoelaces, hairnets, earrings, or certain jackets.[78]

Table 2–3 reports how school districts in the NSBA survey are responding to the increase in school violence. As indicated, the enactment and enforcement of tougher penalties seems to be the most common strategy, with approximately three-fourths of the dis-

TABLE 2–3   School District Strategies to Reduce Violence

Strategy	Percentage of Districts Using Strategy
Suspensions	78
Student conduct/discipline codes	76
Collaboration with other agencies	73
Expulsions	72
School board policies	71
Alternative programs	66
Staff development	62
Conflict resolution/mediation training	61
Locker searches	50
Closed campuses	44
Mentoring programs	43
Home–school linkages	42
Dress codes	41
Law-related education programs	39
Multicultural sensitivity training	39
Parent skill training	38
Security personnel	36
Student photo IDs	32
Gun-free zones	31
Specialized curriculum	27
Drug-detecting dogs	24
Work opportunities	23
Phones in classrooms	22
Metal detectors	15
Parent patrols	13
Closed-circuit TV	11

SOURCE: "U.S. Schools Respond to Violent Society," *School Board News*, 14 (January 18, 1994), p. 4.

tricts suspending or expelling students guilty of committing an act of violence. Many other districts are experimenting with tighter security measures such a campus security personnel, drug-detecting dogs, metal detectors, or video surveillance on school buses. For superintendents, the issue becomes not only which strategy is most effective, but which can the district afford, and what will be the result of taking dollars from instructional programs to spend on violence prevention and intervention.

Workplace Violence

While student-on-student assault may be the most frequent form of violence, superintendents have also been faced with a growing number of assaults on teachers (reported by 24% of the districts in the NSBA survey[79]) as well as on themselves. While the vast majority (95%) of the attacks on teachers have been by students,[80] the same is not true regarding assaults on superintendents. In December 1993, a high school teacher in Chelsea, Michigan fatally shot the superintendent and wounded the school principal and another teacher during a staff meeting. Two months later, a former teacher shot and killed the superintendent of Lee County, Florida schools in his office before turning the gun on himself. Numerous other superintendents report having received death threats.

While this tally does not suggest that the superintendency should be labeled a dangerous profession, it does suggest that superintendents can no longer take their safety and
security for granted. As public figures often placed in the center of controversial issues,
and as the school official with a formal role in student and employee dismissals, superintendents have always been targets for disgruntled parents, students, and employees. However, with the growing violence in society, as superintendents take additional steps to protect their students from violence, they should take reasonable precautions to protect
themselves.[81]

Increasing Pressures and Challenges from Special Interest Groups

One of the more troublesome and difficult challenges facing superintendents in attempting
to make fundamental changes in the public schools is the pressures and challenges coming
from various special interest groups. According to AASA reports, superintendents are
experiencing a significant increase in the number of special interest groups trying to influence school district policies and decisions.[82] And not only is there an increase in the number of challenges coming from special interest groups, but they have become more intense
and are given considerable media attention. According to the Urban Superintendent's Network: "Special interest groups occupy powerful positions that dictate much of what a
superintendent can and cannot do."[83]

Many local special interest groups have come into being as a result of national social
movements. However, unlike those of earlier decades that were interested in building up
institutions such as the schools, the social movements with which many of today's special
interest groups identify are challenging public institutions, including the schools, and are
attempting to make them more responsive to forces outside the local administrative structures.[84] As a result, school boards and superintendents cannot control the groups' agendas
or shape their outcomes as they once did. As a superintendent in a 1993 study of district
politics is quoted as saying: "We've got so much power in special interests that it's very
difficult for anyone to be responsible for the big picture."[85]

Challenges to school district policies and decisions, goals and objectives, specific curriculum or instructional methodologies, or to individual school board members or school
district employees come from any number of special interest groups, from civil rights
groups to environmentalists. Pressure is applied using all avenues and in all forms, from
legal challenges to street demonstrations.[86] However, while challenges have come from a
wide range of groups, the most significant and aggressive challenges in recent years have
come from conservative citizens groups.[87] And while challenges to school curriculum and
practices are not new, the recent challenges by conservative groups are particularly significant, not only because of their increasing numbers, but because of the shift in targets from
those in the past and because of the tactics they employ. Prior to the 1980s the targets of
curricular challenges were usually individual books (e.g., *The Catcher in the Rye*) and
were made by individual parents acting on they own. More recent challenges, however, are
often organized by national conservative groups and often focus on an entire textbook
series, an entire instructional program, or on strategies to redesign schooling.[88] Courses
such as psychology, sociology, and health, as well as instructional units related to sex edu-

cation, AIDS education, values clarification, self-esteem building, and global education are also popular targets. Outcome-based education, a popular reform strategy intended to focus on performance-based student outcomes, is vilified as embodying "affective" learning, values-based education, and replacing basic skills and academic subject matter with subjective learning outcomes.

The implications of this shift in targets for superintendents and others wanting to reform education has been summarized by Martha M. McCarthy, former president of the National Organization for Legal Problems in Education:

> These recent challenges to textbook series, pedagogical approaches, and thinking-skills programs call into question some of the basic assumptions of school restructuring initiatives [e.g., that students should examine alternatives critically and take responsibility for their learning]. Thus they pose far more serious threats to efforts to improve the public school program than do challenges to individual novels.[89]

In their efforts to influence school district policies and practices, the more aggressive and "right wing" conservative groups appear less interested in gaining equal representation in the system than taking it over.[90] In so doing their tactics are reminiscent of old-fashioned ward politics: "dominating discussion at school board meetings and political events, getting sympathizers out to vote, misrepresenting the opposition's views and record, conducting all-out telephone canvassing, developing a thorough mastery of the issues, digging up dirt on their opponents . . . and spouting generalities rather than specifics."[91] In these activities local efforts are often supported by national groups who have developed the resources and expertise for just such purposes.

Obviously, the best way to influence school district policies and decisions is to influence school board members or become a school board member. Accordingly, conservative groups have concentrated their recent efforts on school board elections. The most benign efforts consist of distributing to local churches "fact sheets" on all candidates emphasizing the candidates' positions on issues of concern to the special interest group, as well as actively campaigning for the candidates of the choice. The National Association of Christian Educators/Citizens for Excellence in Education (NACE/CEE) distributes the book *How to Elect Christians for Public Office* to all its 1,600 chapters. Unfortunately, not all the strategies suggested are designed to provide an open forum for discussion of educational issues. NACE's executive director, Robert Simonds, suggests that candidates for public office present themselves as caring parents rather than members of the Christian Right. And in perhaps hundreds of school board elections, "stealth" tactics have been used in which religious conservative candidates have used videotapes, billboards, and campaign literature rather than subject themselves to face-to-face meetings with opponents and voters.[92]

Superintendents recognize the right of citizens to challenge the actions of the school board or themselves. Most also recognize that these challenges serve a necessary purpose in a democratic educational system in that they force us to reexamine and be clear about our goals and purposes. However, when the stated goal of some conservative groups is to "gain complete control of all local school boards . . . [in order to] determine all local policy, select good textbooks, good curriculum programs, *superintendents,* and principals"[93] (emphasis added), and when the principal goal of other conservative groups appears to be to "discredit public education to the point that the entire system will crumble and be replaced with unregulated vouchers that allow parents to select private Christian schools,"[94] the growing concern of superintendents over the increased activism of these groups appears to be both warranted and understandable.

Summary

As the nation approaches the twenty-first century all aspects of its society are becoming increasingly complex and interrelated, presenting issues and challenges to the superintendent of schools that at times seem insurmountable. Superintendents continue to face the challenge of providing a quality education for the children of the district while revenues are declining and mandates are increasing, as are demands for greater accountability and productivity. At the same time, the school reform movement, which began more than a decade ago and has continued largely without the substantive involvement of superintendents, confronts the superintendent with not only the challenge to find a way to become a major player in the movement, but the challenge of adapting to the shift in the existing power relationships in school systems. Superintendents are asked to share their decision-making authority and to become transformational leaders.

The reform movement has not only brought a change in power relationships within the school system, but alternative proposals for restructuring the way schools are organized and administered and how educational services are delivered. One proposal, site-based management, which actually predates the reform movement, challenges superintendents to maintain a balance between decentralization and centralization. The various privatization initiatives present a different set of challenges, as the role of the superintendent has not been clearly defined.

Role definition seems also to be the major issue involved in superintendent–school board relationships. The reform movement, the increasing demands of special interest groups, and the increased politicization of board members themselves have brought increased tensions to what historically has been a strained relationship.

The superintendent today and in the foreseeable future must also face a number of challenges related to the changing demographics of students and staff. The student population is not only growing in size but in the size of the minority population, many of whom are immigrants. Superintendents are challenged to find the teachers and administrators necessary to service this growing population, especially minority personnel and teachers in such areas as bilingual education and special education. Lastly, superintendents must find a way to combat the epidemic of violence that has spread to our schools, and, tragically, into their very offices.

Discussion Questions

1. In what ways has the school reform movement affected the financing of the schools in your state?

2. In what ways can the superintendent be an entrepreneur and remain in the public sector?

3. Assume you are a newly appointed superintendent. What steps will you take to ensure that you communicate effectively with the board?

4. Which of the actions listed in Table 2–3 has your district taken to combat school violence and crime? How successful have these efforts been? Which have been the most successful?

5. What strategies can a poor or rural district use to recruit and retain teachers and administrators? What strategies can any district use to recruit more minority teachers?

CASE 2.1   How "Special" Is Your Special Interest?

At the regularly scheduled March meeting of the Lennox School District Board of Trustees, when the board reached the agenda item that provided for input from the audience, Perry Worth asked to be heard. Mr. Worth, who said he represented the America Only League, spoke long and vehemently against the use of foreign automobile motors in the auto mechanics class. Basically Mr. Worth's position was that publicly supported American schools are undermining American industries and insulting the American worker by promoting the use of foreign-made products. In an aside, he also noted that the superintendent and two of the trustees drove foreign-made automobiles. He requested that the objected-to motors be removed and be replaced by motors from American-made automobiles. The board chairwoman turned to Superintendent Mathis for a response.

Questions

1. What should be Superintendent Mathis's response? Is the superintendent obligated to justify the district's actions to Mr. Worth?
2. If the America Only League were to agree to pay for the replacement of the motors, should the superintendent agree to Mr. Worth's request? Why or why not?
3. What policies might the superintendent recommend to ensure the broad array of community interests are considered in sensitive and important decisions?

Inbasket Exercise

INBASKET 2.1

Cutting the Budget: A Matter of Style

Early in the third quarter it appears certain that state revenues for the current fiscal year will fall short of those anticipated. The projections for next year do not signal any improvement. In fact, the situation may get worse before it gets better. School districts are being told to expect, *at best,* a zero increase in their budgets, and to actually prepare for a budget reduction of 3–5 percent.

Draft a memo from Superintendent Reed to the staff about the budget reduction and how it will be handled. Superintendent Reed may be considered a transactional leader.

Draft a memo from Superintendent Sykes about the same topic. Superintendent Sykes may be considered a transformational leader.

Notes

1. "Leadership," *Education Vital Signs,* a supplement to *Executive Educator,* 15 (December 1993): p. A16.

2. Stanley M. Elam, Lowell C. Rose, and Alex M. Gallup, "The Twenty-sixth Annual Phi Delta Kappan/Gallup Poll of the Public's Attitudes toward the Public Schools," *Phi Delta Kappan,* 76 (September 1994): pp. 41–56.

3. Mark Walsh, "Main Events," *Education Vital Signs,* a supplement to *Executive Educator,* 15 (December 1993): pp. A3–A7.

4. James W. Boothe, Leo H. Bradley, T. Michael Flick, Katherine E. Keough, and Susanne P. Kirk, "This Working Life," *Executive Educator,* 16 (February 1994): pp. 39–40.

5. Allen Odden, "Including School Finance in Systemic Reform Strategies: A Commentary," *CPRE Finance Briefs* (New Brunswick, N.J., 1994).

6. Chris Pipho, "The New Climate for School Finance," *Phi Delta Kappan,* 75 (April 1994): pp. 39–40.

7. Odden, "Including School Finance in Systemic Reform Strategies."

8. Boothe et al., "This Working Life."

9. From an interview with Richard Rossmiller in Anne Turnbaugh Lockwood, "Equity or Adequacy," *Focus in Change,* 13 (winter 1994): pp. 12–14.

10. Odden, "Including School Finance in Systemic Reform Strategies."

11. Pipho, "The New Climate for School Finance."

12. Jerome Murphy, "The Paradoxes of Decentralization," in *Leading the Way* (Boston: Massachusetts Department of Education, Office of Community Education and Massachusetts Association of School Superintendents, 1990).

13. Joseph Murphy, "The 'Maytag Man' of School Reform," *School Administrator,* 2(48) (February 1991): p. 32.

14. Louis V. Gerstner Jr., Rodger D. Semerad, Denis Philip Doyle, and William B. Johnston, *Reinventing Education Entrepreneurship in America's Public Schools* (New York: Dutton, 1994).

15. Ibid., pp. 117–118.

16. Ibid.

17. Douglas E. Mitchell and Sharon Tucker, "Leadership as a Way of Thinking," *Educational Leadership,* 49 (February 1993): pp. 30–35.

18. Seymour Bern Sarason, *The Predictable Failure of Educational Reform* (San Francisco, Calif.: Jossey-Bass, 1990).

19. Kenneth A. Leithwood, "The Move toward Transformational Leadership," *Educational Leadership,* 49 (February 1992): pp. 8–12.

20. Jean Zlotkin, "Rethinking the School Board's Role," *Educational Leadership,* 51 (October 1993): pp. 22–25.

21. Mitchell and Tucker, "Leadership as a Way of Thinking," p. 32.

22. Zlotkin, "Rethinking the School Board's Role."

23. Ibid.

24. Joseph Murphy, "Maytag Man," p. 33.

25. Jerome Murphy, "The Paradoxes of Decentralization," p. 5.

26. Irwin Blumer, "Communication: Building Support for the Value of School-Based Management among School Constituencies," in *Leading the Way* (Boston: Massachusetts Department of Education, Office of Community Education and Massachusetts Association of School Superintendents, 1990), p. 10.

27. Ibid.

28. Jerome Murphy, "The Paradoxes of Decentralization."

29. Mark Walsh, "Beginning in 1995 Edison Project to Manage Two Schools in Wichita," *Education Week* (18 May 1994): p. 9.

30. Martha M. McCarthy, "External Challenges to Public Education: Values in Conflict," paper presented at the Annual Meeting of the American Education Research Association, New Orleans, April 1994.

31. Mark Walsh, "Three Edison Plans Win Charter School Backing in Mass.," *Education Week* (23 March 1994): p. 13.

32. Chris Pipho, "Bipartisan Charter Schools," *Phi Delta Kappan,* 75 (October 1993): pp. 102–103.

33. Pricilla Wohlsetter and Lesley Anderson, "What Can U.S. Charter Schools Learn from England's Grant–Maintained Schools?" *Phi Delta Kappan,* 75 (February 1994): pp. 416–419.

34. Peter Schmidt, "Private Enterprise," *Education Week* (25 May 1994): pp. 27–30.

35. John M. McLaughlin, "Privatization Trend Likely to Continue," *School Board News* (7 June 1994): pp. 4–5; McCarthy, "External Challenges to Public Education."

36. Chris Pipho, "Taxes, School Boards, and Higher Education," *Phi Delta Kappan,* 75 (January 1994): pp. 358–359.

37. Schmidt, "Private Enterprise."

38. "Privatization Update," *School Board News* (7 June 1994): p. 4.

39. McCarthy, "External Challenges to Public Education."

40. John T. Golle, "'You Must Take Care of Your Customer,'" *Education Week* (22 June 1994): p. 44.

41. Barbara McCloud and Floretta Duke McKenzie, "School Boards and Superintendents in Urban Districts," *Phi Delta Kappan,* 75 (January 1994): pp. 384–385.

42. Jack McCurdy, *Building Better Board–Administrator Relations* (Arlington, Va.: American Association of School Administrators, 1992).

43. "NSBA and AASA Sketch Your Roles," *American School Board Journal,* 181 (June 1994): pp. 20–21.

44. "Urban Superintendent Turnover, the Need for Stability," *Sounding Board,* 1 (winter 1992): p. 3.

45. Burton Nygren, "Two Party Tune Up," *American School Board Journal,* 178 (July 1992): p. 35.

46. Lynn Olson, "Redefine Role, Duties of School Boards to Focus on Policy, Report Advocates," *Education Week* (8 April 1992): pp. 1, 14.

47. McCurdy, *Building Better Board–Administrator Relations,* p. 47, citing the 1992 National School Boards Association report, *Urban Dynamics.*

48. Ibid.

49. "Superintendent–School Board Relations," *Sounding Board,* 1 (winter 1992): pp. 4–5; McCurdy, *Building Better Board–Administrator Relations.*

50. McCloud and McKenzie, "School Boards and Superintendents in Urban Districts."

51. McCurdy, *Building Better Board–Administrator Relations.*

52. Thomas E. Glass, *The Illinois Public School Superintendent's Opinions on Key Issues as Reported on Surveys Conducted Between 1986–1993* (Springfield, Ill.: Illinois Association of School Administrators, 1993).

53. Marilyn L. Grady and Miles T. Bryant, "School Board presidents Tell Why Their Superintendents Fail," *Executive Educator,* 13 (May 1991): pp. 24–25; Edward W. Chance and James L. Capps, *Superintendent Instability in Small/Rural Schools: The School Board Perspective* (ERIC ED 350121, 1992); McCurdy, *Building Better Board–Administrator Relations.*

54. Chance and Capps, *Superintendent Instability in Small/Rural Schools.*

55. McCurdy, *Building Better Board–Administrator Relations,* p. 52. (quoting Gosting)

56. Ibid. (discussing Whigham)

57. Ibid., p. 53, citing the 1992 NSBA report, *Urban Dynamics.*

58. Ibid.

59. McCloud and McKenzie, "School Boards and Superintendents in Urban Districts," p. 385.

60. "State of the States," *Education Vital Signs,* a supplement to *Executive Educator,* 15 (December 1993): pp. A24–A31.

61. Ibid.

62. Karen Diegmueller, "Education Bulk of Immigration Costs, Fla. Says," *Education Week* (11 May 1994): p. 14.

63. U.S. Department of Education, National Center for Education Statistics, *Projections of Education Statistics to 2004* (Washington, D.C.: U.S. Department of Education, 1993).

64. U. S. Department of Education, National Center for Education Statistics, *Projections to 2001: An Update* (Washington, D.C.: U.S. Department of Education, 1991).

65. Steven Drummond, "Outlook for New Teachers in Job Market Rosey," *Education Week* (8 June 1994): p. 5.

66. Glass, *Illinois Public School Superintendent's Opinions.*

67. Thomas E. Glass, *The 1992 Study of the American School Superintendency: America's Educational Leaders in a Time of Reform* (Washington, D.C.: American Association of School Administrators, 1992).

68. Robert L. Crowson and Thomas E. Glass, "The Changing Role of the Local School District Superintendent in the United States," paper presented at the Annual Meeting of the American Educational Research Association, Chicago, April 1991.

69. "D. C. Anti-Violence Plan Includes Locker Searches, Police Patrols," *Education Week* (23 March 1994): p. 4.

70. Jessica Portner, "Riley Advocates Multi-Prong Attack on Problem of School Violence," *Education Week* (20 April 1994): p. 16.

71. Pat Ordovensky, "Facing Up to Violence," *Executive Educator,* 15 (February 1993): pp. 22–24.

72. Louis Harris and Associates, Inc., *The Metropolitan Life Survey of the American Teacher. Violence in America's Public Schools* (New York: Metropolitan Life Insurance Co., 1994).

73. Portner, "Riley Advocates Multi-Prong Attack on Problem of School Violence."

74. Ordovensky, "Facing Up to Violence," p. 22.

75. "U. S. Schools Respond to Violent Society," *School Board News,* 14 (18 January 1994): pp. 1, 4.

76. James W. Boothe, T. Michael Flick, Susanne P. Kirk, Leo H. Bradley, and Katherine E. Keough, "The Violence at Your Door," *Executive Educator,* 15 (February 1993): pp. 16–24.

77. Jessica Portner, "Cops on Campus," *Education Week* (22 June 1994): pp. 22, 30.

78. Ordovensky, "Facing Up to Violence."

79. "U. S. Schools Respond to Violent Society."

80. Louis Harris and Associates, Inc., *Metropolitan Life Survey.*

81. Jo Anna Natale, "Your Life on the Line," *Executive Educator,* 16 (May 1994): pp. 22–26.

82. "Leadership," *Vital Signs,* a supplement to *Executive Educator,* 15 (December 1993): p. A16.

83. "The Changing Superintendency," *Sounding Board,* 1 (winter 1992): p. 2.

84. Michael W. Kirst, "A Changing Context Means School Board Reform," *Phi Delta Kappan,* 75 (January 1994): pp. 378–381.

85. Ibid., p. 381.

86. Patricia Howett, "Politics Comes to School," *Executive Educator,* 15 (January 1993): pp. 14–20.

87. Martha M. McCarthy, "Challenges to the Public School Curriculum: New Targets and Strategies," *Phi Delta Kappan,* 75 (September 1993): pp. 55–60.

88. McCarthy, "External Challenges to Public Education," p. 14. (See n. 39.)

89. McCarthy, "Challenges to the Public School Curriculum," p. 56.

90. George R. Kaplan, "Shotgun Wedding: Notes on Public Education's Encounter with the New Christian Right," *Phi Delta Kappan,* 75 (May 1994): pp. K1–K12.

91. Ibid., p. K10.

92. Ibid.

93. Robert Simonds as quoted in McCarthy, "Challenges to the Public School Curriculum," p. 59.

94. McCarthy, "External Challenges to Public Education," referencing R. Buckman and W. Thomas, and M. Ledell.

Leadership Perspectives: The Life of the School Superintendent

The condition of a society determines the type of leadership it desires. So it is with schools. Educational leadership faces a number of challenges today. For example, school leaders must accommodate the needs of diverse populations, establish fair and realistic expectations for students, provide for the placement of advanced technologies in the schools, and collaborate with other community agencies to develop programs that will better serve the needs of children.

Foremost among the challenges facing leaders in education is the need to restore respect for America's schools. Rapid changes in the global society have perplexed business, political, and educational leaders. America's economic competitiveness has been the topic of much discussion during the 1980s and 1990s. Like it or not, ailments in economic competitiveness are most often linked with the education of the work force. When America is ailing, schools have traditionally served as the agency to provide remedies. In decades past, time, although never abundant, served as an ally. Educators had ample time to design new programs and procedures. That is no longer the case. In a society such as ours schools need to be in a continuous state of adjustment. Change has become a constant!

Unprecedented changes, calls for school reform, and new technologies require masterful leadership. School leaders are expected to design and implement educational programs to serve children and society well into the future. The primary responsibility for this grand design rests with the superintendent of schools. It is the superintendent who provides leadership that informs, inspires, and engages the community, empowers teachers, and convinces policymakers that schools can and must carry out the mandates of a diverse and rapidly changing society. The multiplicity of the role serves to make the life of the superintendent challenging as well as rewarding.

While much emphasis has been given to the improvement of the instructional leadership role of principals, little attention has been focused on the executive leadership position. As noted by Glass, "the superintendency as a profession is still very much in a developmental state. The current wave of school reform has created a great deal of discussion and even produced some state legislation aimed at improving training and encouraging extensive internships for superintendents."[1] Hord reported, "many educators believe that as policymakers become frustrated with the slow rate of school restructuring/reform success in the 1990's, there will be a renewed and significant attention paid to executive leadership of school districts, namely, the superintendency."[2]

To fully explain the school executive's work is a challenge and perhaps no single profile can do justice to the complexities of the job. Individuals who seek the superintendency as a profession, however, must clearly understand the lifestyle they are likely to encounter as a school executive. This chapter provides information about the life of a school superintendent—leadership perspectives related to the role, the professional expectations of persons serving as school executives, the importance of constant preparation and study, and the necessity to seek balance between professional and personal life. Its purposes are to describe several perspectives of leadership, to inform readers about the importance of constructing a leadership foundation based on trust, and to identify frameworks that enable school executives to define their professional role so they may carry out the mandates of the position. It is intended to create a picture of the multiplicity of roles a superintendent must play and to encourage current and prospective school executives to reflect on their personal and professional missions.

Just as the frames around pictures focus the viewer's eye, so can they be used to view leadership, work, family, or life in general. In this chapter we intend to draw several frames around the superintendency that will assist the reader in gaining a perspective of the job role. While time and space limit the number of job attributes that can be investigated, we hope the reader will understand the importance of developing a variety of frameworks for viewing executive leadership in schools. We begin with the proposition that leaders must be trusted and to be trusted they must establish an identity that connects them to the work and the people. This professional identity will serve as a frame through which others view them and the effectiveness of their leadership.

Leadership Perspectives, Professional Identities, and Trust

Some people want a leader who performs magnificently in the face of never-ending crises; others want someone to blame when something goes wrong. These two views are widely held and prevail as the dominant mental models of leadership. New times require new leadership, and somewhere in the great expanse between these two perspectives of leadership there exist better, more workable models for those who are drawn to the superintendency.

The professional life of the superintendent centers on how his or her leadership is viewed. Maxcy provides a traditional, but useful, perspective by focusing on three theories of leadership: leadership as a set of character traits, leadership as a set of specific behaviors, and leadership as a function of school climate.[3] The first, leadership as a set of character traits, examines psychological traits of leaders. The theory holds that certain people are endowed with unique aspects of character that make them effective as leaders: dedication, strength, determination, vision and moral fortitude, to name a few. This perspective suggests that leaders "may be more born than made." The second perspective highlights behaviors or styles displayed by leaders. Leaders may exhibit styles that can be best described as intuitive, nurturing, analytical, driving, and so on. Regardless of the description of the behavior, it has been interesting to speculate if the leadership position defined the behavior or if the behavior defined the position. The final leadership perspective is defined in terms of school climate. The assumptions about climate and leadership hold that leaders are more likely to be influenced by norms and beliefs ingrained in the school culture than by more conventional rules or regulations. In other words, the organizational culture, the result of the collective habits and customs of its membership, may shape the behavior of the leader. Each of the three perspectives provides an instructive framework for viewing school leadership.

Other leadership perspectives help to frame the role of the leader: as a visionary, as a person who leads from a principle-centered foundation, and as a builder who creates a capacity within the organization to empower it to be successful in a variety of environments. These leadership perspectives allow us to construct realistic expectations for leaders who serve education. Implicit among the expectations of educational leaders are strong notions about ethical behavior, positive role modeling, and the ability to deliver high-quality educational services for children while recognizing the capability of the community to provide the necessary resources. All of these things appear to work in concert. For example, if, as a result of modeling ethical behaviors and exercising good judgment the leader enjoys a positive professional identity, it is possible to gain the trust of constituents so they will provide both emotional and financial support for quality educational programs. The first step is to build the positive professional identity.

In one sense, professional identities are widely shared mental models created over time and applied to leaders. They are a set of ideals against which quality or expertise are measured. For example, most people use traditional mental models or frameworks to help them define competent physicians, ministers, teachers, or bankers. They apply these models to help them make judgments about each of these professionals. In another sense, the professional identity is constructed and communicated by the individual holding the position. It is a deliberate and highly responsible act. Great care must be taken to honestly portray an identity that communicates the highest expectations to constituents. It is this type of professional identity we will explore. Hughes-Chapman cited several successful professional identity building strategies used by first-year superintendents. She included the construction of identities based on ideals found in reviews of the leadership literature, the development of broad-based school improvement teams, an emphasis on open communication, and immediate involvement in the community.[4]

Many useful perspectives for the construction of positive professional identities are found in the business literature and appear to be universal in their application. Three of those frameworks will be explored in some detail: a framework based on management competencies, a framework based on principle-centered behavior, and a framework developed around a specific organizational purpose. Similarities exist among and between each of the frameworks; the key is to develop an understanding that numerous frameworks exist and can be used as the foundation for building professional identities.

A Framework Based on Vision

The first leadership perspective suggests that through their actions, leaders send overt signals to those with whom they work and serve. The manner in which co-workers and constituents perceive the messages helps establish the professional identity of the leader. As a result of many observations of public and private sector leaders, Bennis defined four competencies that appeared to enable leaders to draw others to them and to sustain those relationships over time. The four competencies are the management of attention, the management of meaning, the management of trust, and the management of self.[5] We believe they serve as a excellent foundation for the development of a professional identity for school superintendents.

The management of attention is linked to the notion that the leader knows what he or she wants. Leaders with the expertise to manage attention possess a clearly defined set of intentions. The term *vision* is also used to describe these intentions. School leaders must have a clear understanding of what and how they expect schools to deliver. The ability to formulate a vision of the school that will inspire people to support it is the first step in building a solid professional identity. It demonstrates for constituents that leaders will not waste their time or that of constituents on issues that are neither critical nor important.

The second competency, management of meaning, addresses the ability to communicate a vision or set of intentions to others so a shared sense of direction can be established. Bennis called this "making dreams apparent to others and aligning people with them."[6] School executives must have both the ability and the courage to continually communicate the intentions of the school and to commission the support of people. It is much more than simple repetition of the vision—it is using communication to create meaning. An effective leader can bring the vision to life. A good example is illustrated by former President John F. Kennedy's vision to place a U.S. citizen on the moon. The vision was communicated as a distinct possibility and then the emotional, financial, and human resources were brought together to make the dream a reality.

Competency three is concerned with the management of trust. Trust is the key to maintenance of a strong professional and personal identity. People who are trusted are reliable and constant. On important issues they do not waffle or shy away from the set of principles that guide them. A key to managing trust is to be focused on the set of intentions that have been shared with constituencies. It means that leaders must live up to the expectations, that they are predictable in matters that involve the vision of the school district. If the superintendent wavers or moves away from the vision during times of crisis, the trust is eroded and eventually collapses along with the leader's professional identity.

The fourth and final competency from Bennis is the management of self. Leaders are most effective when they capitalize on their strength and rely on other team members to perform in areas where they possess less expertise. Implicit in this competency is the idea that leaders must continue to nurture their strength and understand the conditions under which they are most effective. While leaders invest time learning about others, they must also be willing to invest time understanding themselves.

These four competencies, when practiced consistently and in harmony, will help build a professional identity of which the superintendent can be proud. It will serve the school, the community, and the person well.

A Principle-Centered Framework

A second perspective on leadership suggests that people center on ideas and principles to provide their identity and direction, to give them balance, and to empower them with the capacity to take action. Heider, in *The Tao of Leadership,* revealed the thinking of an ancient Chinese writer, Lao Tzu, about centered people. He observed, "The leader who is centered and grounded can work with erratic people and critical group situations without harm. Being centered means having the ability to recover one's balance, even in the midst of action. A centered person is not subject to passing whims or sudden excitements."[7]

Other writers have offered their observations and advice about operating from a center that involves ethical principles. Covey suggests that "the character ethic is based on the idea that there are *principles* that govern human effectiveness—natural laws that are just as real, just as unchanging and unarguably 'there' as laws such as gravity are in the physical dimension."[8] These principles, he adds, are like lighthouses. Some examples of the principles Covey believes to be universal are fairness, honesty, integrity, human dignity, service, and quality. When leadership is based on these principles and combined with the habits Covey has observed to be present in highly effective people, the personal and professional identity of the superintendent is likely to be positive. The seven habits are

1. Be proactive.
2. Begin with the end in mind.
3. Put first things first.
4. Think win/win.
5. Seek first to understand . . . then to be understood.
6. Synergize (learn to put information from a variety of sources together).
7. Sharpen the saw (keep developing your skills and attitudes).[9]

These habits, identified through observation of many individuals who were considered to be effective and successful people, can serve as effective guidelines for school leadership. They contain essential elements that provide direction for individuals and the organizations they lead.

An Organizational Framework

Senge explained the necessity of designing modern businesses and corporations as learning organizations to ensure their survival in a highly competitive, market-driven environment. Learning organizations are described as being focused on creating and adapting; organizations that are constantly learning so they can adjust to the changing conditions of their environment.[10] The leader's role in a learning organization focuses on design, teaching, and stewardship; it is the leader's role to build organizations "where people are continually expanding their capabilities to shape their future—that is, leaders are responsible for learning."[11] The leader is a part of the management team rather than apart from the team.

Senge discussed certain disciplines that must be practiced to ensure learning organizations become a reality. A discipline was defined as "a body of theory or technique that must be mastered in order to be put into practice."[12] We believe this concept is applicable to schools as well as businesses, and further, the professional identity of the leader in this type of organization is based on attitudes and competencies that set him or her apart from the norm. For example, the leader of a learning organization must realize that the he or she cannot learn for the organization; rather, the leader must empower the organization to learn. Senge associated five disciplines with learning organizations; we have adapted them to describe the characteristics that can be associated with the professional identity of contemporary school executives.

Discipline One: Personal Mastery

Senge suggests mastery is a special level of proficiency that enables individuals to realize their goals or dreams. It is a commitment to lifelong learning and to continuously deepening and clarifying personal missions, focusing energies, developing patience, and seeing reality objectively. To be recognized as a professional implies the mastery of a certain set of skills and attitudes connected with the profession. For school leaders these skills include an understanding of human development and behavior, learning theory, curriculum design, instructional strategies, organizational development, the art and science of politics, communications, and resource allocation.

Discipline Two: Mental Models

Mental models are frameworks people use to help them make sense of the world; assumptions and images that influence how they understand actions or worldviews. To lead a learning organization requires constant attention to an examination of our own mental models and creating new lenses through which to view the world. Senge used the phrase "balancing inquiry and advocacy" to describe the process of exposing our ingrained assumptions to constant scrutiny and revising them as necessary. This suggests that rather than promote traditional mental models merely because they represent the way things have always been done, leaders must constantly inquire about the utility of a model and be willing to develop new models to meet new challenges.

Discipline Three: Building Shared Visions

Successful organizations seem to be driven by powerful forces. Many have defined this phenomenon as vision, a shared sense of purpose and direction. Leaders in learning organizations invest an inordinate, but necessary, amount of time building, communicating, and sustaining the shared vision so everyone in the organization can become enrolled in the purpose and direction of the organization. The key element in this procedure is to enroll rather than compel people to share the vision. A person who becomes enrolled in the work of the organization does so because they are committed to the direction of the organization and have a sense that they are important contributors to that direction through their attitudes and actions. This is a stark contrast to people who "work for" an organization but do not connect to its purpose and function.

Discipline Four: Team Learning

Team learning suggests that the collective intelligence of a team is superior to the intelligence of any of the individuals in the team. The key to team learning begins with dialogue, thinking together about the direction of work in the organization. Effective teams produce extraordinary results, while individuals in the team experience tremendous personal growth. Team learning means each member of the team contributes his or her expertise to the project or outcome.

Discipline Five: Systems Thinking

Leaders must understand how events and ideas are connected. Systems thinking is the discipline that allows full patterns to become clearer and helps leaders realize how subsystems or patterns fit together or how they might be rearranged to be more productive. It is the ability to see the big picture and to understand the concepts of linkage and association.[13] These five disciplines provide a leader with a framework for action and help construct a professional identity that clearly demonstrates a commitment to vision, trust, and openness to dialogue about new ideas and the possibilities for change.

The superintendent must understand how things work and must have the ability to orchestrate resources—people, materials, technology, and finances—to ensure that education works. It is a tremendous responsibility, a position of trust. Trust is built on a positive personal and professional identity; to be effective the superintendent must have the trust of all constituencies. The superintendent is believed to be the one person to have the authority to improve programs, implement changes, and provide direction for the district, its staff, and its children and youth. Each of the three perspectives suggests that leaders adopt and follow guidelines that will show them to be people of vision, integrity, and commitment. The professional life of a superintendent depends on building and maintaining an ethical professional identity.

Leadership and Management: The Mission of the Superintendent

The role of the superintendent varies from district to district depending on the size and conditions of the community, but several aspects of the role appear to be universal. Superintendents must have a strong sense of mission—a sense of purpose, a reasoned approach to explain why they do what they do. And while they may have a well-defined sense of purpose and direction, superintendents serve at the pleasure of boards of education. As elected or appointed representatives of the community, school boards establish policies to govern the operation of the district. It is also the first duty of the board to secure the services of a chief executive officer for the district. Districts in crisis may desire a superintendent who will devote their initial attention to management so that confidence can be regained. A stagnant district may want and need someone to provide direction, to set an appropriate course in the near term; while a progressive district may want someone to maintain the current course of action while taking it closer to its expectations. All districts require someone who can think strategically about the future while maintaining present areas of excellence. The life of the superintendent can be a study of contrast between his or her personal mission and the goals and objectives of the board.

Peterson and Finn noted, "practically never does one encounter a good school with a bad principal or a high achieving school system with a low performance superintendent. Ample research about the characteristics of particularly effective schools confirms the conclusions of common sense: the caliber of institutional leadership powerfully influences the quality of education."[14] Griffiths, Stout, and Forsyth offered some generalizations about the leadership role of superintendents:

1. They must symbolize education in the community. Through their public statements they must express, project, and embody the purpose and character of public education.
2. They must be able academicians with the ability to recognize excellence in teaching, learning, and research.
3. They must exercise the wisest kind of political behavior by resolving the conflicting demands of many constituents and, in turn, gaining their support for education.
4. They must be highly competent managers who demonstrate their skill in selecting staff, planning the future, building the budget, and constructing and maintaining the school plant.[15]

The National Association of Secondary School Principals has provided leadership in the identification of common job dimensions for building-level leadership. For each identified job dimension, they designed simulated exercises to assess the leadership potential of prospective school principals. Leaders in the field were trained to administer the assessments through a series of regional assessment centers established at colleges and universities. The assessment centers are known throughout the world. As a result of their work with the Kentucky Superintendent Assessment Program, the organization has identified the leadership dimensions of the superintendent's role as illustrated in Figure 3–1. These dimensions will serve as the basis for assessment centers designed to provide feedback to current and prospective school executives.

The results of the Kentucky study provided a focused summary of expectations related to the superintendent's job role. The expectations of the job were identified as "(1) taking educational initiatives, (2) analyzing and judging educational problems, (3) building and maintaining educational teams, and (4) expanding learnings. In each of these categories, managing the expectations of customers was consistently linked to success."[16] The report emphasized that superintendents viewed their leadership role in terms of being keenly aware of research about instructional strategies and technology, seeing the big picture, and motivating people to understand and implement the mission of education.

For decades, scholars and writers have debated differences in the meaning of the terms *leadership* and *management*. To invest an inordinate amount of time in that debate would trivialize the role of school executives. Do superintendents lead or manage? We assume they must do both at the same time *and* all of the time. Superintendents lead by identifying areas that need to be changed and then procuring the necessary support to implement the change. Leadership involves environmental scanning, coalition building, and long-term planning. School executives manage by maintaining a sense of order and consistency. Management means paying attention to the proper deployment of resources—budgeting, hiring, staff development, and facility maintenance and upgrading, to name but a few. Both leadership and management are necessary to the well-being of a successful organization; superintendents should be prepared to do both.

Simply put, to accomplish their job, superintendents need scholarly credentials (formal preparation), an orientation toward action (leadership and management), and an understanding of human dynamics combined with business acumen and, equally important, high visibility in the school and community.

Educational researchers identified eleven dimensions of the superintendency as part of their work in designing the Kentucky Superintendent Assessment Program. As a result of the study, procedures were designed to help identify the extent to which superintendent candidates possess these dimension. The 11 dimensions are as follows:

Area I: Taking Educational Initiatives

Dimension 1.   Encourage Innovation
   The extent to which an individual is able to generate new ways of doing things or to seek new ways to creatively deal with educational problems or opportunities.

Dimension 2.   Planning and Implementing Strategic Change
   The extent to which an individual develops educational strategies that emphasize long-term strategic change.

Dimension 3.   Serving the Needs of Diverse Constituencies
   The extent to which individuals can modify their approach or behaviors when exposed to situations that require different methods or perspectives.

Area II: Analyzing and Judging Educational Problems

Dimension 4.   Acquiring and Interpreting Key Information
   The extent to which an individual obtains keys facts and distinguishes between relevant and irrelevant information.

Dimension 5.   Resisting Premature Judgments
   The extent to which an individual refrains from taking action until all the key facts have been obtained.

Dimension 6.   Resolving Complex problems
   The extent to which an individual makes high quality decisions that effectively resolve complex problems.

Area III: Building and Maintaining Educational Teams

Dimension 7.   Communicating Expectations
   The extent to which an individual is able to clearly state what is needed from others as well as what others may expect in return.

Dimension 8.   Developing and Empowering Others
   The extent to which an individual teaches, coaches, or helps others to take personal initiatives.

Dimension 9.   Balancing Complex Demands
   The extent to which an individual can organize work in order to set achievable work priorities for self and others.

Area IV. Expanding Learning

Dimension 10. Understanding Personal Strengths
   The extent to which an individual understands his or her own personal strengths and weaknesses.

Dimension 11. Acquiring New Learning
   The extent to which an individual actively pursues developmental activities in order to acquire new learning or relevant educational experiences.

FIGURE 3–1   Superintendent Dimensions

Preparation for the Superintendency

An important aspect of the superintendent's life is a sense of devotion to continuous preparation for the initial job as well as subsequent positions. The knowledge, skills, and attitudes necessary for providing leadership in education change with the larger society. Formal announcements of superintendent vacancies provide some insights about the skills and experiences school boards require from candidates. The job announcement is a litany of attributes the board wishes to consider as they select final candidates from the list of applicants. Boards require information about the applicants' level of formal education, certification, and teaching and building or central office administrative experiences. Also listed as worthy characteristics are excellent communications skills, the ability to serve as a change agent, the ability to work with diverse ideas, a solid foundation in curriculum and instruction, an understanding of budgeting, an appreciation for a variety of cultures, and a sense of mission or a vision for education.

Many boards want a superintendent with an earned doctorate in educational administration, and many request applicants have previous experience as a superintendent. Training is available for some of the desired attributes listed by boards—budget development, curriculum design, familiarity with instructional methodologies, and personnel management. However, many of the key job requirements are matters of attitude and personal style combined with experience and research. These areas include, but are not limited to, the ability to work with diverse populations, expertise as a communicator, providing leadership for change, and establishing a vision for education in the district.

Experiential Background

Most superintendents are experienced as classroom teachers and in building-level leadership positions or central offices, and have proceeded through a series of formal steps to attain their administrative credentials by attending approved college or university programs. While there may be little connection between the type of work a person carried out as a teacher and the work of the superintendent, teaching experience provides the basis for understanding the connection between teachers, learning, and students. School superintendents must understand and support the relationships needed to make a classroom effective and thereby successful for the student.

Building-level leadership serves as an excellent foundation for the superintendency. Because the building is a larger subsystem of the district than the classroom, it provides additional experiences with a wide array of internal and external publics, planning and implementation of programs of study, some budgeting responsibilities, and community involvement. While experience at the building level may be important, it is not the only route to the executive school leadership. Growing numbers of candidates for the superintendency have leadership experience that does not include the principalship, but comes instead from central office experience in budgeting, staff development, or curriculum development. A profile of the superintendency will provide some insight into the preparation and experiential background of those who hold the position:

1. Most superintendents obtained their first administrative position (other than the superintendency) by the age of 30. In larger school systems the first position tended to be an assistant principalship; in smaller districts it was more likely to be a principalship.
2. Over 70 percent of superintendents had experience as secondary teachers. On an average they spent three to five years in the classroom.
3. About half of the superintendents had previous experience in extracurricular activities leadership.
4. The progression of jobs in education has been teacher, principal (for about 30%—central office experience), and the superintendency.

5. About one-third were promoted to superintendent from the "inside." (This is particularly true in larger districts.)

6. Typically, the decision to become a superintendent was made while serving as a building principal or central office administrator.

7. Almost half of the superintendents reported they were assisted by mentors.[17]

Formal Preparation Programs

Preparation programs for many of the professions revolve around a specific body of knowledge unique to its practitioners. Lawyers, dentists, physicians, and pharmacists are required to graduate from professional schools, serve an internship, and pass state or national license exams before they can engage in professional practice. Preparation for the school superintendency is not as clear-cut, and preparation programs and requirements for credentialing vary from state to state. The quality of academic preparation programs for superintendents has been questioned for years. An overriding concern of practitioners and critics of educational administration preparation programs is that they are weak in content and lack extensive or practical internships. Murphy supported this notion by pointing out, "it is not surprising, although it is distressing that inappropriate content ineffectively packaged should be so poorly delivered in many training institutions. It is also disheartening that so little progress has been made in an area so thoroughly critiqued."[18]

Glass asked respondents to his 1992 study of the superintendency to appraise educational administration preparation programs in general; 7.9 percent said they were "excellent," 43.9 percent rated them "good," and 44.2 percent rated them as "fair." The major weakness associated with educational administration programs was "poor or irrelevant course work and the lack of extensive internships or practicum experiences."[19]

Even though concerns about the quality of preparation programs continue, it is a requirement that superintendents are credentialed to serve in the role. That means they must complete an approved program of study at a college or university. Glass reported, "about 96 percent of superintendents in the 1990 sample [superintendents surveyed for the AASA Study Of the American Superintendency] hold a combination of a master's degree, specialist certificate, or doctorate."[20] In 1992, according to the same study, about 36 percent of American school superintendents held doctoral degrees.[21]

Criticism about preparation programs is not new. Although school leaders require a strong theoretical and philosophical base, they desperately need processes, strategies, and models that can be applied to everyday situations. These elements were reported by superintendents in the Study of Beginning Superintendents as lacking in their preparation programs.[22] While preparation programs cannot provide solutions for every situation, they could be expanded to include greater opportunities to engage in learning about communication strategies such as group dynamics, consensus building, coalition building, and conflict management techniques. These skills are called into use almost daily.

In the past, formal programs to prepare school superintendents were collections of courses aimed at providing foundations in areas such as school law, business and finance, organizational theory, community relations, administrative theory, and personnel administration. The capstone experience was usually a research project such as a thesis or dissertation. While these programs continue to be in the majority, alternative perspectives are beginning to guide the construction of formal education programs for school administrators. Murphy and others offer four goals to serve as a basis for preparation programs:

1. to help students articulate an explicit set of values and beliefs to guide their actions. This goal is based on the premise that both knowledge and values must serve as the foundation for action,
2. to help students become educators. Because student learning is the central focus of schools, school leaders must be experts in teaching and learning,
3. to facilitate the development of inquiry skills, or enhancing the thinking abilities of students. Superintendents must be open to and embrace the notion that their work requires constant inquiry so they can construct new knowledge to serve the needs of their constituencies, and
4. to help students learn to work productively with people; to lead in the broadest sense of the term. This key construct is focused on the idea that one part of leadership is to know how to behave toward people and to understand the human condition.[23]

While formal preparation and professional administrative experiences are initially required for entrance to the superintendency, the education of the superintendent is never complete. Changing social conditions, new instructional strategies, and calls for school restructuring require constant updating of the school leaders educational portfolio.

Making Sense of the Superintendency

Does it make sense for someone to want to become a superintendent? We believe the answer is a resounding yes! It is a position of responsibility, trust, and leadership. It demands time and energy like no other position in education, but from the position leaders have the authority and expertise to make a positive difference. The superintendent must be the number one advocate for education in his or her community. The superintendent operates in a community-wide arena and has the opportunity to influence a variety of publics about the condition of education and the promise it holds for the state and nation as well as the community. The superintendency, like any other responsible and visible position, has positive and negative aspects, but for most people, the positive far outweigh the negative.

Metaphors Help Describe the Superintendency

Metaphors can be used to "cut through the fog" when ordinary descriptions seem to fall short of the meaning that is required. We think it is useful to use them to help describe the position of superintendent of schools. First, the superintendent is the lightning rod for the school district; lightning rods were designed to be placed where they could attract attention. The most visible person on the school staff, he or she attracts attention that draws both praise and criticism. Second, it is through the superintendents office that constituencies learn about plans and actions of the board, teachers, and administrative staff. In this circumstance, the superintendent acts as teacher, an interpreter of policy and practice who teaches about the condition of education in the district. Third, catalysts are often necessary to cause changes to occur; the superintendent is the catalyst for educational change. Fourth, the superintendent is a director, casting and recasting roles, constantly adjusting the conditions under which optimum effects can be achieved, and offering guidance to the educational process. The responsibility for creating a Emmy winner rests with the superintendent! Finally, the superintendent is a builder. It is his or her position to build the capacity of the school district to successfully face its future. We believe the role of builder is extremely important and must be nurtured and supported.

The Importance of Visibility

Glass's study concurred with the notion that constituencies expect the superintendent to be a visible leader. He reported, "the contemporary jurisdiction of the superintendent is not solely situated in a district office or in the schools. It extends into the community, where the superintendent is expected to participate and represent the school district."[24] Communities require their superintendent to provide leadership for the school and participate widely in the leadership of community organizations. The school executive likely will serve on the administrative boards of the chamber of commerce, civic organizations, and churches. He or she will be expected to participate in a variety of fund drives for community betterment projects and to support the general well-being of the community. The active and visible superintendent extends his or her opportunity to be with a wide variety of constituents and by doing so has yet another opportunity to focus on the vision and mission of education.

The Expectations of Constituencies

One function of government is to provide for citizens those things they cannot legitimately or realistically provide for themselves. Some examples of these government services include roads, hospitals, libraries, and schools. Schools for the public are open to all students regardless of their religion, ethnicity, or condition in life. These schools provide opportunities for America's youth to be educated in a diverse setting. Because of the diversity of the wants and needs of the public, school executives must deal with requests, suggestions, and mandates from individuals, groups lobbying on behalf of individuals, the courts, and the state and federal branches of government. For example, several groups might register concerns about the absence of prayer at graduation exercises and an equally committed group will seek guarantees that no prayer is offered in the school setting. Or concerned parents may lobby for a comprehensive health education program, while a different group of concerned parents will oppose it.

Growing numbers and descriptions of constituencies dot the school district landscape. The expectations of each constituent group will cover the full continuum. While it is not the position of the board or superintendent, nor is it possible, for them to meet the needs of all constituent groups, it falls to the superintendent and his or her staff to listen with respect to what they have to say. Understanding and negotiating with multiple constituencies are perhaps the most difficult of the superintendent's roles. However, it is not likely to disappear.

Drucker reminds us that growing numbers of special interest groups will occupy the time and attention of leaders in the future. He noted it is unlikely that any one special interest group will represent a majority view, so they may not be able to cause the board or superintendent to *do* something. However, each special interest may have enough impact to cause an action *not to* occur.[25]

Tolerance for the Ambiguous and Uncertain

As mentioned, one aspect of leadership implies the formulation of a vision or direction for the organization and a continuous emphasis on the communication of that vision. One of the aspects of the superintendency that makes it so interesting and challenging is that on any given day events unfold that are cause for an intense examination of the districts plans, goals, and objectives. For example, during a week in the life of a superintendent, an individual or group may present valid arguments (from their point of view) about prayer in school, a court may uphold the separation of church and state, and an agency of the government might provide statistics to indicate the United States is lagging behind other developed nations on certain aspects of education. At the same time, a group of parents may demand removal of a book from the school library because it falls short of the standards they hold, or an emotionally distraught parent may burst into a school and demand to visit with a child of whom they no longer have custody. Many times these events have no connection to one another except their emergence in the school setting. Daily happenings at all levels of the organization demand time and energy from the superintendent and his or her staff. The life of a school superintendent is influenced by all events and most people who live in the community. Tolerance for ambiguity and the ability to shift attention to items needing critical attention is a quality expected of superintendents.

Time and Energy

The life of a superintendent requires him or her meet with a wide array of constituents and discuss a variety of conditions, problems, and opportunities. For the most part, the day involves meetings, schedules, speeches, visitations, discussions with board members, and negotiations. The day begins early and ends late. Superintendents average 12-hour days and 60- or 70-hour weeks. Hughes-Chapman described what a first-year superintendent told her about the work day: "The typical work day extended from 7:30 a.m. to 9 or 9:30 p.m. When I ran out of time during the regular day on my calendar, then I started meeting people for lunch and meeting people for dinner. So consequently, even though I wasn't in my office, I've been getting home at 9 or 9:30 every evening, and my planning time is being usurped."[26]

The work of school administrators is emotionally and physically exhausting. Time demands and the pressures of the job require tremendous and sustainable amounts of energy. There is no time for energy lapses, and so the superintendent should set aside some time each day for exercise, sensible food, and time to reflect on the events of the day and week. School leaders must be aware of situations that cause stress and learn to deal with them in appropriate, effective ways. Like other busy executives, many school leaders may take precautions to guard against job-related stress by beginning their day at the "Y" or a local fitness center so that they arrive at their offices physically and mentally invigorated.

Finally, it is important to establish an agenda that allows for reading about current trends in education, research in curriculum, instruction, and leadership, and activities of state and federal officials. While this is recognized as a desirable and necessary activity, school officials do not engage in professional reading nearly as often as they would like or, perhaps, as often as they should. It is an activity that must be planned and carried out until it becomes routine. Many superintendents set aside time for professional reading during the day, but most find a quiet half hour or so before bedtime to review a journal or read a professional newsletter.

Approach each day with enthusiasm for the work. The superintendent who approaches each day enthusiastically displays a positive attitude for the job and the importance of education in the community. But how does one maintain a high level of enthusiasm day to day? Several suggestions are offered as food for thought. First, remember two things: you chose to become a superintendent, and you did so because you believed you could influence decisions that would lead to good policies for the education of young people. Second, when the day or week seems to have gone poorly and you are wondering why you put in all those hours and attended all those meetings, take a drive to the closest school and talk with the teachers and students. This is the best medicine for a small case of the "wearies," and it will renew your enthusiasm for your work. Many superintendents reported that a half hour spent reading a favorite book to a kindergarten class or observing senior high students in a science lab or speech class rekindled their commitment and reminded them why they chose to do what they do.

Establishing Support by Building Bridges

Politics are a fact of life in education, especially in the superintendency. Politics can be conceptualized as "a set of interactions that influence and shape the authoritative allocation of values"[27] or "the struggle of a group to secure the authoritative support of government for its values."[28] These definitions imply that in any society highly valued resources are usually scarce enough to be a source of conflict. To obtain these resources, societies establish mechanisms to make decisions about how the resources will be allocated. As individuals and groups attempt to influence the authoritative allocation of the resources, they exhibit what we would call "political" behavior.[29] The superintendent and his or her staff are constantly in the process of providing evidence to inform, educate, or convince people at local, state, and national levels about the resources that are necessary to support the educational enterprise. This part of the work is done in school rooms, board rooms, and legislative hearing rooms, or anywhere anyone will listen. By the same token, special interests in the community want time with the superintendent so they can lobby for a point of view. It is the job of the superintendent to build bridges that will keep communications flowing.

Students in kindergarten through grade 12 are not well represented, at least numerically, by lobbyists who take their cases to policymakers. If children and youth are to obtain enough of the scarce resources valued by the educational community, it becomes a primary responsibility of educators, especially the superintendent, to present their case for them.

In the political arena, it is helpful to have allies. The superintendent must be skilled in building support groups and coalitions who can lend their voice to the struggle to obtain the necessary valued resources for education. Once again, communication skills, the ability to explain the vision and mission of education, serve as the foundation for building support.

Some "natural" support groups already exist in most communities. Parent–Teacher Associations (PTAs), school improvement teams, and athletic and activity booster clubs are excellent examples of groups who support all or some aspects of education. They are energetic, dedicated individuals who legitimately work to support education building by building.

At times, however, it becomes necessary to gather broad-based support for bond issues to finance the construction of school facilities or to pass an increase in the school levy. (This is discussed in detail in Chapter 11.) The superintendent must have enough linkages to a wide variety of community interests to build coalitions to support these special issues. The connections are established over time by being available to speak at meetings of civic clubs, by serving in a leadership role in community fund drives, and by taking a leadership role in the local chamber of commerce or industrial development association. Earlier, it was mentioned that one role the superintendent played was that of a builder. That role applies to the community as well as the school. The superintendent builds by establishing the vision for a desirable future in the schools, and he or she also builds coalitions and support groups for education in the community and at the state level.

Opportunities and Obligations

Tenure and Mobility

One aspect of school district leadership that is shared with other executive positions is the length of time the leader serves an organization. In 1992, the average length of tenure for a superintendent was reported to be 6.47 years (up slightly from the previous decadenal study). About one-fourth have held two different superintendencies, and 11.4 percent have held three. It appeared that superintendents in both very large and very small school districts tended to experience somewhat shorter tenures than the average.[30] There are several explanations for this phenomenon. For example, superintendencies in smaller districts are often used as stepping stones to get to a district that is more desirable in size or opportunity. The most cited reasons for superintendent mobility are to obtain leadership opportunities in a larger district and to improve personal finances.[31] There is a certain amount of status associated with school leadership in any district, and this is especially true in larger districts. It is a goal for many school executives to serve in large or prestigious school districts because of the status and recognition it provides.

A second reason for superintendent mobility is related to superintendents' feeling they have accomplished their goals and it is time to move to another location. Finally, some superintendents move because of a conflict with the board. Some conflicts result over confusion about which decisions belong to professional educators and which belong to the board of education. Research by Bryant and Grady reported differences in opinions about the role of the board and the role of the superintendent. For example: "Systems engineers have sought to persuade all parties that the board should make policy and the administrator should execute policy. But life in many districts does not work that way. Boards and superintendents negotiate roles about incidents as they arise. Roles are fluid and a failure to understand this reality often leads to conflict."[32]

To Leave or Stay?
How will you know whether to leave or stay? According to Papallo, "it is not how long you stay in one place, but the quality of your professional life there. A certain amount of tug-

ging and pulling is normal, given the diversity of many communities. But the tug-of-war can take its toll personally and professional. The superintendency is a fragile position."[33] Two things were noted earlier: the superintendent operates in a highly political environment and serves at the pleasure of the board. Board members are usually elected to four-year terms. When elections lead to changes in the board makeup, the board may find it appealing to search for a leader that is more closely aligned with its philosophy. Differences in philosophy between boards and superintendents usually cut short the tenure of the superintendent. This is a constant concern of the superintendent; it is also a fact of life.

The Balance of Professional and Personal Roles

Seek a Balance in All Things

Earlier in this chapter, balance was mentioned as a concept well worth remembering. To this point we have focused on the superintendent's professional role and how that role translates to a leadership role in the community. However, attention must also be devoted to the superintendent's other important roles.

Senge reminded us of one of the myths of leadership when he said, "We are trained to be loyal to our jobs—so much so that we confuse them with our own identities."[34] While he was speaking about the confusion that exists within organizations, we want to extend the idea from the job to the community to the home. Positions of responsibility, jobs, or professions provide an identity for what people do in their work life. But the essence of the person cannot be tied strictly to the job. People have additional obligations as citizens, parents, spouses, siblings, friends, and neighbors. An ancient Chinese philosopher explained how leaders make a difference in the world:

> First you get your own life in order. Ground yourself in the single principle so that your behavior is wholesome and effective. If you do that, you will earn respect and be a powerful influence.
>
> Your behavior influences others through the ripple effect. A ripple effect works because everyone influences everyone else. Powerful people are powerful influences.
>
> If your life works you influence your family.
>
> If your family works, your family influences the community.
>
> If your community works, your community influences the nation.
>
> If your nation works, your nation influences the world. . . .
>
> Remember that your influence begins with you and ripples outward.
> So be sure that your influence is both potent and wholesome.[35]

This teaching does not mention the job for which a person has been trained; it speaks exclusively to the person and is a good reminder that the way people live their whole life is important! Seek to balance the responsibilities of family, work, leisure, and the community.

Stress in the Superintendent's Life

Stress is a factor in almost all executive positions, including school leadership. Setting the direction for a school district, balancing multimillion dollar budgets, managing personnel systems, and dealing with highly inflammatory political issues and the demands of a school bureaucracy, all in the constant view of the media and the public, is a highly stressful job! The nature of the educational enterprise coupled with the uncertainty that exists in the larger society causes a great deal of pressure to rest on the shoulders of the superintendent.

Regardless of the size or location of the school district, stress is part of the day-to-day life of the superintendent. Goldstein talked about stress as natural ingredient of the position: "As a side effect of running a school system, stress is not new. Nor is it spread evenly among all superintendents and all school districts. How much strain a superintendent perceives—and whether it is debilitating—hinges on personality traits and ability to cope, as well as the nature of the job."[36] Some of the stress may be self-inflicted as the superintendent strives to accomplish the goals and objectives of the district or invests long hours on the job. Some of the stress is caused by relationships with staff, boards, and constituent groups. Regardless of the source, stress is as real in the superintendency as it is in any executive position in the corporate arena. The reality of stress suggests there must be ways of dealing with it in a logical manner. Figure 3–2 illustrates some ways of managing or alleviating stress.

While the stress associated with the superintendent's job role should not be discounted, Milstein believes the research about stress in the superintendency may be faulty. He stated, "much of the research is narrow in scope, fails to include physiological data . . . as a validating measure of attitudinal data, and relies on a ranking system that identifies the most stressful aspects of the job, but does not establish how intense these factors are as stressor."[37] He believes stress is not a new problem and, because many school administrators are seasoned veterans, they are comfortable with their positions and the authority they exercise. "Among those who persist," he says, "there is, usually, a positive perception about the role. That is, they view potentially stressful situations as challenging opportunities rather than intractable problems."[38]

Regardless of whether one considers stress to be a motivator, an inhibitor, or a constant companion, it behooves prospective superintendents to think about how they will react to stress in the short term and over the long haul. It is another fact of life!

Families Live with the Job, Too

Many times people speak about the superintendent as if he or she was a position and not a person; sometimes they do not know the name of the superintendent, but they know what they expect of the person in the position. In a sense, school leaders are "on the job" 24 hours a day. As Hughes-Chapman noted, "superintendents were willing to devote whatever time was needed to get tasks done. However, this devotion came at the price of time for themselves and their families."[39] This phenomenon cannot be avoided altogether, but the wise person plans and protects family time the same way other important issues are planned and protected. Family is an important personal investment, and just like other important investments, they need constant attention to grow and prosper.

School leaders and their families are always in the eye of constituents. While people expect superintendents to be normal in all ways, they do expect them and their families to

Successful superintendents develop a variety of techniques to assist them in dealing with job-related and personal stress. Listed below are some useful coping strategies to consider:

- Build a good support system of family and friends.
- Find confidants and allies in the community. Superintendents need to develop a support a support base outside of educational circles; business associates can provide excellent feedback and sometimes serve as good listeners.
- Develop a thick skin; have the self-confidence that what you are doing is in the best interest of the community and school. Learn to understand that criticism is usually directed at the position and not at the person. Be able to separate the two.
- Constantly improve your organizational skills and the ability to manage your time well.
- Plan to spend some time away from the community; even a weekend away can be diverting and relaxing. Do not pass up your vacation time; it is a chance to recharge the batteries.
- Develop a hobby or interest outside of work that will help you relax.
- Enjoy entertainment; enjoy a good movie, a concert, a ballgame, or dinner out with friends or family.
- Maintain a sense of balance in your life by developing a personal philosophy. Determine what is important in your life and maintain the important things!
- Do not take every criticism about school or policy as a personal affront. Learn to depersonalize the criticism—give critics a break; they serve a valuable purpose!

FIGURE 3–2   Strategies for Alleviating Stress

SOURCE: Adapted from Amy Goldstein, "Stress in the Superintendency: School Leaders Confront the Daunting Issues of the Job," *School Administrator,* 9:49 (October 1992): pp. 8–17.

serve as role models in much the same way they expect positive role modeling from clergy, physicians, and teachers. This takes some getting used to by children, spouses, and even superintendents, yet it is another fact of life in the school superintendency. There will be times when the "superintendent's kids" will be viewed as having advantages over other students in the classroom, in athletic competition, or other arenas of the school. The perception may be promoted by those who need excuses for their own poor performance or the lack of performance of their children. By the same token, "superintendent's kids" may be given certain advantages that others do not enjoy. Nevertheless, it is the wise superintendent who addresses these issues early in the life of his or her own children and helps them devise coping strategies to deal with the situations as they arise.

A Sense of Perspective

It is most important to maintain a sense of perspective about the job and its benefits. The superintendency is a high-profile position. The superintendent has access to community resources such as the media, civic organizations, and open public forums that are unavailable to many other citizens. The role is important in the development of human beings and the communities in which they live. As such, the superintendent receives praise when the work of the school is progressing well, and it is a privilege to serve in the position. But the superintendent cannot be all things to all constituencies. So criticism is a companion as well as praise. The idea, it seems, is to keep the job in perspective; to carry it out with dispatch, to do it to the very best of one's ability. It is an enjoyable calling and the rewards are many.

Summary

The school superintendency is a rewarding career. Preparation for the position requires years of serious planning and commitment to a lifestyle that is not unlike that of political or corporate leaders. An important ingredient of the superintendency is the establishment of a positive professional identity built on integrity and trust. With that identity secure, the superintendent can develop a shared vision for the schools in the community and proceed to design goals and objectives that will allow the vision to be realized. If there is one skill that is universal for all superintendents, it is the ability to communicate the purpose and meaning of schools to all constituencies.

One role assigned to the superintendent is that of the builder. By serving in this capacity, the school executive ensures the organization will be prepared and available to meet the changing demands of society. Superintendents build school systems through the development and communication of the vision of the district, the establishment of high expectations, and the empowerment of people to create and sustain the capacity of the organization to meet its future with confidence.

Well-developed communication skills are invaluable to the superintendent. The role demands constant speaking about, for, and on behalf of education and children. Superintendents must be designers of dreams for the future of education, and they paint pictures of those dreams through words and actions—through constant communication.

Multiple constituencies with wide-ranging wants and needs, and the demands of rapidly changing social, political, and economic environments require constant attention. They also place heavy demands on the time and energy of people who chose to serve as school executives. Additionally, they require continued professional development and an unending desire for further learning. Access to information is a necessity for the superintendent. He or she depends on current information about economics, political activity, technology, and demographics, as well as the latest research in the field of education.

Discussion Questions

1. Reflect on your personal mission and your mission as an educator. In what ways are they similar? Are there any major differences between your personal and professional missions? Are your personal and professional missions compatible with the superintendency?

2. Assume you have just accepted your first position as a school superintendent. Use the four management competencies mentioned in this chapter to describe how you would construct a professional identity in the school district and the community.

3. Point out several important reasons for becoming a superintendent of schools. In your opinion, what are the positive and negative aspects of the job?

4. In your opinion, what are the three most important functions of the superintendent of schools?

5. If learning organizations are the direction of the future, why have not more schools adopted learning organization philosophy?

CASE 3.1   We Have Never Done it That Way Before

Greg Stephan, the new superintendent of the College View School District, explained to the Board of Education that he wanted their approval to develop a strategic planning process for the district so it would be well positioned for the future. To guide the process, Dr. Stephan had written a statement that described his vision of the school district as it might look in the future. The statement was well constructed and set forth a clear picture of what the district could become if its staff, board, administrators and patrons would support the concept.

Milt Stoner, a veteran board member, remarked, "the district has never before found it necessary to have a formal statement that described what it wanted to look like in the future—and things have always worked fairly well! I don't think this is a very good idea. What if we don't meet some of our objectives? People may not support us well if they know what we want to look like and then we don't look that way five years from now."

Questions

1. Explain why it is important for the district to have a clear direction where it is going in the future.
2. Assume the role of Superintendent Stephan. Remembering that your role is to design, build, and teach, how would you respond to Mr. Stoner's remarks?

CASE 3.2   Leadership Is a Matter of Perspective

The College View Chapter of Citizens for Fair Taxation invited Dr. Stephan, the superintendent of schools, to their quarterly meeting so he could be available to answer questions about the increase in the school levy. Approximately 23 percent of the population of College View, like that of many other U.S. cities, had children of school age. The average age of the Citizens for Fair Taxation was 58. Many of them lived on fixed incomes and investments. Some were fully employed and looking forward to keeping more of their personal income as income rather than spending it for governmental services. The meeting room was filled to capacity. While they were not a hostile group, they were certainly representative of citizens who had the perception that government in any form did not use their tax dollars wisely.

Questions

1. Discuss the concept of the role of government in providing a free and appropriate education for children, what it means to American democracy, and how it applies to the citizens of College View.
2. Assume the role of the superintendent and assure the Citizens For Fair Taxation that their investment is valid and purposeful for them and for future generations. How would you frame your remarks?

Inbasket Exercise

INBASKET 3.1

The Individual or the Team?

SANDY VALLEY PUBLIC SCHOOLS
WINAWIN, MARSHALL

Dr. Jayne T. Knapple, Superintendent
Sandy Valley Public Schools
10077 Philben Way
Winawin, Marshall 00010

Dear Dr. Knapple:

I regret to inform you that I feel it necessary to submit my resignation as Principal of the Mayfield Middle School. As you know, I have found it difficult to adjust to the team oriented approach you have promoted in the district. I feel that it is the role of the superintendent to set the agenda for the district and tell the principals and others what part they play in carrying out the plan. I cannot understand why you won't tell us what to do!

I have been a long time member of the administrative staff and feel that I no longer fit in. I used to know what I was supposed to do, but now I am confused about my role. Why must I be concerned about conditions in the entire school district if things are alright in my building?

I am sorry the situation came to this, but that is just the way it is.

Regretfully,

Stan Masters

Stan Masters

cc: Joel Billings, President, Board of Education

Response

1. Assume that Mr. Masters is a respected principal and community member, but he has not been able to enroll in the vision of the district. He resents that he is expected to assume some responsibility for system-wide planning. He has appealed to other administrators and found little support, but he does have friends in the community and on the board. What is your response to Mr. Masters?
2. Explain how you would handle this situation with the board of education. What would you do? Please provide a rationale for your action and explain the rationale in full.

Notes

1. Thomas E. Glass, *The 1992 Study of the American School Superintendency: America's Education Leaders in a Time of Reform* (Arlington, Va.: American Association of School Administrators, 1992). p. 19.

2. Shirley Hord, in Thomas E. Glass, *The 1992 Study of the American School Superintendency*, p. 19.

3. Spencer J. Maxcy, *Educational Leadership: A Critical Pragmatic Perspective* (New York: Bergin and Garvey, 1991), pp. 2–4.

4. Carolyn Hughes-Chapman (Research Team Coordinator), "A Study of Beginning Superintendents: Preliminary Implications For Leading and Learning," an unpublished paper presented at the annual convention of the University Council for Educational Administrators, Houston, Tex., 29 October 1993.

5. Warren Bennis, *Why Leaders Can't Lead: The Unconscious Conspiracy Continues* (San Francisco, Oxford: Jossey-Bass Publishers, 1990), pp. 19–22.

6. Ibid., p. 20.

7. John Heider, *The Tao Of Leadership: Leadership Strategies For A New Age* (New York: Bantam Books, 1985), p. 51.

8. Stephen R. Covey, *The Seven Habits of Highly Effective People* (New York: Fireside, 1989), p. 33.

9. Ibid., pp. 46–62.

10. Peter F. Senge, "The Leaders New Work: Building Learning Organizations," *Sloan Management Review,* 32(11) (fall 1990): pp. 7–23.

11. Ibid., p. 9.

12. Peter F. Senge, *The Fifth Discipline: The Art and Practice of The Learning Organization* (New York: Doubleday, 1990), p. 10.

13. Ibid., pp. 6–12.

14. Kent D. Peterson and Chester E. Finn, "Principals, Superintendents, and the Administrators Art," in *Leaders for America's Schools,* ed. by Daniel E. Griffiths, Robert T. Stout, and Patrick B. Forsyth (Berkeley, Calif.: McCutchan, 1988), p. 89.

15. Daniel E. Griffiths, Robert T. Stout, and Patrick B. Forsyth, eds., *Leaders for America's Schools* (Berkeley, Calif.: McCutchan, 1988), p. 7.

16. *Kentucky Superintendent Assessment Program: Interview Findings and Recommendations* (facilitated by the National Association of Secondary School Principals [NASSP] and Paul Hersey) (Fords, N.J.: Applied Research Corporation, 1992), pp. 22–24.

17. Ibid., pp. 19–33.

18. Joseph Murphy, *The Landscape of Leadership Preparation: Reframing the Education of School Administrators* (Newbury Park, Calif.: Corwin Press, 1992), p. 102.

19. Glass, *1992 Study,* pp. 78–80.

20. Ibid., p. 72.

21. Ibid., p. 73.

22. Hughes-Chapman et al., "A Study of Beginning Superintendents."

23. Murphy, *The Landscape of Leadership Preparation,* pp. 141–146.

24. Glass, *1992 Study,* p. ix.

25. Peter Drucker, *The New Realities: In Government and Politics/ in Economics and Business/ in Society and World View* (New York: Harper and Row, 1989).

26. Hughes-Chapman et al., "A Study of Beginning Superintendents," p. 13.

27. Jay Scribner and Richard M. Englert, "The Politics of Education: An Introduction," in Seventy-sixth yearbook of the National Society for the Study of Education, *The Politics of Education* (Chicago: The University of Chicago Press, 1977), p. 22.

28. Frederick M. Wirt and Michael W. Kirst, *The Politics of Education: Schools in Conflict* (Berkeley, Calif.: McCutchan, 1989), pp. 1–2.

29. Scribner and Englert, "The Politics of Education," p. 22.

30. Glass, *1992 Study,* p. 25.

31. Ibid., p. 47.

32. Miles Bryant and Marilyn Grady, "Sources of Conflict in School Governance," *School Administrator,* 2(50) (February 1993): p. 35.

33. S. Papallo, "Steps to Take with the Board to Avoid Walking the Plank," *Executive Educator,* 12 (May 1990): p. 19.

34. Senge, *The Fifth Discipline,* p. 18. (See n. 12.)

35. Heider, *The Tao Of Leadership,* p. 107. (See n. 7.)

36. Amy Goldstein, "Stress in the Superintendency: School Leaders Confront the Daunting Issues of the Job," *School Administrator,* 9(49) (September 1992): pp. 8–17.

37. Michael M. Milstein, "The Overstated Case of Administrator Stress," *School Administrator,* 9(49) (September 1992): pp. 12–13.

38. Ibid., p. 13.

39. Hughes-Chapman et al., "A Study of Beginning Superintendents," p. 13.

═══════════════════════════════
═══════════════════════════════

Organizational Culture and School Leadership

The most important message for leaders at this point is "Try to understand culture, give it its due, and ask yourself how well you can begin to understand the culture in which you are embedded."
—*EDGAR H. SCHEIN*

The significance of organizational culture for the school superintendent has been succinctly underlined by Schein: "The bottom line for leaders is that if they do not become conscious of the cultures in which they are embedded, those cultures will manage them. Cultural understanding is desirable for all of us, but it is essential to leaders, if they are to lead."[1] In this chapter we examine the concept of organizational culture and its implications for school leadership. What is organizational culture? Can it be managed? The answers to these questions and the primary responsibilities of the school superintendent concerning visioning leadership also are discussed in this chapter.

What Is Culture?

Wide differences of opinion exist concerning the nature of culture. These differences center not only on the definition of the term, but also on the question of whether or not organizational culture is something that can be managed by persons in roles of leadership. The difficulties surrounding the study of culture are underlined by Lundberg. He points out that, "for all its contemporary popularity . . . organizational culture remains a phenomenon that is as yet neither fully understood nor agreed upon."[2]

Differing perspectives of culture are revealed in various definitions of the term. Pai states that "culture is the whole of humanity's intellectual, social, technological, political, economical, moral, religious, and aesthetic accomplishments."[3] He views culture as an integrated set of norms that serve to organize human behaviors, beliefs, and thought processes. Rich's similar definition states that "culture is a pattern of human behavior (including thought, speech, and action) shared by a group of people. It also includes the artifacts produced by those people."[4] Rich speaks of material culture and nonmaterial culture. The former includes the artifacts created by society—the tools, clothing, housing, and technology produced and used by a society for survival. The values, beliefs, norms, mores, folkways, and ideologies of a society represent its nonmaterial culture. Rich defines culture simply as "the way a group of people understand their way of life."[5] Lorch's definition, that culture is "the beliefs top managers in a company share about how they should manage themselves and other employees,"[6] represents a marked departure from previously quoted definitions as is Martin's definition that "culture is an expression of people's deepest needs, a means of endowing their experiences with meaning."[7]

An often cited definition of culture, and one that best conveys the purposes of this chapter, is that of Schein. He views culture as

> A pattern of basic assumptions—invented, discovered, or developed by a given group as it learns to cope with its problems of external adaptation and internal integration—that has worked well enough to be considered valid and, therefore, to be taught to new members as a correct way to perceive, think, and feel in relation to those problems.[8]

As suggested by Schein's definition, a given group preserves its existence by inculcating its culture upon its members. Individuals are socialized by learning the beliefs, values, important skills, membership roles, ways of thinking, and future perspectives held by the group. Institutions and individuals within the culture, the school, the family, peers, group leaders, and others serve as the socializing agents. Persons who enter the group learn what is valued, what behavior is acceptable, the penalties and rewards associated with certain behaviors, and the ideas that are important to the culture. What is success? What are the expectations of various group members? These are among the many complex questions that loom important in organizational cultures.

As cultures become more and more diverse, answers to such questions become more controversial; disagreements and conflicts can result. As noted by Smircich, "to study cultures means to study social significance—how things, events, and interactions come to be meaningful."[9] Thus, by giving serious attention to the culture of the school organization, school leaders can gain important and useful insights into how existing problems might be resolved and can uncover new problems that require their attention.

Can Organizational Culture Be Managed?

One school of thought is that culture cannot be managed. Since culture is something that emerges as an abstract, unconscious, and complex expression of needs and beliefs, it is not a maneuverable or manageable entity. On the other hand, cultural pragmatists argue that not only can culture be managed, but it is absolutely necessary that leaders do so. Others stipulate that although it might not be possible to manage culture, leaders can facilitate the development of its identity. Berg holds this view and believes that a true "strategic" change program can make persons aware of the nature of the culture of which they are a part.[10] Barnard,[11] Bennis,[12] and others have pointed to the need for leaders to establish superordinate goals or guiding visions in organizations. Louis[13] uses the expression, "the emergence of local shared meanings," in relation to the development of culture in organizations. He speaks of "planting a culture" by a leader with a vision and the capacity to get others to subscribe to it. Leaders, according to Louis, are distinguished from managers by their capacity to create a clear and meaningful vision for the organization that its members internalize. Siehl supports this contention and reasons that "perhaps cultural management is really this: articulating a possible culture, coming to agree that it is desirable, and then attaining it through the sharing of desired values."[14]

The primary leadership responsibilities of the school superintendent in helping the school system articulate a possible culture, as well as the leadership needed to implement it, are discussed in detail in a later section of this chapter. In the following section, we examine internal and external influences that bear on the behavior of leaders and others in organizations.

Culture and the School System

Concepts of social systems have been detailed by many researchers and writers. A synthesis of various treatments of social systems theory most often concludes that they are peopled; there are specific interactions between and among its members; the system shares a set of common goals; the system is normed—there are expectations for individual and group behavior; and the system's institutions serve specific functions that facilitate, control, and preserve its expectations.

The Getzels–Guba Social Systems Model

Although originally set forth in 1957, the Getzels–Guba Social Systems Model[15] is a useful framework for examining the nature of social systems such as school organizations and the influences that affect them. This model views social systems as having two dimensions, the nomothetic, or organizational, dimension and the idiographic, or human, dimension (see Figure 4–1).

According to the Getzels–Guba social systems theory, the organizational and human dimensions of a social system are always interacting to influence the behaviors of members of the organization and the outcomes of the organization. Social systems can consist of groups of people who share a set of common understandings, or institutions (e.g., governing agencies, policing agencies, educational agencies) that serve the purposes of the social system. Individuals in the system assume specific roles in the system's institutions that are founded on expected role behaviors (e.g., in education, role members include superintendents, principals, supervisors, teachers, support personnel). Although the organization holds specific expectations for various institutional roles, each role is influenced by various role senders, who represent both internal and external members of the organization's environment, and by the individual in the role as well.

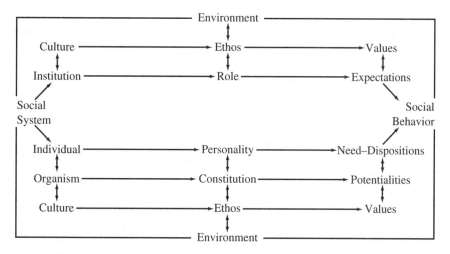

FIGURE 4–1   Social Systems Model

SOURCE: Figure from *Educational Administration as a Social Process* by Jacob W. Getzels, James M. Lipham and Ronald F. Campbell. Copyright © 1968 by Jacob W. Getzels, James M. Lipham and Ronald F. Campbell. Reprinted by permission of HarperCollins Publishers, Inc.

The human dimension of the model includes various individuals and subunits of their varying personalities. Each individual brings a unique set of need dispositions to the organization as a subunit of his or her personality. Thus, according to the Getzels–Guba theory, the observed behavior (B) within a system is a function of the institutional role (R) and the individual's personality (P), or $B = f\ (R \times P)$.[16] The school administrator in any school setting, then, must keep both the organizational dimension and the human dimension clearly in mind if the system in which they are embedded is to be organizationally productive and personally fulfilling for its members. Barnard[17] termed this phenomenon the organization's capacity of equilibrium—the ability to be productive and, at the same time, to satisfy individual employee needs.

The foregoing conceptual model was criticized as having the form of a closed system; that is, the original Getzels–Guba theory tended to view organizations from an internal perspective only. Although internal organizational influences are crucial to leadership and organizational behavior, the external environment affects organizations heavily as well. The aspects of ethos, mores, and values, which are part of any social system's environment, were added to the original model to allow for cultural factors associated with the behaviors of individuals in social institutions.[18]

In brief, the behavior of individuals in a social system is influenced not only by the status roles in the institution and role expectations, but also by the larger environment of which they are a part. Institutions such as school systems are affected by the cultures in which they are embedded; the beliefs and values undergirding these cultures present conditions that both facilitate and inhibit individual and system outcomes. Likewise, individuals in organizations work both in formal and informal settings. The individual's behavior is a product of not only the organization's culture but that of the external cultures present.

Hoy and Miskel note that "the work group develops its own informal status structure and culture, its social organization. This informal organization, with its important group norms and values, becomes another powerful force that affects organizational behavior."[19] The implications of the Getzels–Guba model, and its extension to include environmental influences, for schools and school leaders are far-reaching. Sociological, economic, political, and legal factors, along with other influences, provide both opportunities for and constraints on schools and the roles and behaviors of their leaders. Various individuals and groups in the community, as role senders, give various, often conflicting messages of direction and priority for the mission of the schools. Efforts on the part of school superintendents and other leaders "to read" their environment and to make decisions that can be implemented successfully are essential.

Although various individuals and units within the school system have roles in understanding and influencing the internal and external environments of the school system, the school superintendent is the one individual ultimately held responsible for leadership in understanding, informing, influencing, and promoting the complex phenomenon of school culture. The following section focuses on the overarching responsibilities of the school superintendent relative to culture and the school community.

Leadership Implications for the School Superintendent

The school superintendent must assume three primary leadership responsibilities relative to the school system's culture. First, the superintendent must become personally knowledgeable of the organizational culture and then educate others about this culture. Second, the superintendent must take a leadership role in helping to plant a vision for the school system that guides the organization. Third, the superintendent must assume leadership in implementing the organization's vision for the future.

Davis summarizes the challenges for school leaders in cultural leadership as follows:

> Good leaders must have a vision of the effective school and an understanding of the values that underlie it; then they must work to gain support . . . both within the school and without. They must be aware that the existing culture within the school has emerged as a response to the necessity of contending with the problems of survival of the organization. Attempting to change that culture will create new anxieties and problems. The leaders should know how to address these problems and provide stability within the school until they are resolved.[20]

Conveying Personal Knowledge and Education of Others about the School Community Culture

To assume leadership in helping others understand the culture, the school superintendent must undertake the personal responsibility of self-education. Although gaining an understanding of the culture of any school community is a complex endeavor, embarking on the discovery of the organization's belief system is a key step. Less formal strategies for determining what people in the organization believe include such actions as simply asking them, examining statements of the organization's mission, studying adopted school policies, observing ongoing practices such as school ceremonies, and listening to the stories of school and community members that describe the school environment and important views of its beliefs and values.

Schein removes some of the mystery of deciphering organizational culture. He describes a process for working with organizations on cultural issues that enables its members to identify and evaluate important cultural assumptions. Schein speaks of shared assumptions and states, "a group has a culture when it has had enough of shared history to have formed such a set of shared assumptions."[21] Basic assumptions of an organization evolve from a group's shared values that have been confirmed as successful solutions to existing problems or from a specified process that has led to the group's shared vision of success. These assumptions become firmly ingrained in the minds of organizational members; to an extent, they ultimately are taken for granted and become extremely difficult to change.

To decipher the culture of an organization, one must obtain the commitment of those in leadership to this process's purpose.[22] Through larger group processes, organizational members come to understand that their culture is a learned set of assumptions based on the group's shared history. The group's culture is further refined through the identification of its artifacts (e.g., dress codes, physical conditions, members' behaviors, tools, technology). Organizational values are examined through discussions that center on the "why" of system practices. Underlying assumptions are examined relative to the actual behaviors of organizational members. In the culture deciphering process, much time is devoted to refining and categorizing the group's culture assumptions. Key questions are posed to uncover how each assumption might hinder or facilitate the achievement of desired change. Every effort is made to gain some consensus about the shared assumptions that are an integral part of the group's culture.

The school superintendent can make people in the organization aware of the culture in which they exist by bringing its values, principles, and behaviors to the surface and providing a framework for interpreting what they see. Berg[23] contends that such an approach initiates a creative process that brings a feeling of ownership to members. He emphasizes two basic needs in this educational process. First, leaders in the organization must focus attention on formulating and framing strategic issues facing the system as opposed to developing specific plans. This approach establishes broad conceptualizations of the organization and its future; plans provide narrower suggestions of the means to achieve desired outcomes. Second, educating members about organizational culture requires the development of a clear concept of what the organization is presently in relation to what it can and wants to become. Thus, the school superintendent must assume a leadership role in articulating a guiding vision for the future of the school system.

Visioning Leadership

Follett,[24] as early as 1923, and Barnard[25] in 1938 spoke of the value of establishing superordinate goals in organizations. Follett's concepts of conflict resolution focus on the "integration" of talents whereby all parties in conflict are brought to consider the broader purposes of the organization rather than personal interests only. Barnard viewed the establishment of superordinate goals or purposes as one of the three basic functions of all executives. More recently, Louis stated that "planting a culture . . . seems to require a key person with a vision and the capacity to get others to subscribe to it. In fact, recent work on characteristics that distinguish leaders from managers singles out this capacity to create and communicate a lucid and compelling vision which subordinates internalize."[26]

Leithwood and Stager,[27] Thompson,[28] Senge,[29] Cunningham and Gresso,[30] and others have examined characteristics evidenced by visionary leaders. For example, visionary leaders help determine organizational directions; they are concerned about the human element of the organization; they place emphasis on communication processes; they build and communicate the rationales for determined priorities; and they work to establish ownership on the part of the members relative to the organization's future. Thompson[31] describes several specific behaviors of visionary leaders as follows:

- Learning orientation—a strong desire for self-improvement and personal development of others
- Self-knowledge—a strong knowledge of one's strengths and weaknesses
- Values foundation—strong personal values and ethics
- Values and vision bridging—a commitment to establish a basic system of human values and a shared vision in the organization
- Empowerment—a positive attitude toward people and their abilities
- Organizational sensitivity—an understanding of human behavior

The school superintendent can lead in the establishment of a vision for the future of the school system by applying various strategies. Effective visioning leadership places emphasis on member participation. The superintendent should vigorously avoid being the sole creator of the organizational vision. Unless the vision of the future evolves from members' beliefs of what is possible for the organization's future, it likely will gain limited support and will likely fade rapidly if the leader moves on. Visions that evolve from the thinking and creativity of everyone in the system provide for feelings of ownership, individual initiative, and personal commitment.[32] The superintendent works to develop a common agreement among members regarding the purposes of the organization and the basic assumptions of its culture.

Although organizational leaders often do act as the sole creators of the organization's vision of the future, and indeed might change organizational behavior, it is questionable if such action actually serves to change the culture. As noted by Kiefer, "when the leader is the sole creator of the organizational vision, the members' own ability to envision the future atrophies, and they grow evermore dependent on that leader. When the leader departs, the organization is usually left with key players who lack the ability to create new visions of the future."[33] Feelings of manipulation tend to result, and members consciously or unconsciously resist visions "forced" on them by others.

A Visioning Strategy

A possible strategy for creating a vision for the system's future begins with an in-depth consideration of the school system's past, its historical foundations, beliefs, values, and traditions (see Figure 4–2). Considerable time is devoted to answering basic questions: What has been the purposes of the system historically? What clients have been served? How has organizational and individual success been defined in the past? Responses to these and other important questions are recorded and displayed.

The Past

Phase 1 School members/key leaders, under the superintendent's leadership, consider/analyze the question, "What has the system been in the past?"

The Present

Phase 2 The key question, "What are we now?" is considered/analyzed in depth.

The Future

Phase 3 An in-depth exploration and visioning of what the system wants to become in the years ahead are considered/analyzed.

System Strengths/Needs, Resources and
Actions Needed to Accomplish the Vision

Phase 4 Strengths are assessed and weaknesses identified in relation to successful accomplishment of the future vision. What problems/inhibitors must be overcome?

Selected/Preferred Alternatives

Phase 5 Action is focused on best alternatives. Specific strategic planning is operationalized.

FIGURE 4–2 Model for Visioning

Next, members address the question, What/who are we now? The school system's present purposes, products, achievements, and stakeholders are identified. How is success in the system presently defined? What important basic assumptions undergird what we do? These kinds of questions, and others that shed light on the system's present culture, are discussed at length, and the questions and the products of that discussion are recorded and displayed. These discussions necessarily consume large blocks of time.

In the next phase of the visioning process, the basic question, "What do we want to be or what must we become in the years ahead?" is pursued. What purposes must the school system achieve? How should success be defined for the system and its stakeholders in the future? These kinds of questions and the basic assumptions that support members' responses, once again, are recorded and displayed.

Envisioning strategies must give appropriate attention to the school system's present strengths and weaknesses including available material and human resources that lend toward the implementation of the envisioned future. Consideration of factors that might inhibit the accomplishment of the vision of the future, as well as problems and obstacles that must be overcome, are objectively identified in the visioning process. In the final steps of the visioning strategy, questions related to alternatives for action and procedures for follow-up strategic planning are detailed. At this point, planning strategies, such as those discussed in Chapter 7, are implemented.

Establishing a shared vision is not a product, but a continuous process. Visioning implies cultural change. Change tends to create anxiety and uncertainty for some members. The school superintendent must anticipate such fears and be prepared to implement actions that reduce human problems. Envisioning strategies that incorporate personal development programs, human motivation concepts, personal visions of the future held by members, and implementation procedures that lead to the successful realization of the system's vision are essential.

Implementing the New Vision

Kotter and Heskett[34] emphasize that changing cultures in an organization is complex, takes time, and requires leadership quite different from effective management. Their model for enhancing cultures emphasizes the actions of leaders who institutionalize a new vision and set of strategies that include management's actions, values, and behaviors. Actions focus on the communication of core values and behaviors; values give full consideration to the organization's constituencies; behavior centers on the institution of strategies relevant to the current environment.

Visionary leadership requires more than managing well—bold leadership is required. Cultural change requires leaders who can help plant the system's vision of the future and cultivate the energy required to realize necessary, difficult organizational change. The research literature is clear on one point: effective leadership from people at the top of the organization is the most important factor in the realization of cultural change.[35]

School leaders who try to force or control change through edicts and centralized control are likely to fail. When superintendents lead through personal example, support expressions of shared values, and give personal attention to the school system's envisioned future, leadership toward change is more likely to succeed. Schlechty supports this contention and states, "Leaders who structure the relationship among these elements (people, knowledge, time, and space) in the most imaginative ways will be the leaders who invent the schools for the twenty-first century."[36]

Summary

Cultural understanding is essential for effective leadership by school superintendents. Without a basic knowledge of the school community culture, school leaders will have little success implementing educational programs and realizing changes that lead to program improvement. Education is inextricably related to the culture in which it is embedded. Therefore, the behaviors of individuals in the school system are influenced by both its internal and external cultures. Since the school is an integral part of the culture of its community, it is essential that the school superintendent be highly knowledgeable of this culture and his or her role in working within it.

As a social system, the school system comprises an organizational dimension and a human dimension that are always interacting to influence the behavioral outcomes of its members. The external environment affects both of these dimensions; the beliefs, values, and assumptions of the school system's culture serve to determine its primary goals and policy decisions.

Society establishes institutions that serve its educational, social, and economic purposes. Schools, as social institutions, are no exception. Schools reflect the shared values, beliefs, and collective life of the cultures of which they are a part.

The school superintendent must assume the primary leadership role in educating others about the culture in which they are embedded. The superintendent's visioning leadership role centers on planting a guiding vision for the system by helping members understand past purposes, analyzing basic assumptions undergirding what the system is presently, envisioning what the system must and can become in the future, and implementing strategies and procedures for achieving the vision of the future.

Discussion Questions

1. Consider the culture of the school district with which you are associated or the one with which you are most familiar. Describe in some detail its culture in terms of values, beliefs, ceremonies, artifacts, and traditions. To your knowledge, has the school district's culture changed significantly over the last several years? What do you believe are the reasons for the changes that may have occurred? If no significant changes have taken place in the culture, how do you explain this maintenance of the status quo?

2. Consider the work of the school superintendent in any district at large. List and describe a minimum of five ways in which the culture will likely affect the superintendent's policy recommendations.

3. Discuss the topic of planting a culture in the school system. In your view, to what extent should the superintendent have a personal vision for the system clearly in mind?

CASE 4.1   English Only

The College View School District's administrative cabinet met each Thursday of the month to consider matters of importance to the district at large. At the outset of its November meeting, Principal Black brought up the matter of language problems being encountered at Whittier Elementary School.

"As you all know" stated Principal Black, "the influx of Hispanic and Asian students in the last few years has brought about some real problems for us. Teachers are finding classroom instruction for many pupils ineffective. Our efforts to use bilingual messages in home contacts, and in some of our instructional materials, seem to be contrary to our purposes. If we continue to use this approach, I don't believe we'll ever get some of these kids to speak English."

"I agree," said Principal Wilson. "We've got to get these kids to know our community; we need extended English instruction, not more foreign language."

"May I offer another point of view?" requested Patricia Monte, Coordinator of Elementary School Curriculum. "I think we need to extend language instruction for all children. The parents who objected to our bilingual pilot program at Fairbanks Junior High School last year never really understood our purposes. I believe a second effort, perhaps at another school, is in order."

The room was silent momentarily. Cabinet members looked to Superintendent Kelly in anticipation of some response.

Questions

1. Assume the role of Superintendent Kelly here. From your personal viewpoint, and with the limited information provided in the situation, set forth your response to members of the cabinet.
2. Why is the topic of language so important in discussions of school programs?
3. What external cultural considerations will likely affect the program and the College View School District?

Inbasket Exercise

INBASKET 4.1

Just a Little Suggestion

FORTHRIGHT INSURANCE COMPANY
WYMORE, LAFAYETTE

To: Ward Henson, Supt.
From: Wade Martin, Board President
Date: October 7
Re: PTAs and child care requests

As you will note by the attached request, parents of the Hawthorne and Whittier elementary schools are recommending an early childhood and care program for the school district. In visiting informally with board members Jed Barker and Sally Mariner, we think the idea has considerable merit. Please prepare your thoughts on this matter and send them to me within the week. I want to get my memo out to all board members as soon as possible and tentatively respond to Curothers and Valdez. Please give this some priority.

(Accompanying Letter)

October 3, 19___

Wade Martin, President
Wymore School District
501 Pascal
Wymore, Lafayette 02075

Dear Mr. Martin:

The PTAs of the Hawthorne and Whittier elementary schools request the school board's serious consideration of a district early childhood and child care program.

As the school board is fully aware, our community has increased greatly in the number of working mothers due to one-parent families. An early childhood program with child care facilities indeed is a community need. In our recent discussion of this problem, the large majority of parents viewed this as one of the leading needs educationally. We ask for action to implement this program; we really don't need to "study it" further. The need is obvious!

I have called the PTA presidents of three other schools and they gave us their total support. Your action is appreciated. We understand that there are state monies available for such programs, is this true?

Sincerely,

Twila Curothers

Twila Curothers

PTA President, Hawthorne

Rosemary Valdez

Rosemary Valdez

PTA President, Whittier

Questions

1. Assume the role of Superintendent Henson and write the specific administrative actions you will take here. What additional information is needed? How will this information be gathered? Be specific in your response. Write out the specific memorandums and letters that you send, if any. If telephone contacts are made or if meetings are held, set forth the specific statements you will make and the questions you will ask.
2. What cultural considerations are apparent in Inbasket 4.1 and the accompanying letter that will affect the behavior of the school superintendent and staff?

Notes

1. Edgar H. Schein, *Organizational Culture and Leadership,* 2nd ed. (San Francisco: Jossey-Bass Publishers, 1992), Chapter 1: "Defining Organizational Culture," p. 15.

2. Craig C. Lundberg, "On the Feasibility of Cultural Intervention in Organizations," in *Organizational Culture,* by Peter J. Frost, Larry F. Moore, Meryl Reis Louis, Craig C. Lundberg, and Joanne Martin (Beverly Hills, Calif.: Sage Publications, 1985), p. 169.

3. Young Pai, *Cultural Foundations of Education* (Columbus, Ohio: Merrill, 1990), p. 21.

4. John Martin Rich, *Foundations of Education: Perspectives on American Education* (New York: Merrill, an imprint of Macmillan Publishing, 1992), p. 106.

5. Ibid., p. 113.

6. J. W. Lorch, "Strategic Myopia: Culture as an Invisible Barrier to Change," in *Gaining Control of the Corporate Culture,* ed. by Ralph H. Kilmann, Mary J. Saxton, Roy Serpa, and Associates (San Francisco: Jossey-Bass, 1985), p. 84.

7. Joanne Martin, "Can Organizational Culture Be Managed?" in *Organizational Culture,* p. 95. (See n. 2.)

8. Schein, *Organizational Culture and Leadership,* p. 12.

9. Linda Smircich, "Is the Concept of Culture a Paradigm for Understanding Organizations and Ourselves?" in *Organizational Culture,* p. 63.

10. Per-Olaf Berg, "Organizational Change as a Symbolic Transformation," in *Organizational Culture,* pp. 298–299.

11. Chester I. Barnard, *The Functions of the Executive* (Cambridge, Mass.: Harvard University Press, 1938).

12. Warren G. Bennis, *On Becoming a Leader* (Reading, Mass.: Addison-Wesley, 1989).

13. Meryl Reis Louis, "An Investigator's Guide to Workplace Culture," in *Organizational Culture,* p. 86.

14. Caren Siehl, "After the Founder—an Opportunity to Manage Culture," in *Organizational Culture,* p. 139.

15. Jacob W. Getzels and Egon G. Guba, "Social Behavior and the Administrative Process," *School Review,* 65(4) (winter 1957): pp. 423–441.

16. Ibid.

17. Barnard, *The Functions of the Executive.*

18. Jacob W. Getzels and Herbert A. Thelen, "The Classroom as a Social System," in Fifty-ninth yearbook, Part II, of the National Society for the Study of Education, *The Dynamics of Instructional Change,* ed. by Nelson B. Henry (Chicago: University of Chicago Press, 1960), pp. 53–83.

19. Wayne K. Hoy and Cecil G. Miskel, *Educational Administration: Theory, Research, and Practice,* 4th ed. (New York: McGraw-Hill, 1991), p. 38.

20. John Davis, in *Educational Policy for Effective Schools,* ed. by Mark Holmes, Keith A. Leithwood, and Donald F. Musella (Toronto: Ontario Institute for Studies in Education, 1989), Chapter 6: "Policy and Organizational Culture," p. 122.

21. Schein, *Organizational Culture and Leadership,* p. 12. (See n. 1.)

22. Ibid., p. 147.

23. Berg, "Organizational Change as a Symbolic Transformation," in *Organizational Culture,* pp. 298–299.

24. Mary Parker Follett, "The Meaning of Responsibility in Business Management," in *Dynamic Administration: The Collected Papers of Mary Parker Follett,* ed. by Henry C. Metcalf and Luther Urwick (New York: Harper and Brothers, 1940), pp. 146–166.

25. Barnard, *The Functions of the Executive.*

26. Louis, "An Investigator's Guide to Workplace Culture," in *Organizational Culture,* p. 86.

27. K. Leithwood and M. Stager, "Differences in Problem Solving Processes Used by Moderately and Highly Effective Principals," paper presented at the annual meeting of the American Educational Research Association, San Francisco, 1986.

28. John W. Thompson, "Corporate Leadership in the Twenty-first Century," in *New Traditions in Business: Spirit and Leadership in the Twenty-first Century,* ed. by John Renesch (San Francisco: Berrett-Koehler Publishers, 1992), pp. 209–233.

29. Peter M. Senge, "The Leader's New Work: Building Learning Organizations," in *New Traditions in Business: Spirit and Leadership in the Twenty-first Century,* pp. 81–93.

30. William G. Cunningham and Donn W. Gresso, *Cultural Leadership* (Boston: Allyn and Bacon, 1993).

31. Thompson, "Corporate Leadership in the Twenty-first Century," in *New Traditions in Business: Spirit and Leadership in the Twenty-first Century,* p. 219.

32. Charles E. Kiefer, "Leadership in Metanoic Organizations," in *New Traditions in Business: Spirit and Leadership in the Twenty-first Century,* pp. 175–191.

33. Ibid., p. 219.

34. John P. Kotter and James L. Heskett, *Corporate Culture and Performance* (New York: The Free Press, 1992), Chapter 11: "On the Role of Top Management," p. 149.

35. Ibid., pp. 84, 92.

36. Phillip C. Schlechty, *Schools for the Twenty-first Century* (San Francisco: Jossey-Bass Publishers, 1990), p. 82.

Chapter 5

The New Politics of Education

Guidance systems are essential to all travelers who depart for unfamiliar territory. The devices that establish direction and periodically confirm the position of the traveler in relation to the destination range from simple maps to sophisticated electronic systems aboard space shuttles. Similar systems are necessary to guide nations through changing social, political, and economic environments. Policy is a common form of guidance mechanism for societies. The formulation of policy is a crucial process, and policymakers should be among the most reliable and trusted individuals in a society. In the arenas where policy is molded, exchanges of ideas, clarification of values, and proposals to balance the wants and needs of society with available resources are the order of the day. It is here, in the political system, where courses are charted and corrected.

Politics; at the mention of the word, people break into dialogue about endless rhetoric, spending the taxpayers' money, last minute efforts to trade votes, wielding influence and power, and other assorted conceptions of a system too few will admit to lending their endorsement. Too often, politics or political action is portrayed as the kind of activity in which decent citizens should not want to engage. Unfortunate as that may be, politics, the authoritative and legitimate distribution of valued resources, is as real as air and water. Politics is a necessary part of every social system. Politics, not baseball, is America's favorite pastime, and for the American educational system it is serious business.

For many years, the myth that education was apolitical was sustained mostly by educational practitioners. Education was, after all, responsible for the enculturation of youth and for the preparation of the young for citizenship and work—areas that were viewed as intellectual, not political, endeavors.

Wirt and Kirst[1] provided several reasons for the perpetuation of the apolitical myth. First, education professionals did not wish to be assumed to be aligned with a particular political party. Second, the general public was perceived to be more supportive of education if it were not connected with partisan politics like many of the other branches of local and state government. Finally, educators believed more benefits, status, legitimacy, and money would accrue to them if education was viewed as a nonpolitical function of government. All that aside, the formal distribution of knowledge, a powerful, valued resource, is the purview of the school, and that alone makes the educational arena highly political.

The Reality of Change

During the middle of the nineteenth century, approximately 1830 to 1870, the Common School Movement, inspired by Horace Mann and others, was promulgated on the premise that America could and should be unified through a set of common values taught in the public schools. Hansot and Tyack[2] remind us that the case for common public schools was built on the particular view of history that Americans shared mutual aspirations and a common destiny, the concept that America would serve as a redeemer nation. At the time the movement began, the modal school in the United States was largely rural, with only several students and a young, usually untrained teacher. It was governed and supported by local volunteers. As the movement proceeded and the population became more widely distributed, schools and teacher training were changed.

When the nation entered the twentieth century, leaders in education were inspired by a different vision of public education: a scientific and rational model. These leaders perceived they "could and should control human evolution through improved schools."[3] Unlike the schools that prevailed at the beginning of the Common School Movement, early-twentieth-century schools were increasingly staffed by better trained teachers and career oriented professional educators with expertise in pedagogy and educational management. During the Progressive Era, 1876–1955, schools were reshaped according to guidelines of educational science and business efficiency. One of the designs of that era was to raise the education profession to greater recognition as a legitimate professional endeavor and improve the science of education. Schools and school systems became increasingly professionalized, centralized, bureaucratized, and politicized, albeit still committed to education as an instrument of progress.

Old Reference Points Vanished

By the mid-1980s, some of the traditional reference points once used to measure standing and status among nations were no longer pertinent; some had vanished altogether. For example, time, once measured by the number of days, weeks, or months it took to transform raw materials into a salable good, is now measured in heterojunctions: a measure of time, recorded in nanoseconds, required to electronically exchange wealth among people and nations.

Other reference points have vanished as well. The loyal worker who gave the corporation the time and talent it took to produce goods and services, make the sale, balance the account, or find new markets has been replaced by the knowledge worker who possesses information and expertise that can be useful to multiple users, not merely a single organization. Knowledge workers can and do move to conditions of employment that satisfy their need to make a contribution, rather than spend a lifetime in one organization.

Territory, the space people claim as their own surrounding, where they are free to navigate among familiar landmarks, has taken on new meaning. Television has allowed several generations to experience, vicariously, the cultures of many nations. The Vietnam conflict was the first war to be fought on foreign soil as it was monitored almost minute by minute by millions of people around the world. Improved transportation methods afford the opportunity to leave familiar territory and return to it quickly, as well as inexpensively. Consequently, the worldview of many citizens has been shaped by their capacity to expand their territory. People live in a global society increasingly accessible through electronic media or expanded travel services. The access has provided an opportunity to compare cultures, customs, government, and educational systems. People have discovered their differences, but many have yet to intelligently view how they are the same.

Add to the changing reference points a new concept of age, due to increased life expectancy through advances in medical science; intelligence, by the creation of smart systems, so-called artificial intelligence systems that accomplish some of the routine work people once had to be reminded to do; and life itself, with the discovery of techniques to humanly modify genetic codes. New paradigms or reference points eventually lead to new ways to allocate valued resources. The political system is the arena in which old and new reference points are compared and contrasted, but it is much different from what it was several decades ago: more complex, less hidden from public view, and more accessible to a greater variety of users.

In a society punctuated by difference instead of sameness, it is difficult, if not impossible, to focus on sustainable reference points. Travelers through the political landscape have only the controversies of the day, week, or month to serve as guidelines for policy. The idea of America's destiny as a redeemer nation and the concept of "American" values and ideals serve as historical markers along a trail where traditional reference points seem to have vanished.

The American schoolhouse, the traditional reference point for education of the young, has lost some of its luster due to the vast changes in delivery of information. During the 1980s public education came under intense scrutiny from federal agencies and business interests. The lead report of the decade, *A Nation at Risk,* issued a call for a new era of educational reform. Among other things, the report was critical of America's schools for not helping the country maintain its level of economic competitiveness in the world marketplace. The opening statement that rang out most forcefully was, "Our nation is at risk. Our once unchallenged preeminence in commerce, industry, science, and technological innovations is being overtaken by competitors throughout the world."[4] The report created a reaction similar to that of the Russian launch of *Sputnik* in the late 1950s, when scientists, economists, and politicians declared America had fallen behind in the race to conquer space. In both cases, new reference points were established and schools were expected, as they had done in the past, to place America at the forefront of world leadership, power, and influence.

Before school leaders begin to wring their hands about how to respond to a multitude of demands or requests to change, they must reflect on issues that may cause citizens to become dissatisfied with the educational system. Consider the following scenario: Early in life, people develop a set of mental models, which they constantly use to bring order to their world and make sense of their environments. These mental models are based on individualized perceptions of reality of varying keenness. In times of crisis or when unfamiliar concepts are explored, the old mental models are held up as standards with which the new realities are compared. The gap between an individual's mental model of "how the world should be" and how the world might look according to the new information is cause for concern—especially if this lacuna is big. As old mental models give way to new ideas, new economies, or new techniques, leaders, specifically school leaders, have an opportunity to educate the public about intended change and alternatives that may indeed provide relief for previous concerns. New reference points require study and explanation, not simply reaction and rejection because "things were never done that way before."

The role of reflector, explainer, and interpreter is a natural role for the superintendent. It assists people to gain new perspectives and consider new possibilities. The role may not be new to the superintendency, but it has become an increasingly important function of the job as old reference points vanish and new complexities develop.

The Complexity of School District Governance

Public school systems are units of local government with a broad range of power, including the authority to levy taxes and establish rules in the form of policy. While regulated in part by state and federal laws, first and foremost they serve the needs of local communities and constituencies. School board members, elected as representatives of the community, are entrusted to establish policies for the proper function of the educational system. In some communities, school boards are elected by ward or precinct; in others, members of the board are elected at-large. A typical term of office is four years. Local school board members are accessible, accountable, and very visible in their communities. Like other policymakers, they are evaluated with a variety of measuring sticks by citizens who determine their political fate as lay leaders in the community.

We have mentioned that policy making at the national level was more straightforward when citizens were bound together by similar beliefs and values. Populations were smaller, issues were debated on the basis of what might be best for the country, and loyalties were bound by a national sense of pride. In a sense, this carried over to state and local issues as well. Today, however, the national picture is anything but simple, and the conditions are similar for state and local policy arenas. Local school district governance is as complex as the audiences are diverse. Special interest groups from the right, left, and all points along the continuum pressure boards of education and school executives to adopt points of view, instructional programs, or materials that favor the view of each special interest. Or they lobby against programs proposed by school officials or other special interest groups. This lack of unity is a real condition of the politics of education in contemporary society.

Public school boards and administrators, faced with decisions about what to teach, to whom, when, and how, come face to face with the reality that they are only one of many groups seeking emotional and financial support from citizens. There is intense competition for the psyche, as well as the tax dollar, among and between the various special interests who believe their need is the one that must be filled. Of additional concern to school boards and school administrators is their constituent base. Households with school-age children are in the minority in today's society, and among them are large percentages of single parent, dual working parent, and non–English speaking families. Senior citizens, with their own political agenda, seek relief for health costs and medical benefits from the same governments that help provide funds for the education of the nation's children.

There is also a segment of the population that is dissatisfied with the public schools. The reasons they offer range from concerns over increasing violence in the schools to perceptions about curriculum offerings. Many in this category have removed their children from public schools and have opted to educate them at home or in private schools. The home-schooling movement has created a new market for educational materials and services. Coupled with this is a rise in entrepreneurial schools designed by their creators to offer "high tech," cost-effective educational services for a price. The new competitors for the child and the educational dollar have reconfigured the political arena for educational policymakers.

Understanding the Political Landscape

School board members and superintendents must be keenly aware of the political landscape as they seek to carry out the mission of educating the children of a diverse public. The political landscape seems to be continuously under construction; it is shaped by rapid shifts among the wants and needs of constituent groups, modifications in cultural values, periods of economic stability or recession, the gap between those who possess the material or symbols valued by a society and those who do not, and other equally important variables. School leaders need to develop frameworks to help them navigate the evolving landscape of educational politics. These frameworks must be defensible, legitimate systems to analyze both normal and highly charged situations (see Figure 5-1)

Politics and Values

Easton[5] provided a conceptual framework that viewed societies as a set of systems and subsystems: the economy, education, health and welfare, and so on. One of major institutions, the political system, was described as the subsystem through which the *values* of the society are *legitimately* allocated to members of that society. For example, members of democratic societies elect or appoint representatives and grant them the authority to distribute scarce resources for the general well-being of the society. This idea is based on the notion that in each society there is a constant dialogue about the importance of certain values or ideas. The political system is the forum in which those values are debated and assigned a sense of importance or place and converted into policy that in turn affects the general population. Because there are a number of values that always seem to be in competition in a society, the political system is a highly intense arena. The mission of the political system is to legitimately allocate values either material (money, contracts, land) or symbolic (recognition or status). In a sense, it is a system where the demands, wants, and needs of the society are converted into public policy.

When a legitimate system exists to provide for the allocation of resources, people seek ways to have the system take notice of and approve the values they deem important. Thus a loose description of politics or political action is the struggle of a group to secure the authoritative support of policymakers, at any and all levels of government, for its values. Four key variables that affect the distribution of values by policymakers, as outlined in Wirt and Kirst[6] are quality, efficiency, equity, and choice. School leaders must understand

I. A Framework For Managing Conflict Situations

Leaders, when faced with a conflict situation can use the following frame of reference as a defensible *process* to analyze the situation and determine an appropriate course of action. While time may preclude a written analysis, it is *critical* that the leader takes time to mentally consider the following questions before responding to any conflict situation.

1. **What is really going on? What is the real issue?**
   - Who is involved?
   - What are their behaviors? What emotions, values, or feelings are involved?
   - What do they want? Are their purposes similar to the purposes of the school?
   - Why am I involved? Am I the right person for this situation?
   - Who else in the school/district needs to be involved in this situation? Who else needs to be made aware of this situation?

2. **What are the potential outcomes of this conflict situation?**
   - What are some well-reasoned responses to the situation?
   - What is the bottom line if the outcome is
       —a worst case scenario? (win–lose or lose–win)
       —a middle ground scenario?
       —a best case scenario? (win–win)
   - What are the *long-term and short-term* consequences of each option?
   - What is the risk of doing nothing?

3. **What is the immediacy of the situation?**
   - How much time do we have to respond or take action?
   - What is the potential magnitude of the situation?
   - Is the media involved?

4. **What options or alternatives does the school have?**
   - Is this issue covered by an existing policy or procedure?
   - What resources do I need or have available to me?
   - Who else needs to be involved? (singly or collectively)

5. **Based on analysis of this situation (steps 1–4), what plan of action is recommended for the school?**
   - What school goals or outcomes must be preserved/protected?
   - Who needs to do what? By when?
   - Who else can help implement the plan?
   - How does the school communicate the outcome(s) of the situation? To whom?
   - Does the school need to amend existing policies or procedures or develop new ones to cover this situation?

FIGURE 5–1   Defensible Processes

how these four variables, manifest in statutes, lead to conflict in the political arena. Each of the variables, which are values in and of themselves, is always pursued in relationship to the others in matters of policy formation (see Figure 5-2).

In the politics of education, quality, defined here as the desire for overall improvement of conditions for those affected by a particular policy, can be illustrated by the establishment of standards of performance for schools, teachers, and students. Quality, as a value, should be viewed from the perspective of those who must achieve a certain level of that value. As an example, schools in which communication, science, and mathematics are highly valued would be presumed to maintain standards by which student progress in those areas could be measured over time. The standards are graduated in

In educational politics, the four values described below serve as supports on which policy makers attempt to construct meaningful public policy.

Quality: Issues of quality are concerned with the establishment of standards aimed to produce substantial improvements in conditions for those whom the policy is designed. Quality issues are normally employed as a means to raise other standards or conditions; i.e., the quality of student performance may be assumed to increase the opportunity for college entrance or job placement.

Efficiency: Efficiency is concerned with the minimization of one factor, usually costs, and the maximization of a second factor, usually gains, outcomes, or product. Secondly, efficiency is viewed as a means of accountability. In schools, this value is satisfied when schools provide the best educational possible value for the dollar amount invested and they do so in accordance with state and local policies; economic efficiency coupled with accountability.

Equity: The redistribution of resources by a political authority to provide relief for or satisfaction of a human need. Equity requires two steps; the recognition that a need exists and the resources to fulfill it. Public law 94-142, Education for Handicapped Individuals, is an example of equity.

Choice: Policy makers can decide to adopt a policy or reject it. When provided with the information surrounding a political issue, school board members have to choose to make a

---

FIGURE 5–2 Policy Variables in Education

SOURCE: F. M. Wirt and M. W. Kirst, *The Politics of Education: Schools in Conflict* (Berkeley, Calif.: McCutchan, 1992), pp. 85–86.

---

such a way that as students proceed from simple to more complex ideas, their understanding is continuously improved. Typically, it is believed that the higher the standard, the better the quality.

Efficiency, the second value, has two aspects. First, in terms of expending resources, it means getting the maximum result for a minimal investment. Second, efficiency can be viewed as a yardstick for measuring the accountability of policymakers. When school boards and administrators follow established procedures in accounting or reporting, it is assumed they are being efficient. School boards and administrators are constantly reminded to be efficient with the expenditure of tax dollars. They are sometimes compared on a cost-per-pupil basis; supposedly, the district with the lowest cost per pupil is among the most efficient users of the public dollar. Schools also labor under a highly controlled system of checks and balances via annual audits of general fund expenditures and regular audits of all federal funds. The reports required from school systems to federal, state, and local agencies satisfy the accountability portion of the efficiency formula.

Efforts to achieve equity, perhaps the most noble but least understood and accepted value, are concerned with closing of the gap between what people legitimately need and the capacity to devote scarce resources to that need. Equity is a sophisticated concept. It is a notion that requires discipline and commitment. In a multiple-tiered society, disparities develop between and among the tiers. These disparities or gaps become increasingly difficult to bridge as those who possess a majority of the resources are called on to find ways to redistribute some of them to those who are less fortunate. Because resources are not evenly distributed among a population, the opportunity to have equitable opportunities to access the resources is paramount for some groups while it is taken for granted by others.

The final value, choice, is a fundamental idea in a democratic society. In short, it is the opportunity to make or reject policy decisions. To explain choice we must illustrate the interaction among and between all four values. Let us revisit the idea of equity at the local level. For the most part, citizens accept and understand that all school-aged youngsters in the community should have equal opportunity to access information and gain knowledge through a system of well-financed public schools. This means, regardless of race, gender, geographic location, social status, or economic circumstance, all children will be empowered by the school district with good facilities, excellent teachers, and up-to-date learning materials so that they can meet the established standards of the district (quality). It also means that those who enter the school unprepared to learn should benefit from additional educational strategies so they have an opportunity to compete on a level playing field (equity).

This is where the concept of equity begins to come apart for some people. They view the cost (efficiency), in dollars and time, to be too great to justify the potential gains from this segment of the population, and so they encourage policymakers to be more concerned about efficiency—getting the most from the limited resources they have to invest. If a choice is made in the name of efficiency, the policy to equalize opportunity may be jeopardized, at least for the time being. This type of selfishness with the public dollar seems rampant in modern America. School superintendents and boards of education must educate the public about the needs of children so that quality, efficiency, and equity come into balance. This illustration, although simple, does offer an opportunity to view the interaction among and between the four basic values as they are manifested in educational policy.

Community Power Structures

To the complexity of the policy-making formula is added the concept of power—the kind of power used to influence decisions about the allocation of resources. All communities have a power structure of some sort. In many cases, it is very informal and difficult to observe. In other cases, it is highly structured, formal, and easily noticed.

McCarty and Ramsey[7] provided a valuable tool for understanding community power structures and their political ramifications for school administrators. They identified four broad, community types: dominated, pluralistic, factional, and inert (see Figure 5–3).

The source of political power in dominated communities was associated with an influential individual, family, or group, whereas the pluralistic community was one with a variety of power bases, but no single group interested in controlling a situation. In fact, pluralistic communities were described as those where various points of view were openly discussed with the idea that the best response to the situation would emerge and be approved by a majority of those making decisions and then supported by the entire decision-making body. Inert communities were depicted as listless, without agenda, kinds of places where little action was ever taken. On the other hand, the factional community was perceived as a place where a variety of factions were constantly struggled against each other for authority. Elections were spirited, and those in control only maintained power until another faction mustered enough support to oust them.

In each community the governing boards were influenced by the nature of the community power structure, and the administrative head hired by the board was also at the beck and call of the power structure. Boards or councils in dominated communities served

All communities have some type of identifiable power structure that serves as a basis for action for its policy making boards. These power structures may and do vary from community to community and may manifest themselves in a variety of ways. What is important, however, is for school leaders to understand the concept of community based power and to learn how it is manifested. McCarty and Ramsey identified four basic community types and the power structures that operated within them.

Dominated Community: A community in which the source of power is concentrated in the hands of a dominant individual or family. Community type boards, like the community itself, are directed by the dominant individual or family as is the administrative head of the community board.

 Pluralistic Community: The sources of power in pluralistic communities arise from many centers. Community-type boards are usually composed of representatives from many differing backgrounds. Discussion and consensus characterize the actions of this type of board. The administrative head of the community board is valued as a supplier of alternative plans and information.

Factional Community: The factional community is composed of various interest groups (factions) who struggle with each other for control. Elections are spirited as one faction may try to out-maneuver another for a decisive vote on the board. Argument and control surround issues and power shifts back and forth as factions gain and lose control. The administrative heads of community-type organizations must provide information equally among the factions and be careful not to side with the faction that is in power at the moment.

 Inert Community: The inert community lacks direction and inspiration. It is a status quo operation where community type boards appear to be satisfied with what is already in place. Maintenance is the stimulus unless there is a compelling reason to do something else. The administrative head of a community-type board is viewed as the provider of new information and catalyst for movement.

Note: It is assumed there are many variations among each type of community. The four types provide a framework for understanding community actions and policy decisions.

FIGURE 5–3   Community Types and Structures

SOURCE: D. McCarty and C. E. Ramsey, *The School Managers: Power and Conflict in American Public Education* (Westport, Conn.: Greenwood Publishing, 1971), pp. 15–22.

the wishes of the dominant individual, family, or group, and superintendents, for example, were also expected to carry out the wishes of the controlling party. Pluralistic boards discussed all aspects and alternatives connected with a decision and then decided in the best interest of the community. In these communities, the professionals who served as administrative leaders acted as advisors and provided alternatives and counsel to the board. The superintendent in a factional community needed to be certain not to align him- or herself with any one faction, but to provide information on and speak to all sides of the issue. Constant vigilance by the superintendent was needed as shifts of power changed the decision-making venue on the factional board. Finally, inert boards typically took little or no action without something or someone to guide them. They usually looked to the administrative head for leadership and direction.

While these four descriptors provide an excellent framework for developing an understanding of the rudimentary political landscapes, most communities are not purely dominant, pluralistic, inert, or factional. The point is superintendents must understand the community power structure that exists in their district and be aware of those in control or those who seek control. As the variety and number of special interest groups increase and begin to seek support for their point of view, the political landscape becomes more difficult to transverse.

Since the McCarty–Ramsey study surfaced, America has been through economic, social, and political changes. One of the most apparent changes has already been mentioned: the fractionalization of the population into numerous single-purpose, narrowly focused interest groups. Each group has specific wants or needs, and each lobbies for a singular position. If one or several of these groups is successful in getting a candidate elected to the local school board, the board room becomes the forum for a power struggle, with the superintendent and his or her staff placed squarely in the middle of the fray.

School superintendents are expected to identify and understand where the various sources of political power reside in a community. They must also be adept at negotiating with them for influence that can be converted to resources to advance the education of children. The superintendent, as chief advocate for the education of children, must accept this role as necessary part of the work of educational leadership.

Competing Bases of Power

Earlier in this chapter political action was defined as the struggle of a group to secure authoritative support for its values. Further, the political process was characterized as the authoritative distribution of goods, services, or values to members of a society. The authority most often recognized as best equipped to distribute scarce resources is government at the local, state, or national level. This is probably so because it is commonly assumed that the populous has voice in most, if not all, matters in a democratic society. When the society in question has a set of common wants and needs, the allocation process is fairly simple. As the needs and wants of the society become more diverse, the system charged with the allocation of resources becomes stressed.

Drucker[8] noted that "government will malperform if an activity is under pressure to satisfy different constituencies with different values and different demands. Performance requires concentration on one goal. It requires setting priorities and sticking to them." To add to the dialogue, it has been suggested that America has become a hyphenated nation where identities are defined by differences instead of sameness. There is a tendency for Americans to define themselves in terms of their cultural or ancestral origins, for example, Irish-Americans, Polish-Americans, or African-Americans, instead of "just plain Americans." When applied to public education, these statements raise important questions. Can the same governmental policies that served when we were more closely aligned as national citizens serve us well today? What has caused the body politic to splinter into groups with specific, narrowly defined interests? When those narrow interests are converted into demands, how can policymakers ever hope to satisfy constituencies? How can resources be legitimately allocated among competing power bases?

Consider the type of issues a society asks its policymakers to consider: employment opportunities, access to health care, educational opportunity, equal protection for men and women in the work place, security for older citizens, minimum standards of pay, the subsidizing of agricultural products, housing and low income citizens, and protection from enemies foreign and domestic. All of the issues beg for resolution, and each one needs resources for relief, mostly in the form of money. The money is generated from a single source: taxes!

Money generated from taxation is perhaps the most hotly contested resource in an expanding society. As the mean age of Americans has increased, older citizens compete with children for money to fund programs for their well-being, money that once went to education of the young. Teachers and administrators lobby for more money for their professional expertise and for materials for students, modern facilities are needed to replace ancient classrooms and fixtures, and the need to upgrade advanced technological equipment is unrelenting. By the same token, other governmental agencies experience like demands to meet constituent wants and needs; cities and counties seek the same tax dollar to maintain or expand their infrastructures. State and federal governments join the picture, as they have been called to provide more services for a diverse population! The citizenry, on whom the burden of funding ultimately rests, has become overwhelmed by the constant assault on its pocketbook, and so they have resorted to aligning with groups that speak for taxpayers' points of view.

Money is only one of the resources valued by society. Other key resources such as information, access to knowledge, values, time, and power await legitimate distribution through the political system, and the more diverse the society becomes, the more intense the competition for resources. In fact, if government is ineffective in the distribution of valued resources, the population will exercise its option to chose other means to obtain them. In the case of education, special interest groups may chose to provide the service by pooling their collective talents and resources. Or they may establish privately funded educational institutions to teach the values they desire and exclude the values they do not wish to embrace. What will become of the school for the children of the public? Who will attend public schools and how will they be funded if former constituencies opt for alternative educational programs?

The Public's Schools: What and Whose Purposes Are Served?

The concept of supporting a school system for the masses was founded on a set of well-reasoned intentions. The general public, through its pooled resources, assumed it could afford an efficient, effective school system where the values of the society, and the knowledge, skills, and attitudes necessary for citizenship in a democratic society and employability, would be transmitted to the young. The concept was well aligned when national interests were similar, but as previously mentioned, the nation has become less inclined to agree on common directions and more interested in satisfying individual wants and needs.

When the word "public" appears above the entrance to the schoolhouse, it should be assumed that *all* the public's children are welcome there, and that they will be provided an opportunity to learn. Certainly, it is in the best interest of the public to have well-educated citizens. Schools provided through public funding should function with that ideal in mind. Today, however, it is more accurate to refer to *publics* rather than the singular public. Near the end of the twentieth century, the publics making up American society are diverse, and their interests are varied.

The question worth answering is, who are the publics and what do they want—especially for the youth of the nation? Since the 1950s, public schools have been called on to solve problems that were deeply encased in the collective conscience of the society. As a result, there were claims that American public schools had abrogated their primary responsibility: the delivery of universal literacy to its citizens. Drucker[9] pointed out, "the American school has subordinated its teaching mission to other socially necessary objectives." It is assumed this reference pertains in part to federal and state mandated programs for school desegregation, alcohol and drug education, special education, behavior modification, multicultural education, and so on. To be certain, each of these programs results from public policies designed to address the values of equity and quality, values that must be satisfied at the same time universal literacy is addressed. Or in some cases, before literacy can be addressed. But not all of the publics are interested in quality or equity for children of "someone else."

Special Interest Groups: A Sampler

On one hand it appears that the new politics of America has people building walls to protect their ideas or values from those of others. School administrators must accept, as one of their tasks, the challenge to seek and establish common ground for the various publics who send their children to public schools. Administrators must understand the agendas of special interest groups if they are to accomplish quality, efficiency, and equity in the educational arena.

During the 1980s and 1990s, educational policymakers have learned that special interest groups can muster the necessary financial resources and people to successfully lobby their point of view. A growing problem for school officials is the increased number of special interest groups confronting the schools. School leaders invest much of their valuable time engaged in trying to balance the interests and demands of one group with the issues of others.

Some of the groups that lobby school boards and administrators have been around for quite a while, and regardless of the types of appeals they make, they have come to be viewed as a normal part of doing business. Parent–teacher organizations, coalitions supporting the rights of physically and academically challenged students, supporters of educational opportunities for gifted and talented youngsters, and music or athletic booster clubs have raised concerns in school districts for decades. These are the groups that asked the schools to recognize their needs and provide relief with additional or improved programming. Gender equity in athletics; new band uniforms; additional programs and challenging activities for students; or accessibility to programs or facilities for challenged students: While each group may have carried the banner for a particular cause, they were typically advocates for improving conditions in the school program. By the same token, they appeared to understand that school leaders had to weigh the merits of each asking and determine if and how to prioritize among all the demands on the districts' budget, facilities, and programs. In cases where federal or state law served as a mandate to provide a certain level of service, the school was faced with the modification of existing or proposed programs to meet the needs of the mandate. It was a matter of trying to attain a balance among quality, efficiency, equity, and choice, the four values of educational policy making.

Single-Purpose Organizations

In the mid to late twentieth century, controversy about the success of the public schools and a new sense of pluralism changed the landscape of education history and educational politics. Starting with the civil rights movements of the 1950s, changes in the American social consciousness, an aging population, and economic competitiveness had tremendous impacts on the schools. The reality of changing times catapulted school administrators and school boards into the political arena, sometimes on different sides of the same issue. Special interest and single-purpose lobbying groups demanded to be heard and satisfied. Religious and business interests now shared the spotlight with parent–teacher groups and advocates for handicapped and gifted students, and spokespersons from a multitude of groups advocated everything from tax reform to equality for those with differing ethnic, racial, and sexual orientation.

The final decade of the millennium is characterized by fragmentation and deinstitutionalization. The resources once used to promote and support a system of public education have became the target of a variety of special interests who seek the sanction of government for their values. Drucker[10] described the new pluralism in America:

> It is a pluralism of single-purpose organizations, each concerned with one social task: wealth creation or schooling or health care or forming the values and habits of the young—the new pluralism of society is totally apolitical. The new pluralism of the polity by contrast focuses on power. It is a pluralism of single cause, single interest groups—the "mass movements" of small but highly disciplined minorities. Each of them tries to obtain through power what it could not obtain through numbers or through persuasion. Each is exclusively *political.*

Americans may assume that the government is the only organized center of power, but that assumption is not correct. None of the single-purpose groups is government. In most cases, they are organized and managed but totally autonomous. They operate freely in a system designed to recognize differences in points of view and voices from the political right, left, and center.

While educational leaders had grown somewhat accustomed to groups that demanded quality and equity of programming, many other special interests began to appear at the schoolhouse door. Well organized and well funded, these groups requested quite different favors from those of the constituents mentioned earlier. Some gained their membership from internal audiences. They were professional organizations that represented various categories of employees: associations of teachers, administrators, custodial and clerical workers, and food service employees. Some of these groups were aligned with traditional labor unions, and others resulted from state legislation requiring local governments to engage in collective bargaining with employee groups. In either case, the groups had a single interest: improvement of working conditions for their members. While these associations or interest groups have become common, the goals they sought put them in direct competition for resources with the audiences they served.

Single-purpose groups emerged in the external environment as well. Some of them were dedicated to the reduction of taxes, while others lobbied for removal of textbooks that were offensive to "community interests," elimination of curricula that led to specific objectives or outcomes, and so on. They were different from the other groups: they asked for elimination of programs and materials, were focused on a specific set of values, and were not willing to compromise their position.

The strength of single-purpose organizations lies in their commitment to pursue a unilateral goal until it is reached. For illustration, we will examine some of the interests of single-purpose organizations. Teacher organizations have successfully lobbied for improved working conditions for teachers. As a result, teacher pay and fringe benefits have increased. Groups representing support staff have been equally successful. Coalitions of taxpayers have halted increases in tax levies at the local level, defeated bond issues for school construction, and thwarted attempts by boards to increase school budgets. Politically conservative religious groups have demanded and won the removal of materials and programs that were not in line with their beliefs.

In reality this is the new face of public education. A swarm of single-purpose, politically active groups is each demanding their needs be fulfilled before or instead of the needs of some other group. These demands may seem foreign to educational leaders who operate from the framework that *public* means collectivity or sameness. But the demands are real, and the struggle for equity, efficiency, and quality will take place in a politically charged atmosphere where either the best organized or most convincing party may be victorious. If America's schools are to remain among the best in the world, school leaders must meet this activity with a renewed sense of vision and purpose, not withdraw from it.

The New Face of Public Education

The new face of public education is reminiscent of a familiar optical illusion: the young girl and the old woman. Viewed from one angle, public education remains an open route to literacy for millions of youngsters, a responsive, graceful, and tireless system. From another angle, it appears tired and haggard, beset by years of turmoil over resource allocation, mandates, and the provision of countless services to satisfy yet another societal need.

Enormous educational opportunities have become available to adults and youngsters during the past few years: Internet, CD-ROM technology, electronic pen pals, virtual reality, and so on. This is the new face of public education: information delivered to our homes at any time of the day or night. Vast electronic networks waiting to be tapped for potential sources of learning. Who will have access to the powerful reservoirs of knowledge, and how will they be managed? Will there be request to filter out certain pieces of information while providing for universal distribution of others? Will there be attempts to restrict sources of information to only a privileged few, or will information become so available for such a small cost that virtually all citizens will have unlimited access to knowledge bases? Do these relationships change the nature of public schooling and do they foretell a story about the relationships the public might have with its school system? Tough questions for changing times!

Knowledge: The Ultimate Source of Power

Writing about conflicting interests within the educational arena, Spring[11] reminded us that in America, the public schools are among the major disseminators of knowledge for the young. As a result they are targeted by various groups trying to influence values, ideas, and information. For example, some religious groups have traditionally objected to such issues as human sexuality and evolution being discussed in the public school classroom. The business community wants the school to teach ideas that support their economic interests, while politicians would like the schools to teach political values that support their positions. Social service agencies or social crusaders want the schools to solve the problems ranging from drug use to highway safety by instilling a set of values in students. Add to these groups the wants and needs of campaigners for racial and gender equity, consumer organizations, ecology and environmental organizations, and many more, and it becomes clear that information (knowledge) is power and the power to potentially influence young citizens is a source of conflict.

Knowledge is power; some actors in society would chose to empower all citizens, while others would limit empowerment. This is a reality that educators must understand and accept as a condition of their work. School leaders (teachers, counselors, administrators, and elected boards) must be ever aware of the potential for the conflict of interests that will invariably come to rest at the schoolhouse door. School leaders must establish a clear vision and direction for the program of the school, and it is incumbent that the vision is communicated effectively and often. While this will not eliminate conflicts of interest, it will serve to characterize the school and school personnel as open and communicative.

Public education is a political activity; as such, it is a fertile arena for conflict. Conflict provides opportunity to examine, clarify, and compare the mission (purpose and function) of the school with the wants and needs of the society it serves.

Toffler[12] wrote about three sources of power: wealth, violence, and knowledge. Wealth, because it appears to be concentrated in the hands of few, provides small numbers of people the capacity to influence policy and policymakers. This is not to suggest that policymakers are purchased by the wealthy; however, it does suggest that wealth is an excellent tool with which to gain access to the arenas where policy is made. In some cases, wealth may be used to finance the campaigns of political candidates with the hope that the provider's generosity will be remembered when future policy considerations are debated. Wealth concentrated in the hands of individuals and organizations has been a political tool for centuries.

Violence, or at least the threat of violence, serves to intimidate the defenseless and underorganized and concentrates power in the hands of those with the capability to inflict hardship on others. Violence can take many forms. It can manifest itself as the withholding of necessary services or information from those who suffer hardship, or it can be the actual infliction of severe physical damage to person and property.

Knowledge is a remarkably different source of power. Theoretically, at least, it is available, in the form of information, to all who wish to seek it, and it serves to empower them to compete against or collaborate with their fellow humans. It is easy to distribute and constantly renewable. If it was to become universally available, the balance of power throughout the world would be dramatically shifted. For this very reason, there are those who wish to keep certain kinds of information long enough for the opportunity to convert it into a source of power that will assist them in gaining an advantage over others. Others view it as a liberating resource that, when distributed freely and universally, has the potential to continuously improve conditions for all humankind.

With information and knowledge as resources to be allocated through the political system, the four variables of educational policy become key factors in determining who will receive the resources and how they may be allocated. The politics of knowledge is serious business.

The Politics of Knowledge

If knowledge is a source of power equal to wealth and violence, it is indeed a commodity that humankind will pursue. The right knowledge in the hands of the right people has the potential to end human suffering due to hunger or disease or contamination of the environment. In the wrong hands, this same knowledge could be used to hold an entire population hostage. Public schools are one of the distribution mechanisms for knowledge—they are powerful institutions charged with an awesome responsibility. If policymakers in education believe schooling can make a difference in the lives of citizens, they can literally empower the nation. If they believe that only a certain few can achieve at high levels, their policies can dampen the hopes of humankind. Godwin wrote:

> How long has the genius of education been disheartened and unnerved by the pretense that man is born all that is possible for him to become? How long has the jargon imposed upon the world, which would persuade us that in instructing a man you do not add to but unfold his stores?
>
> Education will proceed with a firm step and a genuine luster, when those who conduct it shall know what a vast field it embraces; when they shall be made aware that . . . the question whether the pupil shall be a man of perseverance and enterprise or a stupid and inanimate dolt, depends on the powers of those under whose direction he is placed, and the skill with which those powers shall be applied.[13]

These words were penned in 1798. They should provide a clue as to how long humankind has wrestled with the potential power of knowledge. It must not be concentrated in the hands of a few; rather, it should be distributed like some life-giving elixir to all who wish to pursue it.

Competition for the Classroom

The classroom is a powerful place. Some might chose to see it as a place where the past and future come together to produce extraordinary designs for the present. Others view the classroom as the safe environment where all children can explore ideas and build knowledge and meaning for themselves. In it, a child or adult can become empowered to achieve success through reading, mathematics, science, history, and the arts. It is a place where ideas are explored, absorbed, and applied. The strength of America's literate citizenry is anchored to the classroom.

The public classroom is an open forum. It operates under the watchful eye of the general citizenry. Herein lies the opportunity and the threat. When citizens of good will comprehend the necessity for critical thinking, universal literacy, testing ideas, debate, dialogue, and the exchange of viewpoints on controversial issues, education is a servant to people. However, if the citizenry continues to splinter into ever-smaller interest groups, the classroom could become quite a different place. Some citizens may wish to have limits imposed in the classroom if their point of view is not upheld up as the dominant one. Given the vast number of special interests who might chose to have that view legitimized in policy, the classroom could become the hostage of a factious society. A classroom free from spontaneity and discovery becomes a darkened environment and will not serve its citizens well.

Of the variety of roles the superintendent plays, none is more important than that of advocate for a free and open public system of education. As an advisor to boards of education, the superintendent is in the key position to provide information about the impact of policy decisions based on past experience and current conditions. The superintendent must also be visible in the community as the advocate for education for all children and, on as many occasions as necessary, point out the ramifications of proposed educational policy at the local, state, and national levels.

A Unified Voice for Children and Youth

Children, every society's hope for the future, are not granted the right to vote until they have reached a certain age, established by policy. The society, through the policies it enacts, develops opportunities for children, but not all children benefit from them equally. While the intent of sound policy is to ensure the values of quality, efficiency, and equity, the fourth value, choice, plays an important role at the level of policy formation. Simply because an authoritative source examines policy options does not guarantee its passage or eventual implementation. Even if it is passed and implemented, interpretation of the policy, a choice of local officials, may render it ineffective for some the intended beneficiaries.

Collectively, children need strong, political advocates who support sound educational opportunities for them. It is here the superintendent has vast potential to exhibit leadership and influence policy decisions. As an example, if a computer lab is requested for children on the north side of town, should not one be built for children on the other sides of town as well? If parents and other advocates for the north side children are articulate and vocal before the board of education, does this mean that the other children, who were not represented by parents or community partners, have no voice? Theoretically, the response is no, but in reality policymakers often allocate resources based on the "squeaky wheel" method. If they are not acquainted with the interplay among the values of quality, efficiency, equity, and choice, the superintendent must make them aware. Without the support of policymakers there will be no unified voice for children.

Closing the Gap

Closing the gap between the haves and have nots in American society is a problem designed specifically for the political system in general, and public education in particular. The distance between poverty and prosperity can be measured by the educational power possessed by an individual or group. It is the power to access, process, and use pertinent information to provide a service or produce hard goods that are needed and wanted by the society. It is also the power to understand systems and how they work. And it is voice—the power to be heard and understood amid the masses so all citizens can be represented in the political arena. This is a job for government, if the will is present! If one subscribes to the theory that government should do for people those things they cannot do for themselves, then the most responsive form of government, the public school system, must be staffed by people who understand and are willing to use the political system to empower citizens, all citizens!

The voice of child advocates must be heard above the voices of self-interest and elitism. There are forces who oppose free, public education for all children. Their voices are loud and clear. They know how to use the political system. The desperate need is for school leaders who understand how and why political action can be used to provide resources to those who most need it. More than that, school leaders must be willing to enter the political ring to fight for the freedom to teach and learn. The new politics demand it!

Summary

Politics has been described as the art and science of government, the methods by which the will of the community is arrived at and implemented. That description, while instructive, explains little about the various publics who make up a community. Special interest groups at the local, state, and national levels each have valid reasons (in their collective opinions) that their values are the ones that should receive the authoritative support of government. In this sense, politics might best be described as the socialization of conflict.

The political landscape can and does look different depending on the type of community in which one resides. McCarty and Ramsey's 1971 study defined four broad categories of community political behavior. Communities were described as pluralistic, where consensus and dialogue were valued; factional, where win–lose was the fare of the day; dominated communities that were reflections of a dominant family or citizen regardless of what kinds of councils or boards were in place; and inert, where the status quo was valued above all else.

Policy making is the act of converting the wants and needs of citizens into legitimate guidelines or policies. It is not simple, given the complexity of wants and needs that exist in a diverse population. Policymakers at all levels of government devote countless hours to the endeavor. The public school system, perhaps the most local of all political bodies in America, is governed by elected and, in some cases, appointed boards of education, who have as their task the formation of policy about how educational opportunities will be made available to all students without regard to their race, religion, social status, gender, or physical and intellectual capacity. Who will have the opportunity, at public expense, for information and knowledge? This question looms large as various special interest groups at the local, state, and national levels compete for scarce resources. It is in the public school arena where administrators and board members alike must listen to constituents and advocate for the welfare of children by designing and implementing sound educational policy through a system of defensible processes.

Discussion Questions

1. Politics was defined as "the authoritative and legitimate distribution of valued resources in a society." What are some of the valued resources that are distributed by the public education system?

2. This chapter identified some of the societal reference points that have vanished during the past several decades. Looking ahead, which of the current societal reference points do you believe may vanish in the near future? What new reference points might replace them?

3. Why is political action necessary as a society grows more complex?

4. What procedures or practices might you introduce to attempt to bring factional groups together on important issues?

5. What conditions are likely to result if the gap between those who have adequate resources and those who do not continues to widen?

6. Name the agencies in your community who act as advocates for children. What conditions or subgroups do they represent? What kind of political influence do they possess? What are you doing to align yourself with them or bring them together under a common umbrella?

CASE 5.1   As Long as the Values Are My Values

Recently, the board of education of the College View School District approved a policy that underlined the importance of stressing all sides of controversial issues in high school class discussions rather than limiting debate to a single viewpoint. The policy was analyzed long and hard in several open, public meetings. Some members of the board believed it was the place of the school to teach a certain set of values, while others argued that having discussions about salient issues would allow students to use their considerable skills to engage in open and honest debate. When the dialogue ended, the board was unified behind the new policy.

At their next meeting, the board of education was challenged by a rather large group of parents and citizens who loudly voiced their disapproval of the policy and asked the board to retract it at once! They claimed high school students were too young to engage in meaningful dialogue about controversial issues, and that the board's new policy was merely encouraging students to question the values their parents had taught them. They also stated that if the board did not meet their demands, they would organize a campaign to have the board members defeated during the next election.

Questions

1. As a member of the board of education, what would your reaction be to the group of citizens who brought the complaint forward?
2. How would you respond to the threat to have you defeated in the next school board election?
3. As the superintendent, what strategies or advice would you offer the board for dealing with this matter?
4. What kind of defensible processes could the school district have in place that would assist them in dealing with this issue?
5. What are the possible consequences of retracting the policy? What are the possible consequences of keeping the policy?

Inbasket Exercise

INBASKET 5.1

Multicultural Education

The state legislature has enacted a law requiring all school districts to devise a plan for the inclusion of a multicultural perspective in their curriculum. When the College View Board of Education met last week, it acknowledged the state mandate and discussed the growing diversity in the United States, the state, and the local school district. The chairperson of the board thanked the superintendent for the information regarding the multicultural legislation and indicated that it was important to encourage tolerance for diversity and to view diversity as a strength.

The morning following the board meeting, the local newspaper carried a front-page story about the board meeting. The headline startled you because it suggested that the board intended to alter the school curriculum. You quickly read the story, which seemed to be accurate, and then telephoned the reporter who was at the meeting to complain about the slant given by the story's headline. While the reporter agreed that the headline alone might mislead a casual reader, she was pleased that you felt the content of the article was accurate. You learned that all story headlines are written by the editor just before the paper is printed. Coincidentally, the editor has just left for a well-deserved, two-week vacation. A message was left for the editor to call you when she returns.

Calls from concerned parents and citizens who referred to the newspaper article began pouring into your office after the morning paper was on the newsstands. Many of the callers remarked that they did not want their children taught about different religions, sexual mores, or alternative lifestyles (such as same-gender couples). Some callers were quite emotional about the issue. They perceived a "hidden agenda" to alter the school's curriculum. Some callers did not believe it was the responsibility of the school to teach about honoring diversity, and they have vowed to fight the issue at every opportunity.

Response

1. Develop a plan of action to address alternative resolutions to this issue.
2. Outline the agencies or persons in the community that you would contact for advice on how to address the issue on a community-wide basis.
3. Politically and educationally, what is at stake with this issue?

Notes

1. Frederick M. Wirt and Michael W. Kirst, *The Politics of Education: Schools in Conflict* (Berkeley, Calif.: McCutchan, 1992), pp. 4–8.

2. Elisabeth Hansot and David Tyack, "A Usable Past: Using History in Educational Policy," in Eighty-first yearbook of the National Society for the Study of Education, *Policy Making in Education,* ed. by Ann Lieberman and Milbrey W. McLaughlin (Chicago: University of Chicago Press, 1982), pp. 1–22.

3. Ibid., p. 5.

4. The National Commission on Excellence in Education, *A Nation at Risk: The Imperative of Educa-*tional Reform (Washington, D.C.: U.S. Office of Education, 1983), p. 5.

5. David Easton, in *The Politics of Education: Schools in Conflict* (Berkeley, Calif.: McCutchan, 1992), pp. 32–33. (See n. 1.)

6. Wirt and Kirst, *The Politics of Education: Schools in Conflict,* pp. 85–86.

7. Donald McCarty and Charles E. Ramsey, *The School Managers: Power and Conflict in American Public Education* (Westport, Conn.: Greenwood, 1971), pp. 15–22.

8. Peter F. Drucker, *The New Realities: In Government and Politics/ in Economics and Business/ in Society and World View* (New York: Harper and Row, 1989), pp. 66–67.

9. Ibid., p. 234.

10. Ibid., pp. 76–77.

11. Joel Spring, *Conflict of Interests: The Politics of American Education* (White Plains, N.Y.: Longman, 1993).

12. Alvin Toffler, *Powershift: Knowledge, Wealth, and Violence at the Edge of the Twenty-first Century* (New York: Bantam Books, 1990).

13. William Godwin, *Enquiry Concerning Political Justice and Its Influence on Morals and Happiness,* 3rd ed. (1798), Book 1, Chapter 4, pp. 43-44, quoted in Brian Simm, *Studies in the History of Education 1780–1870* (London: Lawrence and Wishart, 1960), p. 49, reprinted in Eighty-first yearbook of the National Society for the Study of Education, *Policy Making in Education,* ed. by. Ann Lieberman and Milbrey W. McLaughlin (Chicago: University of Chicago Press, 1982).

Chapter 6

The School Superintendent
and Board of Education

The relationship a superintendent has with the local school board of education is one of the most crucial found in a local educational agency. The nature of the superintendent–board relationship has far-reaching implications and affects the quality of the educational program in untold ways. In this chapter, we discuss the background and context of the superintendent–board relationship, the role and function of the board of education, and the role of the superintendent as chief executive officer of the board. Finally, we present some facets of the superintendent–board relationships.

A historical perspective, as presented in Chapter 1, can provide a view of the superintendency and the development of the school board to help current observers maintain a balanced view of the relationship between the superintendent and the board as the two work in a complex educational and political arena. "Local school boards are among the most venerable of U.S. public institutions, embodying many of our most cherished political and cultural tenants. One of these is distrust of 'distant' government that dates back to Colonial times."[1] In Colonial schools, parochial or public, the person in charge of providing instruction to students was governed by a committee of lay persons or church officials who were not educators; these persons, nevertheless, had the responsibility to see the school functioned according to the wishes of the "community." With the growth of schools and the increased size of community and city schools, school governance was assumed by school boards in Massachusetts "when local selectmen determined that running both towns and schools in expanded communities was too great an administrative burden."[2] With the advent of the twentieth century, the Industrial Revolution strongly influenced the shaping of the school board and ultimately the superintendent–board relationship. Colonial school committees constituted one era of school governance, and the first three-quarters of the twentieth century constituted the second era, which was shaped by many of the characteristics of the Industrial Model.

The third era of school board maturation is now under way, with many changes in the functions of superintendents and school boards. Participatory management and several other school reformation proposals are affecting the interactions between boards of education and superintendents. The model of governance that grew out of the Industrial Revolution is similar to the Model-A Ford—it was great for its time, but its time has passed.

In the current era of school governance, official and unofficial groups of people continue to serve certain power interests. The federal legislative process, translated by a massive federal bureaucracy; the state legislative mandates carried out by state departments of education; numerous special interest groups on the national or the local level; and local patrons expressing multiple sets of educational values all call on local school superintendents and school boards. The laws that prescribe the duties of school boards have had few changes. Public expectations, however, have changed in many ways; greater emphasis is now placed on new kinds of patron involvement and staff involvement in the governance of schools. The mix of demanding agencies is complex, and the expectations of school clientele and professional staff are in transition. At the center of the complex system, the school board and the superintendent must learn how to reshape their own interactions to carry out the cultural, political, and educational mandates placed on them.

Legal Bases for State and District Educational Systems

The school system in the United States has been shaped by and evolved from many influences. Societal influences have, at the same time, shaped the nation's political and legal structure, which have in turn interacted with and influenced the school system. The dominant base of power in American society is entrusted with the electorate; this power then moves to the legislative process, involves the courts, encompasses bureaucracies, moves on to the level of an individual agency, and finally comes to rest with individuals working within an agency. Individuals, especially when frustrated by the system in which they are involved, have expressed the view that their thinking as an individual does not count because "they" control "everything." History has, however, repeatedly shown how citizens "vote" to influence what takes place in the various levels of power within our society. Citizens vote officially at election time; they vote with their expenditures; and they "vote" through their indifference or neglect regarding selected issues. The process of taking the pulse of the electorate becomes increasingly complex as various segments of the populace express differing, often conflicting, interests. School boards and superintendents are not immune to the flow of power; indeed, they are within the hierarchy of the flow of power.

A second dimension of the flow of power can be seen in the locus of power. Federal legislation can be far-reaching because of its comprehensive jurisdiction and relationship to the courts and its access to the federal bureaucracy. Local school boards have a much more narrowly prescribed locus of power with a higher concentration of decision making; therefore, the local impact of a school board can be immediate and more intense than much of the federal legislation. Thus, although the decisions of a local board must be in compliance with federal laws, these decisions become highly personalized and significant at the local level. As superintendents become aware of the flow and concentration of power, they can have a greater understanding of their role in the structure in which they work.

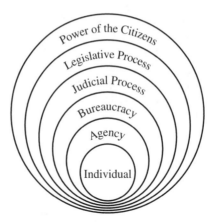

**FIGURE 6–1   Flow of Power in a
Democratic Society**

Constitutional and Legal Bases

The constitutional and legal bases on which public education was founded grew out of educational values expressed by early leaders in the United States, such as Thomas Jefferson. He was credited with the "Bill for the More General Diffusion of Knowledge," in which he set forth in 1779 his belief that an "enlightened" populace was essential for the growth of a nation.[3] Since the authors of the U.S. Constitution did not specify the federal government would be responsible for education, the individual states assumed the responsibility for educating the people. With this responsibility, a philosophical view developed that local school boards were the best structure for a decentralized system to keep the vital function of education in the hands of the people most immediately affected. The local school board, representing the local school patrons, was seen as the representative group responsible for carrying out the mandate of free, universal public education.

Originally, education was viewed as a state responsibility. Although state legislatures passed laws concerned with the organization and operation of local schools, they delegated much to the local school boards. State laws concerning education were, however, implemented and monitored by personnel in state departments of education. Federal legislators were originally concerned with more broadly conceived national interests until the last half of the twentieth century. Then, they became more concerned with school issues that reached into the local level; thus, the separation of federal, state, and local levels of jurisdiction has blurred considerably. Although state legislatures prescribe some of the functions of local boards of education, they also leave considerable latitude for discretionary action. Knezevich wrote:

> The manner in which a particular board interprets and exercises its authorities and responsibilities has a significant impact upon educational administration, the morale of the professional staff, as well as the quality of educational services delivered.[4]

What Knezevich purported in the mid-1980s continues to be true. The relationship between the board and the superintendent emerges as highly significant, particularly because board and superintendent relationships are in an environment and institution in transition.

The American school board evolved into a quasi-governmental structure that was generally separated from municipalities and the political patronage system to better serve the needs of children and youth, without the encumbrance of unsavory political influence. The unique status of the school board, with its tradition of separatism, prevailed largely unchallenged until recently. As socioeconomic conditions changed and as the ethnic balance and expectations shifted, there were calls for many institutions and local school boards to change, to be "reconfigured to meet more adequately . . . interrelated educational, health, and social needs."[5]

How boards, working with superintendents, should become more effective or how they should be reconfigured is still open to debate. In some instances, more involvement and control are advocated for local boards, while at other times suggestions have been made to reduce local board control. As the debate progresses, local board members find

> the area in which school boards exercise discretion has become progressively smaller. The board's discretion is squeezed from the top by increasing numbers of regulations from legislative, administrative, and judicial arms of the federal and state governments. In addition, the influence of private interest groups . . . has been expanding.[6]

At the same time external, top-down forces are affecting local boards and superintendents, an acceleration of diverse demands from local interest groups can be seen, including teacher groups who are asking for greater input into the governance of the local school. As distrust and discontent with a big, distant government become evident, individual citizens sense the need for local control in the operation of the schools. The desire for controlling one's own destiny and the concern over social conditions at the national level can be seen when numerous respondents to national polls point out there are major needs in education at the national level but that the state of affairs is good in their local school district.

The multiplicity of educational values linked with a desire for controlling one's own destiny is also reflected in various forces that compete with local school boards, such as home schooling, the choice movement, and private schools. As forces that compete with public education have grown in number and intensity, legislators' actions have reflected that ambiguity. Societal influences have entered schools through the influences of courts and newly enacted laws and through a wide array of contradictory edicts or permissive provisions. While mandates have required the provision of education for all children and youth, including those with multiple handicaps or from diverse backgrounds, proposals have been set forth to provide support for schooling in an elitist and separate educational system.

Local administrators and board members are confronted with the challenge of maintaining a balanced set of educational values, defining an educational mission, and specifying goals that will ultimately foster a common culture, while at the same time developing an educational system to maximize the growth and development of each individual entering the school. For many decades the schools have not been the sole educators of children and youth; the family, churches, numerous private and governmental agencies, mass media, businesses, peer influences, and many other forces have compounded the complexity of the issues faced by superintendents and boards.[7] Local superintendents and board members feel pressures from state and national interests, from numerous, competing local pressure groups, and often intense pressures from within the school system.

The complex interactions and pressures experienced by school boards make it evident that the simple model of education, with each state assuming responsibility and delegating much of the decision making to the local level, is no longer clear and precise. More actors are involved at all levels, from the federal to the local scene. The complexity of demands, the growth of knowledge regarding governance, and changing expectations of patrons and professional educators suggest a call for the restructuring of the school board's role; such a call will have profound influences on the superintendent–board relationship.

Organization of School Districts

School district structure has grown in response to geographic, economic, political, and educational needs. Some districts provide only K–8 schooling. The most frequent type of district contains grades K–12, or pre-K–12. In many states, districts serve secondary grades only, usually encompassing grades 9–12. Within the K–12 structure, schools may be organized in many ways. Some districts have elementary buildings with grades K–4, 5–8 middle schools, and 9–12 senior high schools. In other districts, the grade configuration may vary, with elementary grades K–6, 7–9 middle or junior high schools, and 10–12 senior high schools. With the growing emphasis on middle schools, the structure of K–5 elementary school, 6–8 middle school, and 9–12 senior high school has appeared more frequently.

Because of the number of small districts throughout the nation, however, the K–6 elementary school and 7–12 secondary school is the most frequent school organization. Secondary schools housing grades 7–12 are structured in two basic ways: one provides for a "six-year" secondary school, in which there are six grade levels rather than three or four grade levels, and the second is the "junior–senior" high school with a separate junior high or middle school program for grades 7 and 8 and a separate senior high program.

In a junior–senior high school building, class schedules are utilized to provide some space and time exclusively for middle level students and for senior high students, and some space and time are allocated for common use by all grade levels. The lunch room is a good example of a common space used by different age groups at different times. Some faculty are exclusively involved with middle school students, some with senior high school students, and some with all grade levels. The art teachers, music instructors, and physical education staff members are examples of those who typically serve all grade levels. The junior–senior high school has two programs, each designed to meet the special needs of a certain age group, in one facility with one staff.

Intermediate or educational service units or districts are found in many states. The intermediate service district was implemented to provide programs for districts too small to afford all needed services. There are also financial advantages for smaller districts associated with intermediate service districts.

Intermediate service districts generally have an elected school board and an advisory board consisting of representatives, usually the school superintendent, from each local district. The elected board is primarily a policy body, and the advisory board usually functions as a program development body. Intermediate service districts have taxing authority, are eligible for federal funding, and can contract for services. There is no specified list of functions that are performed by intermediate service districts. Services provided for local districts are determined by policies made by the elected board and by advisory board members who request services for their districts that fall within the legal parameters prescribed by policy and state law. Many intermediate service districts are involved in staff development activities, educational resource libraries, group purchasing, testing programs, special education services, computer services for management and class scheduling, and general consultation for local school administrators.

School district size continues to affect superintendents and school boards. Of the total of 15,358 public school districts in the United States in 1990–91, 1.2 percent had 25,000 or more pupils; 3.2 percent 10,000 to 24,999 pupils; 6.1 percent 5,000 to 9,999 pupils; 12.6 percent 2,500 to 4,999 pupils; 23.1 percent 1,000 to 2,499 pupils; 11.7 percent 600 to 999 pupils; 14.8 percent 300 to 599 pupils; and 24.8 percent 1 to 299 pupils. Larger districts provided education for the bulk of the students. The 1.2 percent of districts with 25,000 or more pupils enrolled 28.7 percent of the pupils; in districts with less than 600 enrollment, which comprised 39.6 percent of the school districts, 3.6 percent of the pupils were enrolled.[8] As the population in the United States has grown from approximately 124 million in 1930 to 248 million in 1990, the number of school districts has declined from approximately 130,000 in 1930 to 15,500 in 1990.[9] (See Figure 6–2.)

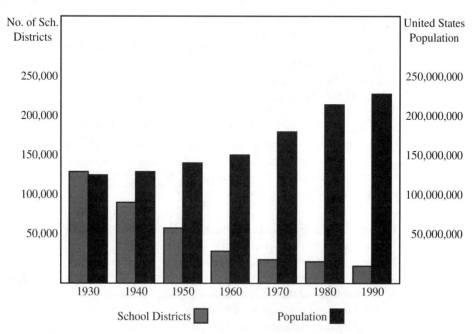

FIGURE 6–2   Comparison of U.S. Population with the Number of School Districts

The Local Board of Education

Local boards of education function as quasi-corporate bodies established by state legislative actions. As elected bodies, boards of education legally operate only as a total body; individual members are not authorized to act in an official capacity. The system is intended to provide for local control through the efforts of elected lay boards who are to perform specified functions as prescribed by law. "The purpose of a system of decentralization is to keep the schools close to the people. The notion is that education is such a personal and private affair and yet so vital to the preservation and improvement of the culture that it must at once be kept close to the will of the people and be as safe from alien seizure as possible."[10] Boards of education are recognized as bodies responsible for setting school policy. The superintendent is responsible for the daily management of the school as board-approved policies are carried out.

In practice, board of education members do not always stay in the policy arena but perform administrative functions as a group or individually. As an example, two board members were unsatisfied with the recommendation a building principal and the superintendent made regarding two teachers. One teacher was on a one-year contract and had not yet earned tenure; the other was tenured. The two board members wanted to terminate both teachers. They went to the school and videotaped each teacher without informing the principal or the superintendent. The board members appeared at the next board meeting armed with their videotapes as evidence to justify their recommendation to terminate the two teachers. A professional organization and legal intervention prevented the board from releasing the two teachers in question; however, at the end of the year the two dissatisfied board members garnered sufficient votes to terminate the contract of the superintendent.

The illustration is extreme, and its like occurs infrequently; but it does show that boards of education can breach legal and/or ethical boundaries of responsibility. They may act as individuals rather than a total board, and they can step over the policy boundary into the realm of administrative duties that should be left in the hands of the superintendent. The distinction of policy as a board function as contrasted to management in carrying out board policy by the superintendent is perhaps the most crucial balance that exists between a board and the chief executive officer.

The statutes and department of education rules in each state specify what responsibilities should be carried out by boards of education. Some board functions can be legislated and some cannot. Bill writers for state legislators have not been able to shape legislation that will control "communication," "rapport," "respect," "vision," or "school climate," all of which are important to the smooth functioning of a local educational agency. Generally, the board of education is responsible for:

1. The selection and retention of a superintendent (and in some instances, terminating the services of a superintendent)
2. The evaluation of the superintendent
3. The development of school policy in cooperation with the superintendent
4. The establishment of district mission, goals, and objectives[11]
5. Attending and conducting all board meetings in accordance with the law
6. Planning for board–superintendent communications
7. Taking action on matters only after the recommendation of the superintendent

8. Providing the superintendent with sufficient resources to carry out the duties of the office[12]

9. Carrying out the contractual powers of the board in conjunction with the operation of the district

10. Conducting review and approval of the budget development and management functions, including the determination of long-range and financial planning and bonding for construction

11. Establishing a local school foundation for soliciting, investing, and disbursing funds

12. Assuring due process will be provided when grievances occur

For any one of these areas of responsibility a host of specifics can be suggested to school boards. Most of the specifics are not detailed in state laws or state department of education rules. The selection and retention of a superintendent is a case in point. Good board practice and conventional wisdom suggest that when a new superintendent is employed there be a period of at least one year of support by the board to "induct" the new CEO into the district.[13] A new superintendent induction program is not commonly provided for in state statutes, and yet a board has the authority to develop and fund such a program.

The school board should transcend the specifics of legal provisions and at the same time operate within the boundaries prescribed by law. Danzberger suggested that frustrated state legislators in the 1980s (during which time it was popular for state legislative bodies to pass laws requiring schools to reform) were dissatisfied with local board leadership. Thus, "state policy makers believed that they needed to take charge of what and how much students were required to learn and of how states would know if students were learning."[14] Boards were perceived as failing to meet the transcendence expectations of their legal domain by:

1. Failing to provide far-reaching or politically risky leadership for reform

2. Becoming another level of administration, often micromanaging districts

3. Becoming splintered by members' attempts to represent special interests or by striving to meet individual political interests

4. Spending too little time on educating themselves about issues or in making educational policy

5. Not providing the leadership required to mobilize other agencies and organizations to meet the health and social service needs of students and their families

6. Not exercising adequate policy oversight and lacking adequate accountability measures while failing to communicate progress to the public

7. Relying on rhetoric

8. Failing to develop positive and productive lasting relationships with superintendents

9. Paying too little attention—or even no attention—to their performance and to their needs for ongoing training

10. Tending either to make decisions in response to the "issue of the day" in communities experiencing changes of major proportions or, by contrast, governing in an effort to maintain the status quo in more stable communities[15]

In response to the perceived limitations and weaknesses found in the traditional school board setting, Danzberger and others from the Institute of Educational Leadership

(IEL) proposed a list of essentials to be accomplished in the restructuring of school boards. The recommendations from the IEL include the following:

1. "Repeal all current laws and regulations that specify the duties, functions, selection, and role of school boards; rename the school board the 'local education policy board.'"[16]

2. Board vision should be manifested through strategic planning and performance indicators for measuring learning outcomes. Moving individuals who may lack vision to a posture of visionary policy leadership will, however, be a difficult challenge for the most competent superintendent. The importance of goal setting has been identified by various analysts, who have also suggested that the National Goals for Education set forth by President Bush and the nation's governors may have a profound impact on "goal setting and resource allocation prerogatives of local school boards."[17]

3. School boards will be responsible, as they traditionally have been, for employing and evaluating the superintendent as well as defining the role of the superintendent and other cabinet level administrators. "The board should establish personnel policies to guide hiring, evaluation, and dismissal of principals and other district personnel but will not be involved in individual personnel decisions." Deleting the legal requirement and practice of having board members approve all appointments in the district is a recommendation that would place the board in a position of lesser responsibility while requiring greater attention to policy development.

4. "Boards will approve the school district budget, ensuring that spending priorities are consistent with the goals and objectives in the strategic plan."

5. "Boards will determine policies and guidelines for negotiating employee contracts . . . but the board will not negotiate directly with representatives of employee organizations." Removing the board from the actual negotiation process would be a departure from current practice in many districts.

6. "Boards will approve curricular frameworks and standards for student achievement."

7. It was also recommended that boards provide "policy coherence by linking policies and reform initiatives to student outcome objectives, curricular framework, and assessment."

8. Further, boards should "establish policies for staff development" that are internally consistent with the mission, goals and objectives of the district.

9. "Boards will develop a system for reviewing individual schools' performance on a periodic basis."

10. A departure from the way in which grievances and conflicts are to be resolved was suggested by recommending that boards employ "law judges (or another type of qualified third party) to hear and decide complaints" involving staff or students.

11. Greater community involvement and cooperation with other human service agencies was recommended.

12. The final two recommendations would require boards to "conduct regular and periodic self-assessments" and "commit themselves to an ongoing process of learning and development."[18]

While the recommendations from the IEL suggest board members will continue with many of the responsibilities they have had in the past, significant changes were suggested in the role and function of local boards of education. If school reform is to be achieved, all segments of the educational system, including the local board of education, will have to undergo substantive changes consistent with the total system of reform.

The composition of school boards in the 1990s remained as it had for several decades; 94.3 percent of all board members were elected by the registered voters in the school district. In some larger districts, board members were appointed by the mayor of the city. As the size of the district decreased, the percentage of board members that were elected increased; in smaller districts, virtually all (99.8%) were elected.[19]

At the national level, Feistritzer indicated that boards of education are "a homogeneous group consisting primarily of white, well-educated, middle-aged males."[20] Local board members are reportedly predominantly white (92%), male (70%), and 36 to 45 years old (71%). In recent decades, the number of women serving on local boards of education has increased, a trend that seems to be continuing.

Generally, a person must be a citizen and registered voter residing in the district or ward involved to be qualified to run for a seat on a school board. There have been instances where 18-year-olds who have just graduated from high school have run and been elected to serve on school boards. Thus, board elections are open to all citizens.

Superintendents' perceptions of the qualifications of board members were reported in an American Association of School Administrators (AASA) study in 1992. Superintendents saw board members as "very well qualified" (16.7%), "qualified" (55.1%), "not well qualified" (26.3%), and "incompetent" (1.9%).[21] Clearly, the expectations and desires of an individual superintendent, along with expressed educational values, will greatly affect how a superintendent defines "qualified."

Board members are generally elected "at large" for overlapping terms with the intent of fostering continuity on the board. The vast majority of board members are elected in nonpartisan elections, while approximately 4 percent are elected from a partisan ticket.[22] The membership of school boards may range from 3 to 20. The most common size is 5 to 9; generally, the number of board members is uneven, although in some states boards consist of an even number of members.

With the interest in involving more persons from a wider range of ethnic backgrounds in the educational process, there was a move from elections at large to a ward election system. The ward election system is like the good news/bad news story and has vigorous proponents and opponents. Ward elections generally result in greater numbers of minority board members. There is, however, a perceived loss of persons with broad views, since there is a tendency for ward-elected board members to vote for programs and policies that help their ward; they often fail to see the broad view of the district as a whole. The "ward mentality," it is argued, can result in competition for resources and a breakdown of cooperation.

Power of the Board to Make Decisions

Legally, board members have the power to make decisions only when they are in official session and acting as a group. Decision making is an area, however, where tensions can develop between a superintendent and individual members of a board of education.

Policies, supported by legal citations, are an important form of documentation to have when working with board members. Board and superintendent unity, a clear understanding of the division of powers, and the legal basis for board power can be achieved through board policies. While the clear majority of board members realize the need for a board to operate as a legal body rather than allowing each board member to make official decisions, it is not a matter that a superintendent can take for granted. There are cases of board members seeking individual gratification, such as special treatment for family and friends, responding individually to a patron, seeking to influence local elections, dictating to coaches or trying to determine who should be the coach, and directing budget development. Such examples suggest the superintendent should work with a board and develop policies so the energies of individual members are directed to legally performed and productive efforts.[23]

Most states have established legal requirements for announcing and holding public meetings that specify the conditions under which a board must operate. In practice, however, the superintendent is faced with potential breaches of the law on the part of some board members as they resist clear role definitions and separation of authority.

The Superintendent as Chief Executive Officer and Educational Leader in the District

The leadership skill shown by the superintendent of schools when working with the board of education is a significant factor in how a school district functions. The superintendent must provide leadership of the highest quality while educating the board. Communication becomes vital when demonstrating leadership and educating the members of the board.

As pointed out previously, superintendents perceive nearly three-fourths of the board members to be qualified to perform their duties and slightly more than one-fourth to be unqualified. It is the responsibility of the superintendent to "lead" and "educate" the portion of the board possessing less than desired qualifications. If a superintendent can educate the one-fourth of the board members who are lacking in qualifications, the level of board competence can be improved and will ultimately enhance the quality of education in the district. Educating, informing, and developing the potential of the board of education members is a never-ending responsibility for a superintendent. Boards change with each election; old members retire or are defeated, and newly elected members begin their service. Consequently, the superintendent must continually work to educate the board of education.

Management styles have evolved as education has changed through the decades. As school administration has moved from the Industrial Revolution–era model into the emerging participatory model, the relationship between the superintendent of schools and the members of the school board has changed. The current "reform movement calls for educational leaders to move away from the traditional, hierarchical, control-and-command environment."[24] In the information environment in which pluralism dominates, superintendents should demonstrate marked skill in both the human domain and in working with technical resources. "The paradigm shift in leadership is depicted in business management literature . . . as a shift toward a more flexible organizational structure based on units that are more lateral and cooperative. It is an organizational structure that values leadership over management and emphasizes collaboration, consensus building, and empowerment."[25] Thus, the leadership, communication style, and education provided for board members by the superintendent must reflect the emerging paradigms in education.

Minorities and Women in the Superintendency

The superintendency in the United States continues to be dominated by white males. In 1992, 92.7 percent of the superintendents who responded to a national survey were men, and 6.6 percent were women. A total of 95.5 percent were nonminority, and approximately 4.0 percent were minority.[26]

Women's perceptions of the superintendency were studied by Grady, Ourada-Sieb, and Wesson. They reported in their national study that women superintendents found job satisfaction from an opportunity to "make a difference," "be involved with change," "provide direction," and "meet children's needs." Some women respondents found satisfaction in power and control. An equal number of respondents found satisfaction working with people. When the respondents were asked how much self-fulfillment they received from the role of superintendent, 65 percent said it provided a "great deal"; 27 percent said the position provided mixed positives and negatives; and 8 percent said the superintendency provided only a "little" self-fulfillment.[27]

The process of employing chief executive officers for school districts has not proven conducive to selecting women or minorities. An interesting conclusion was reached, however, by Grady, Ourada-Sieb, and Wesson: "Both urban and rural women superintendents have leadership characteristics that are similar, and these leadership characteristics do fit a new leadership paradigm. These women superintendents have been hired to be change agents and consensus builders, and both the urban and rural superintendents are finding success in their jobs."[28]

With the changing demographics in the United States, there likely will be changes in the proportions of women and minorities in the superintendency.

Responsibilities of the Chief Executive Officer

The responsibilities of the superintendent can be broken down in various ways. Different authorities have suggested various lists of duties or functions, and in various states the requirements of the law specify different tasks or functions to be performed by the superintendent. After the legal requirements have been met, the superintendent and the members of the board of education should arrive at a mutually agreed-on mode of operations. The combined forces of the National Association of School Boards (NASB) and the American Association of School Administrators (AASA) suggested 11 areas of responsibility to be accomplished by the superintendent:[29]

1. *Serve as the board's chief executive officer and advisor.* What Miller and others suggested over two decades ago is still true:

    The superintendent of schools is the executive agent of the board. Because the board is a board only when in session, the superintendent stands in its place at all other times. He [or she] is the executive agenda in terms of carrying through the decisions it has made. He [or she] is the executive agent in terms of receiving communications to be transmitted to it. Sometimes, he [or she] is the executive agent in terms of making the best immediate decision inadequately covered by policy or delegated authority, always aware that it must be reported to and accepted or overruled by the board.[30]

2. *Serve as the school system's educational leader.*
3. *Keep the board of education informed about the operations and programs of the school.*
4. *Keep the community informed about board policies, programs, and district procedures.*
5. *Interpret the needs of the school system to the board.*
6. *Present and recommend policy options along with specific recommendations to the board when circumstances require the board to adopt new policies or revise existing policies.*
7. *Develop and inform the board of administrative procedures needed to implement board policy.*
8. *Provide leadership for the district's educational programs.*
9. *Develop an adequate program of school–community relations.*
10. *Be responsible for the day-to-day operation of the school.*
11. *Assume responsibility for evaluation of personnel and keeping the board informed about the personnel evaluation.*

Other areas of superintendent responsibility, which can expand this list, are:

12. *Plan, with the staff, for the development of the budget and the management of receipts and disbursements.*
13. *Plan for facility needs and make recommendations regarding maintenance, modernization, or replacement of buildings.*
14. *Become involved in strategic planning.* The superintendent should provide leadership to board members to help them develop a vision, gain an in-depth understanding of the influences from outside and inside the institution that will affect its future, clarify the mission for the district, and develop strategic goals and implement a management plan for their accomplishment.

Additionally, there are some less tangible but significant areas of superintendent responsibilities. One of these is leadership, which is required in all areas of responsibility. The superintendent must also develop a positive climate that can embody a feeling of respect and of trust. Looking ahead to determine future needs in a district is another responsibility faced by the superintendent. Superintendents should not only be a reader of futurists; they should be futurists in their own right. The ability to make projections and to envision what will occur in the future are responsibilities of the superintendent.

The superintendent, serving as chief executive officer of the board of education and fulfilling the role as "educational leader" for the district, faces many audiences, wears many hats, and applies numerous skills. The superintendents who are able to demonstrate a vision and see what is needed to manage the day-to-day operation of the district will ultimately make the greatest contribution.

The Relationships of the School Superintendent and Board

Board of education functions to improve education have been viewed in different ways. By the same token, there are both implied and explicit functions with which superintendents should be involved if they are to lead schools into the future, with its rapidly changing education environment. Perhaps more important than listing the functions of boards and superintendents is consideration of the relationship between superintendents and their boards. Blumberg and Blumberg suggested that the "most critical forum that exists as far as running a school system is concerned [is] that which involves the interplay of the superintendent and the school board."[31]

The relationship between a superintendent and a school board is generally a productive one; however, it can never be taken for granted. Fostering the most productive relationship between the superintendent and the board takes thoughtful planning and the application of good human relations skills. From his vantage point as a school superintendent, Nygren suggested the following items be rated on a 10-point scale (10 highest, 1 lowest) to conduct a checkup on the relationship between the board and the superintendent.

1. Board members work at the tedious chore of setting policy, even though at times they would enjoy dabbling in management.
2. The board develops and works to maintain a sensible, understandable, even believable job description for the superintendent.
3. Each year, the board and the superintendent sit down together and set timely, attainable, and measurable goals.
4. Each year, the board prepares a . . . performance appraisal of the superintendent.
5. On major agenda items, the board insists the superintendent make recommendations and then . . . considers them.
6. Citizen complaints to the board . . . are referred routinely to the superintendent.
7. Board members do not criticize the superintendent, even in social settings. . . .
8. The board holds orientation sessions for new members.
9. During a crisis involving angry parents, the board remains silent and refers news reporters to the superintendent for comment.
10. Board members . . . attend training. . . .
11. At official meetings, the board would find it unthinkable to take a "surprise" action without having given the superintendent an advance word.
12. The board believes the superintendent should continue to grow professionally and provides dollars . . . to help him [or her] do so.
13. Each year the board evaluates its own effectiveness. . . .[32]

Obviously, if superintendents and board members could rate all these items as a 10, superintendents would want to keep their positions indefinitely. Freund suggested the superintendent relationship with the board could be nurtured by:

1. Regular communications and meetings with the board president
2. Planning the board agenda as a cooperative effort by the superintendent and the board president who then is responsible for chairing the board meeting
3. Conducting a "postgame" analysis with the president the following day to make suggestions to improve the meeting
4. Allowing the board president to handle arguments between board members
5. Praising the board president and other members of the board publicly and regularly

6. Inviting the board president to attend professional meetings and encouraging all members to participate in training programs
7. Calling the president first in case of an emergency
8. Informing the board president when he or she will be out of town
9. Recognizing the entire board is serving and being served and all members should be dealt with equally.[33]

Establishing Mutually Acceptable Roles and Functions

It might seem that clarifying roles and functions to be performed by a superintendent and a board of education should not be a complex task. After all, the superintendent is the professionally trained chief executive officer and the educational leader of a school system, and the board is an elected lay body responsible for setting the policy of the district and carrying out, in most states, legislated responsibilities.

On closer examination of their respective roles, however, there are several reasons for possible confusion and debate about the responsibility and accountability of the superintendent and board of education. There are areas of overlapping responsibilities that do not yield to a simple separation. An illustration of this is found in policy development by the board and leadership for the board by the superintendent. While boards are responsible for policy, researchers have found that policies are initiated by the superintendent most of the time. Although board members must approve policy additions or modifications, policies are initiated by the superintendent in approximately two-thirds of the situations, and board members initiate policy approximately 4 percent of the time. Policy initiation was viewed as a shared responsibility approximately one-fourth of the time.[34]

Consider also the area of evaluation. A superintendent of schools, as a professional person licensed to evaluate staff, has the responsibility of evaluating staff and submitting recommendations to the board regarding staff placement, promotion, or retention. A board member may view an elementary school instrumental music teacher acting in a very unprofessional way in dealing with children at a performance. Parents may call the board member and complain about the teacher, and the board member may be aware that student interest and participation in instrumental music are declining. It would be unreasonable to expect the board member not to be influenced by what had been observed and reported by parents, although evaluation of staff was not within the domain of the board member as an individual or as a member of the total board.

Another reason for role ambiguity between the superintendent and the board is that the superintendent is a trained professional, who must juggle many tasks or functions at any one time, and the board is composed for the most part of individuals who are not professionally trained as educators or in board diplomacy. Finally, the board members can terminate the contract of the superintendent at any time they wish; thus, the leadership of the superintendent and the way it is extended must be acceptable to the board. There is an old saying: to do the job of superintendent you have to keep the job. Small wonder that role ambiguity is a major area of concern for many school superintendents.

The importance of school board orientation has been recognized by professional organizations, scholars, and practitioners. Not all board members, however, are willing to participate in formal orientation and training programs, and some who do disregard the information presented. Efforts to improve the understanding and skill of board members have increased as school board association leaders at the state and national level have developed programs and published literature to help board members. Board members receive training from several sources: superintendent (46.2%), other experienced board members (3.4%), school board association in-service activities and literature (15.6%), working with other board members and administrators to learn by doing (27.4%). "Unknown" or "not formally oriented" was reported 7.4 percent of the time.[35] Note that the superintendent heads the list of the ways school board members get training; this suggests that superintendents, to a degree, hold their fate in their own hands.

Role clarification is influenced by the level of confidence a superintendent generates with a board. Equal treatment of all board members and openness and honesty are essential. "Boards have a tendency to place a considerable trust in the good intentions of the superintendent. They might accept countless mistakes and forgive even costly oversights. But once a board becomes convinced its superintendent has committed even one willfully harmful act, trust is irrevocably lost."[36]

Two major functions are fundamental to clarifying the role of the board and the superintendent: strategic planning in which all significant parties are involved (see Chapter 7), and comprehensive policy development. Both strategic plans and school policies should be revisited annually and updated. If a well-conceptualized strategic plan with an agreed-on set of principles, a clear and meaningful mission statement, workable and prioritized strategic goals, and a carefully designed strategic management plan that includes evaluation are in place, the result will be a good understanding between the superintendent and board. "School board members frequently appear dysfunctional because of conflicts between members and the resulting incapacity to chart a clear direction for their systems."[37] In like manner, if a board and the superintendent have developed a well-codified set of comprehensive policies, containing agreed-on definitions of operational authority and management decisions, a positive base is established for a better working relationship between the superintendent and board.[38]

Although superintendents who work with perverse board members might find it difficult to acknowledge that the relationship with boards does not top the list of problems superintendents face across the nation, superintendents rated relations with the board as the eighth most frequently perceived problem (14.1%). Inadequate finances was the most frequently perceived problem (59.0%); involvement with too many insignificant demands followed (51.9%). Other perceived problem areas were state reform mandates (38.0%); collective bargaining agreements (25.4%); and racial/ethnic problems (22.0%).[39]

Every superintendent will eventually face the need to resolve a conflict with an individual board member or the total board of education. Obviously, the best strategy is to prevent the occurrence of conflicts; however, some conflicts will emerge in the best of situations. When conflicts do arise, the superintendent should realize that avoidance is counterproductive, conflict can provide a means of healthy growth, and there are techniques and procedures for dealing with conflict. Every superintendent, to develop human potential among board and staff members, should know the fundamentals of conflict resolution.

When dealing with role ambiguity and conflict resolution, successful superintendents have demonstrated they are astute analysts of the power structure in the community, on the board, and within the school system. The successful leader knows how to harness power in a constructive way. "The key to board–superintendent relationships that work lies not in survival checklists that delineate do's and don'ts for each party. Instead, . . . they are grounded firmly in the basic principles of educational and democratic theory; the rigorous search for truth, genuine understanding, and mutual respect for divergent views; sincere commitment to the common good; and the belief that people . . . are basically honorable, with intelligence and the capacity for judgment."[40]

Preparing the Executive Board Agendas

Laws in the various states that control open meetings of public boards of education and guidelines from professional associations have provided the framework for board meeting agendas. Because of legal requirements, official notice must be posted in advance of the meeting in prescribed ways and for a specified time. Specified procedures are used to call the meeting to order, take roll for the record, and determine if a quorum is present. The minutes from the past meeting are read and approved by an official motion and board action. Communications to and from the board are reviewed, and bills are presented for approval by the board. Provision is made on the agenda to hear any scheduled delegation(s). Committee reports are presented, and any report from the superintendent is given. Unfinished business is brought up for information or action, which is followed by new business.[41] There will be variations from state to state within the basic structure of the board meeting agenda; style and formatting may differ, with larger boards frequently having a more formal format than found in small districts.

Insko explained how agenda items are formatted in the Chapel Hill-Carrboro, North Carolina, school system. Each agenda item "begins with a specific statement of the problem or issue, followed by appropriate background information, relevant data and data analysis, a listing of possible actions the board might take (complete with the pros and cons of each) and, finally, a recommendation for approval or revision by the board."[42] This format lends itself to a "decision/action summary" of directives listing the "specific follow-up action required, the person responsible, the date for completion, and whether the board will need to take further action."[43]

Superintendents have been and remain the primary persons responsible for setting the board agenda. In 76.5 percent of the districts surveyed in the United States, the superintendent was the person who set the agenda. The board chairperson set the agenda in 0.2 percent of the schools, agenda development was a shared responsibility in 22.4 percent of the schools, and in less than 1 percent of the districts the agenda was determined in some other way.

A noticeable difference was reported in how the board agenda was determined in larger and smaller districts. In larger districts, with 25,000 or more pupils, the superintendent developed the agenda individually in 65.3 percent of the districts, and the responsibility was shared between the superintendent and board chairperson in 34.7 percent. In districts with fewer than 300 pupils, the superintendent developed the agenda in 85.5 percent of the districts, while it was a joint superintendent–board chairperson responsibility in 15.5 percent. The difference in agenda development between larger and smaller districts may reflect that larger districts operate more formally and may be more aware of and involved with participatory governance.

Superintendents should acknowledge that sharing the development of the board agenda does not relinquish power and control; the shared approach to agenda development generates greater support from the board president, serves as a means of communicating to and educating the president, and capitalizes on the fact that two heads can be better than one.

The distribution of the board agenda and the accompanying data to board members several days prior to the board meeting is an appropriate, if not essential, practice. If board members are to attend a meeting with sufficient information to carry out their responsibilities judiciously, they must have the agenda and supporting information in hand well in advance of the meeting.[44]

Evaluation of the Superintendent

Superintendents of local school districts exert considerable influence on how they are evaluated. Lay boards typically do not possess the training and experience to be expert evaluators of a superintendent; therefore, they rely on information obtained from the local superintendent, board in-service programs, attendance at professional meetings, and printed material concerning the evaluation procedure.

A natural progression of thought can lead to developing and implementing a plan to evaluate a superintendent of schools. If a board has a clear grasp of the mission and goals of the district, such information can be used to prepare the job description for the superintendent. The superintendent will help clarify the mission and goals of the district in writing a job description, thus influencing those areas that should be reflected in the evaluation of his or her position. When the desired results a board is seeking and a job description are considered, the expectations the board has for the superintendent can be incorporated into the evaluation process.

Glass has suggested that board expectations of their superintendents, when viewed from a national perspective, include (1) skills in human relations (43.8%); (2) knowledge of finance and budgets (39.2%); (3) skill in general management (48.5%); (4) good community relations (13.0%); (5) the ability to provide instructional leadership (40.0%); and (6) skill in planning (11.1%). Other miscellaneous skills were mentioned by 2.5 percent of the respondents.[45] Such expectations could reasonably be reflected in the job description of the superintendent and thus appear in the evaluation process.

Developing a rationale for the need for evaluation and what can be achieved by an evaluation of a superintendent is also a part of the process. Generally the rationale for evaluating the superintendent includes the need for (1) accountability, (2) personal growth, (3) identification of areas of need, (4) building open communications between the superintendent and board through a structured process, and (5) a basis for planning for improvement.

A joint effort can be conducted to evaluate the work of the superintendent and the board of education. Just as there is a rationale for evaluating a superintendent, there are similar points to be considered for evaluating a board: (1) greater accountability, (2) a means to foster better understanding, (3) improvement of the decision-making process, (4) building open communications between the superintendent and board through a structured process, (5) growth in professionalism, (6) growth of insights into the role of the board, (7) a contribution to the orientation of new board members, (8) addressing problems so that they can be resolved rather than ignored, (9) a strategy to help people accept and be comfortable with the discussion of basic issues, and (10) the establishment of a base for planning.

The team review process has been explored for evaluating superintendents and boards in one combined effort. "The mechanics of Team Review are simple enough: Every three or four months, the school board members and the superintendent complete a question-naire that asks them to respond to . . . descriptive statements that cover such matters as communication, trust, and decision making."[46] Through the questionnaire, each board member and the superintendent are asked to make judgments regarding board-to- board relationships and board-to-superintendent relationships. For example:

> TRUST: being willing to discuss concerns with the total group without fear; not taking disagreements personally. Board/Board _____ Board/Superinten-dent ____.[47]

The board members and superintendent are asked to rate items, such as the preceding, on a scale from 1 (needs improvement) to 7 (extremely effective) and to make explanatory comments. The board members and superintendent then discuss, at a regular meeting, the questionnaire responses on any item rated 3 or less.

Even though a clear rationale can be set forth for evaluating a superintendent and a board, it is not universally accomplished. Glass reported that formal evaluation of the superintendent was done in 43.1 percent of the districts; an informal evaluation was con-ducted in 15.3 percent of the districts; a combination of formal and informal evaluation was been carried out in 37.7 percent of the districts; and no evaluation was performed in 3.9 percent of the school systems. In districts of 25,000 pupils or more, the formal evalua-tion of the superintendent was performed in 53.9 percent of the districts, and in schools with enrollments of 300 or less, the formal process was used in 31.9 percent of the dis-tricts. The percentage of districts in which no evaluation was conducted was significantly higher in districts with 300 or less enrollment.[48]

While almost 9 out of 10 superintendents have a formal job description, they are not always evaluated according to the job description. "Job targets," which generally accom-pany job descriptions, and strategic goals approved by the board are not always incorpo-rated in the evaluation process. Thus, in some districts little relationship exists between the evaluation process and the specified expectations of the superintendent.

A superintendent should work out a plan with the board of education that incorporates the expectations of the board and is internally consistent with the mission and goals of the district and his or her job description. If the job description is incompatible, it should be adjusted to be a working document against which the superintendent can be evaluated. The evaluation should be routinely performed and draw on more than one source of informa-tion to accompany any judgments expressed by board members. Ideally, the system for evaluating the superintendent should also incorporate a process for board/superintendent evaluation.

Summary

The relationship between the superintendent of schools and the board of education has evolved from a history and legal framework that has moved through an agrarian society and the Industrial Revolution model of the first half of the twentieth century. This relationship is now changing into a new paradigm for management and has been reshaped to include greater levels of lay participation and decentralization. The superintendent and the local board of today experience more pressure from legislative edicts, continue to respond to court rulings, and encounter confusing signals from our pluralistic society. Moving into the new management arena is difficult in many respects, as traditions die hard.

The role and function of the board of education can be defined very simply—the board is responsible for policy matters. However, with increasing federal influences on education, changing political moods at the national and local level, and continual interest and legislative actions that shift with political winds, local board members often are pressured so that they have less control or influence.

The responsibilities and functions of superintendents are defined in various ways. The superintendent faces a constant stream of challenges from outside and within the district as new management approaches, change, continuity, and inclusions and exclusions are called for by conflicting pressure groups.

The relationship between a superintendent and members of a local school board is key to the quality of education provided to children and youth in a district. A positive, constructive relationship cannot be left to chance. The superintendent should provide leadership for the board that will move the district in a direction to assure quality education as it moves into the future. In many respects, good leadership provided by the superintendent for the board is the most significant function he or she can perform.

Discussion Questions

1. For education to be upgraded and reformed to meet the demands of a changing society, the major components of the total system should be changed; these changes should be in harmony and internally consistent. Is a systematic approach to school reform necessary, and if so, where does the relationship between superintendents and boards fit into the picture? If systematic change is not possible or unnecessary, what meaning does the relationship between the superintendent and the school board have for improving education at the local level?

2. Superintendents seldom get fired because they do not demonstrate the ability to plan a budget or perform tasks typically associated with the office of superintendent. Superintendents lose their jobs because they get into conflicts that are categorized as human relations problems. If human relations problems are generated by the superintendent, by the board, or by other significant actors, what should a superintendent do to avoid job-threatening situations that emerge within this arena?

3. Explain why it has been suggested that a comprehensive set of school policies is essential for a healthy superintendency.

4. Explain why strategic planning has been placed at the same level of importance as school policies to provide a solid base of operations for a superintendent.

5. To understand and achieve a healthy superintendent–board relationship, the areas of responsibility of the board and the superintendent (leadership and carrying out policy by the superintendent, policy development by the board) should be separated. Achieving the appropriate separation of power between the two is sometimes difficult. Why is that the case? When the relationship does break down, what should the superintendent do?

6. Since the relationship between the board and the superintendent is important, and the superintendent is in a place to influence a board of education, what would you suggest a superintendent should do to put a plan together to educate a board of education?

7. Describe what you believe to be an appropriate and adequate process for evaluating a superintendent's performance. How would it be possible to include and involve the board of education in assessing performance?

CASE 6.1   Policy, Administration, or Preferential Treatment

Marshall Hill was the superintendent of a district with 1,500 pupils in grades K–12; the district sprawled across an area 33 miles long and approximately 27 miles wide. The town of Meade, the only town in the district, was located on a north–south state highway that followed the Blue River. Bus routes extended from Meade to all corners of the district and provided transportation for approximately 300 pupils. Bus transportation was typically provided to the elementary and middle school children, while senior high students drove their own cars to school.

Over the years, the practice had been that the bus would pick up students living on ranches at the state or county roads nearest to their homes. Private roads that led from a state or county road to the ranch house were not traveled by the school buses. Since a ranch house could be a half mile to several miles from a state or county road, parents would drive their children to the bus stop or provide a car for their children to drive to meet the bus. Although the routine of having school buses travel only on state and county roads had been discussed periodically, the practice had remained that no buses would travel private roads.

Charley Johnson, the newest member of the school board, was a rancher and lived a mile and a half from the county road. Charley had three children attending the Meade public schools, two in elementary school and one in middle school. Mr. Johnson advocated having school buses travel on private farm roads so that students could board at their front door. He brought up the topic at several board meetings although it was not an official agenda item; each time the city board members had ruled, and his request was not given much consideration before it was rejected.

Superintendent Hill had attended a Thursday and Friday meeting held by the State Department of Education to provide information on new legislative provisions for teacher certification and special education funding formulas. He went to his office Saturday morning to clear mail off his desk and see what items needed attention. Among the numerous items that awaited him was a letter from Lawrence Hutton. Lawrence was in charge of transportation. He drove one bus route, assigned 11 bus drivers, provided training for drivers, was in charge of bus maintenance, and scheduled all drivers for out of town athletic activities.

The message from Lawrence was as follows: "Dear Mr. Hill: I ran into a situation that is serious and I have taken steps to remove a driver from duty. I have looked into the situation and am sure of what has taken place. Charley Johnson has asked me several times if we would run a bus to his place to pick up his kids, and each time I have explained our rules about not driving on private roads.

I learned yesterday (Thursday) that Benny Goodman, the driver on the route that goes past the Johnson ranch, was ordered by Mr. Johnson to come into his ranch house and pick up his kids and that he had been doing that since a week ago Friday. Benny had not told me he was doing this, and when I asked him what was going on he indicated Johnson told him to do it and that I didn't have anything to say.

What I have done is to move Harry Jenkins to the route Benny was on, and then I got Mrs. McDaniels, one of our subs, to drive the route Jenkins has been on. I told Benny I'd be back with him when we get all this straightened out, but that in the meantime he was not driving.

I knew you would want to know what happened.

Lawrence Hutton."

Notes

1. Jacqueline P. Danzberger, "Governing the Nation's Schools: The Case for Restructuring Local School Boards," *Phi Delta Kappan,* 75(5) (January 1994): pp. 368–373.

2. Ibid., p. 368.

3. Edgar W. Knight, *Readings in Educational Administration* (New York: Henry Holt, 1953), pp. 6–15.

4. Stephen J. Knezevich, *Administration of Public Education,* 4th ed. (New York: Harper and Row, 1984), p. 276.

5. Michael D. Usdan, "The Relationship between School Boards and General Purpose Government," *Phi Delta Kappan,* 75(5) (January 1994): p. 375

6. Michael W. Kirst, "A Changing Context Means School Board Reform," *Phi Delta Kappan,* 75(5) (January 1994): p. 380.

7. Van Miller, George R. Madden, and James B. Kincheloe, *The Public Administration of American School Systems* (New York: The Macmillan Company, 1972), p. 14.

8. National Center for Educational Statistics, Office of Educational Research and Improvement, *Education Statistics on Disk* (NCES 94-670) (Washington, D.C.: U.S. Department of Education, August 1994).

9. U.S. Bureau of the Census, *Current Population Reports* (P25-1045 and P25-1112) (Washington, D.C.: Government Printing Office, 1994).

10. Miller et al., *The Public Administration of American School Systems,* p. 25.

11. William F. Schaefer, "Effective Board–Superintendent Communication: A Two-Way Street," *ASBA Journal* 21(4)(1991): p. 25.

12. *Roles and Relationships of School Boards and Superintendents* (Joint AASA–NASB Committee) (Arlington, Va.: American Association of School Administrators, 1980), pp. 3–4.

13. Kenneth Bird, "Critical Factors in Superintendency Transition" (unpublished doctoral dissertation, University of Nebraska—Lincoln, August 1993).

14. Jacqueline P. Danzberger, "Governing the Nation's Schools," p. 368.

15. Ibid., p. 369.

16. Ibid., p. 372.

17. Thomas L. Krepel, Louis V. Paradise, and Marilyn L Grady, "Facing Opposite Directions? Local School Board Responses to the National Goals for Education," *Planning and Changing,* 24(172) (January 1993): p. 2.

18. Quotes in items 3–11 are from Danzberger, "Governing the Nation's Schools," p. 372.

19. Thomas E. Glass, *The 1992 Study of the American School Superintendency: America's Education Leaders in a Time of Reform* (Arlington, Va.: American Association of School Administrators, 1992), p. 41.

20. C. Emily Feistritzer, "A Profile of School Board Presidents," *School Boards: Changing Local Control,* ed. by P. F. First and H. J. Walberg (Berkeley, Calif.: McCutchan, 1992), p. 130.

21. Glass, *1992 Study,* p. 40.

22. "Twelfth Annual Survey of School Board Members: Here's Looking at You," *American School Board Journal,* 177 (1990): p. 34.

23. Marilyn L. Grady and Miles T. Bryant, "Critical Incidents between Superintendents and School Boards: Implications for Practice," *Planning and Changing,* 20(4) (1991): pp. 207–221.

24. Marilyn L. Grady, Theresa Ourada-Sieb, and Linda H. Wesson, "Women's Perceptions of the Superintendency," *Journal of School Leadership,* 4 (March 1994): p. 157.

25. Ibid.

26. Glass, *1992 Study,* p. 55.

27. Grady et al., "Women's Perceptions of the Superintendency," p. 161.

28. Ibid., p. 168.

29. *Roles and Relationships of School Boards and Superintendents,* p. 5.

30. Miller et al., *The Public Administration of American School Systems,* p. 59. (See n. 7.)

31. Arthur Blumberg and Phyllis Blumberg, *The School Superintendent Living with Conflict* (New York: Teachers College Press, 1985), p. 72.

32. Burton Nygren, "Two-Party Tune Up," *American School Board Journal,* 178 (July 1992): p. 35.

33. Sidney A. Freund, "Superintendent: Here's How I Stay Friends with the Board President," *American School Board Journal,* 175(6) (June 1988): p. 39.

34. Glass, *1992 Study,* p. 35.

35. Ibid., p. 36.

36. Joy J. Rogers, "Good-bye Honeymoon," *American School Board Journal,* 178 (September 1992): p. 31.

37. Danzberger, "Governing the Nation's Schools," p. 370. (See n. 1.)

38. Daniel L. Burke, "Sorting Out Roles for School Board Members," *School Administrator, 2*(49) (February 1992): p. 47.

39. Glass, *1992 Study,* p. 46.

40. Elizabeth Donohoe Steinberger, "Superintendent–School Board Relations That Work," *School Administrator, 7*(51) (August 1994): p. 14.

41. Knezevich, *Administration of Public Education,* p. 280. (See n. 4.)

42. Verla Insko, "How to Keep Your Board on Your Side," *Executive Educator* 8(9) (September 1986), p. 22.

43. Ibid.

44. Glass, *1992 Study,* p. 7.

45. Ibid., p. 44.

46. Richard T. Castallo, Janice Greco, and Thomas McGowan, "Clear Signals," *American School Board Journal,* 179 (February 1992): p. 33.

47. Ibid.

48. Glass, *1992 Study,* p. 42.

Chapter 7

Leadership for Educational Planning

Every superintendent plans. Some superintendents have a natural or intuitive ability to do a good job of planning and are able to supplement this talent by acquiring added techniques through experience and observations. Natural and intuitive planning skills need not be the total foundation on which planning takes place; there is a growing knowledge base on which superintendents can draw to enhance their planning skills.

The environment in which planning takes place in a local school district has changed markedly over recent decades. No longer can superintendents sit in the privacy of their offices, develop plans, and send memorandums to each building principal and expect positive results. Nor can meaningful planning be accomplished simply through the use of formulas and technological devices. Planning is largely a people process; a high level of human interaction is required.

Planning to maintain the status quo can be accomplished with relative ease and limited staff involvement. The security generated by planning strictly for maintenance is, however, false. True security comes from envisioning what direction a school district should be moving, enlisting community and board support, and leading staff to plan and implement improvements. As Waterman[1] and Toffler[2] forcefully point out, those who are convinced that the past is equal to the future will have their world shaken and will lose to new leaders and perhaps new agencies. Sound planning is required of superintendents if public education for all American children and youth is to be achieved and public education is to survive.

In this chapter we present information about two basic levels of planning. First, we discuss strategic planning, and second, we focus on operational planning. In this text, both strategic and operational planning are based on systems theory, which we also summarize and relate to the planning process. Planning, especially strategic planning, is closely related to the development of school policy. Just as school policy (see Chapter 5) is basic to a well-organized, smoothly operating district, strategic planning is also a fundamental process for the development of a school system that will not only survive in the future, but contributes to the maximum human potential of all children and youth.

Finally, we argue that planning implies change. Thus, if change is to be achieved in the educational establishment, superintendents should be students of the management of change.

What Is Planning?

Planning is defined and carried out in many different ways. The dictionary contains several definitions of planning. A generic definition, applicable in most settings, is: Planning consists of the formulation of a scheme or program for the accomplishment or attainment of a prescribed outcome.

Planning has been described as occurring at three fundamental levels. *Strategic planning* is first in importance to the superintendent of schools. Second is *long-range planning,* which may extend over several years. The third level of planning is generally referred to as *operational planning.*

Strategic planning came to education from work done in the military, governmental agencies, and the business world.[3] Strategic planning is a process designed to create the history of an institution. Strategic planning is, according to Below, Morrisey, and Acomb,[4] "a framework for carrying out strategic thinking, direction, and action leading to the achievement of consistent and planned results." One of the earliest, yet perhaps most durable, definitions of strategic planning as it applies to education came from Cope[5] when he wrote, "Strategic planning is concerned with the long-term development of an institution, its essential character, its personality, its essence . . . [and] with decisions which have enduring effects that are difficult to reverse." There is a significant dimension to strategic planning that was identified early in its adaptation to education by Olsen and Eadie[6] when they wrote that strategic planning "is a disciplined effort to produce fundamental decisions shaping the nature and direction" of an institution. A key word in Olsen and Eadie's definition is "disciplined." An active leader in strategic planning, Cook,[7] captured the essence from many predecessors when he wrote:

> Strategic planning is the means by which an organization constantly recreates itself to achieve extraordinary purposes. . . . Only strategic organizations can do strategic planning. . . . A strategic organization is *autonomous.* Strategic organizations have the prerogative and the responsibility to determine their own *identity* . . . [and] have the prerogative and responsibility for acquisition and allocation of *resources* . . . for providing the *vision, values* and *leadership* that control, guide, and sustain.

The term *strategy* can convey different meanings. Some planners use this term synonymously with *goal.* Others use a literal definition in which a strategy is used to mean an "organization's preselected means or approach to achieving its goals and objectives while coping with current and future . . . conditions."[8] The term *strategy* is used in this text as the approach or means selected to achieve a goal.

The history of strategic planning in education has been mixed. Ultimately, planning must affect what happens to children and youth, and many plans carrying the label of "strategic" have not helped school personnel bring about desired or needed improvements. Strategic planning, properly done and led by visionary superintendents who possess strong leadership skills, can be the means of moving to the future and determining what that future will provide educationally for children and youth.

Some consider *long-range planning* to be the same as strategic planning. There are, however, some key distinguishing characteristics. Long-range planning is a form of operational planning typically involving a time span of more than one year, such as a long-range plan for roof or bus replacement extending from 6 to 17 years.

Long-range planning does not involve the in-depth analysis of the environmental issues and does not draw on values and political issues to the extent typically found in the strategic planning process. Strategic planning is used to set the compass heading for an institution; long-range planning is typically of lesser import and subservient to the direction set in strategic planning.

Operational planning is an approach to designing ways to accomplish desired outcomes. The outcomes can range from building a district budget, planning for a new building, planning an agenda for a board meeting, arranging for the use of facilities for a professional meeting, planning the yearly calendar, and planning a daily schedule. If a process requires organizing time, space, facilities, equipment, people, or information, the process can be termed operational planning. Operational planning is usually, but not always, considered an effort that will extend for no more than one year. Operational planning might be very informal or casually done mentally. By contrast, the development of a school budget, which is an operational planning process, is much more formal, with legal considerations and specified forms to be used.

Operational planning may be an outgrowth of a strategic planning effort. Typically, once a strategic plan has been developed, in which strategic goals have been specified and prioritized, operational planning teams are selected to devise a plan for reaching the identified objectives or goals. In this sense, strategic planing has been extended and made the transition into operational planning. Most operational planning is, however, carried out with less formal ties to a strategic plan.

Systems Theory

Systems theory provides concepts for looking at planning and gaining insight into how the superintendent's plans can be more workable. The basic concept of systems theory is that an entity consists of parts that enable it to function as a whole. At the same time, each entity or system is related to a larger system.

There are natural systems, such as the universe and its many subsystems; natural systems on the earth include weather systems and river systems, plants and animals. People also create systems, which in turn can be divided into mechanical or technical systems and social or political systems. A pair of pliers is a simple mechanical system, and a spaceship is a very complex technical system. An example of a social system is an informal group of peers who meet regularly to have lunch and discuss mutual problems. Such a system may be loosely coupled and lack formal documentation. By contrast, a government is a much more complex and formalized system, and the educational enterprise or bureaucracy is a subsystem within the total governmental system. A local school system is a subsystem within the total educational enterprise in a given state.

While every system is composed of parts and is also tied or related to a larger system, each system is identifiable and definable as an entity in itself, such as a local school district. A system can also be related to many larger systems in a complex mesh of networks. People who write about the Internet, confronted with trying to explain a very complex set of almost untraceable, yet very real, relations, have ultimately referred to the Internet as a cloud or foggy entity that is made up of many parts and tied together with key subcomponents that enable it to function.[9]

School superintendents who can apply the concepts of systems theory to planning can devise plans that are more likely to be functional. Systems theory concepts key to the development of plans are (a) a system demonstrates a wholeness, as it is an identifiable entity that functions as a whole; (b) a system is made up of parts that work in a synchronized way to enable the whole to function; (c) systems also relate to larger systems of which they are a part; (d) systems are dynamic—they work, and if they do not work they atrophy or are discarded; (e) systems have a life span; (f) systems serve a purpose, either by design or by some natural placement; (g) systems, if they are to survive, must be self-correcting or self-perpetuating; thus, they have a feedback subsystem; (h) systems may be very tightly structured or they may be dominated by loose connections (referred to as "loosely coupled"); and (i) systems are predictable.

The inner workings of a system in which the elements or subsystems function together are synchronized because subfunctions, or parts, are designed to complement each other and work together as a whole. This characteristic of a system is referred to as internal consistency. The feedback process is the means by which internal consistency is maintained so the system can be fine-tuned. Once internal consistency of a system deteriorates or is destroyed, the system will either self-correct or it will stop functioning.

In a complex, loosely coupled system such as a bureaucracy, not only do individual personalities and capabilities enter into the complex nature of the system, but political influences become a major force on the total system. Political influence is typically not identified as a component of a system; however, in a bureaucracy, politics may become the driving force, or subsystem, which determines the ultimate nature of the total system and its relationship to larger systems. A novice observer might well conclude that the political influence makes the total system unpredictable, while the "ward boss" of the bureaucracy may smile and say, "I told you so," after having predicted the outcome that seemed so unexpected to the novice.

Those who look at difficult predictions, whether it be the weather or a bureaucracy, may find greater understanding and the ability to look past the "science of chaos" once they develop more insights to systems theory. The science of chaos, as described by Gleick,[10] has captivated the imagination of some observers impressed with what has been termed the lack of predictability found in many settings. Greater predictability emerges, however, as observers gain insights of how systems theory is manifest in organizations.

The Importance of Planning

Educators have a long history of planning. From the time of Thomas Jefferson through the formulation and application of educational philosophy at the turn of the twentieth century, there have been leaders who, as planners, shaped the direction of the educational establishment. Throughout the decades, the pendulum has swung between educational and political leadership, as movements, such as the Progressive Education Project, were under-taken during the 1930s, the Trump plan of the 1950s and 1960s emerged, or the educa-tional legislation following the launching of *Sputnik* was implemented. Since the release of *A Nation at Risk*[11] in 1984, there have been repeated calls from legislators and the media for educational reform, restructuring, choice, vouchers, site-based management, and vari-ous other approaches—all intended to change the educational enterprise. Unfortunately, many well-intentioned designs to improve education have been ill-conceived.

The calls for improving, or making wholesale changes in, the educational enterprise have grown to a din of confusing signals, as special interest groups fervently call out and charge at the establishment. Amid the clamor for change, thoughtful leaders in education have been trying to sort out ways of improving the structure. Thoughtful efforts are diffi-cult to maintain, as superintendents are confronted with a need to drain the swamp when they are hip deep in alligators. The situation is further exacerbated because the education-al establishment is being condemned for ills in society over which the school has little or no direct influence. Why are schools held accountable for so many adults using illegal drugs, for homes that have changed so radically they have become a major form of disrup-tion in place of a haven for children and youth, or for violence that has been popularized and glamorized?

Increased competition for tax dollars has grown to frightful proportions. State and fed-eral budgets swell with the burden of entitlement programs, and school budget planners work under legislative limitations. School officials have accepted the mantle of teaching values ostensibly as a counterculture movement. But a truism persists—as a society demonstrates disruptive behavior, disruptive behavior will be brought into the schools by the pupils, who come from society.

The need for improving education is clear. The means of making improvements will come from educational leaders who have vision and a high level of skill in planning. Edu-cational planning needs to involve strategic planning. The mission of education should be clarified, and the goals that are to be met specified and prioritized so that educators have a major voice in shaping the future. Operational planning needs to be carefully crafted, with the concepts derived from systems theory incorporated.

The Strategic Planning Process

Strategic planning includes numerous approaches, various techniques, and some inconsis-tency in terminology. Some approaches to strategic planning have involved long-time com-mitments from many persons. In other instances, partially as a reaction to the severe time requirement for completing a strategic plan, quick and dirty approaches have been devised to shortcut the process to give an economical means of generating a strategic planning doc-ument. Experience has proven that the strategic planning process can be compressed through intensifying procedures and using special group processes; however, the quick and dirty economy approaches will typically generate little more than a paper document, pos-sibly slick-looking, but with little or no meaning.

Strategic planning is a part of a planning continuum that starts with a *perceived need,* a *vision,* and a *commitment.* The process then moves into *strategic analysis,* advances to the clarification of a *mission,* followed by identifying *goals* and putting the goals in order of importance. The process then moves forward to *strategic management,* where operational planning and the selection of *strategies* are designed to achieve goals. Finally, the process includes a procedure for *monitoring, evaluating,* and *regenerating.* A strategic planning sequence is depicted in Figure 7–1.

Preliminary Steps to Strategic Planning

Debates occur periodically about whether strategic planning should be grass-roots or initiated by the superintendent. Without vision and commitment by the superintendent, the likelihood of major, planned changes succeeding are like the proverbial snowball in the realms below.

Strategic planning demands the highest qualities of leadership of the superintendent. The superintendent must be able to communicate the sense of urgency and the general vision that is held for the school, while leading others in sharing that felt need and vision. Human relations skills along with the ability to resolve conflicts, to enlist others, and to work effectively within the political realities of the setting are required. The superintendent must also be able to draw on data and the information base to build a sound foundation for planning. The process also calls forth organizational and managerial skills.

Dealing effectively with and enlisting important others are central to the strategic planning process. Although the key person in the strategic planning process, the superintendent cannot do strategic planning in isolation. Successful strategic planning requires the involvement of school board members, staff, parents, and patrons, and representation by students.

The superintendent, working in conjunction with key leaders, should select a group of opinion leaders from the district that will provide a cross section of all segments of the school and community. The number of opinion leaders enlisted may vary according to local conditions. There may be a temptation, when identifying opinion leaders to

FIGURE 7–1   A Sequence of Strategic Planning

SOURCE: Ward Sybouts, *Planning in School Administration: A Handbook.* Reprinted with permission of Greenwood Publishing Group, Inc., Westport, CT. Copyright © 1992 by Ward Sybouts.

serve on the strategic planning team, to identify only persons who are power brokers and who are known to be "on the right side of the fence." While power brokers are important members of a strategic planning council, one must have opinion leaders who represent the broad spectrum of the total community, quite likely including some outside the circles of power. A representative group of opinion leaders is much better than a stacked deck.

The size of the strategic planning team must be decided. Different authorities suggest different limits on the size of a strategic planning team or council. Twenty-four persons on a team usually affords a wide array of people and also keeps the group to a manageable size. If it is necessary to exceed 24 persons on the team, special procedures, such as the Live Modified Delphi (LMD), can be used to actively involve all persons in a constructive way.[12] The LMD is a group process that capitalizes on some of the key elements of the Delphi Technique, such as anonymity, controlled feedback, and recycling content derived from the best thinking of opinion leaders for refinement. In addition, the LMD incorporates some of the elements of the Nominal Group Technique (NGT). The LMD can bring the thinking of a group of 25 to 125 people together in an efficient, effective way. The LMD produces consensus and, at the same time, fosters a high level of ownership on the part of the participants. Finally, the LMD is a time-efficient process.

A person who may play a key role in the strategic planning process is a facilitator. Some school districts have on staff a person trained in the process of strategic planning and qualified to serve as a facilitator. In districts where a facilitator is not available, the superintendent should consider acquiring the services of a person who is competent in the strategic planning process.

While the strategic planning council of opinion leaders is being formed, relevant data for the planning process need to be collected. Some data, such as demographic data, can be collected before the strategic planning process formally starts. Staffing information can be gathered, as well as quality measures of the educational program, assessments of facilities, follow-up data about graduates, socioeconomic conditions in the district, and any other baseline information that may provide insights into the needs of the school. The preliminary data should not be gathered simply to tell what a great job the school district is doing; data should be gathered in a mode of "problem finding." The school district's old mission statement should be included in the documentation provided to the strategic planning council. The superintendent, members of the central staff, or the facilitator may also identify key references or mediated materials that come from credible futurists. These materials can be used to prime forward thinking on the part of the strategic planning council. Data are needed that will present an honest view of conditions as they exist and will also stimulate people to look up from their daily involvements and focus on the future.

Planning the schedule for the strategic planning process is an important task. The schedule must afford the planners enough structured time to accomplish the task at hand. One and a half to three days are generally recommended for the strategic planning teams to go through the initial planning process. With the enlistment of opinion leaders, with equipment, time, and space, and with preliminary information collated and in the hands of the strategic planning council, the formal process of strategic planning is ready to be implemented.

There are three basic components to the strategic planning process: (a) the *strategic analysis,* (b) *clarifying the mission,* and (c) *strategic management.*

Strategic Analysis

Strategic analysis is a process in which the strategic planning council reviews all the environmental considerations they feel have a significant influence on the school system. There is no fixed list of "significant influences." The kinds of information external to the school district that are often considered include the work of futurists, a study of trends related to the district locally as well as trends that draw on worldwide conditions, relevant laws, demographic considerations, cultural climate, consideration of technological advances, economic considerations and projections, political climate, family conditions, and geographic data. The consideration of external influences is referred to as an *external environmental scan.*

An *internal environmental scan* is also needed in which conditions within the school system, which may be analyzed in the form of resources and constraints, are examined in light of their impact on the future of the school. Topics typically covered include data about the student population, an inventory of staffing resources, facilities, equipment, internal politics, and school climate. Along with the internal scanning, a discussion of the philosophy and values that are fundamental to the school system should be included. There may also be data that have come from needs assessments conducted in the district.

At the conclusion of the strategic analysis, the discussion should bring the strategic planning council to a point of agreement on basic assumptions and fundamental issues. Brevity in summarizing the basic agreements allows them to be communicated to all interested persons quickly and succinctly. The form in which conclusions are stated is frequently headed "We Believe"; in other instances, the form is referred to as a "We Agree Statement."

Examples of items contained in a concluding statement of agreement from different strategic planning efforts in schools are:

- We believe that all people are capable of learning.
- We believe education is a lifelong experience.
- We believe public education is fundamental to the existence of a democracy and the mobility of its citizens.
- We believe education is a force for change that both influences and responds to human events.
- We believe excellence justifies the investment.
- We believe diversity enriches life.
- We believe public education benefits the entire community.

These illustrations are only a few paraphrased examples chosen from various documents; they do not present a comprehensive view of what may be contained in a "We Agree" or "We Believe" statement. The content of such statements is important; perhaps equally important is the process that people go through to reach consensus. Through the consensus reached in the process, a base is built upon which all other elements of the strategic planning process, and ultimately the operation and future direction of the school district, will follow.

Clarifying the Mission—Goals and Priorities

Mission clarification is the second major component of the strategic planning process. One can hardly imagine a school district that does not have a mission statement. Mission statements, however, carry greater significance in some districts than in others. Regardless of the status of a mission statement, the statement needs to be reviewed by the strategic planning council to determine if it contains the vision, focus, and clarity deemed appropriate in light of the strategic analysis. Practice has shown that strategic planning councils will revise and edit old statements in most instances. Such changes are appropriate and even desirable, since they are a reflection of the emerging ownership that becomes so important if the strategic planning process is to result in meaningful improvements in a school system.

A mission statement should be brief, visionary, and meaningful. Examples of actual mission statements can illustrate the approach used by some planners:

- The mission of the Alpha Public Schools, home, and community is to ensure all students learn the skills, knowledge, and attitudes necessary for responsible living in a changing global society; this will be accomplished by a staff dedicated to excellence in a safe, caring environment.
- The mission of the Beta Public Schools is to develop independent learners through an educational program, as identified by the school, family, and community, which prepares the learner to be a contributing and responsible member of society by providing

    1. A qualified, innovative, caring, student-centered staff
    2. A comprehensive and dynamic curriculum
    3. An environment conducive to the learning process

Goals should emerge from the mission statement that can be used to translate it into workable, achievable components. Goals may be generated by asking the strategic planning council members to list their best hopes and greatest fears and directing them to indicate how they would achieve their hopes and avoid or prevent their fears. As the list of goals is developed, continual reference should be made to the "We Agree" or "We Believe" statements, as well as the philosophical base and needs assessments, to assure that internal consistency between goals and the basic assumptions is maintained.

Setting priorities: Although it may be known in advance that a school staff will only be able to focus on a few goals for the school at any one time, the list of goals generated by the strategic planning council should not be restricted to what is believed to be a workable list. All goals should be listed for consideration. Once listed, goals need to be put in order of importance. Facilitators, employing such techniques as the Nominal Group Technique, can help the strategic planning council arrive at a set of priorities to be recommended to the school board.

Strategic Management

The third phase of the process is putting the strategic plan into operation. The strategic planning council members may recommend some strategies. They should be informed of progress and conferred with as the strategic management efforts move forward; however, the intense involvement of the council members with the strategic analysis and the clarification of the mission and goals will mark the completion of their primary responsibilities.

The board of education should review the recommended list of goals and determine those which should receive attention. As stated previously, not all goals should or can be acted on immediately. Goals not given immediate consideration should be held and reconsidered at the end of a year as the strategic planning process moves into a second cycle, or second year. Superintendents need to make thoughtful decisions when working with the board and recommending how much can be undertaken. A concerted effort should be made not to try to address too many goals at any given time.

The superintendent is ready, once board approval is given, to assign planning teams to develop operational plans for each strategic goal. Timelines need to be set for the completion of the process. Each planning team should have a chairperson who has expertise in the area under consideration. The chairperson should be allocated the needed support staff and resources to do the job; there should be a task force of six to eight persons who are not only competent in the intended area but who are interested and highly motivated. One of the key resources that an operational planning task force needs is time. The development of an operational plan designed to achieve a major goal in the district cannot be done by people who are expected to plan as an overload to an already full schedule. As much as two to three months may be required to put together an adequate operational plan.

Each strategic goal planning task force needs to have a clear charge from the superintendent and inservice on how to craft an operational plan designed to reach a strategic goal. The task force assigned to develop a plan for each strategic goal should be monitored and supported by the superintendent so that at a prescribed time recommendations for each plan can be submitted to the board for approval. Boards then have the responsibility of reviewing each plan and (a) accepting it, (b) asking that it be revised, or (c) rejecting it. Once a strategic goal operational plan is accepted, the board should authorize the allocation of needed resources to implement the goal. At the end of each school year, the strategic planning documents and the process should be reviewed. Basic assumptions that have resulted in "We Agree" statements need to be discussed and the mission statement scrutinized. As some goals are accomplished, previously listed goals that were not among those initially dealt with should be reviewed, and new and emerging goals studied. Just as the school and community were involved in the original strategic planning effort, so should they continue to be involved in the renewal process each year.

The Operational Planning Process

While it has been suggested there are a number of *steps* involved in operational planning *models,* it is more appropriate to say there are several *concepts* that should be incorporated in the planning *process.* Steps and models give an impression of filling in the squares or painting by the numbers. No great painter created a work of art painting by the numbers, and a parallel can be suggested for planning. Planning is less likely to contain any genius, or even a high level of craft, if it is simply based on steps and models. Planning is much more likely to serve people well if it has incorporated the basic systems concepts in a process that is fluid and adaptable, yet one that is conceptually solid. Elements of a conceptual framework for the planning process are shown in Figure 7–2. We discuss the concepts shown there in the following sections.

1. Review Basic Assumptions

Any planning effort should consider basic assumptions related to environmental elements. The basic assumptions to be considered in operational planning are not a fixed list, but vary

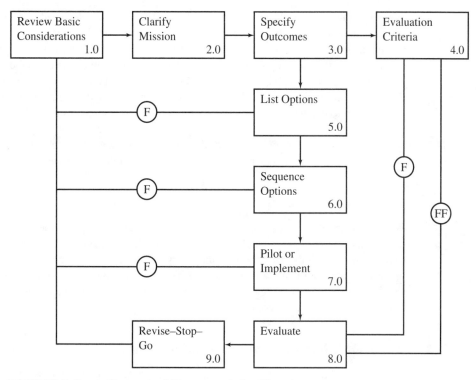

FIGURE 7–2   A Conceptual Framework for Planning

SOURCE: Ward Sybouts, *Planning in School Administration: A Handbook.* Reprinted with permission of Greenwood Publishing Group, Inc., Westport, CT. Copyright © 1992 by Ward Sybouts.

with each project, just as the areas to review in the environmental scanning of strategic analysis differ with each setting. The relevant factors for building a district budget, or financial plan, will obviously differ from the points that may need to be considered in planning to change bus routes. The degree of complexity of an operational planning project will also bear on the detail and breadth of basic considerations. If the system's rationale, that every system relates to a larger system, is valid, it then follows that a plan should be crafted so that the level of compatibility with the larger environment is as great as possible.

2.   *Clarify the Purpose to Be Accomplished*

The purpose of a newly created plan is often self-evident. If, for example, an operational planning effort is to carry out the mandate of a school board by developing a plan to achieve a strategic goal, the purpose is thus prescribed or mandated. Operational plans, however, often involve purposes other than achieving strategic goals.

Focusing clearly on the purpose to be accomplished can be confused with selecting strategies to reach the intended outcome. Making the distinction between purposes and strategies crucially affects how the plan is envisioned, implemented, and evaluated. For example, there may be a need in a district to enable elementary pupils to become more knowledgeable and proficient in the use of keyboards and in accessing information from various data sources. The plan could conceivably call for staff development; the acquisition of additional computer hardware; the construction of a computer laboratory; the acquisition of additional software; and the modification of the curriculum in language arts, science, and social sciences for the proposed computer competence to be integrated into the regular subjects taught. In practice, what has sometimes happened is the acquisition of computers and the renovation of space to establish a computer laboratory, and an announcement has been made: "Our goal is to get this computer lab open for the beginning of the school year." The goal, the purpose, should be to help pupils learn more and better—not to get a lab installed before the start of the school year. Although the establishment of the laboratory is an important *strategy*, building the laboratory should not be interpreted as the purpose to be achieved.

3.   Specify Outcomes

With the purpose for developing the operational plan either prescribed, as for strategic planning, or defined, as is usually the case, the planners are ready to translate the purpose to be achieved into measurable outcomes. Desired outcomes should be clearly stated; this makes it much more likely that they will be achieved. Assessment measures applied to carefully crafted outcomes can provide better information and lead to more accountability than if vague outcomes were involved.

4.   Establish Preliminary Evaluation Criteria

Relatively few planners, at this point in the operational planning process, stress the determination of general criteria for assessing outcomes.[13] While it may be more apparent in instructional planning than in planning from a managerial perspective, it is at the point where specified outcomes are stated that attention should be given to assessment criteria.

Directing attention to assessment criteria immediately after listing the outcomes focuses the planners' attention on final outcomes; it establishes a helpful mental receptivity and awareness. Another point is that it is often helpful to gather pre and post types of information. By thinking about assessment criteria early in the process and before the plan is implemented, there is less likelihood that pre-conditions will be overlooked in data collection. Finally, considering the assessment criteria early in the planning process provides a greater assurance that evaluation, both process and product, will be undertaken. One of the most flagrant omissions in educational planning and program implementation is the failure to evaluate.

5.   Identify Options

There is an old saying that there is more than one way to skin a cat. So it is with planning. When planning, multiple ways should be identified to achieve specified outcomes. Having more options generally allows better choices to be made.

When considering different options, planners should be sure that the options contemplated would lead to desired outcomes. Persons can become enamored with something having little or no relation to the specified outcomes, or there can be political pressure to employ an inappropriate option. In all aspects of operational planning, internal consistency is needed; when identifying and choosing options, the options have to match with outcomes.

6.   *Sequencing Options*

The task of sequencing options varies considerably with the nature of the project being planned. The logic that goes into sequencing the options can become obscure in complex projects. Consequently, some planning projects require specialized planning tools, such as the Program Evaluation and Review Technique (PERT) pioneered by Cook.[14] PERT was first used by space engineers; it was later adapted for the construction industry. Although there have been dozens of reworkings of PERT, Cook's original work has stood out as the basic document for educators. The biggest advance since Cook originally published his manual for the U.S. Office of Education in 1966 has been the development of computer programs to do the detailed, laborious work of creating a PERT chart once the planner has conceptualized the plan.

PERT has proven to be an excellent tool when hundreds or thousands of tasks need to be performed in a project, and it also helps to show the relationships that exist when a project has numerous facets that are conducted simultaneously. Once the plan is displayed with a PERT chart and the project is under way, PERT becomes an excellent management and monitoring tool, because the project director can keep an immediate, clear view of how the project is progressing. By reviewing the PERT chart, the project manager can see quickly if one part of the project is lagging and move resources to the area of need to keep the total project moving forward. PERT is grounded in and makes a clear application of systems theory. Figure 7–3 depicts a portion of a PERT chart. Events are depicted by circles and activities shown with arrows. Events are starting or ending points and use no time or resources. Activities use resources. The event numbers and the activity arrows can be followed sequentially through a PERT diagram. Written documentation is needed to accompany a PERT chart.

A Gantt chart is another diagramming technique; it is actually used more frequently than PERT. Typically, in a Gantt chart, events to be accomplished are laid out on a vertical axis, and then the time frames for tasks in the plan to be completed are depicted with horizontal bars placed along a timeline. Gantt charts are not as effective as PERT for depicting large numbers of tasks, nor as clear in their display of interrelationships among parallel tasks. Gantt charts and PERT were developed in the planning of two different sorts of tasks. An example of a Gantt chart is shown in Figure 7–4.

A flow chart is another means of visually depicting, with the use of icons and arrows, the steps to be completed in a plan or in some managerial process. Each icon in a flow chart carries a meaning, and the arrows show the flow, or direction, of the work to be completed in the process being depicted. Flow charts are excellent tools for displaying procedural tasks carried out in the management of a district. For example, payroll procedures could be displayed by using a flow chart. A flow chart is shown in Figure 7.5.

The LOGOS diagramming technique is applied in many planning efforts. A LOGOS chart is constructed with rectangular figures, called function boxes, and arrows. A caption and a number will be found in each rectangle. The function boxes are connected with arrows that show how one function is related to another and the sequence in which they need to be addressed (see Figure 7.2, a LOGOS chart, which also displays elements of operational planning). All the diagramming and charting techniques mentioned here can be done with computer assistance. Once a planner has conceptualized a process, the charting techniques that will best display the plan, to communicate it to others, can be determined. All charting techniques have been referred to as languages since they are used to communicate the planned project to an audience.

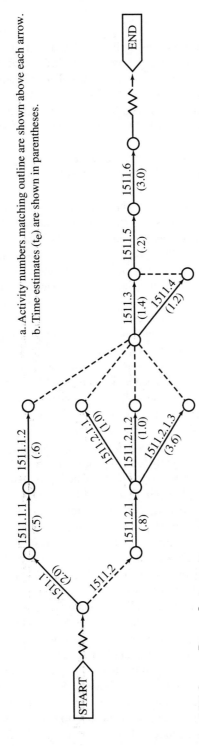

a. Activity numbers matching outline are shown above each arrow.
b. Time estimates (t_e) are shown in parentheses.

1511.0   Prepare Instruments
1511.1   Collect Critical Incidents
1511.1.1   Sort, Input to Computer
1511.1.2   Summarize & Categorize
1511.2   Develop Attitude Scale
1511.2.1   Review Literature – Conduct Searches
1511.2.1.1   Read Osgood
1511.2.1.2   Read Edwards
1511.2.1.3   Conduct Computer Search of Journals, Select, Summarize
1511.3   Construct Attitude Scale – First Draft
1511.4   Construct Likert Scale – First Draft
1511.5   Print Scales
1511.6   Pilot

FIGURE 7–3   Sample Segment from a PERT Chart Showing Instrument Preparation for the Development of Training Materials for School Superintendents, with Accompanying Outline

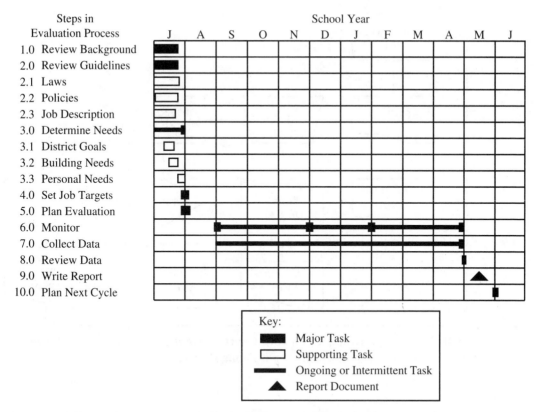

Steps in Evaluation Process	School Year

FIGURE 7–4   **An Example of a Gantt Chart, Depicting the Steps Involved in Evaluating a Building Principal**

Written explanations, referred to as documentation, generally accompany diagrams or charts depicting plans. All PERT charts will have a set of detailed written instructions and contain a cost figure for each phase of a project. Gantt charts and flow charts may or may not have accompanying written documentation. LOGOS charts typically have a written document of explanatory information. The documentation may be no more than a page or two that explains a flow chart or a LOGOS diagram, or it may be as extensive as several hundred pages and contain numerous other diagrams and engineering plans. Good charts or diagrams are an excellent way of helping the planner conceptualize a plan and providing an audience with a conceptual framework and overview of a project.

7.   *Pilot or Implement the Project*

There is some wisdom in the generalization that whenever possible a pilot program should be run before adoption and implementation of a plan. While it is possible to plan and immediately implement some simple projects, as projects get more complex it becomes increasingly important to try out the planned project. A pilot program can be time and resources well invested; it may lead to considerable savings in the long run.

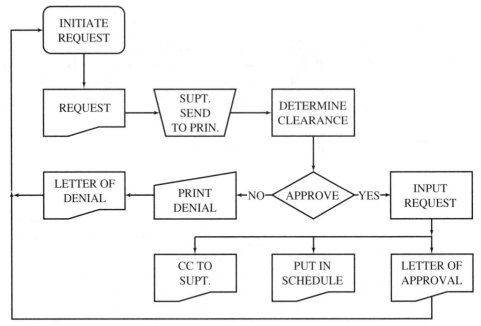

FIGURE 7–5   An Example of a Flow Chart, Depicting the Procedure for Responding to a Request for Records from a Building Principal

Piloting is not the only means of trying out a new project. In some instances, a field test, which is a form of a pilot, is advisable. A field test is a controlled use of a plan in one or a few settings over an extended period of time. Through the test, the entire district will not be committed until it is known if satisfactory results are achieved. In other situations it may be deemed most judicious to run a simulation to see if the plan works. In preliminary planning efforts, the use of scenarios can also help persons involved in the planning consider many options and give thoughtful attention to variables and implications.

The time eventually comes for the decision to implement. Implementation is when the plan is put to work for real; it is where the rubber hits the road.

8.   Evaluate the Project

When implementation of a pilot or field test takes place, the criteria for evaluation that were established with the fourth function come back into focus. The evaluation of each project needs to be tailored to fit its individual characteristics and outcomes. As previously stated, evaluation is perhaps the most unused or misused portion of our efforts in the search for excellence in education. Education is too important to leave alone to find its way home like Mary's Little Lamb. Evaluation is basic to accountability.

No plan should be proposed by a superintendent or a central administration staff, nor should any plan be submitted to the board of education, unless there is, as a component of the plan, a design for evaluation. Evaluation should generally embody both the process, or formative data, and the outcomes, or summate data. Concerted efforts should be made to make a clear linkage between project outcomes and the design of the evaluation. The casual observer might suggest that such an admonishment is unnecessary, that all evaluations are designed to measure intended outcomes. A brief illustration will underscore the need to remind educators of the importance of fitting the evaluation process to the intended outcomes.

In a secondary school in which an innovative program was being instituted, the building principal and the various client groups had concluded they wanted to focus on developing greater problem solving and self-discipline among the high school students. Program outcomes were suggested that focused on greater student use of library and technological resources to gather information. Students were to be provided with opportunities to demonstrate greater levels of responsibility for their own learning, to show better self-discipline (so that truancy and disciplinary problems would be reduced), and to become better problem solvers. At the end of the first year of the newly structured program, a board member asked the question, "Has the new program accomplished what was intended?" The topic was placed on the agenda for the following meeting to give the principal and her staff time to prepare a report. When the report was presented, the only data included were standardized test scores. There were no data collected, pre or post, that related to the specified outcomes for the new program. No tabulations had been made about the student use of the library and data searches, the frequency of truancy or disciplinary cases, or student problem-solving skills. The bulk of the report submitted to the board of education was couched in terms of how the principal perceived the program.

Managerial projects are generally easier to evaluate than instructional programs. Superintendents, and members of the administrative staff at the central office and building level, are faced with the often overwhelming problem of gathering assessment data and making evaluations of instructional programs. Instructional programs can be evaluated using behavior tests, which can cover cognitive, affective, and psychomotor measures of students; performance outcomes; and, in some situations, measures of student competencies. Educational programs can also be viewed through the collection of preassessment data; process (formative) measures that can be made as the program unfolds; outcome measures (summative); and follow-up information. Often, information related to competencies can be considered in follow-up studies.

The writings of several authorities provide solid, basic concepts for evaluation.[15] The works of these recognized authorities have been enhanced by persons like Cronbach, who translated assessment and evaluation approaches into designs for instructional improvement and provided clarity of focus. He wrote evaluation may be defined as "the collection and use of information to make decisions about an educational program."[16]

9. *Feedback*

Feedback is the last component of operational planning. Feedback loops form interconnections among all segments of a plan and, like a nervous system, keep all parts of the total plan, or system, informed about all other parts. If feedback is ignored, a system failure can occur. The persons developing and implementing a plan should be alert to signs and sounds that will provide information about how the system is functioning.

The Management of Planned Change

Plans are only as good as the results they help people achieve. A superintendent of schools can have an outstanding plan, one that is visionary and well conceived. If the superintendent is unable to gain support and enlist the help of staff, board, and community, the plan may have value only as scrap paper. To make a plan come to life and help staff achieve desired results, the planner must be able to manage the change process. Managing change is not something that is done at the conclusion of the planning process; it is fostered all the way through the planning and implementation stage.

Much research and literature is available regarding the change process. Change literature was first made available by cultural anthropologists; then the change process was studied by sociologists; and eventually scholars applied what was known about how change is fostered to such disciplines as medicine, agriculture, and eventually to educa-tion. An important strain of the change literature is the psychology of adult motivation, in which insights have been provided into how behavioral changes are motivated. In an environment in rapid transition, change is inevitable. The important thing to accomplish is change not by chance but by design—to plan not just to react to conditions, but to create an institution that will make a difference. This presents a major challenge for today's school superintendent.

Summary

Every superintendent works amid constant change, and every superintendent is involved in planning to deal with an environment in transition. Strategic planning is a powerful approach to improving the quality of education. Strategic planning is, however, often mis-used. It will help school officials only if it is, as a process, applied appropriately. When applied correctly by a superintendent who provides a vision and leadership for a board, staff, and community, strategic planning can be used as a method to generate a meaning-ful, clear direction for a district, a motivational force to strive for excellence, and a means of rising up and moving toward the creation of an educational system that will maximize the human potential of all concerned.

Operational planning is carried out at a lower level than strategic planning and is not intended to be applied in the same way. Both strategic planning and operational planning can be enhanced if the planner correctly applies the concepts derived from systems theory. Operational planning may be long-range, extending over several years, or it may be used to plan short-term projects.

The application of systems theory to the planning process involves various concepts, which in turn may be brought together as a conceptual framework for planning. Those who comprehend the conceptual framework derived from systems theory are likely to under-stand the intricacies of planning and be able to generate solid plans that yield desired results.

Finally, planning implies change; school superintendents should understand the avail-able knowledge base to gain insights into the change process and how to manage it. The literature about cultural change, as it has developed and been applied to education, and what is known about human motivation can provide a knowledge base from which super-intendents can draw when planning and implementing programs designed to achieve a planned, not imposed, future.

Discussion Questions

1. Many strategic plans have been well conceived and have yielded excellent results. By contrast, some plans, labeled as strategic, have failed to bring any positive influence to a school system. Why have strategic planning efforts been successful in some districts but not others?

2. It has been suggested that evaluation is one of the more difficult aspects of operational planning and is often ignored. Why? What are the implications?

3. What is the meaning of *internal consistency?* What are some examples of the failure to maintain internal consistency that has posed a problem for planners? Also, if internal consistency is not achieved, what can be predicted about a newly devised plan? Why?

4. Discipline in planning, it has been claimed, is essential to develop successful plans. How can a superintendent impose a forceful hand and demand that the discipline of planning be followed in a climate where site-based management is fostered and a high level of staff autonomy is encouraged?

5. What is the difference between a *conceptual framework* and a *model* for planning, and what implications can be derived from the distinction between the two?

CASE 7.1   Planning to Evaluate a Building Principal

The closing session of the state legislature was in April, and the governor began signing legislation into law. One education bill, SB 123, required that each K–12 school district with two or more building administrators submit a plan to the State Department of Education detailing how principals would be evaluated. SB 123 had an emergency provision that made it effective immediately. Thus, William Proxmeyer, Superintendent of the West Port Public Schools, had to devise a workable plan that would be approved by the board and submitted to the State Department of Education in time for implementation in the fall of the coming school year.

William called three superintendents in neighboring districts; they commiserated with each other and made a few jokes about the need for the emergency clause in the legislation. After exchanging ideas with his peers, William began putting together the plan for his district. William had a senior high school principal and assistant principal, a middle school principal, and two elementary school principals. He generally had cordial relationships with the principals, and they informally met the requirements for evaluation as previously required by the law and school board policy. The one exception was the newest elementary principal, Mr. Nelson. He was autocratic and was encountering some problems with staff members and parents. In the new legislation, SB 123, some steps were specified, and more formal procedures were required for evaluating building principals. William Proxmeyer, after reading the legislation and visiting with fellow superintendents, was not overly concerned, since the added requirements seemed to be in a day's work.

At the second board meeting in May, Superintendent Proxmeyer presented a plan for evaluating building principals that was in the prescribed form and contained the required steps specified in SB 123. The board of education chairperson had a most probing query that Mr. Proxmeyer found hard to answer as he asked, "I suppose this plan meets all the new requirements, Bill?" The plan was passed unanimously, and the next day the West Port

Public Schools plan for evaluating building principals was in the mail to the State Department of Education.

The following February, for the fourth time in the school year, Superintendent Proxmeyer met with Mr. Nelson, principal of North Side Elementary School. Mr. Nelson seemed incapable of working with students, parents, and staff, and often "told them off" in a belligerent manner. During the previous year and throughout the first half of the current year, William Proxmeyer had held informal discussions and offered friendly advice to Mr. Nelson, who was seemingly unwilling to accept Mr. Proxmeyer's counsel. Sensing that needed improvements on the part of Mr. Nelson were not materializing and being aware of the state laws that required a severance notice by March 15, Mr. Proxmeyer decided to ask Mr. Nelson for his resignation, to be made effective June 30.

Mr. Nelson returned eight days later with a letter from his attorney and documentation that set forth a number of inconsistencies and failures to comply with the state law. A claim was made that the local district policy was in conflict with the law, and formal written procedures with charges and a formal plan for helping him to overcome the deficiencies, as specified by SB 123, had not been provided.

Superintendent Proxmeyer met with the board and its attorney in executive session and reviewed the situation. Because of the informal approach in practice in the district, he did not have sufficient documentation to ask for the resignation of Mr. Nelson, according to their attorney. Mr. Nelson claimed the district had not provided him with a formal plan to overcome deficiencies (required by SB 123 and established by the most recently approved plan for principal evaluation on file with the State Department of Education) and the plan for principal evaluation was not followed nor was it in agreement with the old school district policy. According to the district's attorney, Mr. Nelson's claims were of such a nature that the district could not ask him for his resignation or release him from his contract. The following year, Mr. Nelson had upgraded his credentials but was still principal at North Elementary School in West Port.

Questions

1. Could there be a question about the internal consistency found between SB 123, the local policy, and the manner in which the process of dismissing a principal in West Port was followed?

2. In light of systems theory, in which it is pointed out a system is a part that must work in a synchronized way and at the same time be compatible with the larger system of which it is a part, what conclusions can be reached about the West Port plan for evaluating building principals?

Inbasket Exercise

INBASKET 7.1

Politics and Planning

The Background and Setting

In the fall of the current school year, the superintendent of the Mayfield Public School District, with full approval from the seven members of the board of education, took steps to launch a strategic planning effort. The board minutes of July 7 contained the formal motion and the roll-call vote to proceed with the strategic planning effort. Board members assured that support would be given to the process and financial resources would be allocated when plans were finalized, subject to the final approval of the board of education. A facilitator who had a good reputation for working effectively with school systems was contracted. A Strategic Planning Council of 24 opinion leaders from the school and community was formed, which included two school board members and two students, one from the middle school and one from the senior high school. The media was kept abreast of the strategic planning effort; parents and patrons received special newsletters and memorandums; and a small group meeting to get answers to questions and respond to suggestions was held. A schedule of presentations was set in motion to provide speakers to all service clubs and churches. Reports were made at each board meeting that followed.

During September, the Strategic Planning Council met with the facilitator and, as a result of the extended planning sessions, came forth with an entirely new mission statement and set of goals. The newly revised mission statement was based on a list of 21 statements of beliefs and philosophy. Seventeen goals grew out of the strategic planning sessions. When the goals were prioritized, three goals stood out as being most important. They were deemed of such importance by Council members that it was recommended to the board that resources be dedicated during the first year of implementation of the strategic planning effort to the three goals.

You, as superintendent of schools in the Mayfield district, personally wrote the executive summary for the strategic planning process. When presenting the set of recommendations to the board of education, you felt very comfortable with the way things were formed and with the priorities recommended. At the November board meeting, the chairman entertained a motion to (a) accept the report from the Strategic Planning Council and (b) instruct the superintendent of schools to appoint planning teams to develop operational plans with the intent of implementing the three top priorities as recommended by the Council. The three planning teams were subsequently appointed, and progress reports were given to the board regularly. The work of the three planning teams had progressed on schedule, and drafts of their plans and accompanying recommendations were being readied and were scheduled for the June board meeting.

The Situation

Approximately 10 days prior to the May board meeting, you sent a note to each board member, in which you reminded them of the upcoming meeting and asked them, as was the practice in the district, if they had items to be included on the agenda. A few days later you received the following correspondence from Mr. Marshall J. Banks, the oldest member on the board in age and tenure. Mr. Banks was in his fourth term as a board member and carried a considerable amount of influence with other board members. The official agenda item suggested by Mr. Banks was accompanied by a memorandum, which he labeled "off the record."

MEMORANDUM   April 29

To: _____, Superintendent
From: Marshall
Re: Board Agenda Item for May 3

Item for the Agenda: Review of the advisability of continued investment in the strategic planning process.

Rationale: The district has spent a considerable amount of time and resources in the strategic planning process during this current school year. In light of the time invested and in light of the direction the strategic planning is taking, it is incumbent upon the members of the board of education to make a careful analysis of what has been accomplished, the direction taken, and consider terminating the strategic planning effort.

Enclosed with this memorandum was the following note, which was marked "personal/confidential." Following the salutation the message read as follows:

I simply want to express my personal concerns to you so that you will know where I am coming from. This is strictly off the record, but you need to know my thinking and what Willis and Jon [two other board members] are also saying. We know our needs and we know our budget limits so we don't want all this time and fuss over strategic goals and all that stuff about a mission statement. There is a lot to lose if we go ahead and keep people thinking that the board is going to approve of a lot of expensive changes. With budget limits, we simply cannot give the teachers everything they want.

There is another thing that is not going down very well with the three of us. We were elected to the board and it is our job to run the school, not a group of people on something called a strategic planning council. Frankly, I personally think this whole thing should be stopped before it is too late.

Your Action

Decide what you, as superintendent, need to do with the request you have been given by one of your board members and what you should do about the "confidential" memo from that board member. Write your response indicating the action you would take and then explain why you would take such action.

Notes

1. Robert. H. Waterman Jr., *The Renewal Factor* (New York: Bantam Books, 1987).

2. Alvin Toffler, *Powershift Knowledge, Wealth, and Violence at the Edge of the Twenty-first Century* (New York: Bantam Books, 1990).

3. E. E. Chaffee, "The Concept of Strategy: From Business to Higher Education," in *Higher Education: Handbook of Theory and Research,* ed. by J. C. Smart (New York: Agathon Press, 1985).

4. Patrick J. Below, George L. Morrisey, and Betty L. Acomb, *The Executive Guide to Strategic Planning* (San Francisco: Jossey-Bass, 1988).

5. Robert C. Cope, *Strategic Policy Planning: A Guide for College and University Administrators* (Littleton, Colo.: Ireland Educational Corporation, 1978).

6. John B. Olsen and Douglas C. Eadie, *The Game Plan; Governance with Foresight* (Washington, D.C.: Council of State Planning Agencies, 1982).

7. William J. Cook Jr., *Strategic Planning,* rev. ed. (Arlington, Va.: American Association of School Administrators, 1990).

8. Lester A. Digman, *Strategic Management: Concepts, Decisions, Cases* (Plano, Tex.: Business Publications, 1986).

9. Ed Krol, *The Whole Internet User's Guide and Catalog* (Sebastopol, Calif.: O'Reilly and Associates, 1992).

10. James Gleick, *CHAOS: Making a New Science* (New York: Penguin Books, 1987).

11. The National Commission on Excellence in Education, *A Nation at Risk: The Imperative of Educational Reform* (Washington, D.C.: U.S. Office of Education, 1983; Cambridge, Mass.: USA Research, 1984).

12. Ward Sybouts, *Planning in School Administration: A Handbook* (Westport, Conn.: Greenwood, 1992).

13. Bela H. Banathy, *Instructional Systems* (Belmont, Calif.: Fearon, 1968); Sybouts, *Planning in School Administration.*

14. Desmond L. Cook, *Program Evaluation and Review Technique Applications in Education* (U.S. Department of Health, Education, and Welfare, Office of Education) (Washington, D.C.: U.S. Government Printing Office, 1966).

15. Blaine R. Worthen and James R. Sanders, *Educational Evaluation: Theory and Practice* (Worthington, Ohio: Charles A. Jones, 1973); George F. Madaus, Michael S. Scriven, and Daniel L Stuffle-

beam, *Evaluation Models* (Boston: Kluwer-Nijhoff, 1983); Lee J. Cronbach and P. Suppes, *Research for Tomorrow's School: Disciplined Inquiry for Education* (New York: Macmillan, 1969); Benjamin S. Bloom, Thomas J. Hastings, and George J. Madaus, *Handbook on Formative and Summative Eval-* *uation of Student Learning* (New York: McGraw-Hill, 1971).

16. Lee J. Cronbach. "Course Improvement through Evaluation," *Evaluation Models,* ed. by George F. Madaus, Michael S. Scriven, and Daniel L. Stufflebeam (Boston: Kluwer-Nijhoff, 1983), p. 105.

References

Banathy, Bela H. *Instructional Systems.* Belmont, Calif.: Fearon, 1968.

Below, Patrick. J., George L. Morrisey, and Betty L. Acomb. *The Executive Guide to Strategic Planning.* San Francisco: Jossey-Bass, 1988.

Bloom, Benjamin S., Thomas J. Hastings, and George J. Madaus. *Handbook on Formative and Summative Evaluation of Student Learning.* New York: McGraw-Hill, 1971.

Chaffee, E. E. "The Concept of Strategy: From Business to Higher Education," *Higher Education: Handbook of Theory and Research,* ed. J. C. Smart. New York: Agathon Press, 1985.

Cook, Desmond L. *Program Evaluation and Review Technique Applications in Education* (U.S. Department of Health, Education, and Welfare, Office of Education). Washington, D.C.: U.S. Government Printing Office, 1966.

Cook, William J., Jr. *Strategic Planning,* rev. ed. Arlington, Va.: American Association of School Administrators, 1990.

Cope, Robert C. *Strategic Policy Planning: A Guide for College and University Administrators.* Littleton, Colo.: Ireland Educational Corporation, 1978.

Cronbach, Lee J. "Course Improvement through Evaluation," *Evaluation Models,* eds. George F. Madaus, Michael S. Scriven, and Daniel L. Stufflebeam. Boston: Kluwer-Nijhoff, 1983.

Cronbach, Lee J., and P. Suppes. *Research for Tomorrow's School: Disciplined Inquiry for Education.* New York: Macmillan, 1969.

Digman, Lester A. *Strategic Management: Concepts, Decisions, Cases.* Plano, Tex.: Business Publications, 1986.

Gleick, James. *CHAOS: Making a New Science.* New York: Penguin Books, 1987.

Krol, Ed. *The Whole Internet User's Guide and Catalog.* Sebastopol, Calif.: O'Reilly and Associates, Inc., 1992.

Madaus, George F., Michael S. Scriven, and Daniel L. Stufflebeam. *Evaluation Models.* Boston: Kluwer-Nijhoff, 1983.

The National Commission on Excellence in Education. *A Nation at Risk: The Imperative of Educational Reform.* Washington, D.C.: U.S. Office of Education, 1983; Cambridge, Mass.: USA Research, 1984.

Olsen, John B., and Douglas B. Eadie. *The Game Plan; Governance with Foresight.* Washington, D.C.: Council of State Planning Agencies, 1982.

Sybouts, Ward. *Planning in School Administration: A Handbook.* Westport, Conn.: Greenwood Press, 1992.

Toffler, Alvin. *Powershift Knowledge, Wealth, and Violence at the Edge of the Twenty-first Century.* New York: Bantam Books, 1990.

Waterman, Robert H., Jr. *The Renewal Factor.* New York: Bantam Books, 1987.

Worthen, Blaine R., and James R. Sanders. *Educational Evaluation: Theory and Practice.* Worthington, Ohio: Charles A. Jones, 1973.

Chapter 8

<hr>

School District Governance: Policy and Regulation Development

Many persons believe that the selection of the school superintendent is the most important task that a school board will ever perform. Although this view has much merit, the school board's responsibility for adopting viable governance policy for the school district is equally important over time. Policies not only provide the direction for accomplishing the mission of the school system, they provide the school superintendent and staff with the freedom needed to determine appropriate administrative regulations for their implementation. The leadership of the school superintendent in policy development is of paramount importance. As stated by the National School Boards Association (NSBA):

> You've heard the expression many times. The Board makes policy; the administration executes it. But the administration does more. It actually runs the policy-making system. It makes it go. Without the guidance and commitment of the superintendent and the help of the administrative staff, a school board cannot function in policy development.[1]

School districts consist of different cultures; the beliefs, values, and understandings of society's divergent groups often result in differences of opinion about the significance of various educational goals as well as the ways to achieve them. A viable set of governing policies and administrative regulations is essential for realizing program direction. As noted by Rich, "all organizations and systems are regulated by policy, and educational systems are no exception. Policy not only regulates the internal operations of a system but also serves to regulate relationships among systems."[2]

This chapter provides information about the development of governance policies and administrative regulations in school systems. We present important differences between policies and regulations. So that governance policies and administrative regulations are organized and readily usable, some system of codification is essential. This chapter presents two widely utilized codification systems.

Although the school board officially adopts governing policy, the school superintendent and staff assume the major responsibility for its development. The chapter includes suggestions for school district policy and regulation development strategies and emphasizes the school superintendent's leadership role in this process.

The Evolution of Educational Goals, Policies and Regulations

It was noted in Chapter 4 that an organization's culture expresses its individuality and uniqueness. Culture is revealed in the values and ideology of the members of a social system as well as in the strategic choices made by those in the system. The goals set forth by a specific culture are evidences of such choices. *Goals* are statements of the guiding purposes of a social system and serve to provide the direction and focus that institutions within it will assume. Thus, school goals are determined within the culture of the school community and are influenced largely by cultural sanctions, the professional judgments of the school staff, and the lay judgments of individuals of the community.

Governing school board *policies* represent local adaptations to educational goals. Policies are related to the question of *what* the school district intends to do. Policies are the result of specific school board action; only the school board can adopt official school district policy, although legislative statutes, state boards of education, and the courts frequently mandate policy for school districts as well. In fact, both federal and state law serve as a buttress for much policy development in education. Policy decisions constitute the primary duty of the school board. Such decisions are logical outcomes of the stated goals and objectives of the board.

In practice, the school superintendent serves as the primary initiator of new policy nearly 70 percent of the time; board members initiate policy decisions less than 4 percent of the time. Policy initiation does vary depending on the size of the school district. As noted in a national study by Glass, "47.6 percent of large-district superintendents took the lead in policy-making, compared to 74.5 percent by superintendents in districts of between 300 and 3,000 students."[3]

Administrative regulations are specific statements related to how a policy is to be implemented. Although it is appropriate for the school board to approve regulations, they are primarily the decision of the administrative staff with input by the total school staff and lay judgments of the school community members.

The bylaws that serve to govern the school board's internal operations affect school governance. *Bylaws* are specific statements that detail the operating procedures of the school board within the limits of law. Bylaws most often include board purposes, membership and officers' duties, setting agendas, meetings and notifications, committee purposes and makeup, parliamentary procedure, quorum stipulations, types of board meetings, voting methods, public participation, and other provisions for board actions.

The central importance of understanding the unique roles of the school board and the school superintendent in the policy development process is emphasized by the American Association of School Administrators (AASA) and the National School Boards Association (NSBA):

In and out of board meetings, effective superintendents and board members know their own jobs, and know how to get them done. They know, too, what their job is *not*. . . . "the most effective board members keep a policy perspective . . . the best superintendents can assess the administrative impact of policy and balance economic realities with student needs. . . ." Those two statements show that the textbook definition of where the board's role ends (policy-making) and the administration's role begins (policy advice and implementation) is alive and well. The two jobs are probably not absolutely distinct in any school district; but there are legal and practical reasons for continuing to strive toward the textbook ideal . . . the law delegates policy-making to the board and, superintendents have the practical training in how to run schools.[4]

The foregoing section presented brief definitions of goals, policies, administrative regulations, and bylaws. Later in this chapter, we discuss specific criteria associated with policies and regulations. The following section emphasizes the need and benefits of viable governance policies and regulations for the school district and its community members.

Benefits of Governance Policies and Administrative Regulations

School Governance and School Reform

Reform, restructuring, site-based shared decision making, empowerment, and decentralization are only a few of the concepts set forth to suggest new arrangements for local school governance. Many groups and individuals have expressed concerns about the quality of school programs and the effectiveness of school governance structures. The report by the Carnegie Forum on Education and the Economy's Task Force on Teaching expressed concern as early as 1986 about America's ability to compete in world markets. The Task Force pointed out that large numbers of American children were not being prepared sufficiently to deal with the nation's future needs. The report noted that many students are dropping out of school and becoming unproductive members of society.[5]

In the governors' 1991 report on education, a subcommittee, headed by then Governor Bill Clinton, indicated that new societal demands were placing increasing pressures on America's schools. The report emphasized that advancing technology and changes in international trade were altering the structure of international competition and recommended new school structures to meet new societal demands economically and technologically.[6]

No educational group has been immune from criticism; administrator/teacher preparation institutions, school administrators, teachers, and school boards all have been included in castigations and calls for educational reform. Some states have passed legislation questioning the authority of school boards. The state of Kentucky, for example, mandated that all school districts would be operating under site-based management by 1996; many school districts in the state already are doing so.

Local school councils establish policy in collaboration with the school faculty. School councils have representation from teachers and parents and most often operate under the direction of the school principal, who chairs the council. Policy matters include decisions about curriculum, assignment of staff, time, extracurricular assignments, and other educational concerns. The relationship of the local school council and the local school board is a continuing topic of discussion and debate. The ambiguity that exists between school boards and local school councils is receiving due attention by the courts. Although authority issues between boards and councils have not been fully resolved to date, some evidence suggests that, in the future, school boards will hold the authority and responsibility for the general operation of the school district while local councils will develop policies for individual schools within the broader school board policies. In any case, school policy development remains a function of paramount importance.

In the state of Texas, every school district was required to have a plan on file by the fall of 1992 for implementing site-based management. The full impact of this mandate is yet to be determined. As was the case in Kentucky, some plan for local parent and teacher representation in the development of local school policy was required by the Texas legislation. The implementation and reactions to the site-based management mandates in Texas varied widely. While site-based management was legitimized in the state, the mandate did not make it occur. The final outcomes of this governance issue will depend on many factors, including further action by the state legislature and litigation. In Texas, as in any state, school governance is a volatile political matter. The future of site-based management will depend in large part on who does and who does not get elected to political office. Such governance matters, along with concerns for accountability, will be topics of debate for many years.

This text advocates the principles of participative management. Yet a representative school board under the strong leadership of a qualified school superintendent is the best assurance of fair and equitable educational programs for *all* students. Carnoy cautions against the implementation of reform recommendations without scientific basis. He speaks about the popularity of restructuring and notes, "For a public demanding educational improvement, any reform that looks promising is immediately attractive."[7] Certainly, societal changes and developments demand wise decisions for new policies in schools. Such decisions require renewed attention to the legislative responsibilities of school boards. The importance of issues surrounding school governance and policy development is underscored by Duke and Canady:

> Until more is known of local policy, we shall be unable to appreciate fully the impact of local control on American education. Local citizens and educators cling to the belief that they are in the best position to know what is good for the young people of their communities. The policies they develop and endorse are the formal expressions of this belief. Only by studying local school policies in a comprehensive and systematic way will we ever be able to determine if the belief is well founded.[8]

How Stakeholders Benefit by Viable School Policies

The school district's stakeholders, parents, students, and other citizens benefit in numerous ways by viable school district governance policies and administrative regulations. Such benefits include the following:

1. Policies reveal the extent to which stated goals actually are encompassed in the school system's mission. Governance policy is vested in the educational goals that evolve from community cultures. Stated policies reflect the philosophy of the school system and the community itself.

2. Policy formulation presents an essential opportunity for meaningful community involvement in school governance. The collaborative process of policy development can result in an improved understanding and personal confidence in the work of the governing board and school staff.

3. Policies and regulations serve as an important communication vehicle between the community and school district. Knowledge about intent and procedure can enhance understanding of the rationale for school practices and provide a basis for support of needed policy and regulation changes.

Policies inform the school district's various publics of board goals. The board's written policy sets forth its positions on matters of vital interest to the citizenry. Only through a close examination of the school district's governance policies can it be determined if the community's expressed desires for the educational program are being attended. Administrative regulations serve as the procedural implementation of these intentions.

How the School Board, School Superintendent, and School Staff Benefit by Viable School Policies

Benefits for School Boards

It is generally recognized that the Tenth Amendment to the U.S. Constitution gives the states the responsibility for public education in America. Thus, school boards are extensions of state legislatures, and their authority to govern a school district comes from the state. State legislatures delegate the authority for general public education to state boards of education and, in turn, to local school boards that operate within the limits of state and national law. In this sense, local school boards serve the legislative function of policy adoption. This fact undergirds the primary benefit that a school board receives from its policy responsibilities; it gives the school board the *control* it needs to set the direction for school system programs and operations. Policy decisions represent the school board's most important function; it adopts policy that focuses on what the school system is to do and to be.

Other benefits of policy and regulation development for school boards include the following:

1. Policy adoption represents a key distinction between the work of the board and the professional staff. Policy adoption represents the legislative function of the school board. The development of administrative regulations represents the executive function of the school superintendent and staff.

2. Policies and regulations constitute an irreplaceable system of communication for the governing school board; they are a fundamental informational source regarding goals and objectives that the board views as significant.

3. Policies and regulations open the way for effective utilization of personnel talents. Policies permit the optimal utilization of discretionary professional judgment and personal experience of personnel.

4. Attention to the process of policy development gives board members opportunity "to know the school district," its status and needs. Such effort lends to the knowledge base of board members and results in increased board confidence that is foundational for public and staff support.

Benefits for the Superintendent and Staff

From time to time one hears comments about "unwritten" governance policy and regulations. Such statements as, "if you put it in writing you'll have to do it" or "all that policy does is to curtail my freedom," reveal a limited view of the purposes of policy. In reality, effective school board policy gives the school superintendent and staff *more freedom* to perform their important executive function. Viable policy sets the direction for what is to be done but also gives the superintendent and staff the discretion they need to operate the school system effectively. School policies were previously defined as broad statements that allow for freedom of interpretation and execution. This freedom represents a primary benefit of policy development for the school superintendent and staff. Other benefits for the superintendent and staff are:

1. Effective policies permit decision making at the most appropriate place in the school system. Thus, both effectiveness and efficiency are facilitated.
2. Board policies represent basic statements of the school system's objectives and therefore enable each employee to implement these objectives more meaningfully.
3. Effective policies and regulations promote greater unity of action, better interpersonal relationships, and improved communication so necessary for goal achievement.

In short, everyone benefits from governance policies that legislate the intentions of the school system. Without them, a school district hardly could function as a system. Over the long term, students are the primary beneficiaries of effective governance policies and administrative regulations; effective policies result in a more effective school environment for students.

Differentiation of Governance Policies and Administrative Regulations

Previous discussion suggested certain criteria that differentiate governance policies from administrative regulations. For example, governance policies are legislature in nature and related to the question, *what* to do? Other criteria that are helpful in identifying policies are as follows:

Policies:
- are assertions of the goals of the school system; they are concerned with aims rather than procedures. They often assign the accountability for their implementation to the superintendent or other school official/unit.
- are general statements related to an area of major importance to the citizenry. They leave room for the use of discretionary judgment by the school superintendent and staff.
- are the major concern of the school board; only the board can *adopt* policy. Thus, policies are legislative in nature and can be changed only by board action or by legal action by appropriate ruling bodies.
- are applicable over long periods of time. Even though regulations for implementing a policy might change, it may not be necessary to alter the guiding policy.

Although the foregoing criteria are useful for identifying policies, they are not absolute. Some policies evolve from specific state statutes or court rulings. Such mandates often are mixtures of policy and regulations; they set forth not only *what* is expected but *how* it is to be accomplished. Nevertheless, there are numerous advantages in the separation of policies and regulations (e.g., division of labor, accountability, freedom of discretionary action). The following criteria are useful in identifying administrative regulations.

Administrative regulations:

- are related to the question, how to do? They focus more on the procedures to reach the goal than the goal itself.
- are executive in nature; they are mainly the concern of the school superintendent and staff. Regulations are precise statements that leave little room for interpretation. As an executive statement, they generally can be altered by the school superintendent without school board action.
- are procedures to carry out or implement policy, although it is possible to have a policy that is not accompanied by a set of regulations (e.g., some policies do not necessitate additional procedures, and in some cases such as court rulings and statutes of law, the procedures are explicit in the "policy" itself).

Although regulations generally do not require board action, a review of all administrative regulations by the school board serves several positive purposes. For example, such a review provides evidence that the school district's administration is meeting its regulation development responsibilities; it has made specific steps to implement stated board policy. Also, such a review by the school board can serve to identify policy areas that might have been misinterpreted by school personnel; steps can be taken to rectify regulations found to be contrary to board intent.

In some cases, board action on regulations is needed for legal purposes. On occasion, the board's approval of a regulation serves to emphasize its total support. Examples of regulations needing board action are those relating to staff salaries, increments, benefits, staff performance evaluation, dismissal, and leave provisions.

Consider the following statement of policy.

Personnel 4111
Recruitment and Selection   4112

It is the responsibility of the superintendent of schools and of persons delegated by that office to determine the staffing needs of the school district and to recruit/select qualified applicants to recommend to the school board.

There shall be no discrimination against any candidate for employment by reason of race, color, national origin, gender, creed, marital status, or age.

It shall be the responsibility of the superintendent of schools to ascertain that persons nominated for employment meet all qualifications established by law and the school board for the positions for which nominations are made.

Appropriate background checks will be completed for all persons recommended for employment within requirements set forth by law.

The foregoing policy statement reveals each of the previously stated criteria for identifying policies. The *goal/aim* of the policy is to set directions for meeting the school district's staffing needs. It focuses on *an area of primary importance to the citizenry,* the selection of quality personnel for employment in the district. The policy leaves room for *administrative discretion* concerning its implementation, although procedures must not be discriminatory. It is *legislative* in nature and cannot be altered without board action. The guidelines set forth can remain viable for a *long time period.* Finally, the policy *delegates responsibility* for recruitment and selection specifically to the school superintendent and to persons delegated by that office.

Similarly, consider the administrative regulations shown in Figure 8.1. These regulations relate specifically to personnel policy number 4112 on recruitment and selection. The regulations are executive in nature, stating the specific procedures to be followed. These regulations can be revised as necessary without change in the guiding policy. Each of the three regulations serves to answer the question of how the selection of certificated and classified employees are to be implemented. The regulations are precise statements that leave little room for interpretation.

Selected Examples of School District Policies and Regulations

This section includes examples of school district policies and their accompanying administrative regulations. These examples also serve to illustrate the specific criteria for identifying policies and regulations. Figures 8–2, 8–3, and 8–4 are examples of a policy and regulations relating to purchasing; Figures 8–5, 8–6, and 8–7 center on the important policy area of employee appraisal.

These policy and regulation examples illustrate the legislative nature of policies and the executive nature of administrative regulations. The following section centers on ways to organize policies and regulations.

The Organization and Codification of Governance Policies and Administrative Regulations

School superintendents and boards have several systems available for organizing and codifying the school district's governing policies and regulations that facilitate their use and maintenance. There is evident need to have district policies appropriately disseminated for use by community members, school employees, and school board members. If the policy manual is to be utilized and kept up to date, its organization must facilitate these purposes.

The following provisions promote ease of use and alterations of the policy manual:

1. Some basic system of coding governance policies and regulations is essential. Major areas of policy must be identified and divided into subareas as appropriate. A coding system must allow for ease of use and expansion of policies and regulations as needed.
2. Policy statements should be separate from statements of regulation. The placement of a policy and accompanying regulations on separate pages is recommended. The use of different colors of paper for policies and regulations also helps to separate them.

Regulation Procedures for Certificated Employees   4112.1

In order to reach the goal of selecting the most competent employees available, the Lincoln Public Schools maintains an aggressive program of staff recruitment. Elements of the program include:

1. Continuous contacts with agencies which supply personnel.
2. Wide-scale advertising of available positions.
3. Staff visits to major suppliers such as college campuses on a regular basis.

Procedures in Recruitment

1. The Human Resources Division receives the notification of vacancy and related job description.
2. A review of employees on leave of absence, request for transfer, promotion, reduction in force and surplus persons, and current applicants is made.
3. Periodic contact with outside sources who can assist in identifying potential candidates is maintained by the Human Resources Division.

Selection

The Lincoln Public Schools shall strive to attract and retain the best qualified personnel available for every position in the Lincoln Public Schools. The selection procedure is uniformly applied to every candidate. Prior to selecting, the information concerning the following areas is included in the applicant's file when applicable:

1. Subject area competence
2. Experience and background
3. Professional knowledge
4. Personal qualities
5. Physical fitness
6. Mental attitude
7. Professional skills
8. Certification
9. Other information related to specific job qualification

This information is accumulated from such credentials as college transcripts, personal references and a personal interview.

Recruitment and Selection Procedures for Classified Employees   4112.2

In order to reach the goal of selecting the most competent employees available, the Lincoln Public Schools maintains an aggressive program of staff recruitment, including:

1. Contacts with agencies which supply personnel.
2. Advertising of available positions with local sources.
3. Any person desiring employment with the Lincoln Public Schools must submit an application to the Human Resources Division.
4. Interviews are conducted by human resources administrators.

Procedures in Selection

1. The Human Resources Division receives the notification of vacancy and reviews the job description.
2. A review of current applicants is made. Persons interested in reassignments are considered.
3. Finalists, identified by the human resources administrators, are interviewed by the supervisor of the vacant position.

Procedures in Selection   4112.3

1. Examination of professional credentials.
2. A structured interview which will be evaluated.
3. An informal interview, often with persons with whom the candidate will be assigned. Frequently a second or third interview may follow.

4. A staffing conference to pool opinions of those involved to synthesize available data.

Modifications and extensions of the selection process may be made for selected appointments but when this is the case, the selection procedure will be announced in advance.

Contacts by candidates for employment should always start at the Human Resources Office.

FIGURE 8–1

SOURCE: *Policies and Regulations* of the Lincoln, Nebraska Public Schools. Reprinted by permission.

3. Only paraphrases or excerpts of state statutes should be inserted in the policy manual except in those rare instances when "exactness of law" demands that full statutes be included. When paraphrases of statutes are utilized, one should cite the legal reference of the statute in the manual.

4. A comprehensive policy manual provides subcategory headings even though policies for these topics may not have been developed to date. Such listings serve to denote the subcategories for which policies have not been determined; these subcategories serve to note policy area needs as the manual is expanded.

Codification Systems

The Davies–Brickell System

The Davies–Brickell System of Policy Development (DBS) and the National Education Policy Network of the National School Boards Association (NEPN/NSBA) are two prevalent codification systems for organizing governance policies. Of course, there is a variety of codification systems in use, and almost all states provide consultant help to school districts for their utilization. The DBS utilizes nine major series for classifying policies and uses a numerical system for coding purposes. The nine major series of the Davies–Brickell System are as follows:

Series	Topical Heading
Series 1000	Community Relations
Series 2000	Administration
Series 3000	Business and Noninstructional Operations
Series 4000	Personnel
Series 5000	Students
Series 6000	Instruction
Series 7000	Construction
Series 8000	Internal Board Policies
Series 9000	Bylaws of the Board[9]

Each major series in the DBS is divided into appropriate subseries, divisions, subdivisions, items, and subitems. Thus, the code entry 4731.24 refers to the major series 4000 (personnel), the seventh subseries, third division, first subdivision, second item, and fourth subitem within the series. Both policies and administrative regulations are coded. The Davies–Brickell System is widely used and is noted for its comprehensive topical headings and its ease of use and maintenance.

Business—Purchasing

The Lincoln Board of Education declares its intention to purchase competitively whenever possible.

Good working relations with vendors who provide materials, supplies and services to the district are desirable. Constructive efforts by the administration to seek the advice and counsel of vendors about how to improve such relationships are encouraged. If equal bids are received, preference shall go to the local vendor, that is, Lincoln first, then Nebraska.

Recommended purchases or projects in excess of $5,000,000 will be presented to the board of education for approval.

Date of Adoption (or Last Revision):   5-12
Related Policies and Regulations:
Legal Reference:

FIGURE 8–2

SOURCE: *Policies and Regulations* of the Lincoln, Nebraska Public Schools. Reprinted by permission.

Regulation
3610.1

Business—Quality/Quantity Purchasing

Quality/Quantity Purchasing

Items to be purchased shall be at a specified quality level selected to meet the instructional or operational requirement of the district.

Consideration of a higher quality level shall include:
1. Use of products on trial basis.
2. Regard for extended life expectancy of the product.
3. Preference for products having a more trouble-free nature that would result in lower per year cost of ownership.

All recommendations shall be made after consideration and consultation with the personnel requesting the goods and services.

The administration is encouraged to purchase supplies, equipment and materials in quantity to take advantage of quality control and price advantages.

Factors to be considered in consolidating like items for purchase in lot quantities shall include:
1. Price advantages to be recognized on basic purchasing quantities.
2. Savings on shipping costs.
3. Cost of money invested in inventory.
4. Cost of warehouse space and personnel.

Date Regulation Reviewed by the Board of Education: 5-12
Related Policies and Regulations:
Legal Reference:

FIGURE 8–3

SOURCE: *Policies and Regulations* of the Lincoln, Nebraska Public Schools. Reprinted by permission.

Business—Soliciting Prices

Soliciting Prices (Bids and Quotations)

Recommended Procedures in Bidding Undergraduate Senior High Yearbook Pictures.

1. Each senior high school representative will review the current specifications. Desired changes will be noted and returned to the purchasing department.
2. The buyer will confirm the tentative specifications with each vendor. Any specifications that are found to be confusing, not practical, or exclusive will be changed or removed. The final specifications will be shared back with each school's representative prior to bidding with an explanation of any changes from the tentative specifications.
3. The buyer will issue the bid, chart the bids, and share the results with all of the schools' representatives. The buyer will, prior to the meeting, contact references given by the top bidders to confirm that levels of quality and service meet Lincoln schools' standards.
4. The lowest responsible bid meeting specifications will be recommended to the Lincoln Board of Education for acceptance.
5. After the purchase order is issued, any questions regarding the meeting or changing of specifications will be processed by the buyer.

Recommended Procedures in Bidding Senior and Junior High Yearbooks/Band Uniforms

1. The buyer will review existing specifications on an individual basis with each school. Desired changes will be noted.
2. The buyer will arrange a meeting with each vendor and each school's representatives. At the meeting, the desired specifications will be discussed point-by-point. This will eliminate any specifications that are confusing, not practical, or exclusive.
3. The buyer will complete a final set of specifications.
4. The buyer will issue the bid, chart the bids received, and review the results with each school's representatives. The low responsible bid meeting specifications will be recommended to the board of education for acceptance.
5. After the purchase orders are issued, any questions regarding the meeting or changing of specifications will be processed by the buyer.

Date Regulation Reviewed by the Board of Education:5-12
Related Policies and Regulations:
Legal Reference:

FIGURE 8–4

SOURCE: *Policies and Regulations* of the Lincoln, Nebraska Public Schools. Reprinted by permission.

Human Resources—Appraisal

The Lincoln Board of Education requires appraisal of all employees. The appraisal shall be by the immediate supervisor or designee pursuant to procedures approved by the board of education.

Date of Adoption (or Last Revision):   5-12
Related Policies and Regulations:
Legal Reference:

FIGURE 8–5

SOURCE: *Policies and Regulations* of the Lincoln, Nebraska Public Schools. Reprinted by permission.

Human Resources Appraisal—Certificated Employees

Appraisal of certificated employees is the responsibility of the building principal or the principal's designee.

Probationary certificated employees will be appraised formally once each year with summative appraisal reports submitted to the Human Resources Division by their supervisors at the end of the school year. During the third year of probation the summative appraisal report will be required on or about March 15 prior to the Lincoln Board of Education action on recommendation for tenure.

Summative appraisal reports on permanent certificated employees normally will be required by June 1 every third year of their service. A formative appraisal shall be made at the conclusion of the first year following a transfer or change of assignment. Other appraisals may be made as determined to be appropriate by the principal or principal's designee.

Certificated employees who work in several buildings will be summatively appraised by the person designated for that purpose by the Human Resources Office.

Leadership of a comprehensive system of staff appraisal is the responsibility of the Human Resources Division. Records of appraisal activity will be filed with the Human Resource Division.

Date Regulation Reviewed by the Board of Education: 5-12
Related Policies and Regulations:
Legal Reference:

FIGURE 8–6

SOURCE: *Policies and Regulations* of the Lincoln, Nebraska Public Schools. Reprinted by permission.

The National Educational Policy Network of the National School Boards Association

The National Educational Policy Network of the National School Boards Association (NEPN/NSBA) is the most widely utilized codification system; it is presented in detail in this section. NEPN/NSBA is based on an alpha coding system and includes 12 major policy classifications called sections or chapters, as explained by the NSBA:

> Each section has its own family of subcategories—that is, subcodes and terms called "descriptors" that provide suggested titles for policy statements. The subcoding also is by letter. Letter coding offers two major advantages over numerical systems: 1) it is more expandable in that codes have 26 separate letters to use compared to only ten digits of numbers; and 2) it requires no decimal points, a feature that tends to reduce the likelihood of copying and filing errors.[10]

> The NEPN Policy Classification System was revised in 1991 and has 12 sections or chapters as follows:

A   Foundations and Basic Commitments
B   School Board Governance and Operations
C   General School Administration
D   Fiscal Management
E   Support Services
F   Facility Planning and Development
G   Personnel

Human Resources—Appraisal of Administrators

General Procedures

The formal administrator appraisal is based primarily upon the procedures and processes defined below. The procedures provide for a consistent and equitable appraisal of important aspects of the administrator's role. They do not, however, specifically include the total range of expectations of the effective administrator. As a result, additional data and information related to the administrative role may be utilized to generate a comprehensive appraisal.

Appraisal Cycle

The formal appraisal is normally conducted in a three-year cycle; i.e., each administrator can expect to be formally appraised every three years with the intervening two years used to improve performance and to grow professionally. The appraisal cycle can be modified to include additional formal appraisals within the three-year cycle. This modification may be at the request of the appraiser or the appraisee.

Appraisal Process

The appraisal process is the responsibility of the appraisee and his/her immediate supervisor. Performance categories serve as the basis for the formal appraisal. During the formal appraisal, data is collected as required to provide a basis for appraising the performance categories. The data will relate to each indicator identified in the performance category. Data collection may include, but is not limited to, survey of staff, student and parents; responses from Superintendent's Executive Committee members and other administrators; statistics received by routine reports; statistics generated by reports specifically designed for the appraisal; visitations to the work site, etc.

The collected data serve as the basis for the final appraisal report. In addition to the final report, each appraisee will receive a detailed version of the data results as related to each performance expectation and indicator. This review will include the appraiser's perceptions of whether or not the given expectation indicator was met.

Final Report

The appraisal process culminates in a final report. The final report consists of a rating of each performance category, identification of specific unsatisfactory or exemplary characteristics of job performance and the performance necessary to correct any unsatisfactory ratings.

Date Regulation Reviewed by the Board of Education: 5-12
Related Policies and Regulations:
Legal Reference:

FIGURE 8–7

SOURCE: *Policies and Regulations* of the Lincoln, Nebraska Public Schools. Reprinted by permission.

        H   Negotiations
        I   Instruction
        J   Students
        K   School–Community–Home Relations
        L   Education Agency Relations[11]

        Each of the 12 sections has several major subcategories expressed as two-letter codes (i.e., under Section A, Foundations and Basic Commitments, there are five subcategories: AA, School District Legal Status; AB, The People and Their School District; AC, Nondiscrimination Equal Opportunity; AD, Educational Philosophy/School District Mission; and AE, Accountability/Commitment to Accomplishment).
        Subsections and subcategories begin are lexicographically ordered. For example, under the subsection AD, Educational Philosophy/School District Mission, the *first* sub-

category ADA is District Goals and Objectives. Similarly, subcategory ADB refers to the *second* subcategory under AD, Drug Free Schools. The *third* subcategory under AD is ADC, Tobacco-Free Schools, and so forth.

Figure 8–8 is the complete Section C of the NEPN/NSBA Classification System, General School Administration. Note that Section C has 13 major subsections beginning with Subsection CA, Administration Goals/Priority Objectives and ending with Subsection CM, School District Annual Report. Note also that Subsection CB has 10 subcategories, ending with CBJ, Superintendent's Termination of Employment. If an eleventh major subcategory were added to Subsection CB, it would be coded CBK with the proper topical heading.

As a further illustration, consider the code entry of CHCA. The first letter "C" denotes the major Section C, General School Administration. The second letter "H" represents the eighth subsection under C, Policy Implementation. The third letter "C" represents the third subcategory under CH, Regulations Communication, and the fourth letter "A" represents the first subcategory under CHC, *Handbooks and Directives.*

The NSBA also publishes a code-finder index that serves as a component of the NEPN. The code-finder index allows the user to locate related policies in the classification system easily. The code-finder, according to the NSBA, "is an alphabetical listing of common education terms as well as the policy titles found in the classification system. It is useful both for locating policies and regulations . . . and for properly coding policies and regulations in the district's policy manual. It also serves as a guide to titling policies, although the exact policy terms and content documents should reflect the local district's needs and approach."[12]

How Governance Policies and Administrative Regulations Are Developed

A previous section of this chapter discussed the basis of governance policy and emphasized its relationship to educational goals determined by the school community. In those cases when school districts have depended heavily on "unwritten" policy or when major revisions in one or more sections of the policy manual are required, it often is necessary to begin anew. In those instances when policies require major changes, it often becomes a task delegated to the school superintendent.

The purchasing of policy services that provide generic, boilerplate type policies for school districts is not recommended, although such policies might meet some purposes (e.g., give some assurance that all areas are covered, be helpful in emergency situations when new policy areas such as AIDS are required, help districts that are simply unable to develop their own policies). Policy development must be viewed as a process rather than a product. Policies that evolve from identified local goals or needs serve the best purposes.

Although the general task of school district policy development most often is assumed by the superintendent, the question of what procedure to follow arises. The answer for any specific school district depends on such variables as human resources, monetary resources, existing staff–board–community relationships, time limitations, and work loads.

In most cases it is not desirable to have the superintendent actually develop the policies, even though that person possesses key knowledge about the school district, its goals and relationships. Policy development is arduous; it requires much time and effort, most

NEPN	NEPN title
CA	Administration Goals/Priority Objectives
CB	School Superintendent
CBA	Qualifications and Duties of Superintendent
CBB	Recruitment of Superintendent
CBC	Superintendent Powers and Responsibilities
CBCA	Delegated Authority
CDB	Superintendent's Contract
CBE	Superintendent's Salary, Compensation, and Benefits
CBF	Superintendent's Conduct
CBG	Superintendent's Professional Development Opportunities
CBH	Superintendent's Consulting Activities
CBI	Evaluation of Superintendent
CBJ	Superintendent's Termination of Employment
CBJA	Dismissal of Superintendent
CBJB	Retirement/Resignation of Superintendent
CC	Administrative Organization
CCA	Organization Charts
CCB	Line and Staff Relations
CCC	Staffing Formulas/Ratios
CD	Management Team/Senior Staff
CDA	Evaluation of Management
CE	Administrative Councils, Cabinets, and Committees
CF	School Building Administration
CFA	School Principals/Building Administrators
CFB	Evaluation of Principals/Building Administrators
CFC	Assignment and Transfer of Building Administrators
CFD	School-Based Management
CFE	School Climate
CFF	Support Personnel for Building Administration
CFG	Elementary School Administration
CFH	Secondary School Administration
CFHA	Middle School/Junior High School Administration
CFHB	High School Administration
CG	Special Programs Administration
CGA	Summer Programs Administration
CGB	School-Based Child Care Programs Administration
CGC	Adult Education/Lifelong Learning Programs Administration
CGD	State and Federal Programs Administration
CH	Policy Implementation
CHA	Development of Regulations
CHB	Board Review of Regulations
CHC	Regulations Communication
CHCA	Handbooks and Directives
CHD	Administration in the Absence of Policy
CI	Temporary Intern Programs
CJ	Administrative Intern Programs
CK	Administrative Consultants
CL	Research/Administrative Reports
CM	School District Annual Report

FIGURE 8–8   Section C—General School Administration NEPN Coding System

SOURCE: Used with permission from the *School Administrator's Guide* to the NEPN/NSBA *Policy Development System, 6th Edition,* (Alexandria, VA: National School Boards Association, 1991). All rights reserved.

often over extended periods. The task of policy development and meeting the many other responsibilities of the superintendency are too demanding. Other policy development strategies can be utilized that allow the school superintendent to serve as a primary consultant throughout the process.

Use of Task Force Groups

One popular strategy for policy development is the use of specialized task force groups. Representatives knowledgeable of the goals and needs in specific major policy sections serve as the primary researchers, developers, and writers of policies for each section. One person serves to coordinate the work of the several task force groups and might also take the leadership in editing and refining the policy statements drafted by each task force group. Major advantages of this approach include a division of the work load and representative participation. When school board members, teachers, administrators, parents, and others are involved in the work, final approval of the resultant policies is smoother. A possible disadvantage of this approach centers on talent and experience; representatives might lack the credentials required for quality results. Understanding of goals, personnel relationships, the school system and community, as well as the process of policy development itself, is essential for effective results.

Use of Outside Consultants

When major policy development is necessary, the school district likely will consider hiring outside consultants. The problems related to purchasing boilerplate policy materials were noted previously. External consultants, who complete the background research necessary for localizing written policy recommendations, can be useful resource persons. Qualified policy consultants are highly knowledgeable of the policy development process and understand what must be done to determine viable local policies for a specific school district. The use of external consultants can reduce the burden on the school superintendent, the school board, and others. One drawback is cost. Since policy development is time consuming, consultant fees generally run high. Too, since the consultants most often leave the district upon completion of the work, they are not always available to answer questions or field complaints that inevitably arise in policy adoption and implementation.

Use of Internal Leadership

Although the use of external resource persons for policy development has proven workable, we recommend that the school district assume the major responsibility for policy development. One person on the school district staff, other than the school superintendent, is delegated the leadership responsibility when major policy development becomes necessary. Clemmer recommends that this person "should (a) be experienced enough to understand the subtleties of board–administrator relationships, (b) show evidence of a logical and organized mind, (c) be able to communicate effectively verbally and in writing, and (d) be able to gain the confidence of the board and the superintendent."[13]

An Operations Model

Various strategies might be used to proceed with the process of policy development. The following operations model suggests several key considerations for the appointed policy development leader.

Consideration 1—Explain to the staff what is being done and why. State the purposes and values of policies and regulations.

Consideration 2—Establish a policy development steering committee to coordinate study group activities, decide on important procedural matters, serve as the editorial board, and to check for gaps and inconsistencies in preliminary policy drafts.

Consideration 3—Solicit the participation and aid of representative groups. Organize activities that gain input and understanding of the community, staff, and other publics of the school.

Consideration 4—Name study and writing groups to develop appropriate policy for the specific policy sections, subsections, and subcategories. Qualified representatives from the district's staff, community, school board, and student body should serve on the work groups. Final approvals and board adoption are facilitated when appropriate participation on study and writing groups is realized.

Consideration 5—Undertake a thorough search of sources of specific and implied school policy. An examination of school records, board correspondence, previous master agreements, staff records and files, legal rulings, and teachers' handbooks are among the valuable resources for potential policies and regulations. Give careful attention to specific goal statements by the school board. Guides and handbooks published by state agencies and other professional groups also should be examined.

Consideration 6—Study and writing groups must determine established objectives and practices concerning the specific policy section under development. This procedure often leads to formal statements of policy.

Consideration 7—Study and writing groups should examine the policy manuals of similar school districts. Such efforts are useful in revealing areas of policy need that can be localized for the district in question. Close examination of the classification categories in the Davies–Brickell and National School Boards Association policy systems will serve to suggest local policy needs as well.

Consideration 8—The school superintendent and school board should review drafted policy statements by the various study groups in special work sessions. One must also have a legal review of the policy drafts. Such a review locates legal inconsistencies and provides support for the acceptance of the total policy package.

Consideration 9—Minimally, the final policy statements should receive a first reading at an official meeting of the school board. Second readings are recommended before final adoption by the board. In any case, adoption procedures must meet the reading and review requirements set forth in law.

Consideration 10—Control measures must be implemented following policy adoption and dissemination. A record of problem areas, gaps, and complaints relative to the new policies should be duly recorded for immediate and future improvements. (Note: An annual review of all policies and regulations by the school board and staff is recommended.)

The foregoing operations model emphasizes wide participation in the policy development process. Such involvement often adds to the complexity of the task. Nevertheless, the fundamental purposes of effective school policy development, adoption, and implementation embrace such collaboration.

Characteristics of Effective Policies

Clemmer states that "there are two questions to ask about every policy: 1. Does it say what it ought to say? 2. Will its implementation produce the intended result?"[14] He believes that strong responses to these two questions are evidence of "better policies." Four specific characteristics of effective policies are identified by Clemmer as follows:

1. *Pertinent.* Only policies on applicable topics deserve development time.
2. *Timely.* Policies should respond to actual needs but they should not be enacted until essential facts are known.
3. *Functional.* The policy should make possible that which needs to be done.
4. *Practicable.* If a policy cannot be implemented, do not adopt it.[15]

Effective school board policies reflect the short- and long-term needs of the school district for which they are developed. Ineffective policies often are founded on the feelings of specific individuals who proposed them for personal reasons. A good policy serves its intended purposes. Policies, as adaptations of educational goals, must facilitate the accomplishment of these goals.

Summary

Policy and regulation development is an essential function of the school superintendent and school board. Although the superintendent and school board must assume specific, unique responsibilities, policy development is a collaborative process.

School goals evolve from the cultures within the school community and serve as the primary basis for determining school governance policy. Viable school policies benefit both internal and external publics of the school system. Policies give direction to the school district. Adoption of school policy is the school board's singular responsibility, although the judgments of the school superintendent and staff, as well as lay judgments, are key in the policy development process. Viable policies reveal the extent to which educational goals are encompassed in school district purposes. They serve as a primary communication vehicle for the staff and community and enhance the effectiveness and efficiency of the school organization.

Several criteria differentiate policy from administrative regulation. In brief, policies are legislative in nature and are related to the question, what to do? They are general statements that represent assertions of school goals; they leave room for the use of judgment and discretion by the school superintendent and staff. Administrative regulations are executive in nature and related to the question, how to do? They are precise statements that leave little or no room for interpretation. Regulations are primarily the responsibility of the school superintendent and staff, although input by lay persons, as well as the school board, is recommended.

The organization of the policy manual requires some system of classification. The Davies–Brickell System and the Educational Policy System Network of the National School Boards Association are prominent codification systems in use today. Each has its advantages. The former system is based on a numerical code and the latter uses an alpha code.

The job of policy development is never completed. Major policy development or revision requires a planned process led by a knowledgeable individual. Due to the time demands of policy development, the school superintendent likely should not serve this leadership role. Rather, the superintendent should serve as the primary resource person and advisor throughout the policy development process.

There are many strategies for approaching policy development. Any strategy selected must carefully consider organization, including communication, participation, coordination, completion of task, and control. Communication necessitates explanations of purpose and procedure; participation assures appropriate representation of the school district's publics in the process; coordination requires the development of task understanding and relationships among and between various study and writing groups; completion of task includes the determination of target dates and progress evaluations; and control focuses on evaluation measures that lend to quality results during and after the primary policy writing and development process.

Discussion Questions

1. Explain the statement that "the school superintendent actually gains more freedom by having a viable set of governance policies."

2. Point out at least one primary benefit of a viable set of governance policies for the school superintendent, the school board, parents, students, school principals, and school district taxpayers.

3. Assume that you are a candidate for the superintendency in a school district. List several specific things that you could learn by examining closely the current school district's policies and regulations.

4. Explain the code CFHB in the NEPN/NSBA system. First, note the section, subsection, and subcategories that each letter represents (e.g., first, second, third, . . . , ninth section, subsection, subcategory) and then write the specific topic heading that each letter denotes.

5. Write an appropriate policy and one accompanying regulation for the indefinite and inappropriate "policy" below.

"No one will be permitted to use school buildings, grounds, or facilities on Sundays."

CASE 8.1   Policy Development? We Tried That Before.

Greg Stephan, new school superintendent of the College View School District, contacted the school board president, George Nelson, about his concerns with the present school board policies.

"My examination of the policy manual caused me some concern," explained Superintendent Stephan. "The manual appears to be a hodgepodge of school rules and school board minutes. It isn't well organized; I wasn't sure what coding system was being used," he said.

"Oh, Greg, I wouldn't worry too much about the policies," replied President Nelson. "We attempted some policy work when Superintendent Merlin George was here. As I recall, it didn't go too smoothly. Policies and regulations tend to draw sharp lines between the board and the school superintendent, and such an effort might cause a split in our relationships."

Questions

1. Discuss the concept of division of labor as it applies to the school board and school superintendent.
2. Assume the role of Superintendent Stephan and give your response to board President Nelson. What primary considerations must be encompassed in your remarks?

CASE 8.2   Just Doing My Job!

Lewis John had just been elected to a three-year term on the six-member College View School District Board. Lewis John's father had been a member of the board several years previously, and he always wanted to follow in his father's footsteps as a board member. Lewis's father had encouraged him to try for the board but "instructed" him to be the best board member that he could be.

On one Saturday morning, board member John called Superintendent Rodriquez. "Paul," said Lewis, "I've been concerned for some time about the procedures being used to select teachers for our schools. Our daughter, Clementina, lost a full year in grade 3 due to an incompetent teacher. At the last board meeting, the board approved a list of several teachers for next year without even knowing them. We didn't even have their credentials to look at."

John went on to say that, "I think I'm going to write a regulation regarding the board's involvement in teacher selection. How can we continue to vote approval on people we don't even know?"

Questions

1. Assume the role of Superintendent Paul Rodriquez and respond to board member John. What key points would you make in your telephone response?
2. What can be done in a positive manner to help new board members understand their policy responsibilities? List several ideas or strategies concerning new board member orientation.

Inbasket Exercise

INBASKET 8.1

Teacher or Tutor?

COLLEGE VIEW SCHOOL DISTRICT
WYMORE, LAFAYETTE

MEMORANDUM

Date: 10/9

TO: Dr. Nelson, Supt.
FROM: Sue B. (secretary)
RE: Mrs. Jackson's son

Mrs. Jackson called on Friday, 10/6. She was very disturbed. Mr. Black, instrumental music teacher at Whittier, told her that her son (Donn) needed private lessons if he wanted to keep up with the band. Mrs. Jackson was told that lessons would be $9.50 for 1/2 hour and lessons could be scheduled for 4:30 p.m. Wednesdays.

Mrs. Jackson asks that you call her (388-1995).

Response

1. What is the major problem or concern regarding the Jackson case? What do you believe is Superintendent Nelson's primary role or responsibility in this situation?
2. Assume the role of Superintendent Nelson and write out the administrative actions that you would perform. Be specific in your actions; write comments that you would set forth in any communication with others. Write the specific memos or letters that you might send as well.

Notes

1. *The School Administrator's Guide to the NEPN/NSBA Policy Development System,* 6th ed. (Alexandria, Va.: National School Boards Association, 1991), p. 4.

2. John Martin Rich, *New Directions in Educational Policy* (Lincoln, Neb.: Professional Educators Publications, 1974), p. 10.

3. Thomas E. Glass, *The 1992 Study of the American School Superintendency: America's Education Leaders in a Time of Reform* (Arlington, Va.: American Association of School Administrators), p. 36.

4. *Holding Effective Board Meetings* (Arlington, Va.: American Association of School Administrators, 1984), p. 8.

5. Carnegie Task Force on Teaching as a Profession, *A Nation Prepared: Teachers for the Twenty-first Century* (New York: Carnegie Corporation of New York, 1986), p. 2.

6. The National Governors' Association, *Time for Results: The Governors' 1991 Report on Education* (Washington, D.C.: National Governors' Association), p. 10.

7. Martin Carnoy, "Restructuring Has a Downside Too," *Education Week* (7 November 1990): p. 32.

8. Daniel L. Duke and Robert Lynn Canady, *School Policy* (New York: McGraw-Hill, Inc., 1991), p. 148.

9. Daniel R. Davies and Henry M. Brickell, *An Instructional Handbook on How to Develop Policies, Bylaws, and Administrative Regulations* (Naco, Ariz.: Daniel R. Davies, 1988), pp. 9–12.

10. *The School Administrator's Guide to the NEPN/NSBA Policy Development System,* p. 13.

11. Ibid., pp. 17–53.

12. National School Boards Association, *Code-Finder Index,* 6th ed., (Alexandria, Va.: NSBA, 1991), p. 1.

13. Elwin F. Clemmer, *The School Policy Handbook: A Primer for School Board Members and Administrators* (Boston: Allyn and Bacon, 1991), p. 238.

14. Ibid., p. 104.

15. Ibid., p. 104–105.

C h a p t e r **9**

The Superintendent and the Law

We assume that the reader of this chapter has completed a basic graduate course in public school law or has knowledge of the material covered in such a course, namely: the American legal system; the impact of state and federal laws; student and teacher rights and freedoms; religion and the schools; tort liability; and precedent-setting U.S. Supreme Court decisions. Accordingly, this chapter will focus on the legal responsibilities of the superintendent, a discussion of contractual and dismissal issues specific to the superintendency, an overview of emerging legal issues, and a discussion of selected federal laws dealing with legal issues that may have significant impact on the operation of the schools.

Legal Responsibilities of the Superintendent

The legal responsibilities of the school superintendent as the chief administrative officer of a public school district vary from state to state, according to statutes as provided in the school code, and further delineated by school board policy and contractual agreements. In most states, the superintendent of a local school district is considered an employee of the district, and state school codes authorize the school board to "employ" a chief school administrator.[1] However, most state school codes do not delineate the specific duties of the school superintendent. Specific duties are outlined by board policy and/or contract.

A common policy of a local governing board stating the legal responsibilities of the superintendent for the legal affairs of the district would be as follows:

The School Board has delegated to the Superintendent of Schools the execution of the board policies, rules, or other directions given by the School Board. The Superintendent must see that the schools and school functions are appropriate under state law, state Attorney General Opinion, and pertinent State Board of

Education rules issued pursuant to law. In addition, the Superintendent is responsible for compliance with Federal laws and regulations that affect the School Board.

In addition to the general policy statement of legal responsibility, many districts are required by statute, policy, or contract to annually evaluate the superintendent's effectiveness. A part of that evaluation typically includes an assessment of the superintendent's effectiveness in fulfilling his or her responsibilities for the school district's legal affairs in the following areas:

Management of the District

- Ensures that all activities of the district are conducted in accordance with the laws of the state, the regulations of the state board of education, and the policies of the governing board.
- Provides suitable instructions and regulations to govern the maintenance of school properties.
- Provides suitable instructions and regulations to govern the transportation of students.
- Remains current on new legislation and implements laws to the best advantage of the district.
- Maintains a liaison with state and federal legislators in an effort to provide information to positively influence legislation for school improvement.

Governing Board

- Takes prompt action to implement all directives of the board.
- Advises the board on the need for new and/or revised policies.
- Provides timely advice to the board on the implications of changes in statutes or regulations affecting education.
- Informs and advises the board about programs, practices, and problems of schools, and keeps the board informed of the activities operating under the board's authority including threatened, pending, and current litigations against the board or its employees.
- Develops and implements rules and regulations in keeping with board policy.
- Supports and implements policies, procedures, and actions of the governing board during interactions with the public and staff.
- Acts on own direction if action is necessary in any matter not covered by board policy, reports such action to the board as soon as practicable, and recommends future policy.

Personnel

- Recommends to the board the appointment or dismissal of all employees of the district.
- Ensures that all employees are evaluated in accordance with the schedule established by the board and in statutory compliance with state laws.
- Recommends all promotions, demotions, and salary changes to the board.
- Administers personnel policies and the language of contracts in a firm, impartial manner.

In fulfilling these responsibilities, the assumption is made that the superintendent will work in harmony with the board and board counsel to protect the district, the board, and its employees from litigation and to maintain compliance with district policies, and state statutes and regulations.

In addition to their contractual obligation, a recent survey of public school superintendents identified several specific areas of law in which the superintendent must have more than a cursory knowledge.[2] One of these areas is in regard to the state *open meeting law.* Open meeting laws state that if a school board is to take a legal action by making a collective decision, commitment, or promise, it must do so at a public open meeting or the action is void. Often, the attorneys for the school district are not present at meetings of the governing board, and the superintendent is expected to provide information on open meeting law procedures. Generally, the open meeting statutes detail procedures for public elected bodies and involve a notice to the public, meeting agendas, minutes of meetings, ratification of votes or decisions[3] after violations are discovered, and exceptions to the public meeting requirement. Violations of the open meeting laws occur mostly in connection with employment-related actions or decisions. Violations of the open meeting laws by a public school governing board can result in civil penalties or monetary fines and removal from office.

Other areas of law superintendents in the survey identified as important to be knowledgeable about were basic contract law, personnel law related to hiring, evaluation, and dismissal of certificated and noncertificated employees, state education statutes, state school board policies and regulations, and certain specific federal laws and regulations. The specific laws and regulations that are the subject of most of the current litigation affecting the schools include the Rehabilitation Act of 1973, Section 504; the American With Disabilities Act (ADA); Individuals With Disabilities Education Act (IDEA); the Family Medical Leave Act (FMLA); the payment of overtime provisions of the Fair Labor Standards Act (FLSA); and the payment of attorney's fees under the Handicapped Children's Protection Act of 1986. Since an important role of the superintendent is to provide direction not only to the governing board, but to the school board attorney, the superintendent must remain current of emerging legal issues.[4] To this end, a brief review of the legal issues under the foregoing important federal laws will be discussed later in this chapter. We first turn, though, to two areas of major concern to most superintendents: the superintendent's contract and dismissal of superintendents.

Contractual and Dismissal Issues

Contract Law Applied to the Superintendent's Contract

An employment contract defines the rights and responsibilities of the parties signing the contract. The general principles of contract law apply to the superintendent's employment contract. That is, the contract must contain the basic elements of (1) offer and acceptance, (2) competent parties, (3) consideration, (4) legal subject matter, and (5) proper form. Beyond the basic elements, the contract must meet the requirements specified in state law and administrative regulations.[5] It is advisable for superintendents to have written contracts; under most state laws the superintendent's contract is required to be written. Additionally, if the contract is for more than one year, the Statute of Frauds may require that it be in writing.[6]

The following terms and concepts are important to a consideration of the superintendent's contract.[7]

The Negotiated Contract

A negotiated contract is one that is negotiated by the parties to the contract. It can be written or oral, and it may or may not express the entire agreement.

The Written Contract

This contract is in writing and usually expresses the entire understanding of the parties; it can incorporate by reference other documents such as employee handbooks. It is usually signed by the parties.

Express Contract Terms

Express(ed) contracts terms are those agreements that have been expressly discussed and agreed on by the parties or terms that arise by implication out of the discussions and agreements. There may be express terms in an implied contract. For example:

> You will work from 8 a.m. to 5 p.m.; you will earn $8500.00 per month; you will have 10 paid holidays; you will be provided medical coverage at the district's expense; you will be entitled to 21 vacation days a year; you will not be terminated except for cause; you will be given a warning of deficient performance; and you will be counseled and told what you must do to bring your performance up to acceptable levels; you will be evaluated annually; [etc.]

The expression may be verbal, or it may be written; it may be stated in the job interview when the employee is told what the job entails; it may be set out in an employee handbook; it may be set forth by posters displayed on the bulletin board (e.g., "This district is an equal opportunity employer."); it may be in indoctrination courses; or it may be in management leadership courses.

The discussion regarding the contract terms of the agreements may be made at any time during the course of the employment relationship, and the agreements can be unilaterally modified in some cases. Generally, the written agreement has a provision for modification of terms based on mutual agreement.

The Implied Contract Term

A term or some of the terms of the contract may not be discussed or agreed on, but may be implied from circumstances in the employment relationship or imposed by outside sources such as public policy, custom, or practice. They apply to oral and written contracts. Some of the more common implied terms are the following:

- *Terms or acts prohibited by public policy.* Public policy forbids parties to a contract from doing or requiring anything that is detrimental to the public good or in violation of law. Every employment contract has an implied term that the employer cannot terminate or punish an employee for "bad reasons," that is, refusing to violate law or public policy. Example: An employee cannot be fired for refusing to violate law or for reporting an illegal act or omission.

- *Terms imposed by custom.*　A contract term can be established by custom even though it is not agreed to by the parties. It is implied into the contract by their conduct. Example: Even if an employer has no handbook or personnel manual that requires termination for cause and even though the employer has never said that termination would be only for cause, if *in fact* the practice in the work place is to not terminate except for cause, that practice may take the place of written or verbal expressions and impose a requirement of good cause to terminate.
- *Terms implied by law.*　These are terms implied into the contract by operation of law even though the parties to the contract never agreed, or even thought of, them, and even though there is no custom concerning it. Example: The covenant of good faith and fair dealing. The implied term requires the parties to deal with each other in good faith and fairly.

The Tort "Duty"

The law imposes obligations on all parties to conform to rules and mores that contribute to the public good and welfare. These obligations are called "duties" in law.

There are certain obligations or duties imposed on the parties to an employment relationship that are common to the public as a whole. For example, one cannot tortiously interfere with the employment relationship of another, one cannot defraud another in an employment relationship, one cannot use his or her position to inflict intentional mental distress on an employee, and one cannot, in an employment relationship, do something to the other party that would violate public policy. These rules (duties) apply to the employment contract and govern the conduct of the parties with or without their consent or knowledge.

The Public Policy Doctrine

Public policy was defined in one legal case as "what is right and just and what affects the citizens of the state collectively."[8] What is "just" and "right" is found in the federal and state constitution, the federal and state statutes, and judicial decisions. For example, one cannot fire an employee for refusing to commit perjury; for political reasons; for refusing to sign a false and arguably tortious statement regarding a co-employee; refusing to submit to a lie detector test; for exercising an employee's right to Worker's Compensation; or for knowingly terminating an employee based on antidiscrimination law.

Tortious Interference with the Employment Relationship or the Employment Expectancy

A person may not do anything that would injure the employment relationship between an employee and the employer or the possibility or expectancy of an employment relationship. This rule applies to co-employees, supervisors, and outsiders. For example, the supervisor cannot get rid of an employee for personal reasons or set up an employee for termination for reasons that are not in the best interest of the employer.

Intentional Infliction of Emotional Distress

No one can intentionally inflict emotional distress upon another without violating the public duty not to injure another. This rule applies to the employment relationship and imposes on the employer the additional duty to prevent others from intentionally imposing emotional distress on an employee. Example: If the employer is aware that co-employees, supervisors, or outsiders are being cruel or mean to another employee, that employer has an independent duty to put a stop to the cruel behavior. If the employer does not, the employer and the tortfeasor can be held jointly and severally liable for the injury to the employee.

Contract Remedies

The usual remedies for breach of contract by the employer include back wages, future damages (including compensation for loss of promotion), benefits, and future wages, attorney's fees, costs of litigation, and prejudgment interest. In contractual torts, compensatory and punitive damages are available. In discrimination actions the remedies include back wages, "front pay," reinstatement to the job, the employee's "rightful place" if promotional opportunities were available, and attorney's fees.[9]

A sample superintendent's contract is presented in Figure 9.1. The contract represents a two-year extension to a previously completed two-year contract. Some states statutes provide only for yearly contracts to school administrators, and others may provide up to three or more years. Generally, a candidate who has been offered a position as superintendent, in negotiating a legally binding contract, may wish to consult a contract attorney to review the contract provisions to ensure that he or she is not waiving an important contract right, and to determine the "fairness" of the contract in case of termination of the contract by either party prior to the expiration date.

In the sample contract, note the *Duties* section and the potential for ambiguity, particularly in the evaluation of such duties. Also note that salary adjustments are based on the annual evaluation, that there is a restriction of consulting activities under paragraph 5, *Other Work,* and the procedure for discharge based on "cause."

As a contractual employee, the superintendent is entitled to the benefits of his or her contract to the date of expiration. If a superintendent does not fulfill the terms of the contract, these actions may constitute a breach of the contract, and the superintendent can be dismissed for cause. The attachments to the contract and exhibits referred to in the contract are an integral part of the contract and are important in determining whether there is a breach of contract. If the governing board wants to terminate the contract prior to expiration and asks for the superintendent's resignation (not uncommon in the superintendency), then the board will be responsible for the remainder of the contractual benefits. The contract will need to be analyzed as to the remaining value of the contract; this can become complex, as benefits such as retirement and medical and life insurance will be calculated as to replacement costs. At this point, sections such as *Vacation and Sick Leave,* paragraph 10, become key in answering such questions as, Does district policy provide payment for unused vacation or sick leave days? If yes, at what rate?

It is not uncommon for a governing board to be split in their support of the superintendent's performance. If the majority of the board do not support the superintendent, a negotiated settlement may be offered to buy out the contract. A settlement agreement constitutes another type of contract and should be entered into only after the advice of a qualified attorney.

If the superintendent's contract is terminated for "cause" or just reason before the expiration of the contract, the superintendent is generally entitled to a due process hearing related to the superintendent's *property interest* in the contract. In fact, in 1985, the U.S. Supreme Court held in *Cleveland Board of Education v. Loudermill*[10] that public employees discharged for cause were entitled to a pretermination opportunity to respond, coupled with a full administrative hearing at a later date. Additionally, depending on the charges, the employee may be entitled to a hearing under a "liberty" interest. (For a general discussion of public employee's property and liberty interest, refer to *Perry v. Sindermann*[11] and *Board of Regents v. Roth.*[12])

In addition to federal constitutional protection related to property and liberty interests, requirements for notice and hearing regarding nonrenewal of superintendents' contracts may be required by individual state statutes or regulations.[13]

Dismissal of Superintendents

A decade of school reform measures has brought sweeping changes to the face of education. Nowhere is this more apparent than in the arena of administrative dismissal. In light of recent educational reforms, differing educational philosophies of governing boards, and decreasing budgets, educational administrators have experienced an increasing number of dismissals and resignations.

The courts have interpreted and clarified the process for administrative dismissal. Although state statutes generally do not vest tenure rights to administrators[14] (some courts, however, have held that the superintendent is a teacher and consequently holds tenure as a teacher[15]), because of the administrator's protected contract interest under the Fourteenth Amendment, due process procedures must be followed by the school board in the dismissal of a superintendent. However, the courts have decided, in some instances, that due process can be satisfied by paying the remainder of a contract to a dismissed administrator.[16]

Administrators, like teachers, can be dismissed for cause. Some of these "causes" include sexual harassment of employees, failure to evaluate assistant superintendents or principals, misuse or misappropriation of district equipment or funds, failure to fulfill the specific terms of the contract, not following the directives of the board, insubordination, personal gain from payoffs from contractors, and providing misinformation related to the open meeting law. There are also numerous instances of unjust terminations based on racial or sex bias on the part of the board.

Dismissal or contract termination may be alleged a violation of a protected constitutional right; however, plaintiff superintendents rarely prevail. For example, in *Bristol Virginia School Board v. Quarles,*[17] the dismissed superintendent sought relief on the grounds of a alleged violation of constitutional due process. However, the Virginia Supreme Court held that the school board's decision to remove the superintendent was based on "ineffective leadership" and "lack of communication with personnel" and did not imply a liberty

FIGURE 9–1   Sample Superintendent's Contract—1995–97, Red Mountain School District #8

AGREEMENT made this first day of June 1995, by and between the GOVERNING BOARD OF SCHOOL DIS-TRICT NO. 8, ("The Board"), and Dr. Ted Cooper, ("Superintendent"), adopted at the Regular Meeting of the Board held on June 1, 1995, and as found in the minutes of that meeting.

IT IS AGREED:

1.   *Employment*—Employment status of Dr. Ted Cooper is hereby amended to extend through June 30, 1997, representing a continuous service to the District from February 26, 1993, as Superintendent of Schools for School District No. 8.

2A.   *Duties*—The duties and responsibilities of Superintendent of this District shall be all those duties incident to the office of Superintendent as set forth in the job description (Board Policy), a copy of which is attached to this Agreement as an Exhibit; those obligations imposed by the law of the State upon the Superintendent of Schools; and in addition, such duties as from time to time may be assigned to the Superintendent by the Board.

2B.   *Goals and Objectives*—The parties shall meet to establish district goals and objectives for the ensuing school year. Said goals and objectives shall be reduced to writing and be among the criteria by which Super-intendent is evaluated as hereafter provided. On or prior to February 1 of each succeeding school year, the parties shall meet to establish district goals and objectives for the next succeeding school year, in the same manner and with the same effect as heretofore described.

3.   *Salary*—In consideration of a salary of **$100,000 per annum**, the Superintendent hereby agrees to devote time as necessary, skill, labor and attention to this employment, during the term of this Agreement, except as otherwise provided in this Agreement, and to perform faithfully the duties of Superintendent of Schools for this District as set forth in this Agreement. The Board retains the right to adjust the annual salary of the Superintendent during the term of this Agreement.* Any adjustment in salary made during the life of this Agreement shall be in the form of an amendment and shall become a part of this Agreement.

*Adjustment to salary shall be done annually by the Governing Board.

4.   *Evaluation*—Annually (but no later than **December 15** of each calendar year), the Board shall review with the Superintendent the Superintendent's progress toward established goals and working relationships among Superintendent, Board, faculty, staff and the community, and shall consider the Superintendent's annual salary for the next subsequent year of the contract.

5.   *Other Work*—Superintendent shall devote his time, attention and energy to the business of the school dis-trict; however, he may serve as a consultant to other districts or educational agencies, lecture, engage in other activities which are of short-term duration at his discretion. Such activities which require the Super-intendent to be absent from the school district for more than one (1) full work day shall be reported to the Governing Board for approval. Superintendent may, at his option, and with the approval of the Governing Board, continue to draw a salary while engaged in the outside activity as described above. In such cases as honoraria to the Superintendent in connection with these activities, he shall be on leave status, or payment made for such activities shall be transferred to the school district.

6.   *Discharge for Cause*—Throughout the term of this Agreement, the Superintendent shall be subject to dis-charge for cause, provided that the Superintendent shall have the right to service of written charges, notice of hearing and a hearing before the Board. If the Superintendent chooses to be accompanied by legal coun-sel at such hearing, all such personal legal expenses shall be paid by the Superintendent. Failure to comply with the terms and conditions of this Agreement shall be sufficient cause for discharge as provided in this Agreement.

7.   *Disability*—Should the Superintendent be unable to perform the duties and obligations of this Agreement, by reason of illness, accident or other cause beyond the Superintendent's control and such disability exists after the exhaustion of accumulated sick leave days and vacation days during any school year, the Board, in its discretion, may make a proportionate deduction from the salary stipulated. If such disability contin-ues for 90 days, or if such disability is permanent, irreparable or of such nature as to make the performance

of Superintendent's duties impossible, the Board, at its option, may terminate this Agreement, whereupon the respective duties, rights and obligations of the parties shall terminate.

8. *Termination by Agreement*—During the term of this Agreement, the Board and Superintendent may mutually agree, in writing, to terminate this Agreement.

9. *Professional Activities and Memberships*—Superintendent shall be encouraged to attend appropriate professional meetings at the local, state and national levels. Within budget constraints, as approved by the Governing Board, such costs of attendance shall be paid by the Board.

10. *Vacation and Sick Leave*—The Superintendent shall receive 30 calendar days of vacation annually, exclusive of legal holidays and shall be entitled to 12 days sick leave annually. Vacation shall be taken at the discretion of the Superintendent and shall be cumulative to 60 days. Earned sick leave shall be cumulative as provided by the Board policy.

11A. *Hospitalization*—The Board shall provide hospitalization and major medical insurance for Superintendent and his dependents during the term of his Agreement in accordance with the basic insurance coverage provided to certificated members of the professional staff.

11B. *Term Life*—The Board shall provide for $50,000 of term life insurance for the Superintendent during the term of this agreement.

11C. *Dental*—The Board shall provide dental insurance for the Superintendent and his dependents during the term of this Agreement in accordance with the basic dental insurance coverage provided to certificated members of the professional staff.

11D. *Deferred Annuity*—The Board in accordance with applicable state and federal laws, and in accordance with the request of the Superintendent, shall withhold such amount of salary as designated by the Superintendent for payment into a tax-deferred annuity program as selected by the Superintendent.

11E. *Automobile and Related Expenses*—The Board shall provide an automobile for use by the Superintendent during the term of this Agreement. An automobile allowance not to exceed $6202 per year to be paid by the district to cover 80% of the automobile lease agreement for the Superintendent's personal vehicle. Gas and oil to be provided by the district supply and at district site.

12. *Notice*—Any notice or communication permitted or required under this Agreement shall be in writing and shall become effective on the day of mailing thereof by first-class mail, registered or certified mail.

13. This Agreement shall be governed in accordance with the laws of the State.

14. This Agreement contains all of the terms agreement upon the parties with respect to the subject matter of this Agreement and supersedes all prior agreements, arrangements and communications between the parties concerning such subject matter, whether oral or written.

IN WITNESS WHEREOF, the parties have caused this Agreement to be executed in their respective names and in the case of the Board, by its President, on the day and year first written above.

interest. Therefore, no due process rights were involved. The court also held that the board had sufficient cause to remove the superintendent based on inappropriate use of school funds for travel expenses with his wife.

Emerging Legal Issues

There several emerging issues being litigated in the courts that have special importance to the superintendent. With many of these issues, administrators are struggling to develop implementation policies without clear guidance from the courts or legislatures. We discuss several of the more important of the emerging legal issues here.

Charter Schools

A charter school may be defined as "a public school established by contract with a district governing board, the State Board of Education, or a State Board of Charter Schools . . . to provide learning that will improve pupil achievement." As noted in Chapter 2, the contract/charter may be issued to the faculty of an existing or proposed school, a group of parents, an institution of higher education, or any other group of individuals sharing similar views about education. The charter school has no legal or financial accountability to the local school district governing board, nor does the board have any responsibility for the charter school unless the charter is applied for and approved by the local governing board. Eleven states currently have legislation approving the charter school concept: Arizona, California, Colorado, Georgia, Hawaii, Kansas, Massachusetts, Michigan, Minnesota, New Mexico, and Wisconsin.

The most obvious concern about charter schools is the constitutionality of the legislation itself. To date there has been only one judicial decision reported dealing with charter schools. In a 1994 Michigan case the judge ruled that the state's newly approved charter school law is unconstitutional; the design of charter schools in Michigan does not meet the state's definition of public schools; and the new Michigan law that establishes the mechanism for creating charter schools usurps the State Board of Education's constitutional power to supervise schools.[18] It remains to be determined whether the Michigan law will be reinstated by higher courts, but the case will certainly fuel the legal arguments of charter school opponents in the other states with charter school laws.

There are other legal issues and unanswered questions regarding charter schools. For example: Are the charters public or private in nature? Do the advisory boards have to comply with the open meeting law? Can charter schools deny admission to special education student applicants? Are teachers in charter schools protected under the state school code statutes and do they have benefits of tenure? Are teachers in charter schools members of the state retirement system? What defines student rights? And, most important to our discussion, if the charter is issued by the local school district, what are the duties and responsibilities of the superintendent regarding the operation of the charter school?

Many state legislatures promoting the charter school concept have not dealt adequately with these legal issues and others in the establishing legislation. Their omissions have opened the door to litigation seeking answers to these important issues.

Prayer in the Schools

Prayer in the public schools is a continuing controversial issue facing superintendents and school boards. While the Supreme Court has issued a number of decisions regarding prayer in the schools, beginning with *Engel v. Vitale*[19] in 1962, there are still unresolved issues. In a recent decision, the Supreme Court in *Lee v. Weisman*[20] held that the school (administrators) may not invite clergy to give prayers at graduation exercises. However, some school attorneys believe the decision is narrowly defined and may not prohibit employees, students, parents, or other visitors to the school from praying individually or at the invitation of student groups within a school building.

There appears to be a controversy among the Circuit Courts of Appeal in the interpretation of the Supreme Court's decision in *Lee v. Weisman.* For example, in *Doe v. Ducanville Independent School District*[21] the Fifth Circuit Court of Appeals upheld the Supreme Court's long-standing ban on prayer in the schools and, supporting *Lee v. Weisman,* concluded that school-sponsored prayers conducted during basketball games or practices was constitutionally prohibited. However, in another decision, *Jones v. Clear Creek Independent School District,*[22] the same court upheld student-led prayer at graduation after the school district permitted members of the graduating class to vote on the inclusion of an invocation at the graduation ceremony led by a student volunteer. The opposite decision was reached by the Third Circuit Court of Appeals in *A.C.L.U. v. Blackhorse Pike Regional Bd. of Education.*[23]

The issue of prayer in the public schools is far from settled, as the passage of new state and federal laws continues to affect the issue. The Goals 2000: Educate America Act, passed by Congress in 1994 (H.R. 1804), includes a provision that "no funds authorized to be appropriated under this Act may be used by any state or local educational agency to adopt policies that prevent prayer and meditation in public schools" (Sec. 1011). In addition, the Elementary and Secondary Authorization Act (H.R. 6), also passed by Congress in 1994, states that funds under this act will be denied to any state or local agency having a policy denying or preventing participation in constitutionally protected prayer in public schools by individuals on a voluntary basis.

At the state level, several states are promoting legislation that permits student-initiated prayer during public high school graduation and at student group meetings.[24] However, a school district, under current federal case law, may not promote prayer within the curriculum, at athletic events, or at the start of the school day. The U.S. Circuit Courts of Appeals and the federal district courts will continue to provide guidance in this area of law for years to come, and superintendents will continue to have responsibility for the development of policy consistent with the emerging law.

Student-to-Student Sexual Harassment

Recent litigation related to student-to-student sexual harassment has received attention, and school districts have debated the development of policies addressing this issue in light of court decisions awarding damages to students prevailing in these cases. In *Doe v. Petaluma City School District,*[25] a federal district court held that a plaintiff student had successfully asserted a claim for money damages under Title IX and could proceed in court against a school district on the theory that its inaction in the face of complaints of student-to-student sexual harassment constituted circumstantial evidence of actual intent to discriminate against the student on the basis of sex.

Addressing the legal issues of student-to-student harassment in 1993, the U.S. Department of Education's Office of Civil Rights (OCR) recognized some district-level responsibility. The OCR found probable cause that a Minnesota school district discriminated under Title IX against a seven-year-old girl and her female classmates because it failed to treat boys who were sexually harassing them as violators of the district's sexual harassment policy.[26] The OCR found the school district in violation of Title IX for "failing to take timely and effective responsive action to address ... multiple or severe acts of sexual harassment."[27] In both of the cases mentioned, the female plaintiffs were awarded out-of-court settlements ranging from $20,000 to $40,000.

In other student-to-student sexual harassment cases where plaintiff students have sought damages, claiming not a violation of Title IX, but a deprivation of their constitutional right to personal integrity and security, they have not been as successful. In a 1990 Virginia case, *B. M. H. v. School Board of the City of Chesapeake, Va.,*[28] the court found no special relationship existed between the student and the school district on which an action for constitutional deprivation could be maintained. In this case, B. M. H., a 13-year-old student, was threatened with rape by a classmate and reported the threat to one teacher, who told another teacher. The student contended that the district had an affirmative duty to protect her from the attack due to the special relationship that existed between herself and the district. The court, holding for the district, ruled that the student "was not so restrained by the mandatory school attendance laws that she was prevented from acting on her own behalf."[29] However, while the court said the district did not have a "duty to protect" in these circumstances, it did not dismiss state law claims of gross negligence against the teachers.

In another case involving the sexual assault of a special education student by a mentally retarded student in the same program, the court reached a similar decision. In *Dorothy J. v. Little Rock School District,* the court held that "public school attendance does not render a child's guardians unable to care for the child's basic needs."[30] The court noted that a duty to care arises only when the state restrains an individual's liberty to the extent he or she is unable to care for him- or herself. Accordingly, the district was not held liable for the student-to-student assault.

Superintendents and school districts must take the issue of student-to-student sexual harassment seriously and address the problem with clear policies and procedures, support the policies and ensure they are publicized and understood, move quickly to investigate, stop the harassment when it is identified, and enforce sanctions for those found to violate the policies. One example of an effective school district procedure and compliance with Title IX occurred when the OCR found a district acted expeditiously in addressing a complaint that a male student had fondled and exposed himself on the school bus. The district immediately investigated the incident when it was reported and disciplined the male student by removing him from the bus. The district also paid for counseling for the female student.[31]

Sexual Abuse of Students by Teachers and Negligent Hiring, Supervision, and Retention of Personnel

The public press has documented the alarming increase in the number of cases against school districts for the negligent hiring and retention of school employees who have sexually abused students. And while plaintiffs have not been successful in claiming the schools have a constitutional "duty to protect" as it relates to sexual harassment from other students, the same has not been true when the abuser is a school employee. In fact, in a recent case, *Doe v. Taylor Independent School District,*[32] the court held that a supervisory school official can be held personally liable for a subordinate's violation of a student's right to bodily integrity in sexual abuse cases if the plaintiff establishes:

1. The defendant learned of facts or a pattern of inappropriate sexual behavior by a subordinate pointing plainly toward the conclusion that the subordinate was sexually abusing the student;
2. The defendant demonstrated deliberate indifference toward the constitutional rights of the student by failing to take action that was obviously necessary to prevent or stop the abuse; and
3. Such failure caused a constitutional injury to the student.

In this case the principal was held liable for his deliberate indifference toward the student's constitutional rights by failing to act on the substantial information of the teacher's inappropriate behavior. The court found that the superintendent's conduct, however, did not rise to this level. The superintendent had instructed the principal to speak to the teacher, personally investigated he matter, reprimanded the teacher, and warned the teacher of the consequences of his misconduct.

One important implication of the *Doe* case is the court's determination that compulsory attendance laws created a special relationship between the child and the state, which required school officials to protect the child. The *Doe* decision was distinguished from *B. M. H.* and *Dorothy J.* in that the sexual assault to the student was by a teacher.

The torts of negligent hiring and retention occur when an employer breaches a duty in hiring or retaining an employee who is incompetent or unfit for the job to which the employee is assigned, and consequently, the actions of that employee proximately causes injury to a third party. The focus of the tort of negligent hiring is on the employee selection process. Negligent retention focuses on when the employer becomes aware or should have become aware of an employee's problems that indicated he or she is unfit or dangerous.

Even in the absence of actual knowledge, a school district can be held liable if a reasonable inquiry would have produced evidence of an employee's dangerousness or unfitness. However, a good faith effort by the district to carefully check the background of prospective employees, coupled with proper supervision, will lessen liability under claims of negligent hiring and negligent retention. For example, in *Medlin v. Bass,*[33] a North Carolina student was sexually assaulted by the school principal. The parents claimed the school district was negligent in hiring and retaining the principal, who had previously resigned from another district after being accused of sexually assaulting another student. The court found the district had adequately investigated an unconfirmed rumor related to the principal's sexual tendencies and the principal had performed satisfactorily for 16 years. Thus the court held the school district neither knew or could have known of the principal's tendencies prior to the incident, and therefore the student had failed to establish an essential element of a claim for negligent hiring and retention.

Litigation is increasing in both the areas of student-to-student sexual harassment and student sexual abuse by teachers. The superintendent must take the lead in addressing these problems head on, quickly and effectively in terms of preventing costly litigation and out-of-court settlements, but more importantly, in providing a safe environment and protecting students from harm. Increased efforts must be made in identifying personnel who have a past record of inappropriate sexual conduct with students and thoroughly investigating any claim of student sexual abuse by a school employee.

Special Education Inclusion

Despite the availability of administrative hearings at various levels, as well as formal and informal mediation processes, there has been a significant increase in special education–related litigation. In particular, there has been a steady increase in litigation dealing with the least restrictive alternative (LRE) provision of the Education For Handicapped Children Act (EHA), P.L. 94-142, amended and renamed the Individuals With Disabilities Act (IDEA).[34] The least restrictive environment is also known as "inclusion," "mainstreaming," or "integration." The issue of placement of special education students in the regular classroom with their peers has been extremely controversial, involving parents, teachers, administrators, public and private schools, state education agencies, the U.S. Department of Education, as well as the courts in the debate. The courts have repeatedly defined the EHA's and IDEA's preference for mainstreaming as the least restrictive environment.

In 1983, the Sixth Circuit Court of Appeals ruled in *Roncker v. Walter*[35] that the LRE requirements of the IDEA prohibited separate, segregated educational placement whenever the services needed by a student could feasibly be provided in nonsegregated settings. Another court-defined LRE standard was put forth by the Fifth Circuit in 1989 in *Daniel R. R. v. El Paso Independent School District.*[36] The court ruled schools must provide an individual education tailored to each child's unique needs that at the same time educates students with disabilities with their nondisabled peers.

More recently, the Ninth Circuit Court of Appeals, in *Board of Education, Sacramento City Unified School District v. Holland*[37] (1994), developed a four-part test to determine whether a placement meets the least restrictive alternative standard of the IDEA:

1. What are the educational benefits from full-time placement in a regular education classroom?
2. What are the nonacademic benefits of a regular classroom placement?
3. What is the effect on the rest of the class from the placement of child with disabilities in a regular education classroom?
4. What is the cost of a regular education placement with proper supplementary aids and services?

The court in *Holland* determined that the student had a right to be educated first in a regular classroom with supplemental aids and services. Some authorities predict that the decision in *Holland* is further evidence that the IDEA should be interpreted to mean that public schools are obligated to attempt a regular education placement for disabled students before trying a segregated placement.

It remains to be seen whether school districts, administrative hearing officers, and the courts support the trend toward inclusion or whether special education students will be integrated into the regular classroom on a case-by-case basis. Recent case law on inclusion supports the costly nature of such litigation in personnel time, district resources, and the ill will that often develops between parents and the school district.

Selected Federal Legislation

It is not possible to provide an in-depth discussion of the growing list of federal legislation affecting the public schools. However, a brief discussion of the implications of several of the more recent and important federal laws should be instructive to both practicing and prospective superintendents. For it is the responsibility of the superintendent to oversee district compliance with these and other federal laws and regulations, appraise the governing board of potential violations and noncompliance, and put forth a documented, good faith effort to comply with the mandates and directives of these important laws.

Section 504, Rehabilitation Act of 1973

An area of growing concern to school districts is the increase in litigation and the OCR's enforcement of Section 504 of the Rehabilitation Act of 1973.[38] The thrust of Section 504 is to accommodate the disabled student with the services necessary for that child to receive the same level of educational benefit provided to nondisabled students. Thus, evidence that the district has failed to evaluate, identify, and provide appropriate special education and related services for disabled students qualifying for Section 504 accommodations may constitute evidence of discrimination and the denial of a free appropriate public education (FAPE). According to the OCR, the regulations implementing Section 504 require school districts to provide a free public education to each child whose disability "substantially limits" a major life activity.

The growth in litigation involving Section 504 is partly due to an apparent increase in the number of students who do not qualify for services or placement under the IDEA, but may qualify for "reasonable accommodation," as well as a free public education under Section 504.[39] For example, in *Lyon v. Smith,*[40] a federal district court held that although a student with attention deficit and hyperactivity disorders was ineligible for special education under the IDEA because he did not meet the eligibility criteria for the "other health impaired" category, he might be eligible under Section 504 because he was "otherwise qualified."

Other disabled students not covered under the IDEA but possibly entitled to an appropriate education under Section 504 are children with AIDS[41] (automatic exclusion is a violation of Section 504); children with tuberculosis and other infectious diseases (a two-step test is required to determine if the student is "otherwise qualified": (1) whether, considering the nature, duration, and severity of the illness, the student poses a significant risk to others, and (2) whether reasonable accommodation will eliminate the risk of communicating the infection); and students with drug or alcohol problems[42] (students with drug addiction or alcoholism are entitled to evaluation for individualized appropriate education). Marginal special education categories such as socially maladjusted, Tourette's syndrome, and the developmentally delayed may also be qualified for Section 504 service. However, students with lack of impulse control or antisocial behavior may not be covered by Section 504 where there is substantial impairment with major life activity, including learning.[43] There are also a number of cases citing the failure of a school district to provide a method of access to handicapped parents that would enable them to communicate effectively with school personnel regarding their children's educational programs. These actions by the schools violate Section 504.[44]

While there are no federal funds reimbursement provisions to school districts for services provided to students under Section 504, the mandates of the law must be met or all other federal funds received by the district may be in jeopardy. And the OCR's authority to investigate potential violations of Section 504 has been upheld by the courts.[45] In fact, every year the OCR does investigate several hundred school districts based on Section 504 and, unfortunately, finds violations in about half. Due to the potential for loss of federal funds and the expenses associated with accommodating disabled students not eligible for services under the IDEA, this area of emerging litigation (and OCR attention) should be carefully monitored by the superintendent.

Americans With Disabilities Act

Section 504 protections have been extended beyond federally assisted institutions by the Americans With Disabilities Act of 1990 (ADA).[46] Under this Act, a disabled person is considered one who has a physical or mental impairment that substantially limits a major life activity; a person who has a past record of such an impairment;[47] or a person who is regarded by others as having such an impairment. Individuals who have AIDS, are recovered alcoholics, or rehabilitated for drug addiction are covered under ADA. There are several practical implications of the law, such as the reasonable accommodation that must be made for employees and the changes to the employee recruitment and selection process to ensure that the rights of "otherwise qualified" persons are protected (e.g., questions about medical conditions are no longer allowed).

The law also affects the extent to which the district has provided accessibility to both employees and invited visitors. This may include wheelchair accessibility, interpreters and/or assistive listening devices for people with hearing impairments, readers and/or large print materials for individuals with vision impairments, audiotapes for the learning disabled, or other accommodations. In addition, some public school students may be covered under the provisions of the ADA.[48]

Family and Medical Leave Act of 1993

The Family and Medical Leave Act of 1993 (FMLA)[49] is an important federal law that entitles eligible employees to take up to 12 weeks of unpaid, job-protected leave each year for specified family and medical reasons. The law contains provisions on coverage; employee eligibility for benefits; entitlement to leave; maintenance of health benefits during leave; job protection after the leave; and other protection for employees. School districts and other employers are required to keep certain records. There are certain special rules that apply to employees of local education agencies, including public school boards and elementary and secondary schools under their jurisdiction. Some of these special rules for schools include intermittent leave, leave near the end of the academic term by instructional employees, and restoration to an equivalent position. The FMLA has raised many questions for school districts, including, How does the FMLA affect collective bargaining agreements? What is the interaction between the FMLA and federal and state antidiscrimination laws? How does the FMLA affect the spouse of a superintendent employed in the same district?

Fair Labor Standards Act

The Fair Labor Standards Act (FLSA)[50] mandates the payment of minimum wages and overtime compensation to covered employees. The U.S. Department of Labor (DOL) has shown an increased interest in school districts who may be in violation of the overtime provisions of the FLSA, which require employers to pay at least time-and-a-half to employees who are required to work more than 40 hours per week.

As one example of what has been taking place nationwide, the DOL surveyed one-third of the nonexempt classified school district employees in Arizona to determine if they had been fairly paid. The federal investigators also reviewed the districts' wage and hour policies. The DOL found that many classified workers who came to work early or took work home, volunteered in classrooms, coached, or provided security at school events were owed back wages. Several of the Arizona districts owed employees money, compensatory time, or a combination of pay and time off for the two-year period under investigation. One school district owed $63,000 in back wages, another owed $169,000 to 69 past and present employees, and one school district owed more than $800,000 in overtime wages to employees.[51] As a result, school districts warned classified employees not to come to work more than 10 minutes before the beginning of the work day and warned instructional aides not to take work home.

Handicapped Children's Protection Act

Another federal law with potential costly implications for school districts is the Handicapped Children's Protection Act (HCPA).[52] The HCPA provides that the court, at its discretion, may award reasonable attorney's fees as a part of the costs to the prevailing parent or guardian in special education cases pending on or after July 4, 1984.

There is some conflict among the federal circuit courts as to the test of what constitutes a "prevailing party." Under one set of standards, a plaintiff must obtain an enforceable judgement or comparable relief through a consent decree or settlement to be considered a prevailing party.[53] By the standard applied by another court, a plaintiff may be considered to have prevailed if it can be shown that the process was a material contributory factor in bringing about extrajudicial relief.[54]

Parents are entitled to attorney's fees at local- and state-level administrative hearings as well as at court proceedings. For example, in *Tenneman v. Town of Gorham*,[55] the court held that parents may recover fees as prevailing parties at an administrative hearing but were not entitled to recover fees and costs associated with a pupil evaluation team (PET) meeting. Parents have also been awarded attorney's fees although no hearing was held and the issues were resolved through mediation,[56] and for attendance at IEP meetings if directly connected to due process appeals. The courts have also awarded fees to parents who received injunctive relief,[57] and to parents who were prevailing parties despite the lack of complete success because the parents through their efforts altered the relationship between the district and the child, fostered the purpose of the IDEA, and achieved their primary objective.[58] However, an award of attorney's fees may not be granted if the parents were not substantially justified in rejecting the school district's settlement offer[59] or if the parents or their attorney were responsible for protracting litigation.[60]

Summary

The superintendent provides direction to both the school district's attorney and the governing board concerning policies, procedures, and actions to be taken to lessen the liability of the school district. Many superintendents are evaluated on their ability to perceive and understand emerging legal issues, as well as how well the district fares in compliance reviews with state and federal laws and regulations.

The superintendent in the year 2000 and beyond must remain alert to both current and pending litigation at the state and federal levels. The superintendent should also be aware of contract law as it relates to his or her contract. The superintendent should also obtain a professional legal review of his or her contract prior to signing. It is not uncommon for superintendents to not have their contracts renewed for any number of reasons, or to be asked to resign prior to the expiration of the employment contract. As an employee of the governing board, the superintendent has certain contractual rights stemming from state law and board policy. In addition, he or she may have additional constitutional protection and procedural guarantees based on dismissal for cause or dismissal based on discriminatory reasons.

The review of case law dealing with superintendent dismissal, emerging legal issues, and litigation related to recently enacted federal laws will, we hope, provide more than an awareness, but a motivation to keep abreast of important legal issues and case law developments affecting the public schools.

Discussion Questions

1. What are the legal responsibilities of the superintendent in the school district in which you are employed? To what extent does the evaluation of the superintendent in your district consider his or her performance of these legal responsibilities?

2. To what extent does the disability provision of the sample contract in Figure 9.1 represent a possible violation of the ADA or the FMLA?

3. What are the statutory provisions related to superintendent dismissal in your state?

4. What are the advantages to the superintendent of being considered a teacher?

5. Choose one of the emerging legal issues discussed in this chapter and discuss some of the aspects that will likely be the subject of litigation in the near future.

CASE 9.1   Shall We Pray?

The senior class at Rhodes High School voted to have three members of the class, one Protestant, one Catholic, and one Jew, to read prayers at the graduation ceremony. The principal demands to review and approve the prayers before granting permission. When the news reaches parents that prayers are to be read, the superintendent receives numerous calls from parents objecting to the prayers, from parents objecting to the principal's possible censorship, as well as from members of the school board, including Reverend Thomas Davis, taking positions on both sides of the issue. A member of the local press as well as the attorney for the local chapter of the A.C.L.U. have called several times for appointments.

Questions

1.   Under what circumstances are prayers at graduation ceremonies permissible? Are these circumstances met in this case?
2.   Are the principal's actions justified in this case? Why or why not?
3.   What actions should the superintendent take to defuse this matter?

Inbasket Exercise

INBASKET 9.1

Design Your Own Contract

You have been hired by the Port Smith School District as superintendent of schools, effective July 1. The initial contract offered by the district is identical in every detail to the sample presented in this chapter except that under Section 1A your contract is for three years. You are in the process of reviewing the contract with your attorney.

Prepare an amended contract, consistent with the principles of contract law and the law covering superintendents' contracts in your state, that eliminates any ambiguity in the contract and represents your understanding of the duties and responsibilities of the superintendent and the appropriate role between the superintendent and the school board.

Notes

1. See, e.g., Arizona Revised Statutes, Section 15-503 (A)(1).

2. Joseph R. McKinney and Thelbert L. Drake, "The School Attorney and Local Educational Policy," *Education Law Reporter,* 93(2) (1994); see also Donal M. Sacken, "The Legalization of Education and the Preparation of School Administrators," *Education Law Reporter,* 84(1) (1993).

3. *Norris v. Monroe City School Board,* 580 So.2d 425 (La.App. 1991).

4. McKinney and Drake, "The School Attorney and Local Educational Policy."

5. Arthur Linto Corbin, *Corbin on Contracts* (St. Paul, Minn.: West Publishing, 1952).

6. See Ibid., pp. 446–452, for a discussion of the Statute of Frauds—Contracts not to be performed within one year.

7. The discussion on contract terms was adapted from case practice materials of R. Kelly Hocker, Esquire, Tempe, Ariz., used with permission.

8. *Safeway Stores v. Retail Credit Clerks International Assoc.,* 261 P.2d 721 (1953).

9. See generally, Dan B. Dobbs, *Remedies, Damages, Equity, Restitution* (St. Paul, Minn.: West Publishing, 1985), Chapters 1–4; and Mack A. Player, *Employment Discrimination Law* (St. Paul, Minn.: West Publishing, 1988), pp. 185–193, for a discussion of remedying violations in employer discrimination.

10. 105 S.Ct. 1497 (1985).

11. 92 S.Ct. 2694 (1972).

12. 92 S.Ct. 2701 (1972).

13. See, e.g., Arizona Revised Statutes, Section 15-503(D). See also *Bakke v. St. Thomas School District # 43,* 359 N.W.2d 117 (1984) and *Hightower v. State Comm'r of Educ.,* 778 So.2d 595 (Tex. App.—Austin 1989).

14. See, e.g., *Hudson v. Marshall,* 549 S.W. 2d 147 (Mo.App. 1977); *Fuller v. North Kansas City School District,* 629 S.W. 2d 404 (Mo.App. 1981).

15. *Oleska v. Board of Education of East Rockaway Union Free School District,* 604 N.Y.S. 2d 227 (1993).

16. *Cannon v. Beckville Independent School District,* 709 F.2d 9 (1983).

17. 366 S.E.2d 82 (Va. 1988).

18. Drew Lindsay, "Michigan Judge Strikes Down Charter Law," *Education Week* (9 November 1994): 1 ff.

19. 370 U.S. 421 (1962).

20. 112 S.Ct. 2649 (1992).

21. 986 F.2d 953 (5th Cir. 1993).

22. 977 F.2d 963 (5th Cir. 1992).

23. Case No. 93-5368 (3d Cir. 1993).

24. See *Ingebretsen v. Jackson Public School Dist.* (S.D. Miss. 1994) WL 518843; see also Norma R. Rankin and John L. Strope Jr., "Prayer at Public School Graduation: What Is a School Official to Do?" *Education Law Reporter,* 89 (1994): 1051.

25. 830 F.Supp. 1560 (N.D. Ca. 1993).

26. See *Educators' Guide to Controlling Sexual Harassment* (Washington, D.C.: Thompson, 1994), p. 1.

27. Ibid.

28. 833 F.Supp. 560 (E.D. Va. 1993).

29. Ibid., p. 561.

30. 7 F.3d 729 (8th Cir. 1993).

31. Liberty # 53 School Dist., OCR 7-91-0119 (1991).

32. 15 F.3d 443 (5th Cir. 1994).

33. 398 S.E.2d 460 (N.C. 1990).

34. 20 U.S.C. Section 1401 et seq.

35. 700 F. 2d 1058 (6th Cir. 1983).

36. 874 F.2d. 1036, 1098 (5th Cir. 1989).

37. 786 F.Supp. 874 (E.D. Cal. 1992), *aff'd* 14 F.3d 1398 (9th Cir. 1994).

38. See Perry A. Zirkel, "Section 504: The New Generation of Special Education Cases," *Education Law Reporter,* 85 (1993): 601.

39. "Letter to Zirkel," *Individuals With Disabilities Law Reporter,* 10 (1993): 134. This OCR policy memorandum states that the regulations implementing Section 504 requires local school districts to provide a free appropriate public education to students who are covered solely by Section 504.

40. 829 F.Supp. 414 (D. D.C. 1993).

41. *District Community School Bd. v. Board of Education,* 502 N.Y.S. 2d (Sup.Ct. 1986).

42. *School Bd. of Nassau County v. Arline,* 480 U.S. 273 (1987); see also Community Unit School District No. 300 (IL), *Education of the Handicapped Law,* 353 (1989): 296.

43. Shasta County (CA) Office of Educ., *Education of the Handicapped Law Reporter,* 353 (1989): 196.

44. Ramapo (N.Y.) Cent. School Dist., *Education of the Handicapped Law Reporter,* 16 (1989): 559.

45. *Education of the Handicapped Law Reporter,* 17 (1991): 412.

46. 42 U.S.C. Section 12101; see also Ronald Wenkurt, "The American With Disabilities Act and Its Impact on Public Education," *Education Law Reporter,* 82 (1993): 291.

47. For further discussion of the Americans With Disabilities Act, see Bernadette Marczeley, "The American With Disabilities Act: Confronting the Shortcomings of Section 504 in Public Education," *Education Law Reporter,* 78 (1993): 199.

48. *Peterson v. Hastings Public Schools, Individuals With Disabilities Law Reporter,* 20 (1993): 252; see also *Individuals With Disabilities Law Reporter,* 20 (1993): 134, for additional discussion related to student coverage under ADA.

49. 29 U.S.C. 2601 et seq.

50. 29 U.S.C. Section 201 et seq.; see also Section 207 related to overtime pay.

51. Mike Padgett, "Federal Probe of Overtime Costs District," *Arizona Republic,* (9 September 1994), Tempe Community Section.

52. 20 U.S.C. Section 615(e)(4)(B).

53. *S-1 and S-2 v. State Board of Education of North Carolina,* 21 F.3d 49 (4th Cir. 1994) (*en banc*).

54. *Combs v. School Bd. of Rockingham County,* 15 F.3d 357 (4th Cir. 1994).

55. 802 F.Supp. 532 (D. Me. 1992).

56. *Masotti v. Tustin Unified School District,* 806 F.Supp. 221 (D. Ca. 1992).

57. *Capiello v. District of Columbia,* 780 F.Supp. 46 (D. D.C. 1991).

58. *Angela L. v. Pasadena Independent School District,* 918 F.2d 1188 (5th Cir. 1990).

59. *Mattew L. v. Woonsocket Education Department,* 793 F.Supp. 41 (D. R.I. 1992).

60. *Johnson v. Bismark Public School District,* 949 F.2d 1000 (8th Cir. 1991).

$$C \quad h \quad a \quad p \quad t \quad e \quad r \quad \textit{10}$$

Fiscal Responsibilities
of the Superintendent

In the 1992 American Association of School Administrators' survey of superintendents, as in previous surveys, school finance was named as the number one problem faced by superintendents.[1] An era of limited resources and competing demands calls on superintendents to demonstrate their acumen in managing the fiscal resources of the school district and in securing the support of the community for budget and capital levies. In this chapter we provide an overview of the primary areas of fiscal responsibility of the superintendent: budgeting, including a review of the various organizational approaches to budgeting and the difficult task of reducing the budget, conducting budget and bond issue campaigns, and a relatively new task, securing alternative revenues.

The Superintendent's Role in Budgeting School District Dollars

As school districts find themselves in increased competition for scarce resources and facing growing demands for accountability, the school budget takes on added importance. And perhaps the most important fiscal management responsibilities of the superintendent concern the development and administration of the budget. In this regard the superintendent's performance is judged by the functioning of the budget process, the quality and adequacy of the programs provided for by the budget, and the administration of the budget (e.g., control of expenditures and budget adjustments) throughout the year.[2]

A school district budget is made up of three elements: "(1) a description of the total educational program to be provided by the school district; (2) an estimate of the expenditures needed to carry out the desired program; and (3) an estimate of the revenues which will be available to pay for the expenditures."[3] The superintendent is a key player in the preparation of each of these elements. The superintendent and his or her staff generally provide the leadership in the estimation of all known revenues and the projection of costs for each expenditure category in the budget, as well as in the development of the educational program. The specific role of the superintendent in the latter will depend on whether the budget is centralized or decentralized. Under centralized budgeting, where decisions regarding such items as staffing ratios, textbooks, materials and supplies, and curriculum and extracurricular offerings are made at the central office, the superintendent's role is evidently greater than under decentralized, or site-based budgeting, where these decisions are made at the unit (or school) level.[4] In either case the superintendent is responsible for ensuring that site administrators "understand the framework of legal constraints, board policies, procedural guidelines, and budget appropriation amounts within which they must operate" and that programs and services are designed to meet student needs.[5]

In some districts, the superintendent is the only school official who reports budget matters directly to the board. And in most cases, it is the superintendent who presents the working draft of the budget to the board. The superintendent (with the assistance of staff) also provides the board with decision packages and recommends budget alternatives to them.

Once the budget is adopted, the superintendent is responsible for implementing the educational plan and for maintaining communication about the budget. In fact, immediately after the budget is adopted the superintendent should inform the community and all school personnel about any major budget decisions and changes. And although the business manager may take care of most of the day-to-day monitoring of the budget, it is the superintendent who schedules financial reports to the board, the community, and to state and federal agencies. And it is the superintendent who supervises the annual evaluation of budget effectiveness: analysis of estimated versus actual revenues and expenditures, and the measurement of the achievement of objectives. Last, a major budgetary responsibility of the superintendent is to use it as a vehicle to communicate an accurate, positive image of the school system to the community, as well as the community's expectations to the board, and as a means of involving citizens through hearings, surveys, and committees and, ultimately, of securing community support for the schools (and the budget).[6]

Properly developed, the budget is a key managerial tool for superintendents in achieving their primary mission—educating students in the most effective, cost-efficient manner possible. The budget provides the opportunity for community review and approval of the educational and fiscal plans of the district. The budget also serves as a significant planning device; an orderly, effective budgetary process requires that some evaluation of past activities take place and forces units throughout the system to plan for future action. The budgetary process can also be viewed as the major political process in a school district; the principal decisions of who gets what are made through this process.[7] Last, in many jurisdictions, it is the approved budget that provides the legal authorization for the expenditure of funds.

Organizational Approaches to Budgeting

The central importance of budgeting to the educational system requires use of a highly organized process to develop and adopt a budget. The six principal approaches to budgeting are incremental budgeting; line-item budgeting; program budgeting; the Planning, Programming, and Budgeting System; zero-based budgeting; and site-based budgeting. Each approach has its particular benefits and disadvantages, as well as its political utility.

In determining a budgeting method, the superintendent thus must consider both its technical advantages and its suitability to the district's belief systems and organizational structure. For example, an attempt to enact a more centralized budgetary process on top of a site-based instructional decision-making process could well lead to serious organizational conflicts. Likewise, the school board's role in the district should be thoughtfully considered in selecting a particular budgeting approach. A board accustomed to getting involved in administrative decisions and operations would be less likely to want a decentralized budgeting approach than a board that sees its role as more policy than administrative oriented.

In addition, the budgeting process used in the past must be considered. This process will have created certain expectations on the part of the community members and school district personnel as to the role they will play, and any significant change could cause conflict in the budget process unless it is preceded by a strong effort to communicate the nature and reasons for the change.[8]

Also, the superintendent's own value structures and attitudes about fiscal control should be consistent with the adopted budgetary approach. "As the person ultimately responsible for the educational and fiscal outcomes of the school district, the superintendent must function comfortably within the organizational structure of the district"[9] "or chaos and discontent will follow."[10]

The major features of each of the principal approaches to school district budgeting, as well as the major advantages and disadvantages of each, are important for the superintendent to consider; they are described in the sections that follow.

Incremental Budgeting
Incremental budgeting historically has been the most common budgetary technique used by school districts. Under incremental budgeting the previous year's budget is used as the starting point for the budget under consideration, and each item in the budget is adjusted up or down from that base. The adjustments are made as a percentage increase or decrease, and each item in the budget receives the same percentage adjustment.

Incremental budgeting assumes that the existing budget represents the proper distribution of resources among existing budget categories and that little programmatic change is needed. Incremental budgeting is also directly related to the methodology used by most state legislatures in making new state appropriations a percentage increase or decrease of the previous year's appropriations. Incremental budgeting may be employed as a technique for building the entire school district budget or in combination with other approaches.

Incremental budgeting is a politically attractive technique because of its simplicity and because it normally generates the least amount of conflict in that each area is treated equally. However, there are disadvantages to a technique that does not relate expenditure decisions to current conditions and that does not require any evaluation of past performance. And while appearing neutral, incremental budgeting can in fact result in overfunding or underfunding of specific categories. Finally, incremental budgeting, because of its mechanical nature, provides for minimal input from the superintendent.

Line-Item Budgeting
Line-item budgeting is similar in some respects to incremental budgeting. Line-item budgeting also starts with last year's budget and presumes that the expenditure for each line

item represents the appropriate base on which to build the new budget. Under line-item budgeting, however, each line receives separate consideration and may be adjusted by a different amount. Under line-item budgeting the *objects* of expenditure, that is, each line item, become the focus of attention. Objects are aggregated across different operations to yield a single line item. For example, all teacher salaries are combined into one line item, all instructional supplies into one line item, plant maintenance into one line item, and so forth.

A common practice in developing a line-item budget is to gather requests for each expenditure category from each building or program. Supplemental information may be required for expenditure requests that represent a big increase over last year or for special requests such as building repairs or renovation. After requests have been received from all buildings and programs, they are aggregated and decisions made regarding proposed appropriations for each expenditure area. Decisions are most often influenced by program performance, popularity, or perceived promise and may be made by the superintendent or by a committee.[11]

Line-item budgeting does provide the opportunity for greater consideration of current needs and more budget evaluation than incremental budgeting, as well as for more input from the superintendent. (In fact, line-item budgeting may be characterized as a centralized, administrator-dominated budgetary technique.) However, line-item budgeting generally does not encourage planning or innovation. Moreover, line-item budgeting tends to perpetuate the status quo. Not only do those programs already in place have constituents ready to defend their budget requests, often the process by which these requests are forwarded to the central office does not require a formal justification of program priorities or expenditures unless a substantial increase is requested.[12] This absence of information, in turn, limits the ability of the superintendent to gather sufficient information about educational programs to determine educational and community priorities and to make informed decisions in times of budgetary shortfalls. As a result, budget reductions are more vulnerable to political and knee-jerk decisions.

The use of line-item budgeting by school districts has declined considerably since the 1960s. However, it still remains the principal budgetary technique employed by school districts. According to Hartman, the solution to the shortcomings of line-item budgeting is to use this technique in combination with other budgeting approaches that will help overcome its weaknesses. In fact, as Hartman also points out, all other budgetary techniques use line-item budgeting as a basic element in organizing and developing the data.[13]

Program Budgeting
In contrast to the previously discussed approaches to budgeting, program budgeting directly relates expenditures to educational programs and support services. Originally conceived of and still referred to in some formats as a function–object budget, program budgeting is based on a budget organized by the major functions of the district. The structure closely parallels the organizational structure of the district and the way responsibilities are assigned. As a result, there is a specific individual who can be identified as having both organizational and fiscal responsibility for every category in the budget.[14]

The budgetary process itself involves estimating (on a line- item basis) all expenditures by fund, function, and object. Depending on the degree of detail desired, expenditures may be detailed to the school and grade level. For example, a General Fund (010) expenditure for instructional supplies at Horace Mann High School might be coded 10-11300-411-13-5 based on the following coding system:

10,000–19,999	=	Instruction
11,000	=	Regular Instruction
11,300	=	High School Instructional
11,300–400	=	High School Instructional Supplies
11,300–411–13	=	High School Instructional Supplies—General Stores
11,300–411–13–5	=	High School Instructional Supplies—General Stores—Horace Mann High School

Program budgeting promotes greater staff and community participation than incremental or line-item budgeting. However, this increased involvement does not come at the expense of the superintendent and school board members, who ultimately make decisions about what programs will be funded. Having budget information at the operational level strengthens the ability of school personnel to present effectively educational needs to the community and increases the likelihood of community support. In addition, having information available at this level increases the ability of the superintendent and school board to achieve a cost-effective balance between increasing program quality and reducing unnecessary costs.[15]

Program, Planning, and Budgeting System (PPBS)

More sophisticated forms of program budgeting, the Program, Planning, and Budgeting System (PPBS) and the Program, Planning, Budgeting, and Evaluation System (PPBES) link the budgeting process to programs through planning and evaluation processes into integrated systems. The addition of the planning and evaluation functions forces attention to outcomes and the relationships between resources and competing program goals. Under PPBS, the budget is organized around organizational goals and objectives rather than organizational structures. The basic concept is that the planning and budgeting process should involve the articulation of the system objectives and the specification and evaluation of alternatives for accomplishing these objectives in terms of their costs and benefits and resource requirements.

The budget cycle that would result from the implementation of a PPBS cycle is illustrated in Figure 10–1.

PPBS and PPBES were highly touted in the 1960s and 1970s and marked the first major attempt to apply accountability measures to the educational enterprise. In addition, their ability to extend the function–object coding system to include analysis of success stimulated the interest of school systems in tracking student progress and measuring their performance against the resources invested, and in so doing marked the beginning of modern productivity analysis.[16] As school districts attempted to implement PPBS and PPBES, however, they encountered a number of problems. One major problem was the inconsistency between program structures and budget categories in the organizational structure. Another major difficulty involved establishing measurable objectives and program structures and developing accurate measures of program outcomes. A third major obstacle was that the data requirements of the systems meant that only those school systems capable of significant investment in personnel and equipment could implement and operate PPBS or PPBES successfully. As a consequence of these difficulties, these approaches have seen limited adoption to school district budgeting.

Despite these problems, according to Hartman, there are many useful features of PPBS and PPBES that can be incorporated into the school district budgeting process without having to use their sometimes cumbersome program structure. These features include

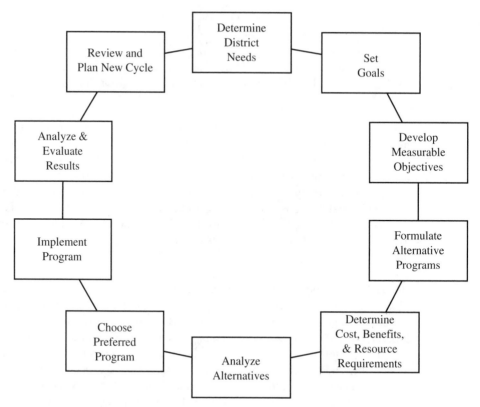

FIGURE 10–1   The PPBS Budget Cycle

"specification of the educational objectives of the district, identification of alternative means of reaching the objectives, multi-year cost estimates of the alternatives, selection of the most cost-effective alternative, and a evaluation of the outcomes for use in future years' decision making."[17]

Zero-based Budgeting (ZBB)

Zero-based budgeting, another form of program budgeting, was initiated in the private sector by Texas Instruments and introduced in the public sector by President Carter. Although some of ZBB's attraction faded in the 1980s—the decade of plenty—some superintendents are now advocating ZBB as the logical budgetary approach for school districts under a mandate to do "as much or more with less."[18] ZBB operates from the basic concept that every budget year the budget it developed from a zero base—nothing is assumed about the previous year's budget, and each budget activity and category must be justified each year. The budget is developed through a process in which *decision packages* that specify program goals and outcomes and the consequences of alternative funding levels are prepared for each activity, project, or program; funds are allocated on the basis of the ranking of these alternatives.

The steps involved in ZBB are as follows:

1. *Identify the decision units for all functions and activities.* A decision unit is defined as "the lowest practical organizational unit that is knowledgeable about the spending request and its impact."[19]

2. *Develop decision packages for each function, activity, or operation.* A function may be a division, school, department, grade level, or any other identifiable unit. An activity may be a total operation or any part of it. A decision package includes (1) a description of the program or activity, (2) a statement of the goals and objectives, (3) a description of alternative methods of accomplishing the goals and objectives, (4) the projected costs and benefits of each alternative, and (5) the consequences of not funding each alternative. Decision packages are of two types: mutually exclusive, which identify the best alternative from among those presented; and incremental, which present alternatives in terms of several levels of funding. With incremental decision packages, a standard practice is to require alternatives to be developed for three levels of funding: the current level, a specified percentage above, and a specified percentage below the current level.

3. *Submit decision packages for ranking.* Once the decision packages have been developed, they must be ranked in descending order of benefit to the decision unit. This ranking is then forwarded to progressive levels in the organizational structure, where these decisions packages are ranked in competition with every other decision package within that span of control. This process forces each successive administrator to study each function and activity, not only providing him or her with information for planning and evaluation purposes, but with a carefully considered prioritization that can be utilized if budget reductions are required or in the rare event the budget unexpectedly increases.

The ranking of decision packages is perhaps the most important step in zero-based budgeting. At each stage in the ranking process, managers and administrators should have the opportunity to defend a decision package. Also, clearly articulated ranking procedures and criteria must be developed and communicated to all units prior to the development of the decision packages. Ranking at each level may be done by a single administrator or by a committee chosen for that purpose. If possible, the committee should include someone from the business department. The final list of ranked decision packages is then submitted to the superintendent for review and approval.

In most instances decision packages in school districts will fall into one of two categories: (1) *mandatory programs or activities,* which are mandated by statute or essential to the basic operation of the school district, and (2) *discretionary programs or activities,* where some discretion exists as to whether or at what level they will be provided. Because mandatory programs or activities cannot be eliminated without violating state or federal statutes or state department of education regulations, or without undermining the basic operation of the school district, it is not necessary to require that they be justified from a zero base each year.

4. *Submit budget document.* The budget represents the final prioritized list of decision packages selected for funding. Operationally, the superintendent may submit the decision packages themselves to the school board for funding, or the decision packages may serve as the budget justification for more traditional budgets (e.g., line-item or function–object budgets).

Zero-based budgeting offers many of the same benefits as PPBS: it makes planning the first step in the budget process; it ties the budget to the school district goals; it encourages involvement of staff at all levels and forces them to closely scrutinize each activity; and it improves the provision of information to the administration.[20] Theoretically, both these forms of program budgeting help ensure that resources are allocated to where they will yield the greatest benefits, and both help constrain the political budgeting process to produce more rational decisions. The particular contribution that zero-based budgeting makes to program budgeting is the richness provided by presenting the budget at more than one level of support. This format arms the administration with the information necessary to forestall otherwise uninformed opposition and to "put the ball back in the other court" at times of budget hearings. That is, many negative responses to specific budget items, especially those representing increases, may be forestalled by the explanatory material accompanying a zero-based budget. In addition, those school board and community members who would otherwise be inclined to demand that the budget be cut across the board by some percentage are instead forced to respond with what specific programs they want to cut, and faced with the consequences of each decision.[21]

As previously implied, zero-based budgeting has not been widely adopted in education and has received many of the same criticisms as PPBS: the large data and resource requirements, and the difficulty in operationally defining and measuring goals and outcomes. However, as with PPBS, it does employ many worthwhile concepts that could be incorporated into a district's budgetary process and that would be particularly useful in times of budgetary cutbacks.[22]

In fact, many school districts have adopted modified zero-based budgeting techniques. One modification involves building the new budget based on a percentage reduction of the previous year's budget, with justification required for restoration. Another modification is to require units to prepare alternative budget scenarios—a growing and useful practice given the frequent uncertainty of revenues.

Site-based Budgeting (SBB)

The school reform movement that began in the 1980s placed increasing emphasis on the importance of the local school in achieving outcomes and improving accountability. The result has been a shift toward various approaches to site-based management that give greater control and involvement in the administration and operation of the schools to those closest to the student—principals, school staff, and community members. Site-based budgeting is an extension of this principle to the area of budget-related decisions. School-based budgeting

> represents the most recent sophistication in learning theory because it finally recognizes the importance of resources at the point of actual utilization—that is resources are only truly meaningful when they arrive at the individual classroom under the care of the individual teacher as applied to the individual student. . . . the special value of this technique is in providing a more holistic and inclusive view of education, making school site budgeting a reality long into the foreseeable future.[23]

As depicted in Figure 10–2, under SBB the budgetary process begins with district-wide strategic planning (including forecasting of revenues) and training of building participants. Each school site council develops its own goals and plan for achieving planning

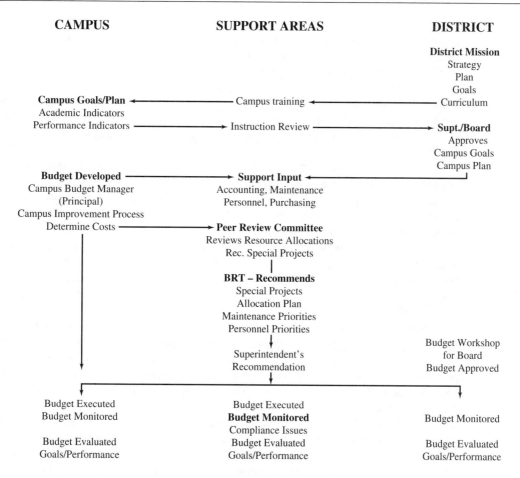

FIGURE 10–2   The Site-based Budgeting Process

SOURCE: Richard A. Griffin and Bill Phipps, "From Power to Persuasion, the Business Official's Role in Site-based Decision-Making," *School Business Affairs,* 58 (December 1992): p. 22.

objectives, as well as a budget designed to meet these goals and objectives. Ultimately all of these must be approved by the superintendent and the school board. Following board approval the budget is executed, monitored, and evaluated.

There is no definitive system of SBB. In some districts that purport to have adopted SBB, schools have budgetary control over only a fraction of the budget (e.g., in Los Angeles they control only instructional supplies and substitute teachers). In other districts, such as Edmonton, Canada, the local school controls as much as 80 percent of the total budget.[24] More commonly, to ensure uniformity and quality, as well as because many personnel matters including salary levels and student–staff ratios are covered by negotiated contracts, the central office retains budgetary control of district-wide functions such as capital outlay, transportation, and administration, as well as personnel salaries. In these cases, because schools are allowed to hire on a average cost basis, there is no financial incentive to hire persons with lower levels of experience or qualifications. Even in those districts where personnel decisions are under school control, there are normally certain positions, such as the principal, that are required to be retained by the central administration.

The money not retained at the district level is usually allocated to the individual schools based on a formula that takes into account the number and types of students to be served. If maintenance and operations expenditures are decentralized to the school site, certain characteristics of the facility, such as its age and relative energy efficiency, may also be considered.

Once the money reaches the school site, the principal and a school council composed of teachers, support staff, parents, and other community representatives are responsible for the development and administration of the school site budget. This does not mean that the central office has no role under SBB. Central office staff may provide technical assistance in budgeting and accounting. In addition, to assist sites achieve economies of scale and purchase wisely, the central office may facilitate cooperative purchasing and develop lists of approved products and vendors. And ultimately, it is the responsibility of the superintendent to ensure that each site is provided accurate and timely data on which to build its budgets, and that each school site budget conforms to state statutes and regulations and school board policies.

The major advantages of SBB are the potential it provides for more accurately ensuring that expenditures reflect student needs and the greater sense of participation and ownership it generates in principals, teachers, support staff, parents, and students. School district participants usually become more sensitive to cost-efficient measures ranging from better use of staff time to turning off the lights in empty rooms. Parents and community participants become more sensitive to the relationship between district tax levies and school services.[25] However, the benefits that will be realized from SBB depend to a large degree on the extent to which superintendents and principals are prepared and willing to share decision making. For this reason, not only must a close dialogue be maintained between the superintendent and other central office personnel and school-based personnel, but the superintendent has to ensure that principals and other participants receive the training necessary to fulfill their expected roles. It is therefore imperative in any district contemplating or attempting to implement SBB that the superintendent provide leadership in preparing the district for the new system and be assertive in insisting that it be supported.[26]

While SBB has numerous advantages, there are several possible disadvantages, the principal one being the potential for engendering inequality among the schools of the district. This can result from varying skill levels of participants in managing available resources, or from unwise decisions, adversely affecting students, made by individual schools to cut or abandon programs and services. For this reason, it is critically important that the superintendent and other central office administrators monitor expenditures and work closely with principals to ensure that district goals are being met and that district standards are being maintained.

It has been said that site-based decision making and budgeting calls for the superintendent to "model shared decision making operationally, focus on student achievement, support positive outcomes, demonstrate leadership by service and training, be goal oriented, be assertive in enforcing the decentralization process, set the vision, articulate the mission, hire and fire principals based on their commitment and ability to carry out the vision, and report progress on the site-based decision-making process to the board."[27]

The Management of Decline

Few districts in the country have escaped the last decade without experiencing some decline in federal, state, or local revenues. When this situation occurs, school districts are forced to go through the difficult process of reducing the budget. The process that is used is key—both for the impact on the educational program and for gaining community and staff support for the necessary reductions. The process can range from edicts issued by the school board or superintendent to broad community involvement. The size of the cuts weighs on the choice of process. Minor cuts without serious impact on programs may indeed be best made by directive. On the other hand, for more severe cuts, with significant program impacts, it is logical to consider large-scale staff and community involvement.[28] For example, when the Consolidated School District #4 in Grandview, Missouri, faced a 6 percent reduction, the task of preparing a prioritized list of recommended cuts for school board consideration was turned over to a 65-person task force representative of the school board, school district personnel, and the community. While acknowledging that this was a large budget committee, the district decided that "if we were going to have to pay a psychic price for reducing the budget, it might as well come sooner rather than later."[29] And by getting the involvement up front rather than at the end of the process, the budget was adopted intact, and without the involvement of just as many people at the end of the process—but involved in the form of angry meetings and bitter complaints.

To reduce the difficulty and trauma associated with making budget reductions, establish criteria to guide the process. This will provide the superintendent and school board with the basis for resolving disputes and will promote rational rather than emotional decision making.[30] The criteria adopted will necessarily reflect the values and priorities of the district. One such set of criteria proposed for a district facing a 10 percent cut in revenues and an estimated 5 percent increase in the cost of living is presented in the following:[31]

> *Criterion 1:*   Any budgetary cut that will be made will save one dollar for every dollar cut. (An example that does not meet this criterion is one that eliminates an employee, but which causes the payment of unemployment compensation.)

> *Criterion 2:*   Although programs may have to be cut, no program will be totally eliminated. However, as many programs as necessary will be reduced in scope in order to meet the expenditure reduction goal.

> *Criterion 3:*   Support services will be eliminated as much as possible before any reductions will be made in students' educational programs.

> *Criterion 4:*   Co-curricular activities (athletic and nonathletic) will be eliminated if they are not self-supporting, with the exception that one female, one male, and one coed co-curricular activity will be offered during the fall, winter, and spring terms. These activities will be supported by regular budgetary means, including local tax funds. Therefore, no contributions will be accepted from individuals or support groups unless these individuals or support groups provide sufficient funds to operate the entire co-curricular activity program at the qualitative level that has been historically expected.

Criterion 5: Program and staff reductions will be made at the senior high school, the junior high school, and the middle school prior to cuts being made at the elementary school.

Criterion 6: Purchasing of supplies and equipment will be reduced to the absolute minimum before the above criteria are considered.

Criterion 7: In addition, all rational and legal income producing activities will be thoroughly investigated.

The Budget Reduction Continuum

Once the criteria have been adopted by the board of education, the district can proceed with the budget reductions. A continuum of budget reduction alternatives, in descending order, is presented in Figure 10–3. The conventional wisdom of making the cuts as far away from the classroom as possible is reflected in the continuum. As evident by the entries on the continuum, not all budget reductions affect the delivery of programs or services. Some are reductions in expenditures resulting from improved efficiencies or modifications in operating procedures. They include a *reduction in prices* for the same products and services resulting from competitive bidding, cooperative purchasing, energy conservation, self-insurance, salary adjustments, lower salary increases, and so forth; *increased productivity;* and *deferred spending.*

The *across the board cuts* approach is normally used to apply small cuts to all programs, including instruction. This is often the more politically palatable approach in that every program and everyone shares part of the budget reduction. The assumption underlying this approach is that all programs will be able to continue to operate with a small, but manageable, reduction in resources without seriously affecting programs and services. However, there are two basic errors in this assumption. First, programs differ in their abilities to absorb cuts: large programs generally can spread the cut over more personnel, supply, and equipment allocations than small programs. Second, while the basic assumption

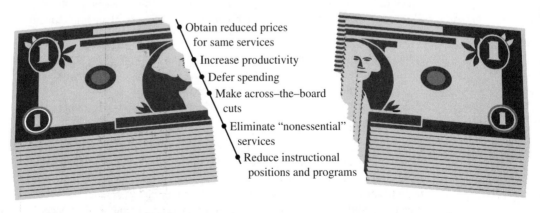

Obtain reduced prices for same services
Increase productivity
Defer spending
Make across–the–board cuts
Eliminate "nonessential" services
Reduce instructional positions and programs

FIGURE 10–3   The Budget Reduction Continuum

SOURCE: Developed from William T. Hartman, *School District Budgeting* (Englewood Cliffs, N.J.: Prentice Hall, 1988).

may hold true for a year or two, a continuation of across the board cuts "will slowly starve the district's programs and negatively impact the quality of education provided."[32]

Elimination of "nonessential" services involves eliminating those services (and programs) that are not required by state statute or regulations; this may include such things as transportation, food services, elective courses, or athletics. While not essential, they are often helpful to and popular with school district clientele and often become the focus of emotional debate in budget-cutting hearings.

The final type of budget reduction is to *reduce instructional positions and programs*. As previously stated, these reductions are typically the last to be made. However, when large budget reductions are required, they may not be avoidable. When this is necessitated, the laying off of personnel will be guided by applicable state statutes, school district policies, or negotiated contracts with employees.

The professional literature is replete with suggestions of how school boards and superintendents can "cut costs, not quality"[33] and "cut without killing."[34] A comprehensive list of possible cuts, the savings that would result, as well as the consequences has been published by the *American School Board Journal* and is reprinted with permission in Table 10–1.

The Superintendent as Development Officer and Entrepreneur

Given the continued resistance to virtually all forms of taxation, it is unlikely that most school districts will see any significant increase in tax revenues in the immediate future. As a result, in an effort both to avoid making budget reductions and to support new or improved programs and activities, many districts have sought ways to increase nontax revenues. In these districts the superintendent plays a key leadership role in directing the activities of staff and interacting with external constituencies.

Nontax revenues may be classified as donor activities, enterprise activities, or cooperative activities. *Donor activities* include direct contributions of funds, services, supplies, and equipment to the school or school district as well as indirect donations to school district foundations or support groups such as booster clubs. The donations are generally tax-deductible for the donor. Another inducement to the donor is the positive publicity that can be gained from the donation.[35]

An increasingly popular vehicle that has been established in many school districts for channeling donations is the educational foundation. An educational foundation is a nonprofit entity, separate from the school district, whose purpose is to develop supportive community and private sector relationships with the school system. Foundations differ from other public school support groups such as the PTA or booster clubs in that they are not situation responsive and do not concentrate on a single issue. "They are not a quick fix; foundations are designed as long-lasting, third party organizations which became important private partners in the support of public education."[36]

The types of programs and activities that are supported by educational foundations vary from school district to school district. Some foundations provide funds to supplant programs or activities eliminated by budget cuts, to build facilities, and even to support teacher salary increases. Other foundations channel funds to more supplemental activities such as enrichment programs for students or minigrants for teachers.[37]

TABLE 10–1 Forty Ways to Cut Costs

1. Hold the line on salary schedule increases this year (but keep step increases intact).

2. Freeze salaries (no increases for anybody).

3. Encourage early retirement of staff by providing a cash bonus or retroactive pay raise.

4. Reduce the number of small classes in secondary schools.

5. Replace credentialed educators in administrative positions with lower-salaried, specialized, full-year/full-time personnel.

6. Adopt new textbooks less frequently (without becoming lax about adoption standards).

7. Collect on lost, damaged, or stolen books—or require student who is responsible to perform work to earn cost of books.

8. Change fees for adult education equal to district's direct costs (with exceptions for low-income and elderly).

9. Place curriculum development projects on a competitive contracted basis (encourage groups of teachers to bid).

10. Reduce the number of specialist teachers, eliminate their formal teacher load, and have them help the regular teachers.

11. Use paraprofessionals instead of teachers for on-the-road segments of driver training instruction.

12. Replace your all-teacher physical education staff with a team of professionals and trained paraprofessionals.

13. As vacancies occur, subject each to thorough reassessment before filling (but be sure this is based on a long-range staffing plan).

14. Perform a cost-comparative study of your schools. Identify high-cost schools and develop plans to remedy differences not justified.

15. Perform a cost-comparison study of programs, identify high-cost programs and develop plans to remedy differences not justified.

16. Study your pattern of teacher absentees and crack down on teaches whose excuses are suspect.

17. Negotiate a new, lower beginning step in employee contracts, not affecting any present employees.

18. Establish "average teaching load" (ATL) factors for secondary-level subject areas and reassign or transfer excess staff to other vacancies.

19. Reduce the number of half-day kindergarten classes by consolidating and assigning teachers to more than one school.

20. Hold all vacancies open for at least two months in all but the most essential positions to find out whether you really need a position.

21. Consolidate evening educational and community programs into fewer schools, on fewer nights.

22. Reduce fuel consumption by turning off fresh-air intake fans after school.

23. Turn off lights when rooms are not in use; cut down on unnecessary lighting.

24. Sweet-talk city hall into letting you use municipal employees (rather than contracting) for repairs to buildings.

25. Cut custodial overtime by starting a second.

26. Collect all direct costs when outside nonprofit groups use school buildings.

27. Implement training program for custodial personnel on small repairs.

28. Evaluate the use of contracted maintenance vehicles. Use in-house mechanics to service transportation equipment.

29. Examine your transportation system to see if more students could walk to school.

30. Review school opening and closing times to develop a new pattern of staggered openings that requires use of fewer buses.

31. Tighten up on money management techniques.

32. Develop and implement a computerized perpetual inventory system for all equipment.

33. Give each subunit in the school system a budget and hold respective administrators responsible for it.

34. Ask administrators to come up with specific suggestions for reducing costs, improving efficiency and productivity on a quarterly basis—in writing.

35. Consolidate advertising for staff to reduce scatter-shot approach to filling vacancies as they occur.

36. Microfilm or scan old records optically rather than retain paper storage.

37. Reduce clerical help and use temporary help and/or high school students for peak periods; plan your staffing needs for average loads only.

38. Devise better control of office copiers.

39. Schedule buying in large lots.

40. Increase fees to faculty to cover full direct costs of lunch.

SOURCE: Alexander H. Decker, Michael Mulheirn, David Sluder, and Shirley Watford, "Cut Costs, Not Quality," *The American School Board Journal,* 179 (June, 1992), pp. 28–30. Reprinted with permission, from *The American School Board Journal* (June). Copyright (1992), the National School Boards Association. All rights reserved.

Internal Revenue Service regulations and state laws will dictate the actual terms and operation of the foundation. The foundation is governed by a board of directors. Foundations vary as to their relationship with the local school board. Depending on state law, the school board may select all or some of the members of the board of directors. Alternatively, the board itself could elect new members, some community group independent of the school board could choose the members, or some combination approach could be used. No one approach is preferable to another. It is a matter of preference of the school board and the persons establishing the foundation.[38] What is important is that the board be representative of the entire community, not just a select part of it.

Having a foundation engage in fund-raising activities offers certain advantages over having the superintendent or school board engage in similar activities:

- The foundation's governing board members presumably would be chosen for their investment experience and financial acumen. By contrast, superintendents and school board members often are not expert in these areas.
- The very existence of a foundation, which suggests a long-term endowment arrangement, is more attractive for potential donors considering bequests and large gifts.
- Many corporations with budgets for making charitable contributions do not make grants to governmental units. The needs of the public education foundation, however, might tie in well with a corporation's charitable giving program.
- Some prospective donors might be reluctant to make gifts directly to the school district, viewing such contributions as the equivalent of paying higher taxes. By contrast, a foundation offers people an opportunity to give money for a different purpose from that of their tax dollars—that is, to provide long-term financial stability for the school district or pay for special programs that otherwise might go unfunded.[39]

The establishment of an education foundation "can be an uplifting experience for a community. It gives school district personnel the opportunity to implement innovative and creative programs while raising the community's awareness of education and the prominent role it deserves in society."[40] An important activity of many foundations is furnishing the community with positive and accurate information about the school district year-round—not just at budget or referendum time. Lastly, the educational foundation provides a vehicle for involving the business community in the schools and allows the school district to benefit from its resources and expertise.[41]

Table 10–2 outlines the organizational steps necessary to establish an educational foundation.

Enterprise activities are revenue generating activities engaged in by a school or school district. Among the enterprise activities reported or suggested in the literature are the following:[42]

1. Impact fees on local developers (not a viable option in slow growth areas).
2. Lease of services the district is not using full time (e.g., food services, transportation, data processing, accounting, and test scoring services).

TABLE 10–2   Steps to Follow in Establishing an Educational Foundation

1. Identify and recruit community members experienced in financial and investment matters to serve on the initial board of directors. Although the board may include any number of members, usually it consists of between three and seven people. If the foundation intends to undertake a major fund-raising program, the board of directors might be much larger.
2. Draft articles of incorporation, and incorporate the foundation as a not-for-profit corporation.
3. Decide how future members of the board of directors will be selected.
4. Apply for tax-exempt status, using Form 1023 under Internal Revenue Code Section 501(c)(3). This preprinted application form asks for information regarding the foundation's anticipated sources of support, the nature of its planned activities, and its relationship, if any, with any other charitable organization or governmental entity. Be sure to apply for IRS status as a "public charity," which is a more favorable classification than the alternative classification of a "private foundation." (For the donor, rules regarding deductibility of gifts are more favorable for a public charity than for a private foundation. From the entity's standpoint, the public charity is not subject to excise tax on investment income or to other restrictive rules governing private foundations.)
5. Complete a registration statement, and file it with the attorney general's office of the state in which the foundation will be located. Reporting requirements for charitable organizations that solicit funds will vary from state to state. Generally, though, these requirements are not onerous.
6. Complete other steps necessary for setting up the organization—including drafting and adopting by-laws, electing offices, and establishing a bank or check-writing money market account.

SOURCE: Gary H. Kline, "Build a Solid Foundation," *American School Board Journal*, 179 (Nov. 1992) p. 32. Reprinted with permission, from *The American School Board Journal* (November). Copyright (1992), the National School Boards Association. All rights reserved.

3. Lease excess and underused school facilities, including classrooms, playing fields, locker facilities, pools, gymnasiums, auditoriums, kitchens, and entire schools.
4. Lease land for farming, grazing, or trapping.
5. Sell oil, gas, or mineral rights.
6. Charge for extracurricular activities and eliminate those that are not self-supporting, or as a alternative, set a maximum percentage of support that will be provided.
7. Charge back to student activity accounts the cost of staff time devoted to maintaining the activity.
8. Harvest timber from school lands.
9. Charge for use of facilities for banquets, social events, arts and crafts, festivals, antique shows, and the like.
10. If not in violation of state statute or constitutions, charge user fees for transporting students, especially transportation such as door-to-door bus service. (The latter was upheld by the U.S. Supreme Court in 1988 in *Kadrmas v. Dickinson Public Schools*, 108 S.Ct. 2481.)
11. Hold an annual computer fair and charge vendors for exhibit space—not only do the district's staff (as well as the staff from other school districts and the public) have the opportunity to learn about the newest hardware and software at no staff development cost to the district, the district may generate revenues.
12. Sell access to school markets, including advertising space and concessions such as student pictures and the operation of vending machines.

Cooperative activities include cooperative agreements and arrangements with other educational institutions and nonprofit organizations, government agencies, and business and industry. This would include activities such as the following:[43]

1. Lease–purchase arrangements whereby a nonprofit agency (e.g., in Florida, the Florida School Boards Association) builds the school and then leases it to the school district. This is an attractive arrangement for districts at the limit of indebtedness or where bond issues have failed.
2. Joint financing and maintenance of a park or playground with the local parks and recreation department.
3. Joining with the parks and recreation department to offer programs (e.g., a tennis program).
4. Joining with other school systems or governmental agencies for cooperative purchasing or warehousing.
5. Joining a regional special education or vocational educational cooperative.
6. Pooling the use of maintenance specialists such as skilled electricians.
7. Joining a transportation consortium for purposes such as bus maintenance.
8. Joining other school districts in offering in-service programs.
9. Establishing a public library branch in a empty classroom.
10. Joining with colleges and universities in writing and operating grants, conducting research, providing in-service, operating cooperative education programs, and hosting student teachers and other interns.

Probably the most publicized and popular cooperative activities are the adopt-a-school and similar partnerships with business and industry. The number of business–education partnerships has quadrupled since the early 1980s, when President Reagan provided popular support for such arrangements with the National Partnership in Education program. The number of such partnership is now well over 200,000. "The continuum of such partnerships ranges from serious attempts at school reform, replete with cash gifts and executive involvement, to crass commercial pitches that many educators find abhorrent."[44] Business–education partnerships offer more potential for urban and suburban districts than for rural districts. Businesses tend to give to schools where they are located, and generally this is not in rural areas.

The conditions giving rise to heightened pursuit of alternative revenues are not likely to disappear in the foreseeable future. And in fact, some school districts have benefited greatly from the infusion of these resources. Thus it seems probable that more and more superintendents will find themselves engaging in at least some of the previously described activities. As they do so, they will need new skills and levels of understanding in dealing with external constituencies. For, as Meno points out, "operating an activity for profit, fund raising in the donor market, and cooperative activities with business and industry are not typical activities in present educational administrative practice."[45]

Conducting Successful Budget and Bond Issue Elections

In some jurisdictions an election is required to approve the property tax levy necessary to support the board-approved budget. In most jurisdictions an election is required to obtain voter approval to levy additional property taxes to balance the budget when the proposed budget exceeds anticipated revenues at the existing levy. Voter approval is also required before school districts can incur bonded indebtedness for the purchase of real property or reconstruction. While one cannot project how many districts will need to hold budget elections in the years ahead, spending on school construction has continued to rise over the last decade and is expected to continue. In 1993, 2,371 school bond issues yielded a record $39.8 billion.[46]

Getting voters to say yes to budget and bond referendums is rarely easy and becomes even more difficult in tough economic times. To be successful requires a carefully planned, well-organized campaign. (Chapter 7 discusses this process in detail.) State and local laws will dictate how directly involved school personnel can be in the campaign. Such laws normally specify that school district resources cannot be used to influence the outcome of the election. This means that school personnel can provide only objective information, and that only private funds and volunteers must operate the campaign. Nonetheless, the superintendent has a major role in planning and coordinating various campaign efforts and is key to its success. The professional literature is replete with stories of successful (and unsuccessful) campaigns and "how to" lists of strategies for winning campaigns. The following strategies are those most often identified with successful campaigns.

Start the Campaign Early

Campaigns are won when voters are convinced of the value of the school program. This cannot be achieved in only a couple of months. Most successful campaigns are begun 8 to 12 months before the election. The campaign should begin with the selection of at least two co-chairs. The chairs should not only be well known and respected in the community, but highly organized and goal-oriented.[47] During the early months of the campaign, attention should be directed toward building community pride in the schools. School board members and school employees should "constantly extol the value of the school system . . . talk about the school system's goals, its programs, and its successes. Then, when the school budget vote approaches, you can turn your efforts to the relatively easier task of getting supporters to the polls."[48]

Conduct a Community Survey

Politically astute school boards and superintendents will evaluate public opinion well in advance of any attempt to raise taxes.[49] The most reliable and objective way to do this is to conduct a professionally developed and executed voter survey. One must know what voters think they can afford and what projects voters are willing to support. Finding this out before the proposal is presented allows district officials and the campaign committee to develop market strategies, and if necessary, do some "polishing, expanding, contracting and in some cases repackaging of the proposal to increase its chances of passing."[50] The survey will also make taxpayers aware that school officials are seeking their opinions. As a result the school district can gain support among those taxpayers who want to have input into the decision-making process.[51]

Establish a Campaign Theme

One should set a theme for the campaign that captures the reason for the campaign as well as voters' attention. And taking a leaf from a recent campaign book, one successful superintendent advises: "Keep it simple, stupid."[52] The theme should also be something that voters will be responsive to, will understand, believe, and support. For example, early in the campaign it became apparent to one California school district that voters were not responding to the message of the "student housing" problem. "By changing the theme to something the voters could relate to, 'Classrooms for Kids,' the campaign picked up momentum and eventually was successful with 73% of the vote."[53]

Recruit Supporters and Funding for the Campaign

Because of the prohibition in many states against school officials campaigning for a tax increase and the spending of public funds on such a campaign, it falls to community volunteers to conduct the campaign. To start things off, an executive committee must be selected made up of a cross section of the community. The initial task of the executive committee is to develop a campaign calendar and detailed schedule of what needs to be done on a week-by-week basis.

In addition to an executive committee, it is usually helpful to have at least two subcommittees: finance and publicity. The finance committee has the responsibility for establishing the budget and raising the funds necessary to conduct the campaign. Local businesses, district vendors, parents, and school employees are logical potential supporters. The better funded the campaign, the more extensive and intensive can be the efforts to get the district's message to the voters.

Focus on the "Yes" Vote

Most tax elections are not won by persuading the general public to voluntarily raise taxes, but by targeting those voters most likely to vote yes, reinforcing their values about education, and encouraging them to vote.[54] The local elections board or county clerk can provide a list of voters who voted in the last school finance election. These are the people most likely to vote in the upcoming election and the ones to be targeted in the lobbying effort. Voter lists can be divided by neighborhood or precincts and volunteers used to identify parents, school employees, and others likely to support the election. At the same time, an attempt should be made to identify those who might be opposed. They should be ignored; "You don't want to lobby them and perhaps encourage them to go to the polls to vote against you."[55]

Register Parents

The key to winning any school finance election is to gain the support of parents. However, the vast majority of the time parents will account for less than 35 percent of the registered voters. This is partly because in most districts less than 50 percent of the parents who are eligible voters register to vote. Thus, an early goal of the campaign should be to register to vote as many parents as possible. This can be done using PTAs, teachers, students, athletic events, or any other event or organization that might attract parents. Remember, 75 percent of the parent registrations become "yes" voters.[56]

Get the Message Effectively to the People

Being effective in getting the school district's message to the community involves several factors. First, the message must be positive. Voters need to be reminded of the benefits provided by the schools, not only to students and their parents, but to the total life of the community. Second, the message should clearly and simply detail the current budget and why it is insufficient to meet the needs articulated in the campaign. Third, the delivery of the message should take advantage of every possible medium. One effective strategy is for the campaign committee (or publicity subcommittee) to organize a speakers bureau made up of citizens, officers of parents' organizations, teachers, administrators, school board members, and the superintendent. The speakers bureau should actively solicit speaking engagements with community organizations so the message reaches as wide an audience as possible.[57] Speakers should be equipped with a 10- or 15-minute video presentation (which can also be distributed to local television stations) that shows what tax dollars have done in the past and what needs to be done now. The video should culminate with testimonials from successful graduates, parents, and community leaders.[58]

Print materials are always important in a campaign. In fact, direct mail sent to targeted voters is among the most effective campaign strategies. It is critical that to the extent possible print material be targeted to the voter. This means that letters addressed to school employees should be different from ones addressed to parents. An effective campaign will feature letters tailored to each neighborhood and signed personally by a community leader or neighborhood member.[59] All campaign literature should be brief, present facts simply, and state the goals directly. Likewise, paid advertising in newspapers, radio, and television should be brief, simple, and appealing.

The last point in getting the message effectively to the people also comes from the politician's strategy book: repetition, repetition, repetition. We know that the more a person is exposed to an idea, the more attractive it becomes to him or her. What the campaign must do, then, is use repetition to make the key points—pick the right words and then wear them out.[60]

Cultivate the Media

The only things many people know about the school district are what they get from newspapers, radio, or television. For this reason it is not enough to sit by and wait for the media to seek out all the good news about the district or to publicize the election. At the very outset of the campaign a press conference should be called and a long list of media people invited. Begin the press conference with a school bus ride around the district pointing out the areas of need and how the tax dollars requested will be used. After the tour, provide the media with a fact sheet containing specific information about the district and its needs.[61]

Throughout the campaign the news media should be provided not only with press releases, but with sufficient information to enable them to report accurately on the financial situation of the district and the needs that brought about the election, as well as to counter the charges of opponents. Whether or not editorial endorsements are sought, the superintendent and the chair of the citizens committee should seek to meet with the editorial staff of the newspapers and television and radio stations serving the district. This provides the sort of open forum the media appreciate. Radio and television talk shows also provide excellent opportunities for presenting factual information about the district and demonstrating citizen advocacy.[62]

Get Out the Vote

During the final three days before the election, the campaign emphasis should be on getting out the vote. This is most effectively done by a phone bank of volunteers calling undecided or irregular voters to remind them of the date, time, and place to vote. Emphasis at this point should be on voting, not how to vote.[63] One public affairs consulting firm that works with school districts suggests that reliance not be placed on volunteers telephoning from their homes, as few will complete their assigned list if left to themselves. Rather, set up the phone bank in a local business where volunteers can work together—the sense of camaraderie will encourage them to complete their calls.[64]

Post-election

After the election is over there are still important things to be done, regardless of the outcome. Not the least is a thank-you letter to all the people connected with the campaign. The letter should be signed by the chair of the citizens committee, the president of the school board, and the superintendent. It is also important to conduct a post-election evaluation of results to analyze what worked and what did not. This can be done on a precinct-by-precinct or school-by-school basis. Feedback can then be given to those who worked on the campaign; the efforts of those who made a difference can be lauded, and the minimal effort of others, especially key school officials like principals, noted.

In addition, much information and experience was gained by those who worked on the campaign. This information should not go to waste; it should be recorded in a campaign file and stored for future reference. Copies of all campaign literature and correspondence should also be kept in the file, as well as committee minutes and reports. After all, this will probably not be the last tax or budget election the district will conduct.[65]

Summary

The successful implementation of the educational programs of the school district depends on adequate resources effectively administered. The superintendent plays a critical role in ensuring that the budget of the school district reflects the educational goals of the school district and provides for their accomplishment. To achieve this, the superintendent must have a detailed knowledge of the budget process and the skills to manage it properly.

In this chapter the most common and current approaches to school district budgeting have been discussed. In addition, two aspects of budgeting where the superintendent's skills and leadership are brought to the forefront were highlighted: budget cutting, and budget and bond issue elections. Lastly, a lengthy discussion was given to an area of growing interest to superintendents as the pressures to do more with less continue—sources of alternative revenues.

Discussion Questions

1. What budgeting approach is used in the district where you are employed? How successful has it been in providing school district personnel and community members with their desired level of input? What have been the political advantages of this approach?

2. If your district has been forced to make budget reductions in recent years, describe the process that was used and the priorities followed. To what extent were these priorities consistent with the budget continuum described in this chapter?

If your district has not been in this position, describe what policies and procedures are in place to guide the budget reduction process. If none are in place, suggest what they should be.

3. List as many as possible of the donor activities, enterprise activities, and cooperative activities operating in your district.

4. Interview a district official involved in the most recent budget or bond issue in your district. Describe the goals of the campaign, the campaign theme, any identifiable strategies and targeted voters, and the various approaches used to communicate the campaign message to the voters.

CASE 10.1   To Bid or Not to Bid?

As the Redfern School District begins to project expenditures for next year, bids are sought for those items estimated to be above $15,000, the level at which statutes require that the district advertise for bids. For items under $15,000, statutes say that contracts may be issued on either the basis of sealed bids or direct negotiation. For the last three years, the only bid submitted for photocopier paper was from the out-of-town representative of Office Warehouse, a large, national office supply company. Redfern is a small district, where the superintendent performs many of the business operations with the assistance of a bookkeeper. This year he is considering negotiating directly with the Office Warehouse representative and not bothering to solicit bids. But before he has taken action, Doris James, a school board member comes to him and asks that he negotiate with her nephew, who has just opened an office supply store in Redfern. As a small business he might be more expensive, she admits, but the action would keep the business in the district.

Questions

1. What are the legal considerations in this case? The ethical considerations?
2. Under what circumstances is it appropriate to give preference to local businesses? Under what circumstances is it not appropriate?
3. What action in this case would best serve the public interest?

Inbasket Exercise

INBASKET 10.1

Responding to Defeat

After months of staff and school board time devoted to budget development and a series of public hearings, the budget of Lakeview School District was submitted to the voters for approval. The budget, judged by the superintendent and the school board to be the "bare bones" budget that would keep intact existing programs, would necessitate a modest tax increase. The budget was rejected on a vote of 4,960 to 4,879. The major organized opposition had come from a large retirement community in the northeast part of the district.

The morning following the election, Dr. Carey, the superintendent, called a meeting of his senior staff. The mood around the table was one of both anger and frustration. "We should call a press conference and just blast those so-called grey panthers," exploded Jim Wade, assistant superintendent for instruction. "Well, maybe not a press conference," countered Anita Aarons, director of personnel, "but certainly a scathing letter to the editor is justified. The paper certainly didn't help us any by given all that space to airing their petty concerns."

"I don't think either one of these suggestions is a good idea," responded Dave Underwood, assistant superintendent for business affairs. "I think that would just further alienate the senior citizens, and we certainly can't afford to have the newspaper against us." Discussion continued. While not in agreement as to form or format, the decision was reached that Superintendent Carey would make some public response to the defeat.

Response

1. Draft the public statement for Dr. Carey. Suggest the form and format for its presentation.
2. Develop a detailed plan for winning voter approval of the next budget election. Be specific in the actions to be taken. Name the responsible parties for each action.

Notes

1. Thomas E. Glass, *The 1992 Study of the American Superintendency: America's Education Leaders in a Time of Reform* (Arlington, Va.: Association of School Administrators, 1992), p. 3.

2. William T. Hartman, *School District Budgeting* (Englewood Cliffs, N.J.: Prentice Hall, 1988).

3. Ibid., p. 2.

4. L. Dean Webb, Martha M. McCarthy, and Stephen B. Thomas, *Financing Elementary and Secondary Education* (Columbus, Ohio: Merrill, 1988).

5. Ivan D. Wagner and Sam M. Sniderman, *Budgeting School Dollars: A Guide to Spending and Saving* (Washington, D.C.: National School Boards Association), p. 25.

6. Ibid.

7. Hartman, *School District Budgeting*.

8. Hartman, *School District Budgeting;* David C. Thompson, R. Craig Wood, and David S. Honeyman, *Fiscal Leadership for Schools* (Boston: Allyn and Bacon, 1994).

9. Hartman, *School District Budgeting*.

10. Thompson et al., *Fiscal Leadership for Schools,* p. 315.

11. Thelbert L. Drake and William H. Roe, *School Business Management* (Boston: Allyn and Bacon, 1994).

12. Ellen Kehoe, "Educational Budget Preparation: Fiscal and Political Considerations," in *Principles of School Business Management* (Reston, Va.: Association of School Business Officials International, 1986), pp. 149–173.

13. Hartman, *School District Budgeting*.

14. Ibid.

15. Kehoe, "Educational Budget Preparation."

16. Thompson et al., *Fiscal Leadership for Schools.*

17. Hartman, *School District Budgeting,* p. 29.

18. Philip E. Geiger, "Zero-based Budgeting Redux," *American School Board Journal,* 180 (July 1993): p. 29.

19. I. Carl Candoli, Walter G. Hack, and John R. Ray, *School Business Administration: A Planning Approach,* 4th ed. (Boston: Allyn and Bacon, 1992), p. 131.

20. Michael E. D. Koenig and Victor Alperin, "ZZB and PPBS: What's Left Now that the Trendiness Has Gone," *Drexel Library Quarterly,* 21 (summer 1985): pp. 19–38.

21. Ibid.

22. Hartman, *School District Budgeting.*

23. Thompson et al., *Fiscal Leadership for Schools,* p. 314.

24. Priscilla Wohlsttter and Thomas Buffett, "Decentralized Dollars under School-based Management: Have Policies Changed?" *Educational Policy,* 6 (March 1992): pp. 35–54.

25. David Peterson, "School-based Budgeting," *ERIC Digest,* 63 (January 1992).

26. Ibid.

27. Richard A. Griffin and Bill Phipps, "From Power to Persuasion, the Business Official's Role in Site-based Decision-Making," *School Business Affairs,* 58 (December 1992): p. 19.

28. Hartman, *School District Budgeting.*

29. Jim Bliss, "Budget Cutting Committee: An Objective Approach to Painful Cutbacks," *School Business Affairs,* 58 (July 1992): p. 40.

30. Jerry J. Herman, "Dealing with Crisis Budgeting: Cutbacks and Planning for More Efficiency," *School Business Affairs,* 58 (February 1992): pp. 35–36, 38–39.

31. Ibid., pp. 35–36.

32. Hartman, *School District Budgeting,* p. 188.

33. Alexander H. Dexter, Michael Mulheirn, David Sluder, and Shirley Watford, "Cut Costs, Not Quality," *American School Board Journal,* 179 (June 1992): pp. 24–30.

34. Thomas E. Glass, "Twenty-one Ways to Cut without Killing, *American School Board Journal,* 175 (January 1988): pp. 26–27.

35. Hartman, *School District Budgeting.*

36. Rene Thomas Rovtar, "Foundations for the Future: Possibilities and Potential," *School Business Affairs,* 59 (February 1993): p. 10.

37. Ibid.

38. Gary H. Kline, "Build a Solid Foundation," *American School Board Journal,* 179 (November 1992), pp. 30, 32.

39. Ibid., p. 32.

40. Rovtar, "Foundations for the Future," p. 12.

41. Ibid.

42. Lioinel R. Meno, "Sources of Alternative Revenues," in *Managing Limited Resources,* ed. by L. Dean Webb and Van D. Mueller (Cambridge, Mass.: Ballinger, 1984), pp. 129–146; Roland M. Smith, "Try These 15 Dandy Ideas for Saving Money and Improving Instruction," *American School Board Journal,* 172 (February 1985): pp. 30, 32; Jay Taylor, "Desperate for Dollars," *American School Board Journal,* 179 (September 1992): pp. 20–25; Wagner and Sniderman, *Budgeting School Dollars* (see n. 5); R. Craig Wood, "New Revenues for Education at the Local Level," in *The Impacts of Litigation and Legislation on Public School Finance,* ed. by Julie K. Underwood and Deborah A. Verstegen (New York: Harper and Row, 1990), pp. 59–74.

43. Smith, "Try These 15 Dandy Ideas for Saving Money and Improving Instruction"; Wagner and Sniderman, *Budgeting School Dollars.*

44. Taylor, "Desperate for Dollars," p. 24.

45. Meno, "Sources of Alternative Revenues," p. 144.

46. "Building and Bonds," *Education Vital Signs,* a supplement to *Executive Educator,* 15 (December 1993): p. A13.

47. Kent Price, "Yes at the Polls," *Thrust,* 20 (September 1990): pp. 19–21.

48. William A. Hanbury, "Getting Voters to Say Yes," *American School Board Journal,* 178 (November 1991): p. 48.

49. Ibid.

50. Price, "Yes at the Polls," p. 20.

51. Hanbury, "Getting Voters to Say Yes."

52. Paul Houston, "Be Your Own Spin Doctor," *Executive Educator,* 15 (June 1993): pp. 14–17.

53. Price, "Yes at the Polls," p. 21.

54. Ibid., pp. 19–21.

55. Hanbury, "Getting Voters to Say Yes," p. 50.

56. Price, "Yes at the Polls."

57. Vickie Bane and Kay Pride, "The $325 Million Bargain," *American School Board Journal,* 180 (October 1993): pp. 24–28.

58. Judy R. Mulkey, "Marketing Your Schools," *Executive Educator,* 15 (July 1993): pp. 32–33.

59. Hanbury, "Getting Voters to Say Yes."

60. Houston, "Be Your Own Spin Doctor."

61. Mulkey, "Marketing Your Schools."

62. Hartman, *School District Budgeting.* (See n. 2.)

63. Robert F. Harris and Terry Blanchfield, "Profiting from Defeat, a Strategy for Passing Budgets," *School Business Affairs,* 59 (February 1993): pp. 13–15.

64. Hanbury, "Getting Voters to Say Yes."

65. Hartman, *School District Budgeting.*

Chapter *11*

Leadership for Facility Planning

The provision of appropriate facilities in a local school district is a major responsibility for the superintendent of schools. In this chapter, we present an overview of the basic elements of school facilities planning, construction, and maintenance. There are two sources on this topic with which every superintendent of schools should be familiar; one is an individual, Basil Castaldi, who authored the basic text about school facilities, and the other is an organization, The Council of Educational Facility Planners, International (CEFPI), which offers assistance in this area with various publications and services.

From a national perspective, concerns have been expressed regarding the condition of the educational infrastructure by Lewis and others. The national view regarding school facilities has been bleak. The nation's school buildings have been judged as (1) inadequate (25%); (2) in need of maintenance and repairs (61%); (3) containing environmental hazards (42%); (4) overcrowded (25%) (while in some rural areas facilities are not efficiently used or are underutilized); (5) obsolete for current educational programs (43%); and (6) structurally defective (13%).[1] Studies done at the state level, such as the one completed for the state of Nebraska by Pool,[2] have revealed findings that are consistent with those reported in *Wolves at the Schoolhouse Door.* In some rural locales with smaller districts, a limited financial base and a declining population, combined with a building that is of retirement age, pose a major challenge.

Providing adequate school facilities is much more than constructing four walls and a roof. If facilities are to provide a positive, constructive contribution to the learning process, there needs to be a logical linkage between the philosophy of the educational leadership in a district and the facilities that are developed. If new facilities are planned, they are generally expected to last for 75 years or even longer. The implications are profound; a new facility carries with it an implicit commitment to the future that will have long-lasting effects on educational accomplishments.

To gain a view of the future of school facility design needs, McMillin surveyed the perceptions of architects, futurists, and educational leaders in a nationwide Delphi study.[3] While the basic question was to consider issues related to future facility needs, the emphasis and implications were clearly related to curricular issues that accompany facility planning. Facilities, according to the respondents to this study, would need to be constructed with careful attention to changes in society and the use of technology. Much of the current thinking emphasizing the use of community leadership and response to community needs, in addition to the needs of children and youth in formal classrooms, was acknowledged. The expansion of human and technological networks and the extension of the school day emerged as needs in the eyes of architects, futurists, and educational leaders.

Builders who plan specifications for the future, as recommended by McMillin, should consider several key points.

1. Electronic media in the areas of curriculum, instruction, and assessment should be expanded.
2. The extension and change of a variety of instructional methods and strategies will be needed; thus, buildings should be designed to facilitate numerous instructional strategies.
3. Expanded use of the school by community groups will continue to be called for as new needs are addressed.
4. *Flexibility* will be a key word as new facilities are constructed.
5. Facilities should be constructed, or renovated, to accommodate changes in the way teachers plan and work together for instruction.
6. Special education spaces will need continued attention when developing facility plans and dealing with curricular issues.
7. School facilities and programs that involve extended hours and a more complete use of the calendar should receive more attention.
8. Cultural diversity will need to be addressed more vigorously in various ways, for example, the use of technology and multimedia for the instruction of foreign languages and cultural issues in the school.
9. School finance, in relation to both facilities and curriculum, will obviously need to be addressed at the local and the state level.
10. Education, with obvious implications for facilities, will become a multilocation and multimedia experience. This could be the most far-reaching of the findings presented by McMillin.
11. School programs, and ultimately facilities, will become more heavily used for before-school, preschool, and after-school programs.
12. Service agencies, especially those involved with economically disadvantaged and students at risk, will be school-based to a greater degree in the future.[4]

Technology is irrevocably tied to facility planning and utilization. The rapid increase of new generations of high-technology devices for school leaders to consider is but one of the complexities in facility planning. It is not easy to ferret out the implications of expanding technologies and search for ways to capitalize on technology, rather than allowing technological devices to dictate what will emerge in the school.

Brubaker[5] suggested several insights into the impact of technology on facility needs. First, the use of technology needs to be integrated into the mission and instructional process rather than appearing as an add-on. Technology should help integrate the educational process with the daily life of the community. "Electronic technology will not only advance the ideas of individual learning but will also make possible the traditional goal of customized schedules for every student."[6] Brubaker further suggested that technology can also encourage the "creation of smaller (urban) schools. . . . One possible scenario: satellite neighborhood high schools for 400 students. . . . Students would spend approximately one-half of their week (in neighborhood schools) with the other half spent in specialized facilities . . . or at a centralized school hub."[7]

The physical arrangements of buildings and organizational structures will not be the only changes to be derived from emerging technology; the individual learning experiences encountered by the students will be involved. In addition to computer laboratories, computers are also used in individual classrooms, as greater accessibility of technology has been recognized as advantageous, even to the extent that libraries are being equipped to check out computers. Specialized high-tech equipment for aiding students with special needs is emerging. Traditional art and mechanical drawing rooms are undergoing a significant transformation as a result of new computer equipment and software; typing rooms are being replaced with keyboarding classrooms that are made available at a much earlier level for elementary pupils. Counselors are able to provide more current and detailed information for students through computer programs.

School officials, when planning buildings designed to facilitate the accomplishment of curricular goals, should address the issue of educational equity in light of the explosion of technology in schools. Students from low-income families will be placed at an even greater disadvantage if they are not afforded broad access to technology. The accessibility of computer labs may be necessary for before- and after-school hours, and systems to check out computers may also be needed. Communication capabilities will be needed in school buildings to enable all students to access electronic networks and databases from their homes through dial-up systems.

Distance learning is emerging as another major factor in the shaping of school facilities. Many locales are acquiring the capabilities of the "information superhighway" to reach library and databases worldwide, and school facility changes are under consideration in many districts and regions. In smaller communities, the use of technology can make the school an information hub that serves not only the K–12 pupils but also the community as a whole. Antiquated community libraries can be supplemented or replaced; adult education needs can be recognized; local medical personnel who work in isolated communities with limited medical facilities can receive and transmit medical information; and the school can actually serve as an economic development component for the community. Technology is changing the shape of school facilities; there are far-reaching implications that suggest the inclusion and integration of technology into the school is far more involved than simply adding electrical outlets to each classroom.

School facility planning often emerges from strategic goals that have been identified in the strategic planning process. In several respects, school facility planning should follow the initial process of strategic planning. If school facilities are not identified as an area of need in a strategic planning effort, this could mean that school facilities were not seen as a high priority and would suggest that the time and resources of the superintendent and staff be directed to other, higher-priority, areas. By contrast, if the strategic planning process placed school facilities among the strategic goal areas of high priority, the superintendent has a base of support on which school facility planning can proceed.

Because of the complex needs and interrelationships involved in providing school facilities, the process should encompass much more than determining how many classrooms are needed to house the student population. School facility planning has evolved into "social planning within a larger context of planning for the entire social environment."[8] By placing facility planning in a broader framework that starts with a global perspective and emerges through strategic planning, better decisions are possible, more judicious financial planning can result, and broad program needs are addressed.

Certain areas of long-range and operational planning that meet facility needs should not wait for strategic planning documents. Schedules for maintenance, which typically involve long-range planning, are simply examples of good management and fiscal responsibility. Many maintenance and cleaning schedules are for a one-year period, while other schedules for facility maintenance, for example, major boiler repairs or replacements for buildings in a district, may extend over a number of years.

Building and maintaining school facilities require people with a wide range of skills. Consequently, the list of persons involved can typically include:

1. The superintendent of schools, who occupies a position of leadership and assumes major responsibilities.
2. The school board.
3. Persons on the central administration staff who have specializations related to facility management. In very small districts, the entire area of responsibility will be the superintendent's.
4. Building administrators and teachers.
5. Maintenance and custodial staff.
6. Specialists from outside the district who are retained as consultants.

The number and type of specialists/consultants needed will vary with the size of the district. In larger districts, a specialist or a staff of specialists may be employed to plan and manage facilities. The list of potential consultants may include (1) school survey specialists, (2) architects, (3) site selection specialists, (4) bonding or financial advisors, (5) construction supervisors, (6) project managers or a clerk of the works, and (7) school facility planners from state departments of education. The superintendent, working closely with the local board of education, is responsible for assessing needs and determining the consultation resources required to embark on a building project.

The Program and Facilities

Facilities exist to facilitate learning. Therefore, planning for new facilities or the revision of existing facilities must start with an examination of what students are to learn and achieve. Once the educational goals are known, facilities can be designed that will enable the professional educators on a staff to realize the desired goals.

The General Curriculum and the Building

The curriculum should influence the shape of the school building. Form follows function. Thus, the school house should not shape the curriculum; the curriculum and the instructional process should influence the shape of the building.

The instructional process, which is the means by which the curriculum is translated into action, should be supported by the school building. In many older buildings, educators have found that selected teaching strategies are inhibited by the rigidity of the building and the size and allocation of spaces. Human ingenuity, however, has overcome many facility limitations, and good instruction can take place in almost any setting. Teachers and principals can attest, however, that if the physical environment for instruction is appropriately designed and built, the school building can facilitate rather than inhibit teaching and learning.

Students with Special Needs and Facilities

With the inclusion of virtually all students with special needs, there have been demands for modifications in the amount and arrangements of space needed. Providing access for the handicapped is one facet of building design, which includes an extensive list of considerations such as (1) accessible building entrances that are equipped with pressure sensitive mats and appropriate time-delayed closure systems; (2) ramps in place of steps and curbs, both inside and outside of the building; (3) carpeted floors to reduce slipping and prevent injuries; (4) classroom doors that are wide enough to accommodate wheelchairs and with visual and auditory exposure to corridors; (5) safety glass in doors; (6) access to toilets and sinks to provide independence for the physically handicapped and visually impaired; (7) light switches and controls for fire alarms within reach of physically handicapped and visually impaired persons; (8) horizontally mounted railings in strategic locations throughout the building; (9) adjustable furniture; (10) accessible storage space for the handicapped; (11) raised or recessed signs to identify rooms and spaces for the visually handicapped; and (12) emergency exits that are marked and accessible for persons with various handicaps.[9]

As school and community officials espouse programs that extend beyond the more traditional K–12 programs and include various preschool and adult education programs, facilities will have to be designed to meet such needs. In order to realize economies by capitalizing on the joint use of space, schools designed for broader use will become more common. As home environments change and disruption in society places greater demands on the local educational programs, school designers will be asked to propose facilities that will accommodate broader and multiple uses.

In many communities, neither school officials nor community opinion leaders have embraced the idea of the school providing extended day care or preschool programs. By contrast, some districts have expanded their services to include preschool, day care, or extended school day care programs. Many school district officials are called on for expanded services, some of which may be coupled with adult education in parenting. Schools do have the credibility, well-trained personnel, good leadership and management personnel, and facilities that can be used for multiple purposes that result in an overall saving to taxpayers.

Criteria or guidelines for designing child care facilities that can be incorporated into a more traditional school building have been proposed by Moore.[10] The standards or criteria suggested by Moore include (1) a network of facilities, some which may be centers for larger group activities and some which may be smaller family day care facilities that are decentralized and closer to the homes of the children; (2) site size and characteristics that afford safe access and an area free of excessive noise or disturbances; (3) a center that will accommodate a maximum of 60 to 75 children; (4) an area for outdoor activities with appropriate facilities; (5) a building that presents an image to the child as "being a friend"; (6) a modified open space concept that will accommodate the needs of children of various ages; (7) resource-rich activity packs for two to five children; (8) a variety of types of spaces; (9) internal spatial zoning that provides separation of incompatible activities; (10) clear circulation for traffic between major activity areas in and around a common core; and (11) transition between indoor and outdoor activities, which contain developmentally appropriate play yards.

Many of the typical secondary school facilities can meet the needs of adult education activities. The breadth and scope of adult involvement in the school, however, will have an impact on the design of the facility. In communities that have a junior or technical community college, the demands for adult learning activities may be greatly reduced. If adult programs are to flourish, the school design can make a difference. If the school library is to serve as a joint school–community library and school computer laboratories and other selected learning areas are to be used by members of the community, the access and flow of traffic must enable adults to negotiate the school with ease.

School Activities

School activities often require more in the way of facilities than many of the academic courses. Although much of the activity program is supported by tradition and public interest, or even pressure from special interest groups, there is a clear and justifiable rationale for their inclusion in the total school program; consequently, there is an equally clear justification for adequate facilities to support school activities.

With the inclusion of sports for girls, there is the obvious need for more physical education facilities. The interpretation of what constitutes equitable facilities for boys and girls has implications for many administrators. In many old buildings, locker room space, gym space, and activity schedules, which include practice time and game schedules, have differed for boys and girls. In some locales, challenges have been raised, and it has been determined that if a girls' locker room is less accessible than the boys' there should be a rotation schedule to allow equal time in equal space. (The rationale has been forwarded, and rejected by federal agencies, that boys need more locker room space than girls because of the bulk of football gear.) In like manner, the schedule for practice time and interscholastic games must be equitable in the use of "prime time." That is, if prime time for athletic contests is considered Friday and Saturday evenings, the number of contests for girls and the number for boys during these evenings must be equal. The provision of equitable facilities and schedules for girls and boys means changes in planning new or revised space.

Auditoriums, used primarily for school activities and for some community functions, may cost 40 to 45 percent more per square foot to construct than regular classroom space. Auditoriums do provide a dimension to the school that can contribute to the student body as well as to the community. Any auditorium planned for a school should be designed for multiple use and users. The biggest argument against the inclusion of an auditorium in a new building, one that frequently prevails, is the cost of construction and maintenance. Joint community and school use of an auditorium becomes a major consideration in many communities. Obviously, the more an auditorium is used, the easier it is to justify the added cost involved.

Swimming pools are typically not found in smaller schools. In most situations the enrollment of the school must be large enough so that physical education classes and inter-scholastic swimming programs keep the pool scheduled to capacity or near capacity. Pools that are utilized to the maximum, with school classes and activities and with community use in the evenings, will gain much more support from taxpayers than pools that are idle much of the time. Joint community–school planning, building, and utilization of pools is advocated. The joint effort generates fuller utilization and builds community support.

Outdoor athletic fields, like auditoriums and swimming pools, should be planned, designed, and operated by school and community leaders to foster joint use. The community and the school district can contribute financially and capitalize on persons who work with both agencies as coordinators, coaches, and maintenance personnel. The key, of course, is cooperative planning; policies and operating guidelines should be developed in advance. For example, during the school term, classes or school activities should receive first priority for facility scheduling.

All spaces for school activities need to be designed so that access is given to the hand-icapped and a hazard-free environment for participants and spectators is ensured. Play-ground equipment for elementary school children needs assurances of safe operation for its intended use. In situations where well-intentioned parents have volunteered their services to build playground equipment on the elementary school grounds, it is recommended that such services be redirected into other productive endeavors and that commercially approved equipment be acquired for the playground.

Programs in Flux

Since educational programs are in transition and constantly changing, the education facil-ities should be flexible. The need for flexibility is quite apparent when older buildings are studied and it is found that load-bearing walls, the size and shape of classrooms, the lack of classrooms for special needs, the inadequacy of the electrical system, and the lack of proper ventilation for selected classes pose serious limitations to converting or upgrading the building. Had there been more thought to flexibility when designing the original build-ing, some of the current shortcomings could have been averted.

People have repeatedly heard, "You will change vocations several times in your life-time"; the same is true of a school building. A given space in a school building may go through several alterations as it is called on to "change vocations." With the expanding potential of distance learning and as more learning takes place in diverse sites and at times other than the traditional school day, there is the consideration that school buildings may be reduced in size and function. This is not to suggest that school buildings will no longer be needed; they will, but often to serve different purposes.

Not only are programmatic changes calling for more flexible structures, but the instructional activities in individual classrooms are demanding modifications in school design. One such modification, referred to as the "L-shaped classroom," was conceptualized in response to changing instructional strategies that called for the accommodation of "small learning groups while providing a sense of separation, because groups working too closely together will experience distractions and nonproductive interaction."[11] The critical features of the modern classroom shape seem to be (1) greater diagonal distance to increase the perception of space; (2) interior corners to increase the feeling of separation and space; (3) compact layout to facilitate classroom management; and (4) economical construction.[12]

Planning for Facilities

Board Commitment

As a need for new or revamped facilities becomes apparent, the superintendent must be sure the school board members are committed. This is not always a transparent set of conditions; possibly, the superintendent will have to educate some board members and use the persuasive influences of other board members to "sell" the board on the need for new or revamped facilities. A building program simply will not progress until board of education members recognize the need and are willing to proceed.

School and Community Survey to Clarify Wants and Needs

The school survey is a basic data collection technique that becomes an important step in considering building needs. The survey helps develop the database used to put together a "plan of action based upon an objective and systematic study of needs, resources, and educational goals of a school district."[13] School surveys are a component of good facility planning; they provide an important database for decision making, create a climate of expectation, foster cooperative efforts, contribute to and support the strategic planning process in a district, and provide a systematic view that can help avoid the pitfalls of planning with a "partial deck."

In medium and smaller sized districts, school superintendents and boards of education commonly go to state departments of education, university specialists, or private consultants for assistance with school surveys. There can be two benefits derived from contracting with a school facility specialist to conduct a survey. First, data can be made available to help in the decision-making process; second, political pitfalls on the local scene can sometimes be avoided when the school facility specialist provides data that are more "objective" than "biased" data that might be generated by local persons.

School surveys can be designed to gather various kinds of information. The most common facility study generally contains:

1. Descriptive information about the district
2. Population trends and demographic information
3. Enrollment histories and projections
4. Program information and projections

5. A financial summary
6. An analysis of existing facilities and site to reveal the discrepancy between the available and recommended space
7. An assessment of the quality of existing space
8. Options for consideration
9. Cost estimates of each option

Several factors go into developing a plan for new or revised facilities: the ability to pay, the scope and nature of the program to be offered, and the number and characteristics of the people to be served. The school facility study is based on the information provided in examining these three factors.

Enrollment projections are typically made using several data sources. The cohort survival ratio method of making enrollment projections is a mathematical process that is based on the number of students in each grade and tracks every group of students as they go on to following grade levels. This method is used to compute an average survival ratio for each grade level, based on a 10-year enrollment history. For example, if there were 100 fourth graders and the next year there were 98 fifth graders, the survival ratio would be 0.98; by contrast, if there were 100 seventh graders in a given year and the next year there were 105 eighth graders, the survival ratio would be 1.05.

Such annual survival ratios are computed for a 10-year period for all grade levels based on enrollment data; thus, a 10-year average survival is obtained. The 10-year average survival ratio for students in one grade level, such as the fourth grade, as they go on to the next grade level, or the fifth grade, is used to compute the anticipated enrollment for each year, which results in a projection for one or more years up to 10 years. If the 10-year average survival ratio for grade four to five is 1.02, then the last year of actual enrollment figures is multiplied by 1.02 to get the first year of projected enrollments. Then the second year of projected enrollments is multiplied by 1.02 to get the third year projection, and this process is repeated until up to 10 years of projection figures are computed for each grade level.[14]

The cohort survival method must be used with caution. In small districts, a few students added or subtracted at a given grade level can cause an unrealistic exaggeration of the mathematical projection, which can easily be misleading. Repeated application of exaggerated average survival ratios over several years compounds the errors they introduce into projected enrollment trends.

While a cohort survival ratio should be used when school facilities are being planned, it never should be the exclusive means of making projections. The cohort survival ratio ignores many human and economic variables. A sound projection should consider: (1) the cohort survival ratio; (2) the general population trend for the state, county, and community (derived from the U.S. Census); (3) the number of births by place of mother's residence (from county health records); (4) the number of housing permits for the area; (5) the population tree (from U.S. Census data); (6) the number of deaths as compared with the number of births; and (7) any economic development information from such sources as local industry or the chamber of commerce. Thus, making enrollment projections is an essential step in facility planning, and several sources of data should be considered.

Demographic data, derived primarily from the U.S. Census, can provide valuable information for a superintendent and school board as they examine program needs and socioeconomic influences bearing on needed facilities and support from patrons. U.S. Census data, which can be obtained for each county in every state, contains (1) the number of persons residing in a county; (2) the education level of adults 25 years of age or older; (3) the ethnic composition of the population; (4) the number of persons in various age categories, e.g., 0 to 4 years old, 5 to 17 years old; (5) the number and type of residential housing units available in the county and the occupancy rate for residences; (6) income levels; (7) employment types; (8) employment rates; and (9) the number and percentage of women in the work force. School facility planners will have a much more informed decision-making base once they have studied the demographic materials for their area.

A *discrepancy analysis* that contrasts the available and recommended space can be valuable information provided by a school facility survey. Space is usually categorized into administrative space; general classroom space; specialized learning areas; and other types of spaces such as food service, storage, rest rooms, mechanical, and corridors. In a discrepancy analysis, the actual space available is computed from measurements from blueprints or actual measurements and compared with the amount of recommended space for the school. Architects, school facility specialists in state departments of education, school study councils or university specialists, authors, and specialists associated with the CEFPI have space recommendations that can be used to compare existing space with recommended space. The recommended amounts of space obtained from various specialists are used for computing the discrepancy analysis and to determine the amount of space to be designed for a new facility.

Examining the amount of space is just one step in the planning process. The specialist who provides the facility study is generally not responsible for drawing plans and developing construction specifications. The adequate size of the building can be derived from the recommendations for space or from a discrepancy analysis; however, the efficient use of the space and building layout is a responsibility of the architect, working in conjunction with the superintendent of schools and staff members. In like manner, planning for energy conservation and structural safety is delegated to the architectural firm with the support of energy engineers.

The *survey of community perceptions* is likely to be more varied and less standardized than the facility survey. The answers sought in most community surveys relate to the willingness of patrons to support a new school facility program. While surveys have some basic components, no two surveys can be exactly alike. They should be tailored for the time and place in which they are used. The steps involved in conducting a community survey may include:

1. Determine or clarify the need to be met or the purpose for conducting the survey.
2. Determine what information to ask for.
3. Develop the individual items or questions to be asked.
4. Pilot and revise the instrument.
5. Determine who to go to for the needed information.
6. Select the sample.

7. Determine how to get the information from the sample, such as by questionnaire, direct interviews, or the use of a phone survey.
8. Plan the data collection.
9. Collect the data.
10. Code and tabulate the data.
11. Analyze the data.
12. Prepare the report.[15]

The question of who should conduct a community survey can cause some debate. Patron involvement is advisable; however, the person who coordinates and directs the process should be knowledgeable and experienced in developing and conducting surveys. Adequate, informative surveys seldom come from inexperienced persons. Good surveys require the application of reliable survey research procedures. Consequently, it is often advisable to use the services of an experienced consultant. The consultant should work with the administration and staff, the board, and the community in developing and conducting the survey.

Community groups, or any committee appointed by the superintendent or board of education to conduct a survey, need to be given a clear set of parameters and a defined set of expectations to be completed within a prescribed time frame. Committees or consultants are to provide information and possibly make recommendations to the board of education. The board of education has the responsibility of studying the data and reaching an official decision. Decision making resides with the board of education in all cases.

Estimating Costs of Construction and Ability to Pay

If a new building is considered or if an addition or a renovation project is planned, school boards, in the early stages of planning, will want to know if they can afford the facility. Preliminary costs figures are based on the number of square feet recommended for the school being considered. The following items are used in computing preliminary or pre-bid building costs:

1. Number of acres and the cost per acre needed for a school site
2. The number of square feet recommended for the building multiplied by the current cost of construction
3. A site development cost of approximately 15 percent of the construction costs
4. The inclusion of movable equipment at approximately 8 percent of construction costs
5. Fees and licenses, which may be computed at approximately 7 percent of the combined construction costs, the site preparation costs, and movable equipment
6. A contingency allowance of up to 10 percent
7. Current bond rates, which can change at any time, coupled with the number of years for the payment of bonds
8. A deduction based on any state aid or reserve or sinking funds that have accumulated
9. The tax base or valuation along with the current tax levy

This list of items can be used to calculate the approximate cost of a building program and how it will affect taxes in the local district. Such data can then be used by a superintendent and board of education to make a preliminary determination of costs and ability to pay.

Site Acquisition

Site acquisition for a new school building can become a political issue in many communities. Often, citizens or board members have in mind a preferred school site that may not meet size standards or the criteria for site selection. Site size recommendations also vary from one agency to another. Some authorities suggest an elementary school site of five acres with an additional acre for each additional 100 students, while other agencies suggest a minimum of 10 acres. Some state departments have site size specifications and some do not. The Council of Educational Facility Planners, International (CEFPI), has suggested the following:

Elementary:

10 acres + 1 acre per each additional 100 pupils

Middle School:

20 acres + 1 acre per each additional 100 pupils

High School:

30 acres + 1 acre per each additional 100 pupils[16]

Site selection is more involved than taking the first piece of land that seems convenient. The steps suggested by CEFPI begin with the identification of a site selection team, consisting of the superintendent or a designee and building specialists, such as an architect, a civil engineer, a landscape architect, and a soil-testing laboratory engineer. Information may be needed from regulatory agencies, such as city or county zoning specialists or state department of education consultants and the Environmental Protection Agency, to clarify the criteria for selecting the site. Information can be requested from real estate appraisers, legal consultants, energy engineers, public safety officials, and city or county planners before potential sites are selected.

A list of potential sites can be generated for consideration. After narrowing the list of potential sites to two or three considered to be most appropriate, soil can be tested and a full site inspection conducted. A recommendation can then be taken to the board of education for approval and authorization of the purchase of land. Legal contracts can be drawn, and the purchase of the site can take place followed by the preparation of the site development plan.[17]

In larger districts, particularly in growing communities, school officials commonly stockpile school sites in anticipation of future needs. If a new area of housing is anticipated, as many as three or four sites may be identified and tested, with the knowledge that only one site will be used for a school building. Those sites not used can then be rezoned and sold to developers. Such a practice assures the superintendent that the most appropriate location is available for a future school, and the investment in multiple sites may actually prove to be financially judicious. Since schools sites should not be finalized until the growth of a new area takes place, the purchase of several potential sites can prove to be a good management procedure.

The following questions should be answered prior to the selection of any school site:

Is the site's location convenient for the majority of students?

Is the site the right size and shape?

Is the topography conducive to desired site development?

Is the general environment aesthetically pleasing?

Is the site safe?

Is the air quality healthful?

Is the site free of industrial and traffic noise?

Does the land drain properly and are other soil conditions good?

Does the site have desired trees and other natural vegetation?

Is water available?

Are there easements of any nature affecting the use of the site?

Is the site suitably oriented for energy conservation?

Is the site located on a flood plain?

Is the site near other community services—library, parks, museums?

What is the relation of the site to existing educational facilities?

How is surrounding land zoned?

Are utility services available?

Is the site served by public agencies—police, fire department, etc.?

Is the site easily accessible to service vehicles?

Can the land be shared with other community facilities and organizations, especially parks?

Will the site provide desirable open space for the community where it is needed?

Is the site available?

Is the site expandable in the future?

Is the site affordable?

Are life-cycle costs reasonable?[18]

Selecting an Architect

Selecting the wrong architect is about as devastating as selecting the wrong spouse. You will not only have to live, at least for a period of time, with the mistake, but future generations will have the mistake imposed on them as well.

Architects may be chosen in a variety of ways. One way is by design competition; the school superintendent presents a design problem to several architectural firms and asks for a preliminary plan to meet the need. The competing firms can, by a specified date, submit plans, which are reviewed by a jury, and the jury makes a recommendation to the board of education. Another means of selecting an architect is by direct appointment based on the reputation of a particular architect. Competitive bidding is also used to select an architect. Bidding on human services is, however, less precise than bidding on the purchase of equipment items. Consequently, bidding is less appealing then other approaches for selecting an architect.

Often, a combination of selected elements from these three approaches is used. Such a combination is referred to as comparative selection, and the following criteria are employed. The architectural firm should (1) be registered and licensed; (2) have experience with school design; (3) demonstrate creativity and inventiveness; (4) demonstrate the ability to cooperate; (5) possess the staff of specialists needed; (6) have a genuine interest in the proposed building project; (7) be able to provide samples of previous work; and (8) provide acceptable references.[19] With these criteria in mind, the superintendent and board can visit schools designed by the firm under consideration and talk to people with whom firm representatives have worked.

Once an architectural firm is identified, a contractual agreement with the firm must be reached. Standard contracts are available, any of which may be amended to fit a local need. The important thing is to specify who is responsible for what functions. Most architectural contracts will include provisions for (1) schematic design; (2) design development; (3) the development of contract documents to be used with builders; (4) monitoring of bidding; (5) construction monitoring if it is to be included; and (6) evaluation. As a part of a contract, a payment schedule can specify what percentage of the architectural fee will be paid upon completion of the various phases of the project.[20]

Bonding Attorney

If the construction project will require the sale of bonds, school districts must employ a bonding attorney in addition to the legal council they normally retain. The bonding attorney is required to advise, meet legal requirements involved in selling bonds, and prepare the appropriate documents. The plan to sell bonds requires (1) legal conditions be met in terms of resolutions in board minutes, (2) legal wording for advertising, financial statements, and specified dates and waiting periods, and (3) various other legally prescribed requirements. Once the bond issue is approved by the electorate, the bonding attorney can advise the school board and superintendent in marketing the bonds.

Project Manager and Clerk of the Works

A school district may employ a project manager who becomes the sole person with whom the architect works. This narrows the number of contacts made by the architect as everything is channeled through the project manager. Project managers are usually employed in larger districts. They often have architectural training and are able to direct the overall process of planning and overseeing construction. The project manager is in a first-line position and is accountable to the superintendent of schools.

A clerk of the works, or construction supervisor, is responsible for supervision of the construction project, but he or she is typically not involved in the preliminary planning of a building project. The scope of the job responsibilities for a clerk of the works is much more specific and less comprehensive than the project manager. The clerk of the works is usually employed for the duration of the construction period by the school district, not the architect. The basic function of the clerk of the works is to see the building is completed on schedule, quality is achieved, and expenses are controlled. A clerk of the works should have knowledge and experience in the construction field, work closely with the architect, and become acquainted with every facet of the building design.

Developing Educational Specifications

In the development of educational specifications for facilities, the superintendent assumes the role of participatory leadership, since the task requires the thinking of several different persons. The superintendent typically does not possess the knowledge and skill of an architect. In like manner, the architect is generally not an expert in education. Consequently, the educational specifications serve as a strong linkage between the educational and building design processes. Through the development of educational specifications, the employees of the district, ranging from custodial and maintenance personnel to classroom teachers and the superintendent or central office staff, can think and develop a dialogue collectively with the architect. The architect becomes well informed regarding the needs to be incorporated into the building design. Through the development of educational specifications, the architect has the conceptual and factual information necessary to translate the educational program needs into a workable design for the new facility.

Educational specifications, according to Castaldi,[21] include three distinct sections: (1) a section devoted to "matters related to the educational program, including a detailed description of instructional and learning activities"; (2) a section dealing with "numerical aspects of the architectural problem," such as the number of students to be housed, the number of grade levels, and the size of groups; and (3) a section concerning "special features that should be incorporated in the school building." Hawkins[22] suggested an additional section in the educational specifications to address spatial relationships. Architects have general guides for the placement of different functions within the school; however, in each situation, community input is needed to help the architect generate a floor plan that will achieve the results desired by local educators.

Planning a New, Expanded, Portable, or Renovated Facility

School boards and community groups often look for ways to construct a building as economically as possible. One way to stretch public funds is by joint use of school–community resources. Recreational facilities are most commonly shared; however, in smaller communities in particular, the potential exists to share various portions of the school facilities with different community groups to bring about significant savings.

Questions emerge from time to time concerning the costs of different types of construction. Masonry construction is the most expensive and has an expected life span of 75 years. Metal construction has been proposed by some advocates to cut costs. The savings per square foot over masonry construction are substantial; the cost of metal buildings has been quoted to be 20 to 60 percent less than masonry construction. Metal buildings have, however, only about half the life span of a masonry building, and they have some maintenance problems not associated with masonry construction.

The renovation of an old building is sometimes proposed to save money. Renovation costs are more difficult to determine than new construction because so many variables must be considered. The feasibility of building renovation implies assurances that the modifications and upgrading of quality will allow its occupants to be involved in a quality learning environment. Before the decision is made to renovate a building, in most cases the district will need to employ a structural engineer to determine if the building is sound. The infrastructure of old buildings, that is, their wiring, plumbing, heating, and ventilation systems, may need to be replaced, or the building may be quite adequate. Such factors make it difficult to generalize about renovation costs compared with new construction costs. Old building renovation and the avoidance of acquiring an expensive new site change the equation in still another dimension. The extent and nature of a renovation project, which can be affected by innumerable variables, make the use of simple formulas to compute renovation costs invalid. Major renovation projects have exceeded 50 percent of new construction costs in some instances.

In addition to the issue of structural soundness and the infrastructure of the building under consideration for renovation, the following factors should be considered:

Adaptability of the building for proposed use

Adequacy of space in the building for proposed use

Adequacy and characteristics of the site

Aesthetic and historical significance and its place in the hearts of the school patrons

Potential operational and maintenance efficiency

Compliance with safety codes and with accessibility requirements.[23]

Portable classrooms are used in cases of rapid growth and shifts in population as a means of securing facilities in the shortest possible time and as a cost-saving approach to providing adequate, safe facilities. Portables, or temporary classrooms, come by their name accurately since most portables are intended to last for 20 years.[24] While costs vary considerably, the cost of the portable itself is only part of the picture. Other costs include the preparation of a pad on which the portable will be mounted, water, sewer, and electrical connections, and sidewalks. Portables may be approximately half the cost of a standard construction classroom, yet they last for a much shorter time.

Teachers who have been assigned to teach in portables give mixed reviews. According to Heise and Bottoms,[25] 15 percent of the K–12 teachers surveyed felt portables were more satisfactory, 58 percent indicated they were the same as a regular classroom, and 34 percent said portables were less satisfactory. According to Adams, Bernay, and DeRuosi,[26] the advantages of portables include:

1. An immediate student enrollment need is met.
2. High quality portable buildings are easily acquired.
3. Buildings on the site can be relocated to other schools.
4. Landscaping is kept to an economical minimum.

The disadvantages, as seen by Adams, Bernay, and DeRuosi, are:

1. A temporary school does not solve a long-term enrollment problem.
2. The facility always appears "temporary."
3. Construction preparation costs cannot be recovered.
4. Dismantling the site may prove costly.
5. There are no "on-site kitchen facilities" or other special learning spaces such as the library, gym, or music room.

Modular construction has been proposed to provide economies in new facility construction. "Basically, modular construction consists of structures built in a controlled environment, then transported to a site for actual installation."[27] Nye suggested the following advantages of modular construction:

1. The controlled constructional environment tends to eliminate construction delays caused by weather.
2. The total construction process can be accomplished more quickly with modular construction.
3. Bulk purchasing of materials by the manufacturer brings about savings.
4. Materials are stored so that losses and waste are reduced in the handling of materials and the elimination of vandalism.
5. Production line supervisors can oversee the construction to ensure quality.
6. Since most of the construction is completed in a factory, there is less on-site disruption.
7. "Unlike an on-site contractor who depends on buying down subcontractors to maximize his profit, a modular construction company maintains skilled tradesmen at the same job day in, day out, who know that their abilities contribute to the company's success. The result is greater quality assurance."[28]

Disadvantages of modular construction include the 30-year life expectancy and the architectural limitations of such buildings.

Every cost-saving facility construction approach has its advantages and disadvantages. No perfect solution applies in all situations. Each situation is different, just as each school site is different; thus, a good answer in one situation need not be a good answer in other situations. Still, however, it is usually safe to say that you get what you pay for.

Financial Planning

Financing facilities is not separate from the total educational system at the local level. Financial planning for facilities is accomplished as a part of the total school operation and is related to the priorities of the district. Facilities involve functions reaching over long periods of time; consequently, financial planning to provide facilities should be accomplished with a long-term perspective. Financial planning should encompass multiple options for building construction, additions, renovations, or improvements. Financial facility planners must set priorities and consider how the facility needs relate to the total budget and the ability to finance education (see Figure 11–1).

The sale of bonds to finance school building construction is the primary source of funding. There are, however, numerous other ways that school authorities finance construction. As outlined by Reider,[29] there are nine options used to finance construction: "(1) pay-as-you-go, (2) state or provincial aid, (3) federal aid, (4) shared facilities, (5) non-tax revenue, (6) leasing, (7) lease purchase financing, (8) bond issues, and (9) state bonding authorities."

The *pay-as-you-go method* of financing school construction is a popular option because finances come directly from operating budgets, without the necessity of getting approval of the district constituents. Most states have options that enable school officials to accumulate funds over a number of years by using a special levy, within prescribed limits, to build a sinking fund for facility construction. Sinking funds can be invested during the time they accumulate, and the board avoids interest payments and gains interest income.

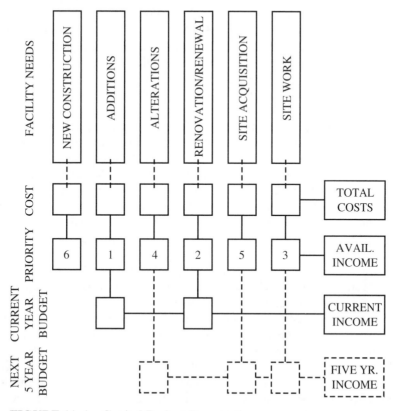

FIGURE 11–1   Capital Budget Preparation

SOURCE: Darwin Reider, "Financing the Capital Program," *Guide for Planning Educational Facilities,* ed. Deborah P. Moore (Columbus, Ohio: Council of Educational Facility Planners, Inc., 1991).

State aid is available for school building construction in some states in the form of grants or loans. Grants for school construction have been used in selected states as incentives for school district reorganization and achieving equalization of educational opportunities. Reider[30] pointed out that various challenges concerning state grants have been taken to court and supported under the concept of equal opportunity to education. Another problem that has been evident in poorer districts is repayment to the state.

Federal funding has been provided to "federally impacted districts" for several decades under the provisions of Public Laws 815 and 874. Because of the federal legislative processes, federal funding has been in a state of some uncertainty from time to time. The provisions and formulas for federal support should be studied and followed closely when such funds are sought.

Shared facilities, in such areas as physical education and recreation, school auditoriums, libraries, and food services, are a reality in communities in many states. Facilities have also been shared been between public school districts and institutions of higher education; buildings are constructed in which teacher education will be conducted with joint involvement between the two agencies. Joint use of facilities is not a major source of funding; however, it is an important way to stretch dollars that has often been overlooked.

Nontax revenue may come from the sale or exchange of property owned by the district. As suggested earlier in the discussion on site selection, medium or larger districts, in which school sites have been stockpiled, have made an investment that can generate revenue through real estate purchases and sales. In some instances, public schools have been rented to technical schools or junior-community colleges, providing a source of revenue.

Leasing and lease purchase financing are means used to cope with overcrowded conditions. Space may be leased from churches, privately owned buildings, or firms that provide temporary or portable classrooms as a short-term solution. Long-term leases are also used, and a contract provides the rent be used as a payment to purchase a facility. In some states, if a bond issue cannot be passed by the voters in a community, it is possible for the board of education to contract with another agency to build a new school. The agency will lease that building to the district, and the rent is applied to the purchase. There is actually no saving to the district, since the builder of the new school must charge sufficient rent to pay the interest on the investment and the management costs. The school district may not have as much control over the construction of the building as under other circumstances; thus, while there are the advantages in finding an alternative to the sale of bonds, there are also some disadvantages.

In some states in which taxing limitations are placed on school districts, which make district bond issues unavailable as a means of financing new construction, a *bonding authority* is an option that is much like lease purchase financing. In such states, a state building authority or other governmental agency may have the authority to sell bonds or levy taxes to build a facility that can then be purchased by the local school by an agreement similar to the lease purchase plan.

The *sale of bonds* by local educational agencies is governed by statutes in each state. Voter approval is required, and taxing limits, as prescribed by law, must be determined. Interest rates on school bonds, which are classified as municipal bonds, vary with prime interest rates, economic factors, and the credit rating, which reflects a district's ability to pay. The duration of most school bonds is 20 years, but this may vary. There is an advantage to financing for shorter periods of time because of the savings in interest. Every state specifies the legal requirements that must be met for the sale of bonds, which include retaining legal specialists. Getting bond ratings, which tells potential buyers of the financial soundness of the district, can be a good investment because the bonds will sell at a more advantageous figure if rated. Bond ratings can be acquired from Moody's Investors Service, Standard and Poor's Corporation, or Fitch Investors Service.[31]

Gaining approval of bond issues from the voters can be a miserable experience for many superintendents. Unfortunately, there is no easy solution. Bond elections are, however, not passed on election day. Bond issues are passed over a long period of time by demonstrating the quality of education year after year; increasing the credibility of teachers, superintendent, and board members over time; developing pride and ownership of the people in a district through what they observe and the way they are involved in the affairs of the school; and through implementing well-conceived strategic planning that enlists the opinion leaders of the district. Planning, credibility, and involvement are the cornerstones on which bond election strategies must be built.

When a bond issue is taken to the voters, the following steps have been suggested to ensure a successful election:

1. Develop a strong public relations program.
2. Pre-plan, study, and analyze timing, need, and options.
3. Review district historical information and demographics.
4. Survey the community to gain a better understanding of their perceptions of the school.
5. Develop the election campaign strategy.
6. Conduct special voter registration.
7. Develop targeted election materials, tools, and techniques for communicating to voters.
8. Identify the "yes" vote, and make sure the "yes" voters get out and vote. Work to educate the undecided, and do not spend too much time and effort on the "no" vote.
9. Plan the election day strategy.
10. Evaluate results and keep records for future use.[32]

Bidding

The size of any building project requires that it be put out for bids. Laws in the various states specify the contract be awarded to the lowest responsible bidder. An advertisement is generally required to ensure that any interested contractor has an opportunity to bid on a building. A timeline is established, which affords interested parties an opportunity to pick up a set of specifications and building plans and the special requirements that are to be met in submitting the bid, such as providing evidence of a performance bond.

Bid opening and awarding of a contract are done in an open board meeting at a predetermined date and place. A contract, drawn with legal advice and review, is signed, and the successful bidder is required to provide a construction schedule. The project manager or clerk of the works, in conjunction with the architect and contractor, should be certain that regulating agency requirements are met. Regulations and codes may come from several of the following national agencies: Building Officials Conference of America, Environmental Protection Agency, Federal Energy Administration, National Electric Code,

National Plumbing Code, Occupational Safety and Health Act, Uniform Building Code, and Uniform Mechanical Code. Local and state regulations and building codes, which differ from state to state and from one community to another, must also be incorporated into the plan to meet fire and panic safety standards; health and sanitation requirements; air, water, and noise pollution control standards; earthquake or hurricane/tornado safety standards; highway and street safety; and accessibility requirements for physically handicapped.[33] The architect will, of course, develop a plan that incorporates all requirements from national, state, and local agencies. As construction starts, the project manager or clerk of the works must confirm that such requirements are being met.

Since the original federal legislation was passed in 1979 and 1982, asbestos control has been a particularly sensitive issue when dealing with renovations and additions to existing facilities. Asbestos not only brings about special requirements for construction, but it poses an ongoing maintenance task for superintendents. The Asbestos Hazardous Emergency Response Act (AHERA) requires all existing school facilities be inspected for both friable and nonfriable asbestos. AHERA regulations require inspection "by Environmental Protection Agency accredited inspectors of all public and private elementary and secondary school buildings . . . and reinspection every three . . . years by an accredited inspector."[34]

Construction of Facilities

Construction time is a busy time. At the outset of a project, the job description for the project manager (PM) or the clerk of the works should be reviewed by the superintendent, the board, and the person serving as PM or clerk of the works. Board members or the superintendent should channel all questions, concerns, or observations through the PM or clerk of the works. All communication to the architect, the general contractor, and all subcontractors should go through the clerk of the works or PM.

While the architect is to be available for consultation when the building is under construction, she or he is not generally responsible for overseeing the construction unless such construction supervisory responsibilities are contracted for in the agreement between the architect and the district.

As construction of a building moves from the planning stage, through the bidding process, and takes shape on the construction site, the "schedule control—construction phase" and the "cost and quality control—construction phase" remain.[35] The schedule control includes:

Construction contract—schedule adherence requirements.

Full-time, on-site team: all issues are resolved at the job site.

Measuring progress against the schedule continuously.

Iron-link connection between progress and payments.

Maintaining a long-range vantage-point overview.

Eliminating potential constraints before they become real.

Expediting decisions.

Protecting the owner's interest and assisting in resolving the contractor's real problems.[36]

Cost and quality controls are concurrent with the schedule control phase of the construction project and include:

Construction contract cost and quality control provisions.

Full-time, on-site management team; issues are resolved at the job site.

Change order control.

Claims control.

Payments linked to progress and quality performance.

A real quality assurance program.[37]

Change orders are a reality in any school construction job. A change order is defined as "a change made in the plans of a building while construction is in progress."[38] The fewer change orders that have to be made, the less the cost and the greater the assurance the building will be completed on schedule. Change orders may be more frequent in renovation projects than in new construction because of the things that are "uncovered" or unpredictable when an existing facility is renovated.

Formal acceptance of a new building is a time when legal documents are signed and the schedule of payments to the contractor, with adjustments that are needed as a result of change orders, takes place. The general contractor is still responsible for assurances and for seeing that any defects are corrected, usually within a 12-month period. The formal completion is the time when the district authorities officially accept and take over the new building. A dedication ceremony will take place at a later date, after the building has been occupied and there is evidence of student involvement and the life of the new school is taking form. Usually, a dedication ceremony, open to the public, is a happy time and one filled with pride and high expectations, which is as it should be.

Equipping New Facilities

Determining Equipment Needs and Bidding

Fixed equipment, such as the furnace, is designed into the plan by the architect and comes as a part of the bid price for building construction. Movable equipment, which as a rule of thumb is estimated at 8 percent of the construction cost, is the responsibility of staff in the school district. A list of all needed movable equipment for a new facility, determined room by room, needs to be compiled by personnel under the direction of the project manager or the superintendent. Building administrators and teachers who will be working in the new facility should be consulted, and their recommendations regarding equipment needs should receive attention. If an old facility is to be vacated, the list of needed movable equipment should be compared with the list of usable equipment to be taken from the old building and placed in the new building.

The superintendent approves the list of new purchases and seeks approval from the board of education. Specifications for the purchase of movable equipment are prepared and bids called for. Then, just as was done with building contractors, equipment suppliers are given an opportunity to bid on needed equipment. Each interested supplier should be provided with the list of equipment to be purchased, the specifications, and the time and place for opening the bids. The success of the bidding process is contingent on the quality of the specifications. Bidding, when done properly, can save the district sums of money ranging from 15 to 40 percent of list prices.

Inventory of Equipment

All movable equipment, as well as much of the mechanical equipment that is a part of the original building, should be inventoried. Computer programs for equipment inventory and maintenance scheduling can be effective. In addition to the actual inventory, a filing system should be set up, in which the equipment numbering sequence used in the inventory is used to keep all manuals, service information, and warranties for each item of equipment. As a part of the filing system for manuals, a procedure needs to be developed for the check-out of references and manuals. It is natural when people are working on an equipment item to overlook returning such information to a file for future use. Consequently, it is helpful to have a designated person responsible for keeping the library of materials updated and seeing that items checked out for use are returned. Movable equipment is a major investment for a school district; therefore, a good inventory and management system is demanded.

Maintenance of Facilities

Custodians and Maintenance Personnel

The superintendent of schools, or a designee from central administration, is responsible for the maintenance of all school buildings and grounds. The actual organizational plan will vary from district to district, but regardless of how the organizational chart is designed, the superintendent is responsible. Some districts have contracted with private custodial and maintenance firms, but even in such contractual arrangements the superintendent assumes the final responsibility. District policies, regulations, and budgetary procedures must provide the framework in which the custodial and maintenance functions are performed. The organizational chart and the job descriptions for the district should be available so all persons involved know who is responsible for performing what tasks and who is accountable to whom.

If a new building is an additional facility in the district, one of the first tasks of the superintendent is to determine how many custodial and maintenance staff members will be needed. Prior experience can be the main source of information when deciding how many people to employ and what skills they will need. Existing criteria can be used to determine the number of personnel needed to clean and maintain a building, the tasks to be completed by the custodial personnel, and the amount of time it should take them to do each task.[39]

A labor union agreement may also influence what custodians are expected to do and the length of time given them to complete their assignment. The detail and focus of labor union contracts with local school districts vary from state to state. There tend to be more extensive points of arbitration in the contract for custodians and maintenance personnel in larger urban area school districts.

The contractor or subcontractors of a new facility are generally required to provide information to custodial and maintenance personnel about the operation and servicing of all the new fixed equipment. As technological advances are made in equipment, increased emphasis will have to be placed on familiarizing custodial and maintenance personnel with computer controls and the management of equipment.

Maintaining Plans on File

A complete set of building plans needs to be kept on file. In fact, the superintendent, the principal, and the person in charge of maintenance should each have a set of plans. A facility that can cost several million dollars is complex and has many subsystems. To care for such an asset, school officials should have a database, including building plans, to work effectively and efficiently.

Key Storage

A key inventory, storage, and check-out system is needed for each building principal. The locks and keys needed to provide security in a school building add up to a sizable amount of money. The key inventory and storage system should be kept in a vault and careful records maintained to show who has what keys. The superintendent and each building principal should formulate a system for key management. The question of whether or not to issue building keys to individual teachers can be a dilemma. Teachers are professionals and should have access to that portion of the building in which they work. If teachers are issued keys to enter the building, however, there may be times when a lost key falls into the hands of unauthorized persons. To exclude teachers from the building is to imply they cannot be trusted, which may cause a loss of productivity for teachers. Keys can become an issue.

Summary

In 1880, Lewis Sullivan stated that form follows function. Thus, "every educational facility should be designed to support, stimulate and strengthen learning. In addition, educational facilities design should reflect a marriage of educational thinking and architectural philosophy."[40] Facilities are needed to support and provide that prime resource—"space"—for all segments of the school program, including special education students, handicapped individuals, a clientele that includes preschool children and adults, and the whole range of school activities.

Planning school facilities is an important segment of the total process since school buildings constructed near the entry point of the twenty-first century will be standing, in most cases, as the twenty-second century approaches. Projected needs in terms of program, numbers and characteristics of clients, and resources must be given careful attention as flexible and expandable facilities are designed.

When construction or renovation issues arise, school superintendents face major demands and challenges as they provide leadership to school boards and patrons. Considerations concerning the architectural firm to employ, the site to purchase, the type of structure to build, the financing of new facilities, and renovation of an existing facility can lead a superintendent into various and diverse paths. Directing a building program is a major undertaking with long-range implications. Consequently, a superintendent should know what human services are needed, how to acquire expertise for the building program, and to whom to delegate responsibilities during the planning, the construction, and the operation of the newly acquired facility.

Discussion Questions

1. It has been suggested that in the early stages of building planning two considerations be kept in mind: (1) involve a large number of staff and citizens as well as a selected specialist, and (2) tie facility planning to strategic planning. Why are these two considerations important? What potential benefits can be derived from them?

2. At what stage of a building program should an architect be contacted and contracted? How do the services of the architect fit with the services of other professionals who may be involved with a building project?

3. How would you define the role of the superintendent when a school facility project is undertaken? What duties should the superintendent perform, and what duties should be delegated and to whom?

4. Analyze the parts of a school facility survey and indicate what value each component would have for a superintendent.

5. When considering an enrollment projection, what information should be considered by the superintendent?

6. In some states, as much as 30 percent of the construction of a new facility is portable. Suggestions have been made that technology and client demands will make centralized facilities less appropriate to meet the needs of all students. What issues do you see emerging from building "flexibility" needs in the future?

7. If the construction price per square foot for a building were quoted at $75, $100, or $125 and the number of square feet was determined from the architectural plans, an estimate of the construction cost can be determined. How does the superintendent explain to patrons that the building will cost much more than the actual construction costs by the time the building is ready for occupancy? What factors will affect the increase in costs?

8. What are the advantages and the disadvantages of facility sharing by school districts and city governments?

9. If board members resisted hiring a clerk of the works, what rationale could be set forth to support acquiring these services?

10. Explain the importance of school building educational specifications.

CASE 11.1   Power Play between the Superintendent and the Board

County Judge A. T. Hobson was a respected figure in the community of Marshall, a small town of approximately 6,000 people in Clarkson County, where he had served on the school board for 17 years. His involvement in church activities, county government, and the school district had won him many supporters; he had received the Senior Citizen of the Year and the Clarkson County Builder of the Year awards for his support in acquiring a new community hospital. Judge Hobson gave true meaning to the term "community leader."

The community of Marshall did not have population growth. During the last U.S. Census report, the population in Marshall had declined 3.7 percent, and the population in Clarkson County had dropped by 5.1 percent. The rural population was following a national pattern common to many agricultural areas; fewer farmers were managing larger farms, and fewer farm children were born. But Judge Hobson was an optimist, and many felt his constant effort to bring industry and business to Marshall had helped sustain the community.

One of the two elementary schools in Marshall had reached the age where replacement was necessary. Superintendent Martha Burns had effectively led community planning efforts; after numerous meetings and publication of proposed building designs, a bond election was passed by a narrow margin. The board accepted a bid with a contractor at a special meeting, and construction was ready to get under way.

One week after the contract was let, Superintendent Burns faced a very full regular board meeting agenda. One item on the agenda for the board to consider was the selection of one of three candidates to serve as clerk of the works for the building project. Superintendent Burns had interviewed each candidate and listed them in order of her preference and recommendation. The professional qualifications for each candidate were listed; the architect's support for each candidate was noted; and the fees for each candidate were outlined.

Before any of the board members were able to raise questions about the three candidates, Judge Hobson said he saw no need for employing a clerk of the works. His rationale was that to employ such a person for the duration of the construction project would cost the district needless money, the bond issue had narrowly passed, and the economy of the county was not good. He noted he had experience working with the addition to the county courthouse and the construction of the community hospital; in his opinion, he and other board members could serve in the capacity of clerk of the works. He finished his comments and looked at Mr. Al Hanson, who was also a long-time board member. Al moved that the suggestion by Judge Hobson be accepted. The motion was seconded, and the question called for.

Superintendent Burns asked to give some information before the vote was taken, and the chairman concurred that she should be heard. She noted all the textbook listings of the importance of a clerk of the works and the functions that were to be performed. She felt that when compared with the total investment in the new elementary school, it was a small price to pay for needed assurances. She listed the Environmental Protection Agency rules, the county water and waste control codes, and the state fire marshal regulations that had to be met. She called the board's attention to the letters of support from other districts who had used the three persons being considered for clerk of the works. Board member Harry Wilcox asked if the item could be carried over to the next meeting. Judge Hobson said that to delay the decision could be detrimental if the building was to be completed for occupancy on schedule. After a few other comments were exchanged, the vote was again called for. Five members voted in favor of using the board in place of a clerk of the works, and one member voted in favor of employing a clerk of the works from the list of names presented by Superintendent Burns.

Notes

1. A. Lewis et al., *Wolves at the Schoolhouse Door: An Investigation of the Condition of Public School Buildings* (Washington, D.C.: The Education Writers Association, 1989).

2. Dennis L. Pool, "Nebraska School Facilities: Educational Adequacy of Structures and Their Funding" (unpublished doctoral dissertation, University of Nebraska—Lincoln, 1993).

3. Kelvin L. McMillin, "Architectural Concerns for Future Learning Environments" (unpublished doctoral dissertation, University of Nebraska—Lincoln, 1994).

4. Ibid., pp. 141–143.

5. Charlie William Brubaker, "The Impact of Technology on Education Facilities," *Educational Facility Planner,* 27(6) (Nov.–Dec. 1989): pp. 4–5.

6. Ibid., p. 14.

7. Ibid.

8. Glen I. Earthman and Kathleen Westbrook, "Planning Professionals," in *A Guide for Planning Educational Facilities,* ed. by Deborah P. Moore (Columbus, Ohio: Council of Educational Facility Planners, International, 1991), p. D2.

9. Harold Hawkins, "Spaces for Learning," in *A Guide for Planning Educational Facilities,* pp. 65–66.

10. G. T. Moore, "Ready to Learn: Toward Design Standards for Child Care Facilities," *Educational Planner,* 32(1) (1994): pp. 5–7.

11. James A. Dyck, "The Case for the L-Shaped Classroom," *Principal* 7(2) (November 1994): p. 44.

12. Ibid.

13. Basil Castaldi, *Educational Facilities Planning, Modernization, and Management,* 3rd ed. (Boston: Allyn and Bacon, 1982), p. 70.

14. Castaldi, *Educational Facilities Planning, Modernization, and Management,* pp. 415–426; Ward Sybouts, *Planning in School Administration: A Handbook* (Westport, Conn.: Greenwood Press, 1992).

15. Sybouts, *Planning in School Administration,* pp. 160–161.

16. Deborah Moore, ed., *Guide for Planning Educational Facilities* (Columbus, Ohio: The Council of Educational Facility Planners, 1991), p. F7.

17. Ibid., p. F3.

18. Ibid., pp. F5–F6.

19. Ibid., pp. D17.

20. Ibid., p. D18.

21. Castaldi, *Educational Facilities Planning, Modernization, and Management,* p. 143.

22. Harold Hawkins, "Educational Specifications," in *Guide for Planning Educational Facilities, Ed. Deborah Moore,* (Columbus, Ohio: Council of Educational Facility Planners, 1991), p. E8.

23. Moore, *Guide for Planning Educational Facilities,* p. N3.

24. Randal Bache and Caroline Edwards, "History Repeats Itself: Another Look at Relocatables," *Educational Facility Planner,* 28(3) (1990): p. 18.

25. B. L. Heise and Jeffrey Bottoms, "Portable/Relocatable Classrooms: A User's Point of View," *Educational Facilities Planner,* 28(3) (1990): p. 13.

26. B. J. Adams, R. S. Bernay, and T. F. DeRuosi, "Miguel Hidalgo Elementary: A Relocatable School," *Educational Facility Planner,* 28(3) (1990): p. 10.

27. Robert Nye, "New Modular Capabilities Mean Quality, Flexibility in Schools Planned for Tomorrow," *Educational Facility Planner,* 30(1) (1992): p. 43.

28. Ibid.

29. Darwin Reider, "Financing the Capital Program," in *Guide for Planning Educational Facilities,* pp. L6–L7.

30. Ibid., p. L7.

31. Ibid., p. L10.

32. Ibid., pp. L12–L13.

33. Moore, *Guide for Planning Educational Facilities,* p. M3.

34. Matthew McGovern, "Asbestos, the Law," *Educational Facility Planner,* 27(1) (Jan.–Feb. 1989): pp. 18–21.

35. Marvin Powell, "Construction Management for Educational Facilities Programs and Projects—Twelve Steps to Success," *Educational Facility Planner,* 27(1) (Jan.–Feb. 1989): pp. 16–17.

36. Ibid., p. 17.

37. Ibid.

38. Castaldi, *Educational Facilities Planning, Modernization, and Management,* p. 363. (See n. 13.)

39. Ibid., pp. 399, 407–410.

40. Heise and Bottoms, "Portable/Relocatable Classrooms," p. 13.

Chapter *12*

Leadership for the Improvement of the Curriculum and Instruction

This chapter discusses the role of the superintendent in a local district with respect to curriculum and instruction. We look at the role of the superintendent in addressing curricular issues and whether the superintendent assumes direct responsibility for curriculum development or delegates the bulk of the responsibilities. We discuss how the superintendent brings planning and curriculum development together, and we review the steps involved in the curriculum planning process. We also address how curriculum and instruction relate to school renewal or restructuring. Some current issues and trends in the area of curriculum and instruction are briefly noted, and finally, the need for a superintendent to draw on the knowledge base regarding the management of change will be referenced.

Superintendents view curriculum and instruction in diverse ways. The interests, training, and background of a superintendent influence how that person chooses to relate to curriculum and instruction. Local conditions can also have a strong impact on how a superintendent views curriculum, as can local, state, and national laws, which can affect what action is taken. A superintendent should make a self-assessment and acknowledge personal interests and expertise while consciously deciding what role to play in the area of curriculum and instruction. Thus, if superintendents are most competent in budget development and management, logically, they will select that area as a prime responsibility on a personal job description. Other superintendents may have interest, training, and experience in the area of curriculum and thus may select that area of responsibility for personal attention while delegating more of the budget management to staff who have budget and business management expertise.

The size of the district will also have an influence on how the superintendent views and becomes involved in curriculum and instruction. Still another factor that may influence the extent and way a superintendent becomes involved in curricular issues is whether the district has a high level of centralized control or is decentralized. A superintendent may, however, choose to have a major involvement in curricular responsibilities in either highly centralized or decentralized districts.

One may ask, "What is the right level of involvement for the superintendent in curriculum and instruction? Is it better to have the superintendent directly responsible for curricular areas, or to have the superintendent delegate such responsibilities?" The right answer is, perhaps, that the best way for the superintendent to address curricular issues is to deploy the administrative staff in a way that uses the expertise of each staff member. In larger systems, a superintendent may have more options for employing experts in various areas of school administration than in smaller systems, where less specialization is available. Consequently, in any district large enough to employ more than one administrator, the superintendent should determine what needs to be done, look at the human resources available in the district, and make decisions regarding how to best deploy the available human capabilities. Ultimately, the superintendent should, by direct involvement or through delegation, arrive at a plan for capitalizing on the staff's expertise to ensure that the strongest possible instructional program and the most appropriate curriculum is made available to each child and every youth enrolled in the system.

The Historical Perspective to Curriculum Planning

When discussing the meaning of curriculum, Ornstein and Hunkins have suggested it is a "*plan* for action or a written document that includes strategies for achieving desired goals or ends."[1] Curriculum is further perceived to involve "*a field of study* comprising its own foundations and domains of knowledge, as well as it own research, theory, and principles and its own specialists to interpret the knowledge . . . [and] can be considered in terms of subject matter (mathematics, science, English, history, and so on) or content (the way we organize and assimilate information)."[2] Walker noted that the "curriculum refers to the *content* and *purpose* of an educational program together with their *organization*."[3] Saylor, Alexander, and Lewis gave a pragmatic definition of curriculum: "We define curriculum as a plan for providing sets of learning opportunities for persons to be educated."[4]

Another way to view the curriculum has been suggested by McNeil. He indicated the functions of curriculum include general education, supplementation, exploration, and specialization. McNeil acknowledged that the curriculum also "performs less recognized functions. They are the *consummation function* (whetting the students demand for material things such as a car or the latest microcomputer), the *custodial function,* and the *socializing function* (allowing students to meet members of the opposite sex)."[5]

While the socialization of a pupil goes well beyond the dating game, McNeil pointed to a significant part of modern curricular functions. Some academically oriented educators decry the idea that a school is to perform any custodial function. It is, however, not possible to separate some of the custodial functions from the formal curricular functions of a school. Actually, while teachers are teaching subject matter to students in a classroom they are also performing a custodial function. The custodial function is much broader than providing for preschool or after-school child care, as has been demonstrated in numerous courtrooms across the land.

The term *program* has been used in a similar way as the term *curriculum,* but often with a broader connotation. The total school program or experience includes (1) required courses or areas of instruction; (2) elective or exploratory courses as the students move from the primary grades to the middle grades; (3) school activities sometimes referred to as extra- or co-curricular experiences; (4) student services in guidance and health; and (5) auxiliary services, including transportation and food. If the philosophical position is taken that everything that happens in the school should ultimately contribute to the learning experiences of children and youth, "curriculum" and "program" may be perceived as interchangeable terms. By contrast, if curriculum is interpreted to mean only the academic and formal course work involved in the total curriculum, the school "program" becomes much different than the "curriculum."

Historically, the meaning of curriculum had its early beginnings in the academic tradition that embraced the classics and only grudgingly acknowledged more applied areas such as surveying, speech, or music. When school activities were reluctantly allowed on college campuses, and later in secondary schools, they were dubbed "extracurricular activities" by most academicians and were not acknowledged as a part of any respectable curriculum. The narrow view of curriculum, which accepts only academic classes as a legitimate part of schooling, is not compatible with the concept that the curriculum should help children and youth learn fundamental academic processes, gain knowledge of scientific concepts, learn about our culture and heritage while fostering a common culture that embraces diversity, and become socialized in the broadest sense of the term.

The urgency of curriculum development is also reflected in the impact of current events on the educational establishment. In 1962, Taba wrote, "Today, as in the 1890s, the ferment in education is caused by the transforming effect of technology and science on society, with criticism focusing on the failure of the schools to solve the problems created by that transformation."[6] Social trends in the 1980s and 1990s have exacerbated these problems of transformation. As a culture we have all the ingredients to build the highest form of civilization and the best quality of life for all citizens; however, there are exceedingly high rates of disruptive behavior, astronomical numbers of babies born out of wedlock, a greater proportion of youth and adults using drugs, a growing population of incarcerated felons, increases in child abuse, and many other indicators of a violent society.

While it is not difficult to develop a strong case for needed curriculum changes, there is a resilience factor that is difficult to measure as predictions are made about the remaining life span of public education. It is certain that major curricular changes are needed, but the timeline with which educators must work is less than clear; there is an urgency involved in the conditions with which educators are faced.

Influences on Curriculum Development

Cultural and Political Climate

"The transmission of culture is the primary task of a society's educational system."[7] Any educational system that does not support and foster the continued existence of the culture in which it resides will contribute to a fractionated nation with no common cultural base. While a common culture is promoted, the primacy of the individual must be acknowledged. Thus, curriculum planners have a delicate balancing act to perform.

The forces within our society have always had a primary influence on schools and, consequently, the curriculum offered and how instruction was carried out. Walker has suggested the "curriculum is a cultural artifact."[8] Schools mirror society and at the same time contribute to the improvement of society in many ways. Thus, through a loosely coupled system, schools are shaped by society and, at the same time, school personnel are filling the role of reconstructionists as they contribute to a changing society.

The curriculum in American schools is shaped by many influences that are often manifested as special interest groups. All special interest groups, and the individuals who are listed formally or informally as members, feel they have constitutionally protected rights, which include waging campaigns to achieve their desired goals. It was during a period that Glatthorn called Romantic Radicalism, which occurred from 1968 through 1974, that the national agenda was going through major changes in which "'rights,' not responsibilities, was the dominant slogan."[9]

Every superintendent should have policies to help school officials effect changes in the curriculum, choose instructional materials, and deal with the innumerable curricular and instruction issues that can arise. All curricular policies must be aligned with the constitutional requirements of the United States so that human rights are protected and there is adherence to both state and federal laws.

Federal Government

Practicing educators active for 10 years or longer can identify various circumstances in which the federal government has assumed additional areas of responsibility and influence over the curriculum offered in local educational agencies. Federal requirements for equal access and equal treatment of individuals regardless of race or gender are examples where the federal government, with judicial support, has continued to extend its influence on education at the local level.

While the U.S. Constitution does not provide for education, and thus the courts have said the individual states have jurisdiction over education, this interpretation does encounter several gray areas. Clearly, the federal government has assumed a major role in conducting the affairs associated with educating the children and youth of the nation. From the time the federal government established land grant colleges, the Smith–Hughes Act to invest federal dollars in vocational education, several programs within the broad range of federal legislation enacted during the Great Depression, the G.I. Bill of Rights following World War II, and the support of a broad range of focused programs following *Sputnik* in the late 1950s, federal legislators have felt compelled to invest federal dollars in education. A "new focus" and the discarding of some of the primary issues addressed by the previous administration has come with each new administration. The pattern is clear, however; the federal government is involved in a major way in financial support and legal mandates.

During the decade following *Sputnik,* referred to as Scholarly Structuralism,[10] there was a "frenzy" to catch up with the Russians. Federal programs were funded to develop and disseminate curriculum. "Initially these federally funded generic curricula seemed successful. . . . However, resistance to . . . federal efforts to transform the curriculum through direct intervention began to increase."[11] While various federally funded curricula were introduced, frequently without carefully considering how change takes place in education, the results were not encouraging. Critics of education focused attention on falling standardized test scores and increased levels of disruption in schools. They saw no bene-fits that could be documented as a result of federal interventions in curricular areas. Even in areas where positive results could be documented as a result of federal investments in education, the popular critics of the day voiced dissent and decried the failing educational systems with such persistence that the good news was often lost in the din.

Perceiving that the vast amounts of funding for education had fallen short of expected results, the Reagan and Bush administrations suggested less federal funding and more local initiatives. In 1990, during the Bush administration, the governors from the 50 states came forth with the list of six goals for the nation's schools. By the year 2000, (1) all children would start school ready to learn; (2) the high school graduation rate would increase to at least 90 percent; (3) students would leave grades 4, 8, and 12 having demonstrated competency in English, mathematics, science, history, and geography; (4) U.S. students would be first in the world in science and mathematics achievement; (5) every adult would be literate and possess knowledge and skill needed to compete in a global economy and exercise the rights and responsibilities of citizenship; (6) and every school would be free of drugs and violence.[12]

State Legislatures

State legislative bodies have pursued various legislative paths in search of ways to improve education. In some instances they have been motivated to pass legislative support to fund federally mandated programs. Legislation introduced at the state level can also be traced to conferences attended by state legislators, in which information was shared about current legislative movements.

The active involvement of state legislative bodies in education is evidence the educa-tional process has become highly politicized. In sincere efforts to improve education, state legislators have struggled with plans to broaden the tax base, achieve accountability, enhance quality through expanding time on task for instruction, lengthen the school year, mandate specific subjects and testing, and increase graduation requirements. State educational legis-lation, in a pattern similar to federal legislation, has not always generated the desired results; however, state legislators continue to struggle with the limited taxing capabilities and high demands for tax dollars while they search for ways to make a positive impact on education. The curriculum in the local school is often the focus of state legislation.

Courts

Federal and state courts have had a hand in shaping the curriculum in American schools. As constitutional rights are brought before a court for clarification and laws of various types are considered in court cases, an ultimate influence reaches into the school program. Rights of freedom of speech, privacy, and equal access are but a few of the areas that have been taken into court for clarification; eventually rulings in such cases have an influence on the curriculum of a given school.

Court rulings have had an increasing influence on local school policy; curricular poli-cies in a local school district should cite court cases to substantiate their appropriateness. School policy is shaped in numerous ways by the law and the court rulings that have fol-lowed legislative actions or come about as a result of some complaint the court was called on to adjudicate.

State Educational Agencies

Every state has a state educational agency, or bureaucracy, created by the state legislature, that is charged with varying degrees of specificity and emphases, for the conduct of the educational program within the state. The state educational agency, typically referred to as the state department of education, is headed by a chief executive officer called the commissioner or superintendent of instruction. The commissioner of education heads a staff of persons who carry out the mandates of the state legislature by monitoring and providing direction to local school districts as a part of the total state system of education. The most noticeable variation from the pattern just described is found in Hawaii, which has just one school district.

Personnel in state departments of education translate state laws into rules and procedures that control much of what goes on in education, including the curriculum. When a state legislature mandates certain content in the curriculum, the state department of education is responsible for seeing the legislative mandate is carried out in the local districts. If a state law is passed requiring a specified number of hours to be spent on instruction during the course of a year, the state department is responsible for seeing the mandate is carried out at the local level.

Professional Organizations

From the time of John Dewey and leaders in the National Education Association who helped form the Seven Cardinal Principles, various professional organizations and government commissions have had platforms where the best thinking of leaders in education has been brought together to point the way for educators and the general public. The literature, conferences, and professional leadership provided to the educational establishment by professional organizations, from the national level to the local setting, has been invaluable. Superintendents who capitalize on information provided by professional organizations may be tapping one of the most valuable resources available for curriculum development. An effective way to benefit from professional organizations is to have staff actively involved as participating members of professional organizations.

Recognized Scholars and Leaders

Every era has had, and seemingly continues to have, scholars who provide invaluable leadership in curriculum development. From the ranks of philosophers to the individuals who conduct research and those who translate research findings into best practice, outstanding scholars have pointed the way in the areas of curriculum development. The work of leading scholars is disseminated through the literature and their appearances at educational conferences.

Local Opinion Leaders

There are local opinion leaders in almost every district, who seemingly fall into two or more categories. There are those who are continually among the dissenters and critics; by contrast, there are those who school officials can count on for positive leadership and support in curricular issues. As a pluralistic society moves forward into areas of disagreement and debate over educational values, superintendents are often at the eye of the storm. There are no easy, simplistic, or singular answers when dealing with dissenting opinion leaders. The superintendent cannot avoid conflicts that arise.

The superintendent who can involve opinion leaders from various segments of the community and include them in resolving conflict, clarifying mission, and developing policy will resolve discordant mental power into a positive force.

Media

The media, especially newspaper editors and reporters, can exert a powerful influence on program or curriculum development. Every document published on public relations has sections explaining how to live and deal with the media. Good relations with the media can be invaluable, and to a large extent it is the responsibility of the superintendent of a school to build constructive media relations wherever possible.

Commercial Publishers of Printed and Software Materials

Authors and publishers of textbooks have for decades had a major influence on the curriculum that is made available for children and youth in the nation's public schools. From time to time, concerns are expressed that publishers have compromised the content of their texts to gain acceptance of special interest groups who have found historical interpretations or scientific knowledge in their region unacceptable in light of regional perceptions or value systems. At other times, publishers of textbooks are accused of failing to have sufficient rigor or to include challenging materials in their texts. Regardless of charges or expressions of concerns about the content or inaccuracy of textbooks, when the dominant position the text occupies in the instructional process is considered, it is clear that the content of textbooks has a major influence on the curriculum of the school. With the growth of increasing numbers of computer software packages, videodiscs, the CD-ROM, and the use of electronic mail to link into networks to reach databases, the single textbook is no longer a single dominant factor in the schools. Publishers of textbooks, computer software developers, and designers of various technological means of accessing data all have an influence on shaping the curriculum.

Pressure Groups

The pluralistic nature of society, the political climate at the national and local levels, the presence of well-organized national special interest groups, and radical or extremist claims in the media about the failure of education have generated what could be called the heyday for pressure groups. As mentioned several times, the superintendent who has involved the opinion leaders in the community to help carry out strategic planning, clarify the mission of the local schools, and set goals and priorities, and who has sound policies and regulations will have a great advantage when dealing with special interest or pressure groups who seek to influence the curriculum of the school.

Parents and Patrons

Parents of students and patrons who express an interest in the quality of education in the local district can be among the best advocates for curriculum development. If, as sociologists have suggested, the family is the most influential and society the second most influential force in shaping the life of an individual, it would seem logical that superintendents should implement strategies to bring the home, society, and the school into a closer working relationship when developing curriculum for the schools.

Pupils

The input of students into the curriculum development process may emerge in several different forms. Obviously, students can and should be consulted about curricular issues. Course evaluations and student feedback are other ways to obtain information from young people. Follow-up surveys of high school graduates can provide invaluable information for curriculum development efforts. Ongoing follow-up procedures should be in place in every school district.

Boards of Education

Board of education members are legally charged to perform specified duties and make policy decisions that affect all aspects of the district, including decisions involving curriculum. In terms of curriculum development, perhaps one of the most demanding responsibilities of a superintendent is to educate the members of the board regarding curricular matters; local boards of education need to have an understanding and clear focus of the mission of the school and the development of sound curricular policies.

Local Staff

Professional teachers are the specialists in curriculum and instruction. They must be involved in the planning and development of curriculum and supported in carrying out the curriculum mandates of the community and the state and national bodies that require the inclusion of certain curricular components. The superintendent should provide the prime resources needed by staff members for curriculum development. Following the planning and development of curriculum, teachers need continued support as they face the demands of translating curriculum into action.

Leadership in Instructional Planning

The leadership of the superintendent is crucial in program planning and the instructional process. The role of the superintendent in curriculum and instruction is best built on a foundation of strategic planning and is best conducted with the support of well-defined, comprehensive policies.

Letting People Know Where You Stand

The staff, board, and community want to know the stance of the superintendent on curricular issues. Even if staff members do not completely agree with the superintendent, they will be more comfortable if they know the expectations of the superintendent than if they are uncertain about the superintendent's views on curriculum matters. The ideal, of course, is total agreement between the staff and superintendent about the direction taken and procedures followed in curriculum development. Planning is often the key to achieving congruence between the views of the superintendent, staff, board, and patrons. In the planning process, the superintendent's stance can become known to all involved, as educational values are revealed and priorities emerge in the total planning process.

How a superintendent works with various groups in the development of program is also revealing. The superintendent who can tolerate other views, and who solicits and encourages important others to contribute, creates a climate vastly different from the superintendent who is a controller and rejects input from others. Even if they disagree on some points with the superintendent, staff members will become more secure in the curriculum development process if they know the superintendent genuinely wants their input and values their expertise as professionals. Conventional wisdom and numerous researchers and scholars have suggested that the best decisions are made when those who are most immediately affected are involved in the decision making. Teachers are most closely involved in curricular decisions.

A Clear Philosophy, Vision, Mission, and Goals

Curriculum specialists have noted that no curriculum development can be successfully implemented without first establishing a clear philosophy of education. When a clear philosophy is coupled with a strong grounding in the psychology of learning and an understanding of the developmental stages through which children and youth progress, as well as insights about instructional methodology, meaningful, predictable curriculum planning can be undertaken. A vision of education in the future and a clear mission are needed if the superintendent is to provide leadership on curricular matters. The mission can be translated into the goals to be achieved as the superintendent works with all significant stakeholders. The philosophy, vision, and mission become cornerstones on which the superintendent demonstrates the leadership needed in curricular matters and at the same time sees that internal consistency is achieved in planning and implementing the curriculum.

Curriculum Policy

When differentiating between policy and rules, it has been suggested that policy states what directions will be taken to accomplish desired outcomes, and rules prescribe how the intended direction will be reached. In practice, much that could be defined as rules has been stated as policy. This is true when curriculum policy is defined legislatively, at the state and local levels. As suggested by Glatthorn, policy "designates the set of rules, criteria, and guidelines intended to control curriculum development and implementation."[13] In considering what curriculum policy should accomplish, Walker has indicated:

The most basic function of policy is to coordinate the curricula of schools and class-rooms throughout some jurisdiction, . . . [and] policy serves to symbolize and express cultural values, . . . [while] policy performs the important economic function of allocating scarce educational resources among competing curricular priorities.[14]

Delegating Responsibility for Instructional Planning

The superintendent can only expect to achieve needed curriculum development in a district if the major elements of curriculum and instruction are delegated to staff. Staff perform the instructional duties necessary to provide learning opportunities for students. They must, in like manner, be delegated the professional domain of curriculum development. Such delegation is not to imply that the superintendent does not provide leadership in the curriculum development process. The leadership and support, along with the management and allocation of prime resources, are high-priority responsibilities of the superintendent and are the elements used by a superintendent to support staff in curricular issues.

The titles of people, or the wording that appears on job descriptions coordinated with an organizational chart of a school district, vary considerably. In some districts, a person is designated to be responsible for curriculum matters under the heading of assistant or associate superintendent. In others, the curricular function is carried out by the directors of curriculum. In smaller districts, the principal of a building is often delegated the responsibility of curriculum development. Principals frequently delegate portions of the curriculum development function to department heads and teachers on the staff. Intermediate service units who service districts may have curriculum specialists who act as resource persons in curriculum planning. The size of a district and how it is organized will have an influence on the delegation of curricular responsibilities. The superintendent, however, is responsible for the organizational framework that will facilitate curriculum development. This includes specifying the role and function of the superintendent in curricular matters and providing appropriate staff with clear job descriptions and support to see that the process of improving programs is achieved.

Superintendent's Role in Supporting Staff Development

Creating the climate is but one element to generate movement in curriculum and instruction. Climate should not occur by chance. A superintendent has the information resources to help build and maintain a healthy school climate. The characteristics of a good school climate have been identified and elaborated on by Anderson.[15] Several characteristics of a positive school climate are in agreement with that proposed for site-based or school-based decision making. Good rapport among all significant actors, cooperativeness, shared decision making, careful attention to the reward structure, open communications, a clearly articulated mission, an emphasis on educational outcomes, and a commitment to excellence are major ingredients in creating a healthy school climate.

Even if a superintendent is not a curriculum specialist, he or she should become aware of trends and be informed regarding curriculum. The superintendent must show that curriculum is a high priority, not just pay it lip service.

Providing prime resources for curriculum development is but one way a superintendent can demonstrate its importance. *Time,* a crucial, critical resource, must be allocated to the process of curriculum development. It is not realistic to assume that staff can be involved in developing a better curriculum by attending an end-of-day meeting once a week. If curriculum development is to be a high priority, time has to be allocated for curriculum planners. *Human resources,* from within the staff and from outside sources, need to be made available. The better the quality of the human resources allocated to the planning effort, the better the results will be. The acquisition of staff with the needed expertise is not automatic; it must be planned and monitored. Support staff, such as clerical persons or technicians, are often needed for curriculum development. *Space and facilities* are prime resources that should be made available by a superintendent when developing new curriculum. Finally, *information* is a prime resource to be made available for curriculum planners. Information may be available through the human resources used to support curriculum planning efforts, but other sources must also be tapped; for instance, visitation to other school sites; professional literature; attending conferences and workshops; and drawing on electronic data sources should be utilized in curriculum planning. The basic knowledge and research findings that can help in the process of improving a program should not be ignored.

How Curriculum Planning Interfaces with Strategic Planning

Planning for the improvement of a program can be initiated in several ways. There may be a problem that calls for attention, or a new state regulation may be announced. Of the variety of ways in which new emphasis on program development may come about, strategic planning is one of the most significant and potentially fruitful ones. Strategic planning, as suggested in Chapter 7, can be a major force in shaping the future of a school district, including program or curricular matters. The potential of strategic planning will be realized only if done with careful attention to the process, by strategic management, and by the monitoring and evaluation of the effort and all its subparts.

Centralized versus Decentralized Curriculum Planning

Modern management theory, if applied to curriculum development, advocates a decentralized approach to curriculum development as the most fruitful. If viewed from the concepts contained in Total Quality Management or if viewed from what is known about human motivational forces, the knowledge base tilts toward the distinct advantages of a decentralized approach. The advocates for site-based management or school-based decision making can find strong support for their position. In the realm of curriculum development and instruction, the rationale for decentralization is stronger than it is for centralization.

Steps in Curriculum Planning

The steps involved in curriculum planning have been variously described. When reviewing the systems or plans of leading curriculum specialists for curriculum development, however, it is possible to identify common concepts among the various leaders in curriculum. Consequently, it becomes less important for a superintendent to implement the five steps listed by one specialist or the nine points of a curriculum planning model of another specialist than it is to understand fundamental concepts to be employed in the curriculum planning process.

Models of Curriculum Specialists

Taba's[16] paradigm leads curriculum developers through seven steps that include diagnosis, formulation of objectives, selection of content, organization of content, selection of learning experiences, planning learning activities, and evaluation. Saylor and Alexander[17] presented a process model that specifies the need for goals, objectives, and domains that evolve from environmental and philosophical considerations. The actual curriculum design, according to Saylor and Alexander, involves decisions about content and how it is to be organized and delivered. Curriculum implementation and evaluation follow. While differences can be seen in the language and structure posited by Taba as contrasted to Saylor and Alexander, and those contrasts could be carried on to include Ralph Tyler,[18] another early leader in curriculum development, the conceptual base is strikingly similar and serves as the platform from which more recent curriculum specialists have built improved curriculum models.

Hunkins[19] refined early curriculum models with the inclusion of closer adherence to systems theory. Hunkins listed the same steps included by earlier curriculum specialists; however, he added the concepts of the feedback loop and curriculum "maintenance" or a renewal process. More recently, Glatthorn[20] presented a "goal-based model" that includes a broader definition of elements that should be included in the curriculum planning process. Glatthorn recognized the importance of change management in the curriculum development process and discussed change strategies needed to ensure adoption of a new curriculum. Similar concepts, but with more detail, have been provided by McNeil regarding the process of curriculum development.[21] Thus, the work of curriculum specialists over several decades reveals that common, basic concepts have survived as expanded and more sophisticated refinements in the process have emerged.

The Generic Systems Planning Approach

Good curriculum planning is, simply stated, good planning. Good planning may be accomplished by following various approaches. Good planning does, however, involve several concepts contained in the generic planning model presented in Chapter 7.

A superintendent of a school system, working with staff members, needs to consider basic assumptions, which include a clear set of educational values and a philosophy to provide a foundation on which a curriculum can be developed. This especially includes considering the environment, in all its various dimensions, and giving special attention to the needs of the children and youth to be served in the school. The framework in which this takes place can be clarified and become much more meaningful if strategic planning has proceeded the curriculum planning effort.

The mission of the school district should be clarified and translated into a working document that serves as a guide to the curriculum planning process. Internal consistency must begin with the basic assumptions and carried through the clarification of the mission and on to all remaining aspects of the curriculum development process.

Goals, objectives, and outcomes need to be developed. It is not uncommon, at this point in the total curriculum development process, to hear debates about the definitions these terms. The definitions used for an objective, a goal, or an outcome, however, are not crucial. What is important is that the mission is broken down into manageable parts that may be considered in courses of study and individual courses, and specific learning outcomes identified so staff members may use an agreed-on, common set of terms. A staff can use definitions from the literature; however, they will still have to clarify the definitions they find usable and meaningful as they move into the curriculum development process.

Once staff members know what they want to accomplish in specific terms, agreement can be reached about the criteria that are employed to evaluate the results. As suggested in the generic operational planning process, early planning for evaluation is important.

Options for delivering a curriculum can be considered. Identifying multiple options can increase the chances of enriching the curriculum.

Sequencing the learning options and activities is, in a general sense, developing the scope and sequence for a curriculum. For a single course, sequencing the learning options becomes student-related and reflects the daily events in the classroom in the actual instructional process.

If a new or revised curricular area is to be considered, the planned curriculum should be piloted or field tested. In actual practice, it is not always possible to make a trial run with a new curricular effort. Regardless of whether a trial run can be made or whether it is simply a matter of full implementation, an evaluation needs to be conducted. The evaluation should involve process and product measures that encompass psychomotor skills, cognitive learning, and attitudinal or affective measures; pre and post measures may be included. Finally, after full implementation has taken place, follow-up data become important. Evaluation data should come in many forms and be drawn from multiple sources.

Curriculum renewal decisions should be made based on evaluation results. Feedback, in various forms, can be used throughout the entire curriculum planning and implementation process. Superintendents and staff working with curriculum and instruction can do a better job of planning and implementing when they are aware of and capitalize on the feedback loops that are ever present in the planning and operation of a program.

Tying Curriculum Planning to the Total System

For the superintendent, there are several factors to consider concerning a K–12 curriculum. The scope of the curriculum, referred to by Ornstein and Hunkins[22] as the "breadth and depth of its content," is a constant curricular consideration that has grown in complexity with the information age. As teachers had to make choices from many content areas and realized they could not teach all areas in depth, the term "post holing" was popularized.

Integrating the curriculum, akin to assuring internal consistency, refers to joining the areas of the curriculum together both horizontally and vertically. "Integration allows the learners to obtain a unified view of knowledge and an in-depth meaning of the subject matter . . . [while] *sequence* fosters cumulative and continuous learning, or what is referred to as the *vertical* relationship among curricular areas."[23]

Superintendents are ultimately responsible for assuring articulation of the curriculum takes place. Articulation guarantees all components or parts of the curriculum are interrelated, so that unnecessary duplications are not found from one grade level to another and the curriculum is designed and delivered through the instructional process in a smooth sequence. Along with articulation is the question of balance in the curriculum. A balanced curriculum is one in which there is a planned and appropriate weight given to all aspects of the curriculum. Debates occur regarding the balance of school activities, especially interscholastic athletics, in the total program or curriculum. If school activities are considered as a part of the total program or the definition of curriculum is broadly conceived to include school activities, the curriculum planners can better determine the proper balance of school activities with respect to the total program. In the domain of curriculum balance, the superintendent may well take the leadership in developing school policies to provide a structure for curriculum planners.

Relating Curriculum to Instruction

Instruction brings the curriculum to life. Through the instructional process the purpose of the curriculum is either achieved or lost. A curriculum, or a course of study, can be developed that could be truly outstanding; however, if a teacher elects to ignore the planned curriculum, time and effort have been wasted on curriculum planning. Teachers who are deeply involved with curriculum development are much more likely to implement the curriculum through appropriate instructional strategies or teaching models. The organization of a given school can also have an influence on relating the curriculum to the instructional process; teachers in a collaborative arrangement are more likely to carry out and deliver the intended curriculum than those teaching in isolation.

The superintendent, in addition to supporting the curriculum planning process, is also responsible for providing teachers with the needed tools to provide appropriate instruction. The finest curriculum plan in the world may be rendered impotent if the needed instructional resources are not made available. It is the responsibility of the superintendent, working with staff in attendance units, to see that needed resources are made available so the curriculum plan can become a reality through the instructional process.

Allocating Prime Resource for Curriculum Development and Instruction

The educational process has been growing in complexity. The idealistic scene of Plato sitting on one end of a bench and an enthralled student sitting on the other end is scarcely appropriate for education in the information and communication age. Plato, the master scholar, had within his head all the knowledge that was deemed necessary. Since he possessed all knowledge, he was considered the source of knowledge and the one most capable of transmitting that knowledge. Plato's students were very selectively chosen, and they were from a homogeneous culture that fostered a similar set of values. And although they spoke of diversity and questioning as they strove to understand their environment and find truth, they did so in a relatively static society. Life was simple.

In contrast to Plato, teachers in classrooms being readied for the twenty-first century have a much more complex environment and a greater amount of knowledge with which they must work. They live in a pluralistic society that is often facing disruptions of major proportions, and they experience technological changes of great dimensions at exponential speed. Teachers in modern schools who work in an evolving culture within the information and communication era need support from the superintendent through appropriate allocation of prime resources. These consist of time, space, human resources (supporting and supplemental), equipment and supplies, and information. The superintendent speaks the loudest and most clearly by setting expectations and supporting educational priorities for the staff members responsible for curriculum and instruction.

Technology

Interactivity, data sources, multimedia, and distance learning are only a few of the dimensions of the technology explosion that are reaching into schools. With a new generation of computer technology emerging every 18 months, it is virtually impossible to keep technology and the level of staff expertise in a school abreast of the world outside the school. Practically every school system has access to personnel with expertise in the area of technology. Mid-sized to large districts are able to employ staff members highly skilled in computer science and the use of local area networks, as well as other forms of emerging technologies. Most smaller districts have access to expert consultation through intermediate educational agencies.

Every local district, regardless of size, should have access to expert consultation regarding the acquisition of technology hardware, software, and staff development. Superintendents can no longer recommend to board members that they wait until technology is developed and then make purchases, for there is no endpoint to the development of technology. For example, once a computer laboratory is put into a school it may serve the needs of the students for several years; however, the facility will need to be upgraded in a relatively short time and may become obsolete in but a few years.

Perhaps the greatest challenge that superintendents face with respect to the use of technology is not the selection of hardware or keeping current with the latest networking software, but how to lead a staff to a level of sophisticated use where the most fruitful applications of technology are made to the curriculum and the instructional processes. In many schools much of the technology-related curriculum activity consists of (1) an addition to the curriculum and (2) a continuation of the instructional process and the current curriculum with the added expense of computers. Knowing the potential of technology and determining how to employ technology to help reshape the curriculum and the instructional process, rather than having technology dictate the shape of the curriculum, is the challenge facing school superintendents.

Staff Development

The staff is the highest-priority resource with which the superintendent works. Curricular or program development will be meaningful only after staff development has taken place. Staff development is much more than preschool in-service days or allowing staff professional days to go to conferences. Staff development is a continuing, constant process. The superintendent should be a consummate staff developer—a maximizer of the human resource. Development should be a constant thread woven into the total fabric of the professional experience of every staff member by a carefully designed process directed by the superintendent. The growth of staff members involves the (1) school climate; (2) how priorities are set; (3) the allocation of resources; (4) the verbalized informal and formal statements and the behaviors that express and acknowledge the mission, goals, and priorities established for the district; (5) the planning and ordering of all resources, which can include how the school is organized and structured; (6) the reward structure; (7) the study and the discourse of ideas and information; (8) the use of data; (9) the emphasis on evaluation; (10) and a myriad of efforts and subtleties that ultimately help teachers do a better job of curriculum development and instruction for the benefit of children and youth.

Where Curriculum and Instruction Fit in School Restructuring

Restructuring, reform, or whatever the term applied to changing education for the better, will centrally involve curriculum and instruction in the change process. As mentioned, and as has been demonstrated repeatedly in the educational establishment, change of any major proportion requires that all major segments of the total system be involved. Curricular issues and instructional practices will be in the center of the vast, complex set of processes demanded for major educational changes. School superintendents, working with members of their staffs who are delegated the major responsibilities for curriculum development and delivery of instruction, will be required to acknowledge the pivotal position of curriculum development and instruction at the center of school improvement efforts.

Program Trends and Issues

As our pluralistic society, blending with unimagined technological changes, evolves, school superintendents meet many trends and issues; these trends and issues shape the curriculum and the instructional process in many ways. It would be a major undertaking and the source of much debate to attempt to identify the top 20 trends or issues faced by superintendents. Consequently, the following items are presented randomly rather than in any sequence or set of priorities, and the list is not intended to be all-inclusive.

Providing for Students with Special Needs

Students with special needs have been recognized, and programs have been developed and often funded by legislative bodies as evidence of their perceived importance. The trend, in progress since the passage of federal legislation establishing special education, poses a continual set of needs for school superintendents. Filling out state forms, putting a program in place, employing trained staff, and making budget provisions for special education are but a few of the superintendent's responsibilities. Refinements in the management and delivery of programs for students with special needs are ongoing. There are conflicting public demands on the schools, and staff indifference and lack of willingness or skill in dealing with students with special needs remain a concern.

Other students who have special needs and are categorized as gifted pose a different set of challenges for a superintendent and staff. As is typical of many areas related to education, parents of gifted have often become a special interest group.

The Federal Role in Education

It would be almost futile to attempt to give a definitive answer to the question about the role the federal government should play in education, and specifically in curricular matters. The question itself is far too politicized. The National School Board Association did undertake the task of making such a definition.[24] It was suggested the federal role should be to:

1. Define and clarify the responsibility of the federal government in education
2. Take steps to increase the nation's competitive edge through education
3. Advance equal educational opportunities for all people
4. Promote the effective use of existing and emerging forms of technology
5. Provide assistance in strengthening the quality of teaching
6. Assist in providing for the needs of students with special needs
7. Help to improve and to fund rural education
8. Support, on a continuing basis, urban education
9. "Increase the federal interest in education"

The statement provided by the National School Board Association is helpful, but the debate about the amount and nature of federal support for education will continue.

Alternative School Programs/Magnet Schools

Alternative schools have come and gone for various reasons. The evidence found in some locales can be used to support the magnet school concept. Schools, however, whether they are magnet or comprehensive, are good schools because of the staff and the curriculum. Organizing the district to provide magnet schools does not ensure quality. Quality comes from more than school organization. School organization can, however, help improve the quality of education provided youth in a community. While magnet schools have proven to be most appealing in urban centers, there has been little or no emphasis placed on magnet schools in rural areas.

The Year-Round School

The bulk of the population in the United States has views and habits that continue to support the concept of the academic school year in preference to the year-round school. Arguments to support the year-round school, such as economic considerations, overcoming the loss that occurs on the learning curve in the summer, and providing for 12-month home–school–work relationships, seem to be set aside by parents and taxpayers when the issue of going to the year-round school comes to a formal vote. The debate that continues over the achievement scores in mathematics and science of American students as contrasted to scores of Japanese and German youth has not yet convinced parents and citizens to accept the year-round school as a possible means of making America more competitive. The issue of the year-round school remains an open debate in some districts and, at least for the time being, a closed issue in others. The final decision regarding the year-round school is yet to be made.

Sex Education/AIDS

A variety of approaches have been used with respect to sex and AIDS education. Placing sex and AIDS education in the curriculum and selecting instructional materials and teaching strategies have proven difficult in most schools. The reality and volatility of the issues, coupled with values demonstrated in a pluralistic society, compound the problems faced by superintendents. Even if a superintendent and school board, with community involvement and support, have clarified the mission statement of the school, have clearly focused educational goals and sound policies, follow the state mandates, and monitor and evaluate the programs in place for sex and AIDS education, there is no guarantee the program will run smoothly. Of the various curricular issues superintendents face, sex and AIDS education are perhaps among the most difficult issues.

Censorship and Selection of Materials

Special interest groups, some of whom openly embrace the role of watchdog, have camped on the schoolhouse door step in many communities in an effort to keep the school officials from selecting what they perceive to be inappropriate educational materials. The selection of instructional materials and library books, especially those closely linked to sex education and AIDS instruction, has engendered a wide range of interest from numerous groups. Some patrons, often with support from a national organization, have expressed a special interest in social studies texts, science books, multicultural literature, and references dealing with economic principles.

Superintendents should take a proactive stance regarding the selection and reconsideration of instructional materials and library references. A superintendent should:

1. Develop policies for the selection of instructional materials that include a definition of instructional materials and reference such policies to state and national laws related to schoolbook selection and reconsideration when some book is challenged.
2. Affirm, in policy, the teachers' right to teach and the students' right to learn with statements of support for academic and intellectual freedom.
3. Examine the laws, policies, and academic intellectual freedom statements to ensure internal consistency between policies, philosophy statements, educational goals, and objectives.
4. Involve opinion leaders from all strata of the community in the initial stages of the policy development process.
5. Develop the selection and reconsideration policies, in clear statements, before a challenge occurs.
6. Publish and disseminate selection and reconsideration policy information to staff and community after feedback has been gathered from teachers and community leaders and formal board approval has been granted.
7. When a challenge does occur, use the policies and procedures that have been developed.[25]

Religion

The judiciary is repeatedly being called on to define or clarify the separation of church and the state. Special interest groups voice strong views about the inclusion or exclusion of religion in public schools. Legislators strive to redefine or clarify the point of separation of church and state through the legislative process. Ultimately, school superintendents and their boards of education come face to face with the reality of religion in the halls of the school, as the attention of the community, including all its diversity, mores, and accompanying emotions, is focused on the school. The same proactive stance on the part of the superintendent should be used to fit religion into the school program as suggested for dealing with the selection or reconsideration of textbooks.

Education versus Training for the World of Work

A curricular consideration with far-reaching implications is the purpose of education and how that purpose is translated into "training for the world of work," as contrasted to helping every student become an "educated person." Should the curriculum of the school be focused on teaching skills that will be needed in the work place and exclude such things as music, art, and poetry? Should the school provide a curriculum that helps young people find out more about themselves and develop a greater understanding of how to get along with other individuals in a constructive way? Various analysts over several decades have suggested that the rise of the divorce rate, the increase in family disruption and abusive behavior to children and spouses, and the rise in the use of illegal drugs are areas that the curriculum in public schools has not adequately addressed. People do not lose their jobs or their spouse because they are not knowledgeable in mathematics or chemistry. Perhaps the basic question still is to be answered: What is an educated person?

School Activities—Co-curricular

Every superintendent in a public school system will face many questions and feel innumerable pressures with respect to school activities. School activities exemplify some of the best educational planning and some of the worst. For individual activities or events, coaches and sponsors have demonstrated outstanding planning and a high level of expertise in conducting the activity. By contrast, when it comes to the overall planning of school activities some of the worst examples of planning and executing programs have been witnessed. To a large degree, school activities have been left to the individual coaches and sponsors, as they draw on their own devices and do their own thing. When considering the level of importance to youth, the contradiction that is evident in some schools is not only difficult to explain, but educationally inexcusable.

The fact that in some school districts school activities are referred to as "extracurricular" activities is an indication of how they are viewed and the philosophical base from which they operate. School activities can be categorized as (1) performance activities, which include athletics, music, drama, publications, and forensics; (2) leadership activities that encompass student council, National Honor Society, social events, and rally squads; and (3) class-related activities that include subject-related clubs, assemblies, field trips and tours, and culminating events such as commencement. Every teacher who works with secondary students faces potential contractual considerations with respect to school activities.

Although not a major portion of the school budget, the amount of funds needed to carry out an activities program is considerable and becomes complicated by the fact that tax dollars and funds raised from student activities are co-mingled. The use and maintenance of facilities for school activities is a time-consuming facet of the total school activity program. School activities are a high priority for the bulk of the secondary student population in most schools, and they are viewed with more enthusiasm by parents and patrons than most aspects of the school program. It is hard to justify school activities being relegated to a place of "extracurricular." Even when special interest groups have challenged the existence of school activities, the preponderance of public opinion has been supportive of school activities. Clearly, school activities are going to be a part of our public school programs. To ensure a quality activities program, superintendents should provide the leadership, policies, and support for principals, secondary staff, and students. The activities program should be kept in balance with the total school program and consideration given to legal implications.

Affluence

During the last several decades, the United States has occupied a place of affluence among world cultures. Although in some states financial limits on school districts have had devastating effects and most educators have searched for ways to expand the financial resources available for education, American society has been the most affluent in the history of humankind. The American public spends significantly more when constructing new homes; consumes more energy per capita; purchases more expensive cars; spends more on recreation, clothing, travel, and food; and purchases more illegal drugs than ever before in our history. In spite of the rise of the homeless and the number of persons who do not have health insurance, the American public is basically an affluent society.

The impact of affluence on individuals has not yet been fully analyzed. An ever-changing set of public expectations and priorities has emerged from the growth of affluence in society. While needed attention has been given to children and youth from homes at or below the poverty level, little attention has been given to the issues surrounding affluence in the school curriculum or total program. Dealing with affluence is not a matter of setting forth a single policy that will answer a host of complex questions. Dealing with the influences derived from affluence in our society will demand thoughtful considerations that may reach into the mission statement of a district, be reflected in educational goals and policies, and be evident in classrooms and at school activities.

Relating Curriculum Development to the Management of Change

Superintendents will be called on to demonstrate a high degree of skill and an in-depth understanding of how to manage change when curricular issues are considered. Difficulties may arise when changing an insurance program in a district or payroll procedures as new computerization is employed; however, such changes are typically more easily accomplished than innovations in the curriculum. Also, superintendents are challenged because in most instances they are not in direct or immediate command of curricular issues but have delegated them to middle management.

Knowledge about leading a staff into an innovation has expanded greatly over the last few decades. Superintendents no longer have to rely on some vague or undefined set of techniques to accomplish change. Sociologists have formulated change models applicable in the field of education. Studies have been conducted on educational change and the strategies and techniques used to lead a staff through the change process. The politics of change has been explored, and greater insights have been provided school officials to help them manage the change process.

The management of change can be linked to the planning process so that the concepts for operational planning can be used for the framework on which change processes are manipulated.[26] Another growing field of knowledge used to support change in a school district has been found in the literature regarding human motivation. Total Quality Management and Organizational Development specialists translated concepts developed in industry to the field of education. Numerous strategies have been brought together in educational settings, under the heading of school-based or site-based management, that capitalize on techniques and organizational strategies to involve people to bring about change. School superintendents have access to a considerable knowledge base when managing changes in the school curriculum and instructional approaches employed by individual classroom teachers.

Summary

Superintendents work in a complex, loosely coupled system in which curricular issues are surrounded by many influences that require some things or prevent other things from taking place in the program of a school. The leadership provided by the superintendent on curricular issues is crucial to the success of the school. It matters not whether the superintendent assumes direct responsibility and control of curriculum development or whether that function is delegated; the priority the superintendent places on curriculum will determine to a large degree the quality of the educational program made available for children and youth in the district.

The superintendent is called on for the highest order of leadership, as significant others are involved in the process of program planning and carrying out the instructional process. Strategic planning can set the stage and clarify the mission for a district in ways that foster good curriculum planning. Curriculum planning, as much or perhaps even more than other forms of planning, requires the allocation of prime resources to ensure the process is accomplished. To move beyond the planning phase of curriculum and instruction, the superintendent should be knowledgeable about the management of change. The best possible design for curriculum becomes meaningless if the plan cannot be implemented. The implementation of a newly designed curriculum typically involves changes and improvements, which can only be accomplished if people change. Thus, leading staff and community through innovative efforts, or managing change, is a key responsibility of the superintendent.

Curriculum development cannot be done in isolation. As the curriculum is reviewed and improvements planned, there is the need to maintain internal consistency in the scope and sequence of the curriculum itself, as well as acknowledging that the curriculum ties into the budget and that at numerous points the school policies and procedures interface with the curriculum. The total school curriculum or program, including areas that are not in the formal classroom but which involve school activities, should be coordinated and designed to achieve the mission of the school. Evaluation of the school program is also needed to provide information for program improvement and to be accountable to all stakeholders.

Discussion Questions

1. How should a superintendent determine whether the area of curriculum development is a primary responsibility to be included in the superintendent's job description or whether it is an area which should be delegated?

2. How should the scope of the curriculum, or the total program offered in a school, be determined? How should a determination be made regarding what place such areas as guidance and counseling, student health services, school activities, and auxiliary services including food and transportation should occupy in the total school program?

3. How can a superintendent, especially one who has made a determination that curricular issues will be delegated to other staff, maintain control of the curriculum planning process if a site-based, or school-based, organizational structure is employed?

4. If you were to review the concepts found in the literature on human motivation and apply that information to the organization of a school district, with curriculum improvement in mind, how would you recommend that a district be organized for efficient, effective program improvement?

CASE 12.1   The Curriculum and Special Interest Groups

The gifted program in Centerville had been in place for approximately 10 years. The percentage of students identified for inclusion in the gifted program was almost constant from year to year. The state legislature passed legislation that contained new provisions for including a wider range of "gifted" students who demonstrated talents in more specialized areas, such as mathematics and science, music, art, and language arts. New testing and expanded identification programs were introduced in Centerville as a result of the new legislation, and consequently more students were acknowledged as gifted.

At approximately the midpoint of the fall semester, after the newly instituted gifted program had been introduced, some of the parents of the gifted music students appeared at the board meeting and requested a completely separate gifted curriculum for those students identified for special attention in the area of music. The parent representatives had met with the assistant superintendent in charge of curriculum and the secondary school principals and discussed their interests prior to the board meeting; however, they perceived they were not receiving the appropriate responses concerning a change of curriculum for the music students. Their concerns were centered around the fact there were no new courses added to the music curriculum, and there were no courses reserved for the exclusive use of gifted music students. In addition to requesting a curriculum expansion in the area of music, the parents wanted their students to be excused from some courses required for graduation. The reduced graduation requirements would permit the gifted music students to take additional courses and be involved in special performance groups in music.

The parents of the gifted music students had done their homework. They had followed all required procedures to make a request of the board of education and had followed the chain of command in the process. Their request was supported with articles from leading journals, a copy of a report given at the Hampton School of Music symposium that specified needs for a music curriculum, and a newspaper reprint of a report in which traditional music programs were described as being inferior in many public schools. Two letters were included in the materials from students in the community who had chosen to go to an exclusive fine arts institute in a nearby city in preference to attending the local public school. Finally, the parent group had obtained budget information from the district; they had a breakdown of the expenditures for special education students and the numbers of students involved in special education as contrasted to the number of students in the gifted program.

The request presented by the parents of the gifted music students was made in the form of a "recommendation for consideration," and not a demand. They requested the following: (1) the addition of six new music courses to be offered exclusively to the gifted music students; (2) gifted music students be excused from the one year of required physical education and the one year of computer awareness required for graduation; and (3) gifted music students be required to take only one year of science and one year of social science in place of three years of each under the current graduation requirements. The presentation was made to the board, and the topic was tabled to allow the staff to respond and the board to explore the subject in depth.

At the following board meeting, the staff in charge of curriculum and the building principals from the four high schools in the district presented a case in opposition to the proposal by the parents of the gifted students in music. The board again tabled the issue to allow for further examination of the topic. The local newspaper devoted a considerable amount of space to the growing debate. At the third board meeting, the debate continued, and both sides of the issue presented additional arguments and supporting materials. The number of parents in attendance at the board meeting who favored the gifted program had doubled. Parents of students who were in the special education program sat silently in the back of the board room. Over the three-month period since the issue was presented, the battle lines had become quite distinct. The parents of the gifted music students, with the support of the parents of other gifted students, spoke as a solid block. The school officials spoke in a unified voice and gave counterarguments, with the recommendation that the request of the parents representing the gifted music students be rejected.

A motion was made to approve the request of the parents of the gifted music students. The board voted five to four in favor of the request made by the parents, with the provision that the new courses and graduation requirements go into effect at the beginning of the following school year.

Inbasket Exercises

INBASKET 12.1

Letter from a Parent

2224 W. Bullock Dr.
Anytown, U.S.A.
November 21, 199x

Dear Superintendent Byrd,

My daughter, Cindy Clifton, is in the tenth grade and was required to purchase a hand held calculator for a sum of $124.00 for her Algebra II class. She was told she would also be able to use the calculator for math classes she would be taking in the future.

As I have visited with Cindy two questions have emerged. First, is there any evidence that using the calculator will help her learn mathematics better? It would seem to me that students must first know how to work their mathematics and how to work formulas rather than, as the kids say, "Punching it out on the calculator." My second question concerns the teacher, who does not seem to give assignments in which the calculator is used very often. During the first few weeks of the semester he gave the class instruction on how to use the calculator, but since then there seems to be almost no assignments requiring the calculator. I would feel better about paying for a calculator if I knew it would help my child learn better and if I could see, once it has been purchased, that it is being used.

Respectfully,

J. C. Clifton

J. C. Clifton

INBASKET 12.2

The Academic–Activities Conflict

Date: April 3, 199x
To: Supt. T. Byrd
From: Ken Follet, Principal
Re: Spring schedule

Last spring we set up this year's track schedule and this last winter we had to adjust it because the time of the conference track meet was changed since Bufford High School did not get lights installed on their track. We kept the same dates for the conference meet which will be May 4 and 5, a Thursday and Friday. We were scheduled to start at 3:30 P.M. on Thursday afternoon and at the same hour on Friday afternoon which would have meant our kids would be dismissed from class at 2:00 P.M. in order to go to Bufford. Now with no lights for a night meet, the conference has voted to keep the meet on Thursday and Friday but start the meet at 10:30 A.M. on both days which means we will have to leave at 9:00 A.M.

The science and the social science teachers, who have been working on a major environmental project with an integrated curriculum approach, are up in arms over the morning time for track meet. Senator Nyland Sommereset is to be here for the environmental project, with television coverage, on Thursday, and Governor H.J. Benson is to be here on Friday morning. We met to resolve the issue without much luck. You should know the science and social science teachers are calling on parents for support. They are getting parental support and support from the editor of the *Journal*. They are preparing a proposal to send to you and to the board of education asking that the athletic conference be petitioned to hold the track meet on Friday P.M. and all day Saturday, May 5 and 6. If the conference petition fails, the science and social studies teachers say they will challenge the track meet because we will fall short of the number of hours required for classroom contact hours as spelled out by State Department of Education Rule 21-3. We are right on the border of meeting the required number of hours. I have polled conference members, and they have rejected the idea.

As I mentioned above, I thought you would want to be advised of this problem. Do you have any thoughts on what would be the best course of action?

Notes

1. Allan C. Ornstein and Francis P. Hunkins, *Curriculum Foundations, Principles and Issues,* 2nd ed. (Boston: Allyn and Bacon, 1993), p. 9.

2. Ibid.

3. Decker Walker, *Fundamentals of Curriculum* (New York: Harcourt Brace Jovanovich, 1990), p. 4.

4. J. Galen Saylor, William M. Alexander, and A. J. Lewis, *Curriculum Planning for Better Teaching and Learning,* 4th ed. (New York: Holt, Rinehart and Winston, 1981), p. 27.

5. John D. McNeil, *Curriculum: A Comprehensive Introduction* (Glenview, Ill.: Scott, Foresman/Little, Brown Higher Education, 1990), pp. 107–108.

6. Hilda Taba, *Curriculum Development: Theory and Practice* (New York: Harcourt, Brace and World, 1962), p. 1.

7. Ornstein and Hunkins, *Curriculum Foundations, Principles and Issues,* p. 146.

8. Walker, *Fundamentals of Curriculum,* p. 27.

9. Allan A. Glatthorn, *Curriculum Leadership* (Glenview, Ill.: Scott, Foresman, 1987), p. 131.

10. Ibid., p. 129.

11. Ibid.

12. *National Goals for Education* (U.S. Department of Education) (Washington, D.C.: Government Printing Office, 1990).

13. Glatthorn, *Curriculum Leadership,* p. 15.

14. Walker, *Fundamentals of Curriculum,* p. 303.

15. Carolyn S. Anderson, "The Search for School Climate: A Review of Research," *Review of Educational Research,* 52(3) (fall 1982): pp. 368–420.

16. Taba, *Curriculum Development: Theory and Practice.*

17. J. Galen Saylor and William M. Alexander, *Planning Curriculum for Schools* (New York: Holt, Rinehart, 1974).

18. Ralph W. Tyler, *Basic Principles of Curriculum and Instruction* (Chicago: The University of Chicago Press, 1950).

19. Francis P. Hunkins, *Curriculum Development Program Improvement* (Columbus, Ohio: Merrill 1980).

20. Glatthorn, *Curriculum Leadership.*

21. McNeil, *Curriculum: A Comprehensive Introduction.*

22. Ornstein and Hunkins, *Curriculum Foundations, Principles and Issues,* p. 237.

23. Ibid., p. 238.

24. *A National Imperative: Educating for the Twenty-first Century* (Arlington, Va.: National School Board Association, 1989), p. 355.

25. Peggy Fedler, "Schoolbook Selection and Reconsideration Policies for Managing Challenges to Schoolbooks in Nebraska School Districts" (unpublished doctoral dissertation, University of Nebraska—Lincoln, 1991).

26. Ward Sybouts, *Planning in School Administration: A Handbook* (Westport, Conn.: Greenwood Press, 1992), pp. 239–267.

Chapter *13*

Working with Employee Groups: Collective Bargaining

This chapter examines the work of the school superintendent in relation to employee groups. The discussion centers on the development of power within employee groups and its impact on the role of the superintendent. We devote much attention to collective bargaining and its implications for the work of the superintendent. The nature of the collective bargaining process, the role of the superintendent in the process, and requirements relative to the administration of the master contract agreement are included.

Employee–employer relationships have realized extraordinary changes historically. For example, in 1806 employee groups were found guilty of conspiracy to raise their wages. In this Philadelphia Cordwainer's case, such organized action was declared illegal by the courts. Yet years later, the Wagner Act gave strong support to collective bargaining. The political viewpoints of national groups on employee–employer relations have reversed themselves as well. In 1960, for example, a National Education Association (NEA) resolution stating that "representative negotiations are compatible with the ethics and dignity of the teaching profession" was soundly defeated by convention representatives in Los Angeles;[1] two years later this stand was reversed. By 1992, the membership of NEA had risen to 2,145,577 and membership of the American Federation of Teachers (AFT) in 1991 was approximately 780,000. By 1993, 40 states had passed legislation concerning collective bargaining in the public sector. For school superintendents today, working with employee groups and collective bargaining are a way of life.

How superintendents view relations with teachers' unions or associations varies widely. Glass's national study of school superintendents found that 40.7 percent of them "almost never" or "never" felt that relations with teachers' unions/associations were troublesome. Only 16.6 percent answered "very frequently" or "frequently" that such relationships were troublesome for them. As might be expected, 42.0 percent reported that such concerns were troublesome for them "sometimes."[2]

When major problems occur between teachers' unions and school boards, disruptive events such as strikes can occur. Diegmueller reported there were 55 strikes in the nation's schools in 1986. This figure rose to 87 in 1988. By January 1991, 61 teacher strikes already had been recorded.[3] School superintendents in striking school districts, or ones that have continuing problems with teachers' groups, face conflicts that test both their competency and stress level. The superintendent's leadership role in the event of such conflicts also is discussed in the chapter.

Employee Unions

The term *union* is repugnant to many educators. Terms such as *professional teachers' association* or *teachers' organization* are more appropriate in the views of many individuals. Cresswell and Murphy raise the key question: "Are the teachers' organizations unions?"[4] The answer depends in large part on the definition of a union.

Lunenburg and Ornstein define a union as "an organization of employees formed for the purpose of influencing an employer's decision concerning conditions of employment."[5] Tannenbaum states that "unions are organizations designed to protect and enhance the social and economic welfare of their members."[6] Blumberg points out that unions must attend to two basic concerns if they are to remain viable: "the collective bargaining process and strong support of teachers during such matters as grievances and arbitration."[7] An often quoted definition of union, set forth in 1920 by Sidney and Beatrice Webb, states that a union is "a continuous association of wage earners for the purpose of maintaining or improving the conditions of their working lives."[8]

These definitions contain several common factors: (1) unions represent organizations of employees; (2) they strive to influence conditions of work for their membership; (3) they protect and enhance the economic welfare of members; (4) they demand the use of collective bargaining in determining salaries and conditions of work; (5) they lend strong support to members in matters relating to grievances and arbitration; and (6) they represent a continuous association of wage earners. The response to the previous question—whether teachers' organizations are unions—is an obvious "yes"; teachers' organizations meet all of the foregoing criteria in the definitions presented. The point here is not an attempt to judge the positive or negative aspects of teachers' unions; rather, it is an effort to substantiate that teachers' organizations are unions as we know them in other private and public sectors. For our purposes, the terms *teachers' association* and *teachers' union* are synonymous.

The Development of Teachers' Unions and Collective Bargaining in the United States

The development of teachers' unions is traced most directly by examining the historical development of the National Education Association, the American Federation of Teachers, and the escalation of collective bargaining practices in both the private and public sectors. An examination of the growth of employee associations, the changing political posture of such associations, and the legislation that has affected contract relationships reveals the evolving nature of employee–employer relationships. Important developments over the years in these areas include the following:

1794—The Society of Associated Teachers was formed in New York City.

1845—The state of Massachusetts established the first state teachers' and school officials' association.

1857—The National Teachers Association was established; later, it became the National Education Association. Membership totaled 43.

1870—The National Education Association (NEA) was established. This was 46 years prior to the establishment of the American Federation of Teachers (AFT).

1886—The American Federation of Labor (AF of L) was established.

1916—The American Federation of Teachers was organized in the United States. Membership was approximately 3,000.

1920—High school teachers in Oregon attempted to organize a union in relation to a salary dispute. The court agreed with the school board's ruling that teachers did not have such a right.

1926—The Railroad Act gave strong support to collective bargaining. The U.S. Supreme Court upheld its constitutionality in 1930.

1930—By this date, the objectives of the AFT were well established. The right of teachers to organize, due process for teachers, teachers' participation in the administration of schools, increased salaries for teachers, and other provisions related to conditions of work set the pace for the Federation's activities.

1932—The Norris–La Guardia Act curtailed the involvement of the federal courts in labor–management relations by removing the courts' authority to interfere with a broad range of union activities.

1935—The Wagner Act (National Labor Relations Act) established employees' rights to bargain (employees involved in interstate commerce) on matters of wages and conditions of employment.

1947—AFT voters retained the organization's no-strike policy. This policy was not altered until after 1960.

1947—The Taft–Hartley Act, although applicable only to interstate commerce, clarified employee rights in collective bargaining and added a set of unfair labor practices by unions. Its ultimate influence on bargaining in the public sector proved to be far-reaching.

1954—The AFT's membership grew to approximately 56,000.

1959—The first state collective bargaining statute granting rights to public employees passed in Wisconsin.

1960—The United Federation of Teachers (UFT) called a strike for its members in the New York City schools. The one-day strike reportedly included between 4,500 and 15,000 teachers. The lower number was the one reported by the board of education; the higher one by the UFT.

1962—The AFT Local 2 won the right to bargain for the 40,000 New York City public school teachers. The union replaced more than 90 previously existing bargaining units. This event served as the catalyst for the NEA to pass its historic resolution, in Denver, that insisted on the right of professional associations to participate with boards concerning matters of teachers' salaries and conditions of work. A highly competitive, often bitter relationship between the NEA and the AFT has continued since that time.

1962—Executive Order 10988 by President John F. Kennedy approved bargaining for federal employees. This Order opened the way for the establishment of unionism for government workers and led to similar actions by local and state government employees nationally.

1965—By this date the NEA had organized a reported 33 departments under its jurisdiction. The concept of an "all servicing" professional organization was exercised.

1967—Membership in the AFT increased to approximately 140,000.

1968—The NEA passed a resolution that, for the first time, included support for "withdrawal of services" by teachers when the situation demanded it. The Association's opposition to collective bargaining changed in 1962. Now NEA changed its opposition to teacher strikes.

1969—Executive Order 11491 by President Richard M. Nixon brought labor relations at the federal level more in line with those in the private sector. The Order gave support to extended legislation in the public sector, including employees in education.

1970—By this date 27 states had passed legislation granting collective bargaining rights in the public sector.

1970—The NEA strengthened its hand by adopting its unified membership strategy. NEA membership requirements stipulated that an individual could not belong to only the local, state, or national NEA affiliate, but had to join all three units. In turn, NEA established a program of field representatives who could work more closely with local and state teacher groups.

1972—The New York State Teachers' Association and the New York State Federation of Teachers merged to form the New York State United Teachers. The merger added 200,000 new teachers to the AFT. By 1975, AFT membership rose to about 470,000.

1975—Nonclassroom teacher groups had disassociated themselves from the NEA by this date. Relationships with previous member groups such as school administrators were severed by the NEA. Teacher membership in unions between 1964 and 1974 realized the greatest membership increase of any major employee group.

1980—By the early 1980s a reported 40 states had passed legislation permitting the right of teachers' organizations to bargain collectively. Competition between the NEA and the AFT for membership continued at a vigorous pace.

1990—Although teacher welfare continued as a major focus of teachers' unions, new emphasis was placed on political influence and matters concerning teacher empowerment. The movement toward site-based management was attributed by many persons to a ploy by teachers' groups to gain power in school governance. Collective bargaining was entrenched in almost all school districts, although some trends toward win–win bargaining approaches were evidenced. Even in those states without legal provisions for bargaining between school boards and teachers' associations, "meet and confer" and/or "participative problem solving" procedures were practiced. In 1992–93, 51 teacher strikes were reported by the NEA.

The foregoing chronology shows that teachers' unions have become influential in educational policy, program practices, and personnel matters. Their voice has extended beyond personal interests of salary and conditions of work; teachers' groups now can exercise their political strength to influence important educational legislation. Educational innovations and changes now require the input, and often the approval, of teachers' groups prior to their adoption in many school districts.

One text points out three changes in the power structure of education brought out by the growing teachers' movement.[9] Teachers are much more astute politically today than previously; their organizational focus has made them a highly influential force in political matters at all levels. Collective bargaining has given teachers' groups a strong voice in decisions concerning their salary and conditions of work. Most every budget matter now is a concern of teachers' associations. An increasing percentage of the school district's budgeted dollar now goes to staff salaries, an estimated 85–90 percent of the total operations budget. Finally, authority relationships between teachers and various supervisors have changed dramatically. Some persons refer to today's school administration as being "AMA," administration by master agreement. Certainly, the day of the unquestioning, silently following teacher is gone forever.

Today's school superintendent, regardless of his or her attitude toward teachers' associations, faces the reality of working with them. Superintendents must develop working relationships with teachers' groups if school missions are to be realized. The following section examines this working relationship. Following that discussion, the collective negotiations process is considered in depth.

Working Relationships: The School Superintendent and Employee Associations

The Superintendent and Employee Groups

"Regardless of the focus or substance, a seemingly absolute condition of the superintendency is that there are only rarely days when the superintendent is not called upon to make a decision that will create some conflict, or is not involved somehow in conflicts not of his own making. All of this seems to occur irrespective of the person involved."[10] Blumberg's statement sums up the essential meaning of the school superintendency and the statement: living with conflict. Although the major source of conflict for school systems comes from their external cultural publics,[11] conflicts between the school superintendent and employee groups are continuing realities in many school settings.

The nature of working relationships between school superintendents and teachers' associations differs from state to state, school district to school district. Superintendents, as individuals, deal and cope with employees' groups in varying ways. That 60 percent of school superintendents nationally report problems or concerns with teachers' unions "sometimes," "frequently," or "very frequently" was mentioned earlier. Other research further highlights problems in the relationship between school superintendents and teachers' unions. For example, collective bargaining agreements ranked fourth among 13 major inhibitors of the superintendent's effectiveness in a 1992 national study.[12] Additionally, relations with unions was named among those issues that, if not corrected, would most likely cause superintendents to leave their current position.

School superintendents continue to serve as the chief negotiator for the school district's bargaining team in the plurality of instances nationwide, and superintendent–staff relationships figure prominently in the superintendent's performance evaluation.[13] Evidence points to the increasing use of internal or external negotiation experts, especially in larger school districts. The involvement of the superintendent in the negotiation process is discussed in more detail later in the chapter.

Working with Teachers' Associations

School boards generally expect that the school superintendent will represent them in the area of employee relations. In this sense, the superintendent serves as the director of the school district's employee relations program, although various responsibilities are delegated to other units in the school system. In the role of employee relations director, the superintendent assumes four key responsibilities. *First, the school superintendent must serve as the primary liaison between the school board and employee groups, and between the school board and school administration on matters of employee relations.* Although support for this responsibility is provided the superintendent by the human resources unit of the system, labor relations personnel, and others, the superintendent must assume the role of coordinator, interpreter, and facilitator in matters of employee relations.

Effective communication with employee groups is essential. Efforts to keep teachers' representatives informed of pending actions on program needs builds the mutual trust without which communication is aborted. Likewise, the superintendent must disseminate needed information to school board members relative to concerns of employee groups in the school district. If such communication takes place effectively, the school board will have few unpleasant surprises concerning employee needs and problems.

Alert superintendents not only keep themselves apprised of local association matters, they gain insight into probable employee concerns by observing the trends and problems of teachers' groups at the state and national levels. Through anticipation the superintendent can plan and strategize more effectively; needed communication and teacher involvement can be programmed before the full brunt of a problem reaches the local scene.

The development of positive working relationships with teachers' associations requires keeping them informed and involved in matters related to school goals, problems, and crises. Open communications serve to build mutual understanding and foster the establishment of areas of common ground whereby the school board and teachers' group can be educational advocates, not educational adversaries.

We give the foregoing recommendations understanding that the realities of the leadership required to meet the superintendent's responsibilities as director of employee relations are intricate and difficult. Specific issues, problems, and challenges facing the superintendent in the area of employee relations were discussed in Chapter 2. Development of mutual trust, effective communications, and gaining cooperative action are never simple and sometimes go awry even with one's best efforts. Such leadership by the superintendent *can* be successful, often resulting in improved relationships and lending to the development of "advocacy" between the board/superintendent and personnel in the school district.

A second key responsibility of the school superintendent is the development of viable employee relations policy for the school district. The superintendent is the primary actor in setting forth the vision of what the school district can become. Cuban posits two obligations of the superintendent for accomplishing the system's goals. First, the superintendent must "imagine what the organization can become; define the mission; set the goals." Second, he or she must "promote certain values that give the organization a distinctive character."[14] Cuban's general obligations serve superintendents equally well in their responsibilities for employee relationships. The superintendent must work cooperatively with union leadership and others to foster the mission of the school system. Further, the superintendent works to ensure that employees are well compensated for their services and that conditions of work are positive. Such efforts not only serve to develop positive relationships among board, superintendent, and employees, but they give the school district a good reputation that helps attract and retain effective personnel. Thus, the superintendent must define and support policies that foster a positive climate in the school system.

Although some would argue that the master negotiated agreement sets the policy regarding school district–employee relations, the superintendent's involvement in such matters is essential. What's more, such involvement provides additional opportunities to constructively influence employee relationships.

A third major responsibility of the school superintendent concerning employee relations is to lead the instruction of school administrators and other personnel regarding the implementation of the master contract agreement and the administration of grievances related to the contract. The superintendent must coordinate program activities for informing school principals and other personnel about the provisions and agreements set forth in the contract. Ubben and Fulmer point out that the school official with the most direct contact with teachers is the local building principal. The principal becomes a first-line supervisor in a labor–management sense: he or she deals with specific grievances regarding alleged violations of the master contract agreement.[15]

Information sessions must focus on the terms and conditions of the agreement and provide clear understandings of the specific terms utilized, interpretations of specific provisions, and the stated obligations of both the administration and the employees. Such informational efforts support an equitable implementation of the agreement throughout the school district and can reduce the number of grievances filed.

The question of whether the superintendent should include teachers or their representatives in such information programs is one of debate. Some argue that the involvement of teachers in superintendent-sponsored information sessions about contract agreements increases cooperative action, lessens possibilities of conflict, and reduces grievances. Others maintain that it is not the school board's or superintendent's place to instruct association members on contract agreement conditions and terms; this is the responsibility of the employee association. In fact, in certain instances, teachers' representatives might refuse to participate even if asked. Whether teachers and others in the district's employee groups are to be included in such instructional sessions depends on the case at hand. Such programs, however, can serve to help avoid misunderstandings and to enhance mutual trust. School personnel are employees of the school district, not of the union. The school district, therefore, must assume commensurate responsibility for their understanding of school policy and regulations and of agreed-on contractual obligations.

The school superintendent sees that the master contract agreement is equitably administered. The superintendent must take the lead in monitoring the implementation of the agreement and helping the school board and other administrative personnel meet their commitments relative to the contract terms. The superintendent must also ensure that the employee group covered by the agreement meets its obligations as well; we discuss these responsibilities later when we consider collective bargaining.

A fourth major responsibility of the school superintendent is to serve as the school district's representative in matters of paramount importance concerning employee relationships and school district practices in this area. Mandated responsibilities of the school superintendent are those stipulated in law or contractual agreements. These mandates differ among the states, but they include those responsibilities relative to employee relations that the superintendent "has to do." One text emphasizes that

> the public schools, like all other institutions in society, operate within the framework of laws—laws generated by the federal government, the state government, and the courts (case law). The operation of the schools is also subject to a multitude of ordinances, rules and regulations promulgated by numerous federal, state and local agencies, and government agencies. All aspects of the employment relationship, including recruitment, selection, placement and transfer, evaluation, promotion, compensation, suspension and dismissal, and mandatory retirement, have been the subject of legislative and executive pronouncements and judicial interpretation.[16]

Matters of employee relations in such areas as affirmative action, desegregation of schools, labor relations, due process, and others face school districts and school superintendents on a daily basis. School districts are called on frequently by various agencies to report, explain, justify, and defend their programs and actions. The superintendent must assume the leadership role in representing the school district in such vital matters before various regulatory bodies. Although other district personnel or legal representatives often assume a spokesperson's role in cases of hearings or litigation, it is the superintendent who must serve as the school district's official representative.

Thus, the superintendent has employee relations' responsibilities that "must be done" and others that are "wise to do"; both perspectives should serve to promote mutual trust and build the groundwork for cooperative working relationships with employee groups.

In summary, the school superintendent must assume the following key responsibilities for employee relationships:

- The superintendent serves as the primary liaison between the school board and employee groups and between the board and the school administration on matters of employee relations.
- The superintendent develops viable employee relations policy for the school district with the school board and with input from other groups in the school district.
- The superintendent assumes the leadership role in the instructional program of school district administrators and others in the implementation of the master contract agreement and the administration of grievances related to the contract.
- The superintendent serves as the school district's representative in important matters concerning employee relationships and related school district practices.

A further major responsibility of the school superintendent in employee relations is in collective bargaining. This responsibility is discussed in the following section.

The School Superintendent and Collective Bargaining

A brief chronology of the development of collective bargaining in education was presented earlier in the chapter. It also was noted that school superintendents serve as their school district's chief negotiator more than any alternative arrangement.[17] Glass points out that demand on the superintendent's time in collective bargaining was less in 1990 than in earlier studies in 1971 and 1982.[18] He suggests that collective bargaining is perhaps becoming a more routine management function.

The national study of superintendents revealed that those in smaller districts served as chief negotiators for their districts, or assist a board member in the process, more often than those in larger districts. Whether this phenomenon is due to budget factors, lack of central office personnel, or other factors is not clear. Younger superintendents were found to be serving as the chief negotiator for their districts more often than older ones. Larger school districts use a professional negotiator from outside or inside the district more often than other arrangements.[19]

The Nature of Collective Bargaining in Education

The Labor Management Relations Act (Taft–Hartley Act) of 1947 provided guidelines for collective bargaining in the private sector that have greatly influenced bargaining in the public sector as well. Although the Act applied only to interstate commerce, it provided further expansion and clarification of employee rights in the bargaining process. The Act's major employee–employer guidelines for bargaining are as follows:

1. Collective bargaining is the performance of the mutual obligation of the employer and the representative of the employees to meet at reasonable times and confer in good faith with respect to wages, hours, and other terms and conditions of employment.
2. Collective bargaining also includes negotiation of an agreement or any question arising thereunder and the execution of a written contract incorporating any agreement reached if requested by either party.
3. Such an obligation (to bargain) does not compel either party to agree to a proposal or make a concession.

The provisions of the National Labor Relations Act spilled over into education and has served as a model for almost every state statute for negotiations in the public sector. It is not surprising that education initially adopted the distributive bargaining model used in the private sector, whereby strategies are designed to realize the greatest possible gains through demonstrations of authority and power. Later, a quasi-distributive model of negotiations was adopted in education; this approach attempts to avoid a power struggle between the two parties and uses a quid pro quo strategy exemplified by a give-and-take approach. The quasi-distributive model is still dominant in most school districts nationally, primarily because original bargaining legislation in the public sector modeled the private sector and educators were trained to use this approach.

The term *win–win bargaining* is used somewhat loosely in education. The term is used by some persons in relation to either distributive or quasi-distributive bargaining when both sides meet their objectives and are satisfied with the final results. The term *win–win* is used more appropriately in reference to integrative approaches to bargaining. In integrative bargaining, or joint problem solving and creative bargaining, win–win refers to the elimination of adversarial relationships between the two negotiating parties and the achievement of an agreement that truly reflects their common interests.

Problem-solving approaches in collective bargaining came into prominence in education in the early 1990s, possibly for three reasons. First, some school districts, after bitter experiences with adversarial approaches to collective bargaining, decided that there must be a better way to determine salaries and conditions of work. Second, education in the early 1990s was encountering serious image problems and public calls for educational reform. The adage of "hang together or be hung separately" gave impetus to the mutual concern of survival. Third, most every school district was facing severe economic problems; money was scarce. In simplistic terms, there was really no money available to argue about. Thus, many school boards and employee groups felt that the scarce funds were not worth the turmoil and conflict often associated with other bargaining approaches. Certainly the win–win strategy is not universal among school districts. This is evidenced in part by the previously reported 51 school districts that went on strike in 1992–93.

Operational Model for Win–Win Bargaining

Existing conditions suggest when a problem-solving approach can be used successfully in collective bargaining. Schoonmaker recommended that a joint problem-solving strategy be used when the two parties clearly have common interests. If the vested interests of the negotiating parties are in conflict, it sharply reduces the chances of reconciling areas of disagreement.

A win–win approach is also enhanced when the power of the two parties is about equal. When either the board or the employee group is clearly in a situation to gain its objectives due to its power position, other bargaining strategies likely will be more successful for that party.

Schoonmaker further suggests that win–win approaches should be emphasized when the need or desire for harmony between the two sides is present. In most all cases, integrative bargaining is less disruptive. Trust between the negotiating groups also is an essential ingredient for joint problem solving. If trust is not present, or if one team is merely acting as if it is problem solving, negotiations soon deteriorate or revert to distributive strategies.

Lastly, in those instances when the implementation of the final agreement may face opposition, joint problem solving best suits the purpose.[20]

When a joint problem solving approach is being considered, the following basic operations should be implemented:

1. Readiness—Each party must objectively examine current conditions and determine the probability of success for a win–win approach to bargaining. The previously discussed conditions recommended by Schoonmaker should be assessed and the key question answered objectively: Are the conditions favorable for a successful joint problem solving strategy? If the answer is "yes" for both sides, Step 2 should be implemented. If "no," other bargaining approaches should be considered.

2. Goal Assessments—Each bargaining team establishes its goals and priorities and uses appropriate information to forecast the goals of the other party. The school superintendent works closely with the school board, building principals, and others to determine school board negotiation objectives. Employee grievances during the previous year, requests by teachers' groups in other school districts, teachers' journals and newsletters, and conference topics are useful in determining the probable bargaining goals of the teachers' association. Teachers' groups have access to such information as school board minutes, professional journals of school boards, and results of bargaining in other districts for anticipating school board bargaining goals. With the foregoing information at hand, an assessment is made of likely areas of agreement between the two sides; possible troublesome areas are identified as well. Consideration is given to how the areas of disagreement might be reconciled.

3. Informal Discussions—Prior to formal table discussions, time is given to the development of relationships that enhance mutual trust and respect among members of the negotiating parties. During these meetings, information is exchanged and areas needing more data are determined. No attempts are made to reach agreement at this time; the primary concern is that of fostering positive relationships and understandings that will facilitate a win–win, problem-solving approach.

4. Formal Discussions—The two parties move toward the completion of an agreement; areas of agreement are identified and confirmed. Differences between the two parties are identified, and integrated solutions are determined. Attention is given to joint solutions for areas of specific disagreement. Emphasis is placed on superordinate solutions, those solutions that set aside personal or vested interests and focus on what is best for the system and all concerned.

5. Control Measures Are Implemented—The implementation of the agreement is accepted as a primary obligation of all team members in cooperation with the superintendent. The administration of the agreement is closely monitored, problem areas are identified and remedied, and both parties work cooperatively to see that the agreement is administered equitably.

Operational Model for Quasi-Distributive Bargaining

That education historically has utilized the quasi-distributive bargaining process was noted previously. We discuss this model in detail in this section.

The general operations model for quasi-distributive bargaining encompasses five major considerations:

1. Planning and preparation for collective bargaining.
2. Determination and recognition of the bargaining unit.
3. Determination of the composition of the bargaining team, including the chief spokesperson.
4. Determination of the initial bargaining procedures and appropriate table strategies.
5. Administration of the master contract agreement.[21]

Planning and Preparation for Collective Bargaining

Inadequate planning is the root of much unsuccessful bargaining.[22] Preparation and planning in bargaining are continuous activities that require data collection and costing of various proposals and anticipated requests, setting bargaining goals and priorities, determining the ground rules under which bargaining will be conducted, considering the scope of items to be negotiated, and discussing mediation/arbitration procedures to be utilized in case of impasse.

Costing is a crucial task of a bargaining team. Projected cost figures for salaries, collateral benefits, and anticipated expenditures related to working conditions are essential for making wise decisions during table negotiations.

The superintendent, working with the school board, the board's chief negotiator and team members, school principals, and others, assumes the leadership in establishing the goals and priorities for negotiations for the school board. Hughes and Ubben emphasize the importance of the school principal's role on the management team: "Formal negotiations recognize that a principal must be part of the management team. . . . Principals should be represented, because to a great extent negotiation topics represent areas of direct concern to the building principal. In many cases the ensuing negotiations result in the erosion of the power or responsibility of the principal, often reducing administrative effectiveness."[23] Since the goals and objectives for negotiations guide the entire process and weigh heavily on results, the building principal's role in the early planning is essential.

The matter of using mutually acceptable ground rules in negotiations is controversial. Some contend that ground rules that govern the negotiations process should never be agreed on by management. Others believe that such rules serve a necessary purpose in conducting successful negotiations. As mutual trust is established between the two parties, ground rules become less significant. Establishing ground rules for negotiations can be troublesome and, if not determined formally or through mutual trust, need to be considered prior to table talks. Thus, understandings on matters of team authority, meeting agendas, time and place of table negotiations, team membership, procedures, impasse provisions, and other arrangements should be determined in advance.

Determination and Recognition of the Bargaining Unit

The composition of the bargaining unit is determined generally either by statute, by mutual agreement of the bargaining parties, by an outside authority such as a labor relations board, or by unilateral decision of the school board. The bargaining unit is a group of employees designated as the official unit for purposes of negotiations. The negotiated contractual agreement applies to the members of the bargaining unit, although nonmembers often benefit by the bargaining unit's gains as well.

Lieberman and Moskow speak of community of interest represented by employees who hold like employment interests and mutual concerns.[24] For the most part, a community of interest has similar compensation bases, works under similar conditions, and has similar professional needs. Walter points out the major task for the school superintendent relative to bargaining units: to work to establish bargaining units that do have common interests but at the same time to avoid the establishment of several different bargaining units with which to deal.[25]

Some employee groups have adopted a strategy of wall-to-wall bargaining whereby every employee in the district is represented by the same bargaining unit and covered under the same master contract. That is, all certificated and noncertificated employees in the district become one unit for the purposes of collective negotiations. Such an arrangement gives the employee bargaining unit a concentrated strength in pursuing employee demands. Wall-to-wall bargaining brings a new dimension to employee relationships in school districts as well as a host of new questions and problems for school boards and the school superintendent.

Determining the Composition of the Negotiations
Team, Including the Chief Spokesperson

Experienced negotiators contend that the selection of the members for the negotiations team is a key for success. The purpose of negotiations is to reach an agreement, not to win a debate. Thus, team members must possess personal qualities that lend themselves toward successful results: poise, emotional stability, patience, knowledge of the bargaining process, and the personal fortitude needed to participate in the demanding process of negotiations.

Opinions differ concerning the use of the superintendent as chief spokesperson in the negotiations process. Some contend that the superintendent is the best person to serve as a spokesperson for the school board's negotiation team. The superintendent is highly knowledgeable about the school system's goals and needs and most always has the confidence of the school board as its representative. Other arguments supporting the superintendent as chief spokesperson or as a member of the board's negotiations team are that (1) the superintendent is known and trusted by the teachers; (2) teachers are not militant; (3) teachers are not using the services of a professional negotiator; and (4) contract is policy.[26]

In their early work, *Collective Negotiations for Teachers,* Lieberman and Moskow captured the dilemma of superintendents regarding their role in negotiations:

> Superintendents under pressure behave in different ways. . . . If there is no way to commit themselves without antagonizing powerful individuals or groups, a neutral ground seems attractive indeed. For example, suppose the superintendent feels that the teachers should receive more money but his own position is too precarious to press the case vigorously with this board. In that case, he may prefer to have the teachers negotiate with the board while he stands by. If the teachers press their case and the board asks his advice, he can give it. . . . if he acts as the agent of the board in rejecting teacher demands, this may injure his ongoing relations with teachers. Like anyone caught between conflicting pressures, the superintendent would like to avoid antagonizing any major interest group. Thus there is the prima facie attractiveness in saying that the role of the superintendent in collective negotiations is that of resource person, mediator, consultant, or neutral third party vis-a-vis the school board and the teacher organization.[27]

Conran, author of the *School Superintendent's Complete Handbook,* who served as school superintendent in Ohio and elsewhere, states that she successfully negotiated with a board member experienced in labor negotiations. She notes that "at the table the superintendent served both teams as a resource while the board member was on the firing line. It was possible . . . for the board member and the superintendent to work as a team. With careful preparation of what was possible to give away and trade off, the board member took the lead, allowing for the superintendent to state implications for practice of various items being discussed."[28]

Those individuals and groups that oppose the use of the superintendent as chief spokesperson point out that the rigors of bargaining and its time requirements take a disproportionate amount of time from other superintendent responsibilities. Additionally, the adversarial relationships that tend to accompany quasi-distributive approaches to bargaining can subvert positive superintendent–employee relations. Conran also set forth reasons that the superintendent may not want to be on the negotiations team: (1) the superintendent or teachers have an axe to grind; (2) the teachers are using the services of a professional negotiator; and (3) the negotiations process is time consuming and detracts from other administrative functions.[29]

It was noted previously that many school districts now use an outside professional negotiator or a highly qualified internal official. Such a practice allows the school superintendent and other school personnel to concentrate on other educational matters. Additionally, the professional negotiator most often brings experience and expertise to the negotiations process. Such expertise can save time and expedite negotiations by focusing on only those matters of importance in the overall process. It should be emphasized that team membership and spokesperson roles often are determined by state statute.

Determination of the Initial Bargaining
Procedures and Appropriate Strategies

Cresswell and Murphy capture the essence of quasi-distributive bargaining procedures:

> Collective bargaining requires a number of sessions. In each session negotiators for each side propose and discuss terms of a contract, and they eventually agree on the specific language of that contract. As we have noted, the terms proposed by both sides are in conflict, that is, they are incompatible. The fundamental purpose of the bargaining process is to turn incompatible terms into an agreement. This can happen if one side abandons its terms and accepts the other's, if both sides modify their terms (make concessions) so that the results become compatible, or if the parties discover and accept new terms, better in some way than either of the original proposals.[30]

Thus, procedures during formal table negotiations involve a process of give and take designed to reach a mutual agreement that satisfies the objectives of both parties. This does not imply that both sides must fulfill each of its objectives before negotiations can be considered successful. As noted, objectives can be modified by both parties so that the results are compatible or altered in such a way that the new terms represent improvements over the original objectives. The quid pro quo process must continue until an agreement is reached. Team members have the major responsibility to see that both sides keep talking. Once talking stops, negotiations break down; negotiations in such cases, at least temporarily, are unsuccessful.

The achievement of compatible terms requires a willingness to compromise, or in quid pro quo terms, get something for what is given. A bargaining team uses a planned strategy to achieve its objectives by giving something desired by the other party for something it values. Bargaining strategy, then, consists of tactics that lead to the achievement of a team's objectives by making concessions, or finding different, better, terms.

Strikes.   A difference or disagreement between the bargaining parties that reaches an unresolvable stage and results in a stoppage of table discussions is termed an impasse.[31] Resolutions to impasses are sought through the use of mediation, voluntary and compulsory arbitration, or last—best—offer arbitration. When these means do not resolve standing disagreements, a work stoppage or strike can occur. As stated by Cresswell and Murphy, "The main function of strikes is to 'change the bargaining position of the other side.'"[32]

Conran states that

> Whatever occurs during the negotiations process, it is incumbent on the superintendent to remain professional. Stick to the facts, communicate the district's position on how it will handle the strike. That is, will the schools be open or closed? Will regular programs be maintained? Will there be one-to-one replacements for strikers? Will there be security? Will attending school be dangerous? Will grades on school work done during the strike count?[33]

Preparation for a strike must take place far in advance. This necessitates attention to ways to keep the schools open during the strike, effective communication procedures with persons inside and outside the school system, the establishment of a decision base or office to coordinate all activities during the work stoppage, potential sources of personnel who would replace the striking personnel, legal implications, clarification of roles and responsibilities of nonstriking personnel in the system, security measures for school personnel and students, and strategies for reopening negotiations between the two parties.

The superintendent must implement the necessary actions to complete the planning just discussed. In case of a strike, the superintendent takes the leadership role in implementing the strike action plan for the school district. Unless there is clear evidence that the security of personnel or students is in jeopardy, the responsibility of the superintendent is to work to keep the schools operating.

Administration of the Master Contract Agreement

The result of a negotiated agreement is a master contract ratified by the school board and the bargaining unit. Written agreements differ in format from state to state and district to district, although their content often is set forth in statute. Master agreements generally include a statement relative to the recognition of the specific bargaining unit covered in the agreement, the nature of the agreement as to its coverage and time commitments, specific terms concerning salaries and conditions of work, responsibilities of both sides for the implementation of the agreement, and provisions for handling contract-related grievances.

Throughout the previous discussion, the role of the superintendent in collective bargaining has been emphasized. The following discussion summarizes the specific responsibilities of the superintendent in this area.

As pointed out, the belief that the superintendent should not serve as a member or chief spokesperson for the school board's bargaining team is increasing in practice. Approximately one-third of the nation's superintendents do lead the board's team at the table, and in certain situations this arrangement may best serve the school district. The superintendent must play an integral role in the bargaining process as the primary resource person and advisor for the board's bargaining team. Three primary responsibilities are performed by the school superintendent as follows:

1.   Leadership in the Planning for Collective Bargaining

The superintendent serves an integral role in the development of bargaining goals and objectives in cooperation with the school board, administrative staff, community advisory groups, and other staff personnel. Although the superintendent works directly with the management team, he or she understands the benefits of being able to recruit and retain a staff of highly qualified personnel. Thus, the superintendent must work to enhance the quality of work life for all school employees and for compensation levels that serve to attract and retain a stable, quality staff.

The superintendent is instrumental in helping to select the school board's negotiations team. The importance of team membership for successful negotiations was discussed previously. Members of the school board's bargaining team should be selected for their knowledge, ability, skills, and temperament for negotiations. Diversified representation on the board's team is relative. That is, although it might be advantageous to have representatives from the principals' group, personnel unit, business office, instructional unit, and so forth, team members do not represent their units as such but are members of a unified team representing the interests of the school board and the school district generally.

2.   The School Superintendent as a Primary Resource Consultant, Strategist, and Liaison with the School Board and District Administration

Because the superintendent is highly knowledgeable about the school system and its goals, his or her expertise is invaluable in the bargaining process. Although the bargaining team must have the authority to speak for the school board during table negotiations, the superintendent's advice and recommendations on strategy, supporting documentation, alternative objectives, problems, and terms are essential.

The superintendent works as an advisor to the school board's bargaining team but does not attempt to circumvent the board team's authority by "negotiating" matters on the bargaining agenda with employee team members independent of the board's team. During negotiations, it is the selected board team that represents the school board in the bargaining process.

3.   The Superintendent's Role in the Administration of the Contract Agreement

The responsibilities of the school superintendent in the administration of the contract agreement were discussed briefly earlier in the chapter. Additional responsibilities in this regard include the following. Before the master contract is ratified by the school board, the school superintendent should examine it carefully. Contract language, for example, is of major importance. The statement that contractually, "you get what you write," applies directly to negotiated agreements. Additionally, the contract agreement should be reviewed with the legal advisor for the school board. Once the school board has ratified the agreement, the superintendent assumes the leadership role for seeing that all district personnel are well informed and instructed about its provisions. The superintendent must see that personnel in the district understand the terms of the agreement and that the integrity of the agreement's terms and conditions is maintained.

The superintendent, in cooperation with other units of the school system, serves as the primary advisor concerning the clarification of the master contract, acts as the administration's primary advisor in grievances filed by employees related to alleged contract violations, and serves as the administration's initiator of grievance procedures in cases of contract violations by employees in the district.

The school superintendent faces the pressure and stress that accompany a position highly political in nature. Various groups may believe that the superintendent "is their person" and that he or she must support and promote their group's particular points of view. The superintendent, as a member of management, is responsible to the school board in relation to collective bargaining. Views of the superintendent as the "one in the middle" between the board and teachers' union are not sound. It is not that the superintendent does not work for the best compensation and working conditions for the district's employees; it is clear that the superintendent must do so.

The position that the superintendent "must be him- or herself" in negotiations also is unrealistic. Certainly the superintendent, as an individual, has beliefs, values, needs, and a leadership style unto his or her own. In matters of employee relations and collective bargaining, however, the school superintendent is responsible to the school board and to the general school community in establishing the best possible conditions educationally for all concerned.

Summary

The task of working with strong teachers' associations is a common expectation for today's school superintendent. Teachers' unions have evolved to the point that few if any differences can be found between them and employee unions in other settings. The National Education Association in 1962 moved from a position that opposed collective bargaining to one that "demanded" the right for teachers to bargain with school boards on matters of salaries and conditions of work.

Teachers' unions have built strong financial bases to support their causes. Their numbers and monetary support have enabled them to be highly influential in political matters, including the election of supportive persons to political office. Such influence, along with developments in collective bargaining, has brought about new tasks and responsibilities for the school superintendent in employee relationships. In working with employee groups the superintendent must serve as the primary liaison between the school board and employee groups, and between the board and the school administration. The superintendent must work for the development of viable employee relations policy for the school district and must assume a leadership role in the administration of the master contract agreed on by the board and employee groups. The superintendent also serves as the school district's representative in matters of paramount importance concerning employee relationships and associated school district practices.

Collective bargaining became prominent in education during the 1960s and now is commonplace in school districts nationally. The quasi-distributive model of bargaining, based on a give-and-take process, has been the most widely used in education. Since this model tends to emphasize adversarial relationships, the win–win or problem-solving approach has become more popular in education.

The school superintendent nationally continues to serve on school board's negotiation teams and as chief spokesperson in about 30 percent of the nation's school districts. The superintendent must assume leadership in the planning for collective bargaining for the school board and must play a key role in the selection of team members for the board's bargaining team. Additionally, the superintendent serves as a primary resource consultant, strategist, and liaison person with the board's bargaining team and the school administration along with assuming a leadership role in the administration of the negotiated contract agreement.

Discussion Questions

1. Review the evolution of teachers' associations nationally. What were the major events that changed them from a "service" organization to a more earnest, political organization?

2. Consider a teachers' association with which you are familiar. How do you characterize its activities as related to educational improvement? Militancy? Political influence?

3. Discuss the responsibilities of the school superintendent in the area of employee relationships. Ideally, what specific responsibilities do you believe the superintendent should perform? From your perspective, what responsibilities do superintendents actually perform?

4. This chapter pointed out the increasing belief that the school superintendent should not serve as a member or chief spokesperson on the school board's bargaining team. Present your viewpoints on this matter.

5. Briefly describe the "model" of collective bargaining used in your school district or one with which you are most familiar. What model does it follow? That is, does it assume more of a win–win or a distributive approach to bargaining?

CASE 13.1   Resource Person, but for Whom?

Principal Melanie Rose was in her first year as an administrator at Whittier Elementary School. Previously she had served as an elementary school teacher in the district and as president of the school district's teachers' association. During her term as association president, the teachers' association made substantial gains in the area of compensation, insurance coverage for health care, and leave provisions.

During the course of the current year's negotiations, Principal Rose had been asked for advice by the teachers' association team on several occasions. Rose freely gave her opinions and recommendations to the teachers' group, believing that teachers' gains were of benefit generally to the district as a whole.

Upon being apprised of Principal Rose's actions, the chief negotiator for the school board, Angeline Wilson, complained about the matter to Superintendent Nelson George. "Her behavior is undermining our strategy and is unethical in my opinion," stated Wilson. "Someone needs to talk to her."

Questions

1.   Discuss Principal Rose's actions in this case. Can you agree with her position? Why or why not?

2.   Assume the role of Superintendent George. Present the specifics of your follow-up actions in this case. Would you speak with Principal Rose on this matter? If not, why not?

Inbasket Exercise

INBASKET 13.1

A Closer Association

WYMORE TEACHERS ASSOCIATION
WYMORE, LAFAYETTE

To: Superintendent Henson
From: Paul Benson, President
        Wymore Teachers Association
RE: WTA Resolution—Teacher, Administrator/Board Relationships
Date: October 11, 19__

At its recent board meeting, WTA passed the following resolution. Our goal is to improve teacher/administrator/board relationships. Your reaction to the resolution and recommendations for its implementation are needed at this time. The Association truly appreciated you recent speech concerning the need to work as a team.

RESOLVED: The Wymore Teachers Association, in the desire to improve teacher, administrator, and board relations, does hereby resolve that (1) a nonvoting teacher representative be selected to sit with the administrative cabinet of the school district and with the Wymore school board. Be it further resolved that while the representative shall hold no voting rights, that he/she be permitted to participate as a professional in ongoing discussions.

Question

Assume the role of Superintendent Henson and write the specific administrative actions that you will take. Be specific in your responses; write the memorandums and letters that you decide to send, and set forth specific statements that you will make by telephone or in personal meetings with others.

Notes

1. L. Dean Webb, Paul A. Montello, and M. Scott Norton, *Human Resources Administration: Personnel Issues and Needs in Education,* 2nd ed. (New York: Merrill, an imprint of Macmillan College Publishing, 1994), p. 283.

2. Thomas E. Glass, *The 1992 Study of the American School Superintendency: America's Education Leaders in a Time of Reform* (Arlington, Va.: American Association of School Administrators, 1992), p. 49.

3. Karen Diegmueller, *Education Week* (17 April 1991): p. 14.

4. Anthony M. Cresswell and Michael J. Murphy, *Teachers, Unions, and Collective Bargaining in Public Education* (Berkeley, Calif.: McCutchan, 1980), p. 57.

5. Fred C. Lunenburg and Allan C. Ornstein, *Educational Administration: Concepts and Practices* (Belmont, Calif.: Wadsworth, 1991), p. 491.

6. Arnold S. Tannenbaum, "Unions," in *Handbook of Organizations,* ed. by James March (Chicago: Rand McNally, 1965), p. 710.

7. Arthur Blumberg, *The School Superintendent: Living with Conflict* (New York: Teachers College Press, 1985), p. 100.

8. Sidney and Beatrice Webb, *History of Trade Unionism* (New York: Longmans, Green, 1920), p. 1.

9. Thomas J. Sergiovanni et al., *Educational Governance and Administration* (Englewood Cliffs, N.J., 1987), p. 197.

10. Blumberg, *The School Superintendent*, p. 1.

11. Myron Lieberman and Michael H. Moskow, *Collective Negotiations for Teachers* (Chicago: Rand McNally, 1966), pp. 370–373.

12. Glass, *1992 Study*, p. 46.

13. Ibid., p. 43.

14. Larry Cuban, *The Managerial Imperative and the Practice of Leadership in Schools* (Albany: State University of New York Press, 1988), p. 59.

15. Gerald C. Ubben and Barbara Fulmer, "The Relationship of Collective Bargaining to the Decision-Making Power of the Public School Principal," *Journal of Collective Negotiations*, 14(2) (1985): p. 141. Baywood Publishing.

16. Webb et al., *Human Resources Administration*, p. 251.

17. Glass, *1992 Study*, p. 92.

18. Ibid., p. 91.

19. Ibid.

20. A. N. Schoonmaker, *Negotiate to Win* (Englewood Cliffs, N.J., 1989), pp. 12–13.

21. Webb et al., *Human Resources Administration*, p. 286.

22. Lewis T. Kohler and Frederick W. Hill, "Strategies of Successful School Negotiations,"

American School and University, 51(2) (October 1978): p. 68.

23. Larry W. Hughes and Gerald C. Ubben, *The Elementary Principal's Handbook* (Boston: Allyn and Bacon, 1989), p. 283.

24. Lieberman and Moskow, *Collective Negotiations for Teachers*, pp. 128–130.

25. R. L. Walter, *The Teacher and Collective Bargaining* (Lincoln, Neb.: Educators Publications, 1975), p. 25.

26. Patricia Cannon Conran, *School Superintendent's Complete Handbook* (Englewood Cliffs, N.J., 1989), p. 459.

27. Lieberman and Moskow, *Collective Negotiations for Teachers*, p. 375.

28. Conran, *School Superintendent's Complete Handbook*, p. 459.

29. Ibid.

30. Cresswell and Murphy, *Teachers, Unions, and Collective Bargaining in Public Education*, pp. 248–249. (See n. 4.)

31. Webb et al., *Human Resources Administration*, p. 291.

32. Cresswell and Murphy, *Teachers, Unions, and Collective Bargaining in Public Education*, p. 348.

33. Conran, *School Superintendent's Complete Handbook*, p. 460.

C h a p t e r 14

Human Resources Administration

The effectiveness of a school program is inextricably related to the quality of its human resources. Because the human element is so critical in the achievement of school goals and objectives, the human resources function is a primary concern of the school superintendent. The superintendent must be a leader in the development of policies and regulations fostering an organizational climate that maximizes the human potential of the school system. As stated by Conner, "the success of a school administrator will depend more upon his skill in selecting, improving, and dealing with the human element than upon any other factor. . . . There is no more important administrative responsibility than effective personnel administration."[1]

This chapter focuses on the human resources function in education and its related processes. The nature of the human resources function and its impact on the success of the total school program is a central theme. We also emphasize the responsibilities of the school superintendent in the development and administration of an effective system of human resources for the school district. Board policy usually holds the school superintendent responsible for program results. Personnel activities administered in the school system generally are those delegated by the superintendent. The superintendent, therefore, must be well informed about the human resources function and the nature and importance of its related processes.

The human resources function in education developed rapidly after World War I. Moore notes that, "personnel administration as the term is commonly understood, began with World War I. The recruiting, training, and paying of masses of workers in war production forced assignment of such responsibilities to specialized personnel."[2] "By the 1980s, personnel administration had become soundly entrenched as an integral function in school districts."[3] In the early 1990s, however, changing governance structures in school districts emerged that greatly affected personnel practices. These reform movements led to shifts in authority and to major changes in the administration of the human resources function.

Other factors such as strong teachers' unions, collective bargaining, decentralization of administration, and various legal rulings also have affected human resources practices. The utilization of human resources and quality of work life will continue to be primary concerns of school leadership. School superintendents, to be successful, must give high priority to human resources concerns. Successful leadership in this area requires a thorough understanding of the processes encompassed within the comprehensive area of human resources. This consideration, along with the matters just touched on, is the focus of this chapter.

The Human Resources Function in Education

By the early 1990s, what previously was known as personnel administration became known in business, industry, and education as human resources administration. The more contemporary term *human resources administration* extended the concept beyond that of utilization to include both the environment and human development. Figure 14–1 illustrates the human resources function, its three broad components, and its 12 related processes. The broad component, *human resources utilization,* encompasses the eight processes of planning, recruitment, selection, orientation, assignment, collective negotiations, compensation and welfare, and stability. The component *human resources development* includes the evaluation and the development processes. The human resources component *environment* encompasses the processes of organizational climate and protection.

Although the three broad components of utilization, development, and environment serve to classify the 12 human resources processes, all processes are interrelated. For

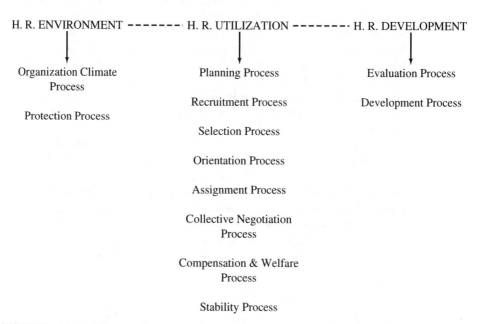

FIGURE 14–1   **Human Resources Function, Components, and Processes**

example, the planning process, placed in the utilization component, not only relates to the other processes of that component, but also links to the evaluation, development, protection, and organizational climate processes of the other two components.

The Human Resources Processes

The following discussion of the human resources processes reveals the comprehensiveness and complexity of the human resources function in education as well as its implications for effective leadership by the school superintendent. Each process is important to the achievement of school goals.

Human Resources Utilization

1. The Planning Process. The purpose of human resources planning is the same as planning in any other educational function: to determine what decisions, programs, activities, and resources are necessary to achieve the right results. Effective planning serves to identify the goals that the human resources function must achieve; it fosters effective administration and promotes optimal work performance on the part of school staff.

> Planning is a systematic and continuous process which prepares for change or attempts to shape and control change. As such, planning involves:
>
> - Forecasting—looking toward the future and assessing probabilities.
> - Designing—creating plans of action, directed at specific goals.
> - Strategizing—defining strategies and activities to meet stated goals and objectives.
> - Organizing—using a systematic approach to decision making.
> - Participating—involving those in the decisions who will be affected by them.
> - Cooperating and collaborating—using all possible resources in order to achieve the best possible results.[4]

Clearly, strong leadership is essential for effective planning. The following opening statement of a superintendent's job description underlines the expectations of the school board concerning planning responsibilities:

> The Superintendent is the Chief Executive Officer, responsible for overall planning, operation, and performance of the district. He provides staff support and recommendations to the Board with respect to decision-making policies and planning, and is the Board's agent in all relationships with the staff. He selects, organizes, and gives leadership to the management team, oversees planning, staff development, and reward systems throughout the district, and ensures adequate operational and financial control.[5]

Planning strategy was named as the sixth highest expectation of school superintendents by school boards in Glass's national study.[6] The same study found strategic planning among the major issues and challenges facing the superintendency; planning ranked fourteenth of 39 such issues.[7] A comprehensive discussion of planning is presented in Chapter 7.

2. The Recruitment Process. The primary purpose of recruitment is to establish a pool of qualified candidates to meet the human resources needs of the school system. Recruitment serves as a preselection process that assures the school system of having the necessary supply of qualified personnel to meet its needs. Glass found that recruitment and selection was ranked by nearly 75 percent of national school superintendents as one of the major issues and challenges facing them. Recruitment activities include the determination of recruitment procedures, formalizing interview and rating procedures, and establishing responsibilities of the staff in implementing recruitment strategies. Griffiths named the obtaining and developing of personnel as one of the four major parts of the superintendent's job.[8]

3. The Selection Process. The process of choosing personnel who will be effective in the roles assigned is difficult and complex. Effective selection of staff not only enhances the achievement of school goals but also reduces the administrative and staff problems within the system. In a national study, the issue of nonproductive staff ranked fourth among 12 major issues that would likely cause superintendents to leave their positions if not corrected.[9] Procedures for improving employee selection are an ongoing topic of discussion. In an attempt to reduce the subjectivity in staff selection, structured interviews, simulation strategies, prescreening instruments, videotaping, and other group strategies have been implemented to supplement traditional selection procedures.

The selection process is considered by many school superintendents as the most important process performed by the school district. Although staff selection is a shared responsibility and one that has become more decentralized over the last several years, it is a responsibility most often placed directly on the school superintendent by the school board. This is illustrated by the following excerpts from a school district's policy manual:

> The Lincoln Public Schools, through an effective recruitment program, will endeavor to employ an effective, well-qualified staff. . . . It is the responsibility of the superintendent of schools and of persons so delegated to determine the personnel needs of the school district and to locate suitable candidates to recommend for employment to the Lincoln Board of Education. . . . It shall be the duty of the superintendent of schools, or designee, to see that persons nominated for employment shall meet all qualifications established by law and the board for the position for which nomination is made.[10]

4. The Orientation Process. The orientation process is "the complex of activities designed to gain congruence between institutional objectives and employee needs. It begins with the job application and continues on an ongoing basis for as long as the employee or the organization views it as necessary."[11] Research has given strong support to the importance of orientation activities. Positive morale has been linked closely to induction practices and personnel assistance given to teachers new to the school system.[12] Special attention to the needs and concerns of beginning teachers, such as student discipline, student evaluation, administrative routines, relationships with system offices and personnel, and financial problems, is of paramount importance. Other matters, including work schedules, parent conferences, community orientation, work load, reporting, and per-

Regulation
4230.1

HUMAN RESOURCES

Orientation—Certificated Employees System-Wide Basis

Orientation of new certificated employees will be the responsibility of the Human Resources Division with assistance by subject area consultant, district administrators and other designated staff.

School Building Basis

The principal is responsible for the orientation of new certificated employees. Principals should give information and general directions in regard to the following:

1. The names of certificated employees, the office staff, cafeteria personnel, custodians and other special staff personnel assigned to the building.
2. Physical facilities of the building.
3. Teaching materials: courses of study, guide books, textbooks, and supplementary materials for grade or subject.
4. Method of ordering books and supplies, securing audiovisual equipment, methods of getting material duplicated, disposing of lost and found articles.
5. Regulations for students in building and on school grounds; uses of entrances, exits, lavatories, playground areas, equipment and activities; regulations for students during, before, and after school hours.
6. Directions about building meetings, in-service training meetings, other meetings, assignments to school committees, fire drill regulations, policies concerning certificated employees' absence, attendance dismissal, excuse of students from school, and procedures for suspected child abuse, etc.
7. The goals of the Lincoln Public Schools.
8. School system policies and regulations.

Date Regulation Reviewed by the
    Board of Education: 5-12-____

Lincoln Public Schools
Lincoln, Nebraska

FIGURE 14–2   Regulation—Orientation of Certificated Employees

SOURCE: *Policies and Regulations* of the Lincoln, Nebraska Public Schools. Used by permission of the Lincoln Public Schools.

sonal safety, also are integral considerations in fostering a positive work environment and, therefore, a part of the ongoing orientation process.

The size and organization of the school district help shape how the orientation process is administered. A school board policy statement such as, "The College View school administration will conduct appropriate orientation sessions for all new employees," is sufficient to develop the necessary administrative regulations for its implementation. The school superintendent most often delegates responsibilities for orientation to other units and local school administrators. The example from the Lincoln, Nebraska, Public School District's policy manual shown in Figure 14–2 illustrates a regulation that places responsibilities for the orientation of certificated employees on the human resources unit and the local building principal.

As stated by Van Zwoll, "the most important single factor in getting the best that a school employee has to offer is how he feels about his work, his associates on the job, and the school system in which he is employed. Everyone has the need to regard his work as worthwhile and to take pride in it. Through orientation the employee is inducted into his work, works in relationship with his administrative, teaching and nonteaching associates, and develops some feeling about his job and the school."[13]

5.   The Assignment Process.   Not only is the placement of personnel in positions that match their interests and qualifications of importance to program quality, but work load, conditions of work, supervision practices, evaluation methods, and other staff utilization provisions tie closely to the quality of work life for personnel as well. The assignment process encompasses the placement of persons in positions most suitable to their talents and interests, the use of talents in the best interest of all concerned, and attention to conditions that affect work quality. As stated by Rebore, "the placement of employees within the school system is the responsibility of the superintendent of schools. The planning required in making assignments is a very complicated task, demanding the full-time attention of at least one personnel administrator in most metropolitan-area school districts."[14] As emphasized by Drucker, "the final but perhaps the most important element in managing people is to place them where their strengths can become productive."[15]

The American Association of School Administrators (AASA) set forth three basic principles of assignment as follows:

> the teacher's preferences should be respected whenever this is feasible; whenever possible, the lighter loads should be reserved for beginning teachers; and, the superintendent of schools should be made responsible for the assignment of all personnel.[16]

6.   The Collective Negotiations Process.   Collective negotiation is the process of determining the compensation levels and matters related to conditions of work by representatives of the school board and employee groups through mutual agreement. School superintendents named negotiations, strikes, and teacher militancy among the leading issues and challenges facing them. Further, superintendents nationally reported that collective bargaining agreements were the fourth leading inhibitor to their effectiveness.[17]

Many persons believe that the human resources function has been influenced more by collective negotiations than by any other single development in education. Although negotiations practices in education vary widely among the states, negotiations play a major role in the lives of school superintendents. Nationally, approximately 30 percent of the school superintendents serve as the chief negotiator for their school board's collective negotiations team. In fact, the use of the school superintendent as chief negotiator leads all other arrangements, including the use of outside professional negotiators, other inside negotiators, or the use of a school board member or board attorney.[18] When not serving as the board team's chief negotiator, the superintendent frequently serves as a team member or as a chief consultant for the board's negotiations team. Chapter 13 discusses collective negotiations and the responsibility of the superintendent in this process in detail.

7.   The Compensation and Welfare Process.   School finance continues as the leading problem in the minds of most school boards and superintendents. A recent national study of superintendents found financing schools as the number one issue and challenge facing them.[19] The matter of determining the allocation of basic salaries for personnel, including methods of incentive pay, adds to the complexity of the superintendent's responsibilities. The compensation and welfare process encompasses such administrative considerations as developing viable compensation policies, establishing the system's position structure and the monetary value of the various positions, ascribing monetary value to individual position holders, and implementing and controlling the compensation plan. As previously noted, the negotiations process ties closely to compensation and welfare and carries further implications for the work of the school superintendent.

The matter of fringe benefits for staff has become a major financial problem for America's schools. Reports indicate that such benefits represent approximately 50 percent of wages and salaries. Cost of benefits (COB) has become a leading problem in the financing of businesses, industries, and school systems. The solution to this problem has yet to be determined. Such programs as employee assistance programs, health and dental preventative programs, and part-time employment arrangements are indicative of efforts to reduce fringe benefit program costs. Many persons predict that the future will see the employee assuming a greater percentage of costs for health care and other provisions presently provided through school districts' compensation packages. The fiscal responsibilities of the superintendent are detailed in Chapter 10.

8. The Stability Process. Maintaining a viable work force requires special attention to employee health and safety, staff turnover, employee absenteeism, staff counseling services, and the substitute teacher program. Problems of maintaining a stable work force are reflected in many ways: troubled workers; reduction in force; leaves of absence; staff separations due to resignation, dismissal, and death; transitions within the system; and absences of various kinds. Each of these matters directly affects the school system's stability and often reflects negatively on the school district's ability to provide quality programs for children and youth.

It is not the purpose here to discuss each of the aforementioned problems. We give the following example of the troubled worker to underline the effects of the foregoing conditions on the worker and, in turn, on the stability of the school program. A troubled worker has personal problems that inhibit effective work performance and lead to excessive absenteeism, accidents on the job, and the filing of more grievances than normal employees. A national study by Norton found that as many as 15 percent of the teachers in some schools were "troubled," although slightly less than 50 percent of the participating personnel directors judged 1–5 percent of the teaching staff in this category. Medical health problems, problem drinking, mental/emotional health problems, marital/family problems, employer/supervisor relationships, personal crises, financial problems, drug/chemical problems, and work/peer relationships were named as the leading problems of employees in the school districts studied.[20] Nearly 65 percent of the personnel directors who reported in the national study were of the opinion that the troubled employee was a problem for the district. Troubled workers had much higher or higher absentee rates than other workers in these school districts; they filed far more or more grievances than other employees; and they consistently received lower performance evaluations than other district employees.

Human Resources Environment
1. The Organizational Climate Process. The school superintendent holds a major responsibility for what the school system is and what it might become. Of the several pri-

mary objectives of the human resources function, the development of an environment that fosters positive human relationships and promotes optimal human development is foremost. "Organizational Climate is the collective personality of a school or school system. It is the atmosphere that prevails in an organization and is characterized by the social and professional interactions of the people."[21] Human resources administration serves a strategic role in meeting the requirements for a healthy work environment. Leadership responsibilities include attention to personnel policies and regulations, principles of human motivation, participative management strategies, community cultures, and best practices in orientation, assignment, protection, and development of personnel.

Establishing and maintaining a positive, open environment was viewed as being "very essential" or "essential" by more than 90 percent of superintendents nationally.[22] Clearly, the superintendent must be highly competent in human relations to be effective in communities of great diversity. Leadership skills require that the superintendent serve as a model as an advisor, mentor, and instructor of effective interpersonal relationships. The largest school district in Arizona set forth several specific human relations skills expected of its superintendent. The superintendent's job description states that he or she should:

- Be personable and friendly.
- Be accessible to employees, parents, and the district's many publics.
- Be caring, and compassionate with the ability to empathize with people of various cultures and ethnicities, genders and ages.
- Be respectful and sensitive of the faiths and beliefs of others.
- Have a sincere interest in the education of youth and children.
- Be innovative, sensitive, cultivated and articulate.
- Be dynamic and results-oriented.
- Enjoy working with people and have a good sense of humor.
- Present self professionally in personal appearance, voice, and mannerisms.
- Model behavior that inspires and motivates.[23]

The reader might suggest the addition of "ability to walk on water" to the foregoing requirements. Yet the importance of these human skills is self-evident. As pointed out directly by Conner, "the majority [of administrators] fail because they lack the skill to deal adequately with the human element connected with the school board members, staff, citizens and pupils."[24] In regard to school board expectations of the superintendent, possessing skill in human relations ranked second in a national study to skill in general management.[25]

2. The Protection Process   Staff tenure, due process, secure work environments, academic freedom, individual rights, grievance procedures, liability protection, and safety provisions are among the many considerations of the protection process. Castetter states that "the decade from 1965 to 1975 produced the greatest advances in the area of individual public rights since the birth of the nation; at the same time, it produced the greatest threat to the economic security of public employees."[26] School superintendents face the dilemma of protecting the rights of employees and at the same time dealing with problems of incompetent personnel, demands for educational equality, and litigation related to employee grievances associated with performance appraisal, employee discrimination, due process, and other personnel matters.

Tenure for teachers is a controversial matter that superintendents must face. Tenure protects teachers from dismissal without specific reasons; it guards against capricious actions concerning the teacher that are unfair and unwarranted. On the other hand, the public and others often view tenure as a provision that "freezes" mediocrity into the school system's teaching staff; it gives lifetime employment regardless of the quality of teaching performance of the individual. The termination of a tenured teacher for cause is a difficult, complex procedure. The superintendent must be knowledgeable of the legal procedures that must be followed in matters of dismissal and also be certain that other administrative personnel understand them as well. Failure on the part of the school district to provide appropriate performance documentation, to follow due process procedures, or to provide improvement support in areas of unsatisfactory performance can result in negative court rulings against the school district.

Leadership requirements for meeting the objectives of the protection process are far-reaching. Strategies for determining and understanding the human needs within the system, knowledge of school law, expertise in policy development, and the possession of a genuine caring attitude are among the essential qualities for school superintendents in this area of human resources administration.

Human Resources Development

1.   The Evaluation Process.   Performance appraisal is a process often delegated by the school board directly to the superintendent of schools. Although other central units of the school system and local school administrators share appraisal responsibilities, final accountability devolves to the superintendent. Leadership in performance appraisal is instrumental in the implementation of school system goals and in meeting personal development needs within the system. In this sense, performance appraisal serves the formative objective of determining staff strengths and needs; strengths can be utilized optimally, and weaknesses can be remedied. In those instances when remedial actions are ineffective, summative appraisal procedures must be implemented, and in some cases, dismissal actions must be exercised.

Staff and administrator evaluation was named as a leading issue and challenge for school superintendents; nearly 64 percent of the superintendents expressed this belief in Glass's study.[27] In many school districts, performance appraisal leads the list of litigation cases in the courts. Due process procedures, appraisal criteria, evaluator subjectivity, and racial or sexual discrimination are among the reasons for lawsuits regarding employee evaluation.[28] For these reasons, superintendents must take the lead in planning, designing, and implementing performance appraisal programs that meet effectiveness criteria, including the training and certification of qualified evaluators. The significance of this process was underlined when nearly 92 percent of the superintendents nationally viewed it as "very essential" or "essential" in their performance responsibilities.[29]

2.   The Development Process   The progress of a school system depends largely on the personal and professional development of its personnel; this fact emphasizes the importance of the superintendent's leadership in the human resources development process. The determination of viable staff development policies and the implementation of effective development programs are major concerns of the superintendent. A 1992 national study of school superintendents named the issue of nonproductive staff number four among all the issues that would likely cause them to leave their positions if not corrected.[30]

The development process is the primary means for helping each employee meet professional growth needs and to realize personal potential. Such provisions as mentoring, teacher centers, assessment centers, clinical supervision, skill labs, workshops, career development planning, job rotation, formal college coursework, and quality circles are among those practices utilized by school systems nationally. In short, the school superintendent is expected to provide the necessary leadership for the implementation of a comprehensive program of staff development for all employees.

School district requirements for professional growth differ widely. Some districts require only those activities and credits required by state statute or state certification regulations. One common procedure is for districts to require a specified number of growth points over a determined period of time. Such "credits" can be earned through participation in such activities as formal college classwork, taking adult education classes, participation in special in-service workshops, teaching college or adult classes, conducting workshops, supervising student teachers, producing professional publications, serving on various system-wide or other professional committees, and educational travel. Although these activities are generally planned and implemented by other units and individuals in the school system, the school superintendent commonly is given the responsibility for ensuring the development of all personnel in their respective areas of personal and professional competence.

The School Superintendent's Leadership Role in Human Resources Administration

The foregoing discussion focused on the several processes of the human resources function and the importance of the school superintendent's leadership in meeting the objectives of each process. In this section, we present the basic leadership responsibilities of the superintendent in the administration of the human resources function.

Although leadership roles of the school superintendent do vary in school systems of different sizes, Glass found that the perceived importance of various major performance areas was viewed similarly by superintendents of both large and small districts.[31] The essential importance of performance areas such as curriculum, organizational climate control, evaluating for quality, money matters, and others was not significantly different among varying school district sizes. Although the specific involvement of superintendents might vary according to district size, the overall leadership responsibilities for the human resources function are essentially the same.

Competencies Required of the School Superintendent

There are several ways to examine the specific responsibilities of school superintendents for the human resources function. One way is to note the specific personal competencies required of the superintendent for effectiveness in human resources administration. The identification of several selected competencies required of the superintendent in this area serves two purposes. It provides insight into the responsibilities of the superintendent in the administration of human resources processes, and it emphasizes the personal skills and knowledge required for the superintendent's successful job performance.

"Competency refers to the ability to accomplish a task at a satisfactory level of performance. To be competent is to possess sufficient skills and knowledge to meet a stated purpose or to have the capacity equal to the requirements of the task."[32]

Norton and Farrar identified major tasks and competencies for school superintendents in human resources administration. Figure 14–3 reveals several selected tasks and competencies required for effective performance by superintendents.

Although the statement in Figure 14–3 includes only a partial listing of needed knowledge and skills, it emphasizes that the superintendent must be far more than a casual overseer of the human resources function. Rather, he or she must possess specific abilities and knowledge that foster the achievement of important major tasks.

The Superintendent's Job Description

The job description of the school superintendent almost always sets forth specific human resources responsibilities. To further illustrate these leadership responsibilities of the superintendent, we give excerpts from several job descriptions in Figures 14.4, 14.5, 14.6, and 14–7. Note that only references to human resources duties have been included in these job descriptions.

In summary, these excerpts set forth expected responsibilities of the school superintendent relating to the following human resources activities: recruitment, selection, assignment, orientation, transfer, motivation, esprit de corps, development, appointment, promotion, dismissal, evaluation, record keeping, job descriptions, staff relations, policy development, development of regulations, personnel supervision, payrolls, salary placement, demotion, planning, reward system, delegation, salary recommendation, communication, effective use of personnel, meetings of personnel, vacation leaves, compensation, certification checks, informing staff of board policies, negotiations, and contracts.

The Implementation of General Responsibilities

The comprehensive nature of the human resources function makes it a shared responsibility—one that requires direction and coordination under a central administrator. The authority for administering the human resources function most often is delegated to a human resources director, who assumes the major responsibility for its daily administration. Even in these situations the school superintendent assumes general leadership responsibilities for directing the human resources function in the system. "The superintendent is the prime person in the school district in developing a sense of mission, establishing a positive climate, and overseeing the implementation of the mission."[33] These responsibilities are discussed in the following sections.

The First Responsibility

The superintendent's first responsibility in administering the human resources function is recognizing that effective human resources in the school system depends largely on the superintendent's leadership. The superintendent must understand the comprehensive nature of the human resources function, and accept it as an administrative function that identifies the policies and procedures that gain the support of the board, staff, and community. Although every unit in the school system shares in effective human resources, it is

Human Resources Tasks	Human Resources Competencies
Task 1.0 To provide for recruitment, orientation, development, utilization, evaluation, separation, and compensation of district personnel.	1.1 Demonstrates skill and understanding of modern practices in all processes related to the task.
	1.2 Ability to determine needs of personnel for growth and professional improvement.
	1.3 Ability to recognize and utilize individual differences among personnel.
	1.4 Demonstrates knowledge and understanding of the concepts of human motivation and utilizes this ability to gain optimal employee performance and satisfaction.
	1.5 Ability to provide for resources processes through the use of data obtained from appropriate and related assessments.
	1.6 Ability to facilitate personnel development by providing opportunities for personal and professional growth.
	1.7 Ability to understand and appreciate the immediate and long-range implications of labor relations and professional negotiations.
	1.8 Ability to work effectively in a multi-cultural setting.
Task 2.0 To provide for supervision and evaluation of personnel.	2.1 Ability to organize and administer an effective program of personnel supervision.
	2.2 Ability to establish an effective personnel performance appraisal system.
	2.3 Ability to delegate responsibilities related to the task and to hold these persons accountable.
	2.4 Demonstrates knowledge of the legal aspects of employment.
Task 3.0 To provide an atmosphere conducive to discussion of human resources issues, problems, and recommendations.	3.1 Ability to maintain an open attitude through active involvement of students, parents, teachers and others in meaningful discussion of the district's programs, goals, and objectives.
Task 4.0 To maintain effective communication and professional relationships with employees.	4.1 Ability to provide for two-way communication and to utilize, when appropriate, information and recommendations of the central personnel unit and of district personnel.
	4.2 Ability to communicate as necessary with individuals when they are not meeting job requirements.
Task 5.0 To provide for a system of compensation and benefits for personnel.	5.1 Ability to develop and analyze job descriptions, current labor practices, salaries, and agreements.
	5.2 Ability to supervisor the implementation of the payroll system for the district.
Task 6.0 To establish a personal plan and demonstrate a commitment to a program of personal professional development.	6.1 Ability to make a critical self assessment of the areas needed for personal and professional growth.
	6.2 Ability to develop a plan for personal professional development.

FIGURE 14–3 Selected Human Resources Tasks and Competencies Required of the School Superintendent

SOURCE: M. Scott Norton and Roger D. Farrar, *Competency-based Preparation of Educational Administrators: Tasks, Competencies, and Indicators of Competency* (Tempe: Department of Educational Administration and Supervision, Arizona State University, 1987).

General Responsibilities

Coordinates the work of the administrative staff members, provides counsel and motivation, and fosters an esprit de corps.

Accepts responsibility for the general efficiency of the District, for the development of the school staff, and for the educational growth and welfare of students.

Personnel

Recommends for appointment, election, or employment all employees of the District, and assigns, transfers, and recommends for dismissal any and all employees of the Governing Board.

Recommends to the Governing Board for final action the promotion, salary changes, demotion, or dismissal of any employee. Accepts the responsibility and leadership of maintaining adequate written personnel evaluation records, reflecting both objective evaluation data and subjective observations.

Makes and records assignments and transfers of all employees in keeping with their qualifications.

Defines the duties of all personnel, subject to the approval of the Governing Board.

Delegates at own discretion to other employees of the Governing Board the exercise of any powers or the discharge of any duties with the knowledge that the delegation of power or duty does not relieve the superintendent of final responsibility for the action taken under such delegation.

Summons employees of the district to attend such regular and occasional meetings as are necessary to carry out the educational program of the district.

Communicates directly or through delegation all actions of the Governing Board relating to personnel matters to all employees; and receives from employees all communications to be made to the Governing Board.

Approves vacation schedules for all salaried employees.

Records

Maintains directly or through delegation such personnel records, pupil accounting records, business records, and other records which are required by law and by Governing Board policy.

Policies

Advises the Governing Board on the need for new and/or revised policies.

Exercises power to make rules and gives such instructions to school employees and students as may be necessary to implement Governing Board policy.

FIGURE 14–4 Superintendent's Job Description—Excerpt

Source: *Superintendent's Job Description,* Paradise Valley Unified School District No. 69, Paradise Valley, Arizona. Used by permission.

the duty of the superintendent to make certain that every unit and each employee understands this fact.

Working with the staff, community, and school board, the superintendent leads the school system in developing a written statement that expresses the district's goals and objectives concerning effective human resources administration. In order that the statement becomes an official part of the school board's guiding policy, the superintendent makes certain that it is approved through formal action of the board and made known to all concerned through appropriate means.

This policy statement expresses the purposes of the system's human resources function and provides for the delegation of authority deemed necessary to facilitate the implementation and achievement of stated purposes. Commitment to the purposes of the human

Responsibilities

Responsible for all phases of school administration, including accounting, budget making, property management, personnel supervision, and curriculum organization. Clears teacher certification, district payrolls and salary placements.

Recommends for appointment, demotion or discharge of all employees of the district.

Supervises all personnel of the district, both certified and classified.

Directs the assignment of teachers as soon after appointment as practicable.

Responsible for providing a program of induction and orientation of new teachers and members of the administrative staff.

Keeps the Board informed as to how policies are being carried out, the effectiveness of such policies, and the condition and efficiency of the different branches of services in the district; to this end maintains a competent system of financial accounting for budget . . . competent business and property records and competent personnel.

Responsible for the formation of school policies, plans, and programs, and otherwise, by presentation of facts and explanations, assists the Board in its duty of legislating for the school.

FIGURE 14–5   Superintendent's Job Description—Excerpt

SOURCE: *Superintendent's Job Description,* Peoria Unified School District No. 11, Peoria, Arizona. Used by permission.

resources function is demonstrated through the allocation of both financial and human resources needed to fulfill its expectations. Figure 14.8 is an example of a policy statement that meets the purposes expressed in the foregoing discussion. The overarching goal of the school district relative to human resources is set forth in the statement's general purpose. The specific responsibilities of the school district, as employer of the staff, then are set forth in four specific statements.

The Second Responsibility

A second responsibility of the superintendent is to ensure that the human resources point of view is duly considered in reaching important program decisions. This responsibility necessitates ongoing communication with the central human resources unit and with local school personnel.

A reservoir of information is essential to the human resources process. The system must maintain a research program that provides information about such matters as future enrollments, projected needs, staff transitions and turnover, work loads, exit reports, staff mix, changing demographics, and other databases that help to ensure the best use of the sys-

In demonstrated ability the superintendent should:

Possess the ability to select, assign, motivate and evaluate competent staff to achieve high standards of excellence in education; inspire confidence and trust of the Board, staff and community by building a vision of the District's future to ensure the effective use of human and financial resources; encourage the participation of others, build consensus, delegate responsibility appropriately, be accountable and hold others accountable.

FIGURE 14–6   Superintendent's Job Description—Excerpt

SOURCE: *Superintendent's Job Description,* Mesa Unified School District, Mesa, Arizona. Used by permission.

Basic Responsibility

The Superintendent is chief executive officer, responsible for overall planning, operation, and performance of the district. He provides staff support and recommendations to the Board with respect to decision-making policies and planning, and is the Board's agent in all relationships with the staff. He selects, organizes, and gives leadership to the management team, oversees planning, staff development, and reward systems throughout the district and ensures adequate operational and financial control.

Primary Duties

Ensure the development and operation of adequate recruiting, selection, appraisal and compensation systems to meet district objectives.

Develop the competence of teachers, staff, and management to the maximum extent possible in the best interests of the individual involved and to meet district objectives.

Establish a performance monitoring system incorporating test data results and consumer judgments to meet the needs of performance information throughout the organization.

Oversees staff negotiation and contract administration.

Maintain effective relationships with and among staff at all levels of the organization.

FIGURE 14–7   Superintendent's Job Description—Excerpt

SOURCE: Richard A. Gorton and Gail T. Schneider, *School-based Leadership: Challenges and Opportunities,* 3rd ed. (Dubuque, Iowa: Wm. C. Brown, 1991), p. 140. Used by permission.

tem's human resources and serve the accomplishment of its goals and objectives. The superintendent is instrumental in developing this research posture within the school district.

The Third Responsibility

A third responsibility of the superintendent is to establish a human resources unit in the school system staffed by qualified personnel. Although the size of many school districts, or other conditions, makes a separate unit with a director impractical, the primary responsibility for human resources services in these instances should be placed with some existing unit or person within the system. In many cases, the school superintendent must assume this responsibility personally. "Data are not available for determining a correlation between the size of a school district's enrollment or staff and the existence of a central human resources administrator; there is no cutoff for such a position relative to school district size. Some schools with fewer than 1,000 students have a central human resources administrator; other much larger districts distribute personnel responsibilities among various units within the system."[34]

Organizational structures for administering the human resources function continue to change. The decentralization of various processes is a reality in practice. Regardless of the organizational arrangements, the central administration must work cooperatively with individual schools in the determination of specific responsibilities, authority, and accountability. Human resources always has been a shared responsibility among the central and local units of the school. This circumstance will continue as a necessary feature of human resources administration in schools.

The Fourth Responsibility

A fourth responsibility of the superintendent is to be certain that effective communication is maintained among and between the various school units relative to human resources

Policy
4000

HUMAN RESOURCES

General Provisions

It is a general goal of the Lincoln Public Schools to select the most competent employees available and to maximize the effectiveness of each staff member in achieving the goals of the Lincoln Public School District.

The school district is the employer of the staff and has the responsibilities for staff which are part of the employer's role.

It is assumed that the maximum effectiveness of all staff described in the general goal will be achieved if the district will:

1. Provide for the best contribution of each staff member to the common goals of the district through a rational and effective organizational structure.
    a. Develop within each staff member a consciousness of the organizational structure, its function, and their role in the structure.

2. Stimulate staff members to contribute their best efforts to the common goals of the district by developing a healthy organizational climate.
    a. Provide programs of staff development which help staff members to contribute to the maximum of their capabilities.
    b. Provide staff opportunities for leadership participation and decision making as appropriate.
    c. Provide recognition for work well done.
    d. Encourage each staff member to personify and exemplify the human relations characteristics basic to an open society operating according to democratic principles.

3. Encourage an organizational point of view which sees purposeful change as an opportunity for improvement.
    a. Provide mechanics for institutionalizing the change process.
    b. Provide planning which insures a self-renewing characteristic for that organization.

4. Improve the individual contribution of staff members to school district goals through a cooperatively developed program of evaluation aimed at retaining the most highly qualified staff.

Date of Adoption (or Last Revision)   5-12-____

Related Policies and Regulations

Legal Reference:

Lincoln Public Schools   Policy and Regulation Manual

Lincoln, Nebraska

FIGURE 14–8   Statement of General Purpose—the Human Resources Function

SOURCE: *Policies and Regulations* of the Lincoln, Nebraska School System. Reprinted by permission.

activities, problems, and research findings. For this reason, most directors of human resources report directly to the school superintendent. If the school district has an administrative council or cabinet, the human resources director should be a member of it. The director of human resources and support staff should be included in the school system's studies and deliberations regarding human resources both because of what they can contribute and what they can learn. In this way, the human resources unit functions in a counseling capacity to the governing bodies, board, cabinet, and local councils of the system.

The Fifth Responsibility

Finally, the superintendent has the general responsibility of demonstrating by example the vital importance of the human resources function in meeting the goals of the school system. Just as the human resources unit is vital to the central administration and school board because of its ability to provide special services, so too can it be of service to all units and individuals within the system. Many persons believe that the school district's personnel policies are the best evidence of what it really believes about the value of its human resources. The school superintendent supports this contention through a sincere effort to develop, execute, and evaluate policies and programs that enhance the human resources goals and objectives of the school district.

In summary, the school superintendent's general responsibilities in the area of human resources are the following:

- To recognize that effective human resources in the school system depend largely on the superintendent's leadership.
- To make certain that the human resources point of view is duly considered in reaching important program decisions.
- To establish a human resources unit in the school system staffed by qualified personnel.
- To be certain to maintain effective communications among and between the various school units relative to human resources activities, problems, and research findings.
- To set the example in demonstrating the vital importance of the human resources function in meeting the goals of the school system.

Summary

The human element within any organization directly affects program outcomes. The school superintendent must be highly knowledgeable and active in the area of school personnel administration.

The human resources function developed rapidly in American schools following World War I, and a central unit for its administration today is commonplace. Yet many school superintendents still must perform many of the processes of the human resources function without the services of a central unit director. Even in those school systems where a central personnel director exists, the leadership of the school superintendent is essential.

The human resources function in education encompasses 12 major processes. Each process ties to the others, directly or indirectly. The human resources function is a shared responsibility requiring cooperation between central offices of the school system and local schools. Even in those school systems that have implemented site-based management, cooperative efforts between the central office of the district and local schools are necessary.

The 12 processes of planning, recruiting, selecting, orienting, assigning, negotiating, compensating, stabilizing, fostering climate, protecting, evaluating, and developing require specific personal competencies on the part of the school superintendent. Additionally, the job descriptions of superintendents nearly always contain specific duties for the administration of the district's human resources.

The superintendent in any school district has five general responsibilities of leadership regarding effective human resources administration. These responsibilities are recognizing that effective human resources depend on (1) the superintendent's leadership, (2) ensuring full consideration of the human resources point of view in decision-making processes, (3) establishing a human resources unit in the school system staffed by qualified personnel, (4) maintaining effective communication among and between various school units relative to human resources activities, problems, and research, and (5) demonstrating by personal example the importance of the human resources function in goal achievement.

Discussion Questions

1. Consider the following three human resources processes: selection, organizational climate, and development. Discuss each process as a shared responsibility. Identify what you believe to be the school superintendent's primary responsibility for each process.

2. Research reveals that nearly 30 percent of school superintendents serve as the chief negotiator for the district's collective negotiations agreement with teachers. Present your views concerning the appropriateness of this role for the superintendent. In view of all considerations, what do you believe to be the superintendent's primary responsibilities for the collective negotiations process in school districts?

3. Assume that site-based management is proposed for the school district in which you serve as superintendent. Present your specific recommendations for the responsibilities of local schools and the central administration office for the human resources function.

4. Review the section concerning required tasks and competencies of the school superintendent in human resources administration. Then list several additional competencies in this area that you believe to be important for school superintendents.

CASE 14.1   That's What They Hired *You* for!

Superintendent Martin was new to the College View School District. He was hired on a unanimous board vote; the district was in dire need of a leader with Martin's public relations skills.

During Superintendent Martin's fourth month on the job, the director of personnel, Patti Sharón, met with him about a problem of the central personnel unit. "I'm having a problem trying to get the commitment of the local schools for implementing the objectives for the personnel development program that we agreed on in last year's retreat," stated Sharón. "The principals readily admit that they approved the program plans, but they are really not taking the steps necessary to gain teacher involvement and interest at the building level." She continued, "We need help in gaining the cooperation of everyone if this development program is to be successful."

"Well," retorted Superintendent Martin, "It seems to me that's what they hired you for."

Questions

1.   First, comment on the case generally. What circumstances do you believe likely led to the current situation concerning the personnel development program?

2.   Comment on Superintendent Martin's position in this matter. Do you agree with his view? Why or why not?

3.   Assume the position of Patti Sharón. What steps and/or actions are necessary to realize a positive outcome in this matter?

Inbasket Exercise

INBASKET 14.1

A Question of Merit

AMERICAN ASSOCIATION OF PROFESSIONAL WOMEN
WYMORE, LAFAYETTE

4753 Elm Row
Wymore, Lafayette 02075

October 1, 19__

Superintendent of Schools
Wymore, Lafayette 02075

Dear Dr. Henson:

At the last meeting of our local chapter of A.A.P.W., we studied the recent report of Dr. Terry Clark (University of Lafayette) regarding *Merit Pay for Teachers.* As stated by Dr. Clark, "How can we move from a single salary schedule that recognizes only training and experience to one that rewards superior teaching in the classroom?"

Your recent speeches on "quality" intrigue our association. Doesn't quality and superior teaching go hand in hand? How can the school district purport to promote quality and, yet, continue to live with the single salary schedule, an innovation of the early 1920s? If we are able to evaluate teachers annually and give marks for performance, why can't outstanding performance be recognized through merit rewards?

We will have a follow-up discussion session on this topic on October 25. I'd appreciate your immediate response to this inquiry for distribution to our membership at that session. Our follow-up recommendations will be determined soon thereafter.

Sincerely,

Emily Rose Miller, President

Emily Rose Miller, President
A.A.P.W.

Response

1.   Assume the role of Superintendent Henson and respond administratively to the matter as presented by Emily Rose Miller. What actions would you implement? If you would write or call Emily Rose Miller, outline the specific statements that you would set forth in your remarks.

2. Most every school superintendent will face the matter of merit pay in the school district at some time in their career. Write two or three paragraphs that present your personal philosophy concerning merit pay for teachers in education.

Notes

1. Forrest Conner, Foreword, in James Van Zwoll, *School Personnel Administration* (New York: Appleton-Century-Crofts, 1964), p. iii.

2. Harold E. Moore, *The Administration of Public School Personnel* (New York: The Library of Education, The Center for Applied Research in Education, 1966), p. 3.

3. L. Dean Webb, John Greer, Paul Montello, and M. Scott Norton, *Personnel Administration in Education: New Issues and New Needs in Human Resources Management* (Columbus, Ohio: Merrill, 1987), p. 13.

4. Susan Paddock and Nancy Mercure, *Planning Handbook* (Tempe: Arizona State University, 1980), p. 5.

5. Richard A. Gorton and Gail T. Schneider, *School-based Leadership: Challenges and Opportunities,* 3rd ed. (Dubuque, Iowa: Wm. C. Brown, 1991), p. 140.

6. Thomas E. Glass, *The 1992 Study of the American School Superintendency: America's Education Leaders in a Time of Reform* (Arlington, Va.: American Association of School Administrators, 1992), p. 44.

7. Ibid., p. 45.

8. Daniel R. Griffiths, *The School Superintendent* (New York: Center for Applied Research in Education, 1966), pp. 70–71.

9. Glass, *1992 Study,* p. 50.

10. *Policies and Regulations* (Lincoln, Neb.: Lincoln Public Schools), Human Resources, Selection and Recruitment, Policy 4200.

11. Webb et al., *Personnel Administration in Education,* pp. 163–164.

12. W. W. Berglas. "A Study of Relationships between Induction Practices and the Morale of the Beginning Teacher," *Dissertation Abstracts International,* 34(5) (November 1973): 2189-A.

13. James Van Zwoll, *School Personnel Administration* (New York: Appleton-Century-Crofts, 1964), p. 138.

14. Ronald W. Rebore, *Personnel Administration in Education: A Management Approach,* 2nd ed. (Englewood Cliffs, N.J.: Prentice-Hall, 1987), p. 138.

15. Peter F. Drucker, *Management: Tasks, Responsibilities, Practices* (New York: Harper and Row, 1973), p. 309.

16. American Association of School Administrators, Thirty-third yearbook, *Staff Relations in School Administration* (Alexandria, Va.: AASA, 1955), pp. 44–45.

17. Glass, *1992 Study,* p. 46.

18. Ibid., p. 92.

19. Ibid., p. 46.

20. M. Scott Norton. "Employee Assistance Programs—a Need in Education," *Contemporary Education,* 60(3) (fall 1988): p. 24.

21. Webb et al., *Personnel Administration in Education,* p. 30.

22. Glass, *1992 Study,* p. 67.

23. Mesa Unified School District, *Job Description of the School Superintendent* (Mesa, Ariz.: Mesa School Board).

24. Conner, Foreword to *School Personnel Administration* by Van Zwoll, p. iii. (See n. 1.)

25. Glass, *1992 Study,* p. 44.

26. William B. Castetter, *The Personnel Function in Educational Administration,* 5th ed. (New York: Macmillan, 1992), p. 441.

27. Glass, *1992 Study,* p. 45.

28. Webb et al., *Personnel Administration in Education,* p. 156.

29. Glass, *1992 Study,* p. 68.

30. Ibid., p. 50.

31. Ibid., pp. 82–84.

32. M. Scott Norton and Roger D. Farrar. *Competency-based Preparation of Educational Administrators: Tasks, Competencies, and Indicators of Competency* (Tempe: Department of Educational Administration and Supervision, Arizona State University, 1987), pp. 2–21.

33. Robert L. Crowson, "The Local School Superintendency: A Puzzling Administrative Role," *Educational Administration Quarterly* 23(3) (summer 1987): p. 60.

34. Webb et al., *Personnel Administration in Education,* p. 62.

Chapter *15*

The Superintendent and Student Personnel

Students are at the heart of the professional responsibilities of the school superintendent. Campbell et al.[1] supported that notion: "one of the most time-honored principles of American education is that schools exist to meet the needs and serve the interests of students." When budget problems appear to be overly complex or when the politics of education become intolerable, most superintendents have only to visit an elementary or secondary classroom to reconnect with the reasons that they selected education as a profession. When they see the faces and hear the voices of students, it reminds them that they are responsible for providing a safe, caring environment for learning, for closing the gap between those who have and those who have not, and for making certain that all the resources of the district are used to benefit the educational needs of students. It also reminds them that education is a noble task and that their work is important.

In 1985 the Committee for Economic Development issued a series of recommendations for America's schools. The introduction to the section containing those recommendations included the following words: "When public schools are successful, they become a national treasure. They can instruct and inspire our young people. They can give life to local communities, contributing to their economic growth and social well-being. . . . In our pluralistic democracy, the schools can forge a common culture while respecting diversity."[2] For the reasons just listed, successful school are desired by all communities; yet the issue of how to determine the success of schools has always been in question. Increasingly, schools must satisfy the wants and needs of a growing number of audiences, and each audience measures the success of schools and the impact of schooling on students in their own way. The school exists to serve the needs of students and their families. Because of this mission, school leaders are challenged to focus on the condition and needs of students as they design productive school environments.

American school superintendents serve as the executive leaders of their school districts. The role implies visionary leadership, the building and maintenance of relationships with a wide variety of publics, strong fiscal management, expertise in planning, and a willingness to have their success measured by the quality of their products.[3] The general public presumes one of the "products" of the public schools to be a capable high school graduate. The business community expects a product that is ready to enter the work force. Colleges and universities anticipate that the product should be prepared for self-directed inquiry in advanced fields of study. Parents want their sons and daughters to be adaptable to changing job and educational environments and capable of obtaining and holding a good job.

Educators view students as much more than products. Rather, they see students as unique individuals with potential, and education as the process to assist students in the construction of skills, attitudes, and knowledge they can apply to future work, leisure, and continuous learning opportunities. Educators, through the programs they help develop and the expertise they supply to the learning environment, provide a valuable service that enables students to gain confidence and mature as learners throughout the educational process.

Among the major concerns that confront school leaders are the relationships that develop between students and their teachers. When students enter their first classroom and meet their teacher, the relationship among the learner, the environment, and education begins. During the entire process of education, a variety of these crucial relationships are formed between learners and educators. Teachers are at the very heart of the learning process, and the classroom is the front line for learning. When superintendents focus on what is best for students, one of their primary concerns is to assure that positive relationships exist among and between students and their teachers.

Teachers and students need continuous support for their work to be successful. At the building level, principals, counselors, and other staff provide financial, material, and professional support for the student, the teacher, and the educational process. These services add value to the student experience by expanding opportunities to obtain additional materials, services, or support that enhance their classroom experience. District-level educators coordinate, facilitate, and advocate for students by working with the community, politicians, and others to gain the necessary resources to ensure the child and the teacher have what they need to do the job. The superintendent is at the head of the entire team, but he or she does not usually work with students on a day-to-day basis. There is no doubt that the superintendent is always mindful of the first-line client. The educational welfare of students was the primary reason most educators entered the field of education, and regardless of how far they are distanced from the classroom, their goal remains the same: to provide high-quality, equitable, educational services for children and youth!

The superintendent serves an influential role as an educational policymaker at the local and state level. Although superintendents may not always have day-to-day contact with students, the advice and counsel that they provide to school board members and state legislators must always be directed to benefit the student. This chapter examines the superintendent's unique relationship with the student population. While they work for the benefit of students, superintendents generally do not work with them directly. Superintendents must be constantly aware of the social, economic, and educational conditions facing students. Also, the superintendent should associate with students in a variety of formal and informal settings so that he or she can observe the relationship among and between educators, the school environment, and students. The responsibilities of the superintendent, as applied to the welfare of students, involve advocacy for the rights and responsibilities of students, recruitment of a well-educated and caring staff, planning, organization, and implementation of the educational program to meet the needs of students, allocation of resources to the programs developed for students, and providing for the safety and security of students.

The Condition of Children and Youth

Children do not have the right to vote; they must rely on others to advocate for them in the political arena. Votes can be powerful weapons when segments of society polarize and the welfare of children falls victim to the presumed needs of others. There is growing concern that America's children, especially those in urban settings, do not have the ear of policy-makers. Kozol[4] visited homes and schools in more than 30 urban environments. "It occurred to me," he stated, "that we had not been listening much to children in these recent years of 'summit conferences' on education, of severe reports and ominous prescriptions. The voices of children, frankly, had been missing from the whole discussion." Kozol's words raise questions about who advocates for children of poverty, children of color, or children, in general. The chief executive of the local school must be a voice for all children if the dream for education in America is to be realized.

Kirst and McLaughlin[5] concluded that "today's schools build on yesterday's notion of 'family' and on children's environment in both form and function. The social institutions upon which schools build have shifted dramatically." Certainly, most people acknowledge the sweeping changes that have affected the American family in the past several decades. The two-income family and the single-parent family stand as monuments to dramatic changes in society. The number of minority children eligible to enter school has increased, and the number of children in poverty has risen dramatically. The implementation of new technologies in every field from banking to medicine has changed the way the nation conducts business and how those with illnesses are treated. An information explosion has created an overload of data. Yet of all the influences that have served to change the way Americans think, act, and work, the most profound have been the changes in family structure. Hodgkinson[6] reported that "nearly one-third of the nation's children were at risk of school failure before they enter kindergarten." His studies highlight the spectacular changes that have taken place in the conditions for children during the past several decades. His findings included the following:

- Since 1987, nearly one-fourth of all preschool children in the United States have been in poverty.
- At least two million school-age children have no adult supervision after school. Two million more are being reared by *neither* parent.
- Between 50,000 and 200,000 children are homeless on any given night.
- Mothers addicted to cocaine during their pregnancy give birth to about 350,000 babies per year. Many of these children suffer from severe learning disabilities.
- Approximately 15 million children are being raised by single mothers who make less than $11,400 per year.
- There were 2.2 million reports of child abuse or neglect during 1987—triple the number from 1976.

These alarming statistics point out that children in America are fast becoming an endangered species; it will take the combined efforts of schools and other social service agencies to reverse the conditions created in a society that apparently lacks the knowledge or will to deal with its problems. These figures have profound implications for school. According to Hodgkinson,[7] "schools will be responsible for education increasing numbers of the kinds of students they have found most difficult to teach in the past. More children will be entering school from minority and poverty backgrounds, single-parent households, and homes in which the parents are not married. . . . These changes in socio-economic backgrounds of students will place unprecedented demands on the schools."

One consequence of this cultural shift has manifested itself as increased pressure on schools and other social agencies to perform some of the functions formerly provided by the home. For example, because of a lack of adequate skills on the part of a large segment of parents, schools may need to invest more time with entering students to teach such basic skills as language and identification of letters, colors, and numbers. Schools have also become the breakfast and lunch place for many children who lack access to proper nutrition at home. Finally, many schools will continue to provide afterschool care for children who might otherwise leave classes at the end of the day to return to empty houses.

Hodgkinson's work points to deteriorating conditions for approximately one-third of the nation's children. He states that "although America's best students are on a par with the world's best, ours is undoubtedly the worst 'bottom third' in any of the industrialized democracies."[8] These conditions must not be allowed to remain. When such conditions exist for large portions of the general population, they create long-term negative impacts on the welfare of the entire nation.

The Superintendent and Students

In 1993 the American Association of School Administrators (AASA) developed a set of professional standards for the school superintendency. Introductory statements indicated, "to a great extent, the quality of America's schools depends on the effectiveness of school superintendents. . . . their vision and performance must focus on creating schools that will inspire our children to become successful, caring, Americans, capable of becoming contributing citizens of the world."[9] In all, eight standards were developed to serve as a framework to define the role of the superintendency and to help measure its effectiveness (see Figure 15.1). While it is clear that children are at the heart of the work of the superintendent, it is also clear that the job involves regular contact with a wide array of other audiences: mostly other policymakers, business leaders, parents, citizens, and professional educators. Even if there is little day-to-day or direct contact with children, the superintendent must be an expert on children, how they learn and develop, and the conditions that affect their lives. In actuality, the superintendent devotes a major portion of his or her time to work on behalf of students but may have precious little time to be with them.

The National School Boards Association (NSBA), in collaboration with the AASA, developed a publication to explain the roles and relationships of school boards and superintendents. One of the statements from that work read, "realizing that schools alone are unable to meet every need, the board and superintendent must work together with families, community organizations, and other public and private agencies to for the benefit of the whole child and the entire community."[10] Once again, students were mentioned as the focus of the work of boards and superintendents, but nothing indicated it was in the purview of either party to meet regularly with students. So it is: school leaders are focused on the welfare of students, but the actual teaching and working with students falls to other professional educators. This seems to be the way things work. And so, it falls to the superintendent to be the chief advocate for children as they pursue an education in the public schools. One of the principles that should guide the work of the superintendent is to do what is best for children. This guiding principle serves as a focal point for educational decisions.

When superintendents plan for changes in school programs and services, they must be constantly aware of the conditions faced by families and children. Traditionally, schools were organized to teach youngsters to read, write, and compute, but changes in the larger society have changed that role. While schools continue to teach reading, writing, and arithmetic, they also have become providers of child care, food service, health care, and counseling services for school-age youth and, in some cases, the families of children and youth. The role of general care provider coupled with the growing educational offerings for disabled youth has changed the landscape of the traditional K–12 school district.

Already-scarce resources for schooling have been spread thinner to meet the diverse and increasing demands of children from dysfunctional homes or poverty. Yet when appeals are made by school officials to increase the amount of resources available from local and state sources, they have resulted in public outcries to cut school spending. At the same time, politicians and special interest groups call for a complete reform of education to stimulate the productivity of the American economy. These conditions cause one to wonder if citizens are unaware or simply do not care about the conditions that face many children in America.

The superintendent must resolve to remain focused on the mission of the school. Conceptually, schools are organizations designed to serve the educational needs of youth. The espoused educational theory implies that schools are places where all children can learn, regardless of their social, economic, racial, or ethnic backgrounds. It suggests that schools should be provided with reasonable resources to accomplish their task and that those resources will be invested in caring, well-educated teachers and administrators, effective learning materials, and safe, modern facilities. In many educational settings the theory, as practiced, finds children grouped by age or ability, a lack of educational resources due to local economic constraints, and school facilities that have been neglected. If the dream of an education for children is to be realized, schools must change. Yet as organizations, schools have been slow to change. As the demands for change intensify, school leaders will be faced with a variety of decisions about school structure and the role of the schools as service providers for children, youth, and families.

The future offers many opportunities for and threats to schools. Opportunities are available to integrate the services of schools with social service and health agencies so that families and children can obtain multiple services in a single location. With involvement from parents and the larger community, schools have an opportunity to define new levels of service through partnerships with business and the community. On the other hand, decreasing financial and emotional support from school district patrons and state and federal governments threaten the services that schools can and should provide. As serious as that lack of support may become, it is tradition and an unwillingness or inability to acknowledge changes in social conditions and demographics that are perhaps the greatest threats to schools and consequently to children and youth. The school superintendent is responsible for communicating the needs of children and youth to the community and organizing the resources of the school to meet the needs of all students.

In 1993, the American Association of School Administrators developed Professional Standards for the Superintendency to inform practitioners, university preparation programs, accreditation agencies, and school boards about the roles and responsibilities of the school superintendent. The are aimed at the development of effective school systems to serve children.

Standard 1: Leadership and District Culture

Major Indicator:

The school superintendent must demonstrate executive leadership through the development of a shared vision that guides the direction of the school district.

Relationship to student needs:

Sets academic standards for students, empowers others to reach high levels of performance, encourages diversity, builds self-esteem in staff and students.

Standard 2: Policy and Governance

Major Indicator:

The school superintendent works with the board of education to develop sound policies and standards for the school district.

Relationship to student needs:

Defines procedures and policies to implement programs for students

Standard 3: Communications and Community Relations

Major Indicator:

The school superintendent communicates the mission and priorities of the school to the community and media—builds support for school programs.

Relationship to student needs:

The superintendent works to persuade the community to support initiatives that contribute to the welfare of students.

Standard 4: Organizational Management

Major Indicator:

The superintendent collects and organizes data to develop priorities for the school district—includes budgeting, planning, delegating, and empowering.

FIGURE 15–1   Professional Standards for the Superintendency

SOURCE: Excerpted from the American Association of School Administrators, 1801 North Moore Street, Arlington, Virginia 22209; (709) 875-0748.

Organizing Schools to Meet the Needs of Students

Equipped with information and knowledge about rapidly changing societal conditions, the needs of youth, and the resources available for educational and related services, the school superintendent bears the obligation to organize the schools to meet the needs of today's children and families. Superintendents must exercise great care to ensure that the organizations that are created will serve to enhance the capacity of students to learn rather than simply the ability to control the student. Roth,[11] writing about positive and negative aspects of modern educational institutions, stated, "the task of creating rational, autonomous persons falls initially to pedagogical institutions. Their goal is to produce young bodies and minds that are self-governing; failing that they try to make their graduates governable." As the superinten-

Relationship to student needs:

The superintendent develops plans to acquire and use resources in such a way to ensure successful learning programs for students.

Standard 5: Curriculum Planning and Development

Major Indicator:

The superintendent designs a curriculum that enhances teaching and learning.

Relationship to student needs:

Creates programs that are appropriate for the age and developmental levels of students and provides a means to measure the effectiveness of the programs as they apply to student learning.

Standard 6: Instructional Management

Major Indicator:

The superintendent demonstrates knowledge of instructional management and uses research to maximize results for students.

Relationship to student needs:

Deals with classroom management, teaching methodologies, assessment of student progress, use of resources to support learner outcomes.

Standard 7: Human Resources Management

Major Indicator:

The superintendent is responsible for staff development, staff evaluation, staff compensation packages—all aimed at improved performance.

Relationship to student needs:

Students benefit by working with a well educated, motivated, and satisfied professional staff.

Standard 8: Values and Ethics of Leadership

Major Indicator:

The superintendent serves as a model for appropriate behavior, values, and ethics—moral leadership. Also knows the role of education in a democratic society.

Relationship to student needs:

The superintendent can balance complex community request so they benefit all students—has an opportunity to serve as a role model for ethical behavior.

---

dent and his or her staff prepare to structure the school organization to best serve the needs of students, it is suggested that the following steps be considered:

1. Review the current conditions in the school district. (This information is available from local and state industrial development corporations, the local chamber of commerce, the Census Bureau, and city and county government officials.)

   a. Collect and analyze data about the community: levels of employment, stability of the population, job development/new business starts, the capacity of the community to generate revenue from sales/income/property tax, availability of adequate housing, construction activity.
   b. Meet with business and civic leaders to verify and seek clarification of the data.

2. Conduct a review of the educational program offered by the school district. (It is suggested that this activity be completed on an annual or biannual basis.)

a. Review how well the program is articulated from the primary through the secondary levels.
b. Be aware of how the needs of all learners are being met. For example, determine if alternative programs are available for students who are learning disabled and for those who are academically talented. Search for evidence of tracking of students.
c. Examine the program for breadth and depth. This process may uncover areas in need of additional programming and classes that are no longer applicable.
d. Utilize the current research on school organization, program offerings, and skills needed in the work place as a guide for the evaluation of the existing program in your school.

3. Collect data about the levels of performance of the student body.

a. Examine the levels of achievement on state and national examinations, level of job placement after high school, drop-out data, and student attendance levels.
b. Study the participation rates in internship or work-study programs.
c. Examine the student participation rate in school-related activities: academic clubs, athletics, drama, music and other performance groups.
d. Survey students to determine their satisfaction with school.

4. Review the qualifications (expertise) of the faculty and staff.

a. The staff should be well versed in the use of technology.
b. There should be evidence that the professional staff has been involved in meaningful developmental and skill-building activities.
c. Determine whether current assignment of staff meets the needs of the school program and the students.

5. Assemble a group of staff, several board members, administrators, students, businesspersons, retired persons, parents, patrons, and other interested parties to serve as a strategic planning group or school improvement planning team. Use the data to explain the condition of the school district and ask for their assistance in planning for the current and future needs of the district and its students.

a. It is advisable to limit the size of the group to 25 or 30 people.
b. The backgrounds of the participants should be diverse, representing a variety of points of view.

6. Communicate data and plans to the faculty, staff, board, and community, and move toward implementation of the plans once they have been approved by the board of education.

The steps outlined here can be modified to suit the needs of the local district. The crucial factor in this process concerns the involvement of people who participate in the school program (students, administrators, faculty, and staff), those who benefit from the success of the school (parents, businesspeople, school district patrons, and retired people), and those responsible for developing educational policy (school board members and the superintendent).

During the planning process it is always wise to investigate educational settings that provide alternatives to the traditionally organized school. It is recognized that all children and youth do not and cannot learn in the same manner or in the same type of setting. Some students, particularly those who are disenfranchised from mainstream society, may experience success if their educational program is directly linked to a work-study program or their school is an alternative educational facility. Schools were created to serve students; the superintendent must be aware that several different programs and organizational structures may be needed to fulfill that obligation.

Many sources of data are available to the superintendent as he or she makes plans for the current and future needs of students. There is a constant stream of research from colleges and universities, professional associations, business groups, and state and federal sources. A report released by the Secretaries Commission on Achieving Necessary Skills (SCANS) is an example of the type of information that can assist school leaders in effective program planning. The Commission was asked to "define the skills necessary for employment, propose acceptable levels of proficiency, suggest effective ways to assess proficiency, and develop a dissemination strategy for the nation's schools, businesses, and homes."[12] The report indicated that schools were expected to do more than prepare people for work, but SCANS was directed to study only that part of education that prepared young people to take their place in the work force. It was also mentioned that the report should not be construed as calling for a "narrow, work-focused education."[13] While its authors focused on the student as a potential worker, they acknowledged schools had a responsibility to prepare students for all areas of life.

The SCANS report listed five competencies that were valued in the work place and suggested ways the school could assist students to develop those competencies (see Figure 15–2). Along with the SCANS report, there are numerous other reports and research studies that can be used by school leaders to help establish frameworks for the educational programs for students.

Another technique used to examine the capacity of the organization to meet the needs of students is to study how decisions are made in the organization and who is involved in making them. An organization that is highly centralized may not be able to respond effectively to the needs of students at the classroom level. The reason for this is simple: if the executive

---

1. **Workers must know how to identify, organize, plan, and allocate resources.** The resources most commonly used by workers were time, money, materials and facilities, and human resources.
2. **Workers must possess interpersonal skills.** Listed among the interpersonal competencies were participation as a team member, helping teach a new skill to others, building relationships with clients and customers by providing service, exercising leadership, ability to negotiate, and ability to work with diversity.
3. **Workers must be capable of acquiring and using information.** The competencies included acquisition, maintenance, interpretation, and communication of information. Use of the computer to process information was listed as a necessary skill.
4. **Workers must understand complex interrelationship.** The capacity to understand systems and see the "big picture" were listed as major workplace competencies.
5. **Workers must be able to use a variety of technologies.** An understanding of the technologies available in the workplace and how to select appropriate technologies to accomplish a task were identified as key competencies.

FIGURE 15–2   Five Competencies for Work (as identified by SCANS)

SOURCE: Adapted from U.S. Department of Labor, *What Work Requires of Schools: A SCANS Report for America 2000* (Washington, D.C.: U.S. DOL, 1991).

leader is not involved with children on a day-to-day basis, he or she may lack critical data or information about individual students. Clearly, teachers and principals are in a better position to respond to student needs. A possible solution is to create a more open organization that allows more people to be involved in the process of educational decision making.

Some schools have implemented site-based decision-making programs that call for faculty and staff to make important educational decisions at the building and classroom levels. Lunenburg and Ornstein[14] described site-based management as "a change in how a school district is structured, that is, how authority and responsibilities are shared between the district and its schools." Under this model, the individual school building becomes the site for school improvement. Principals and teachers, while still responsible for accomplishing the district's mission, are provided with autonomy to arrive at decisions for how to best address the needs of students in their building. This might involve participation by parents and students in decisions that affect the education of children. While the superintendent and his or her staff continue to serve as the architects for school improvement at the district level, they also become resources to assist the buildings to meet the needs of their unique populations.

This organizational shift can be a positive influence on student progress while building a sense of professionalism for teachers and building-level administrators. Newman[15] reminds us that "a site-based management structure . . . gives no assurance that the commitment will be exercised toward any particular educational vision." For this reason, it is crucial to support the mission of the school with strategies designed to enhance student success. In this case, schools that implement participatory management models should be able to tie that concept to school improvement and student success.

Under a site-based decision-making model, one must determine where the various types of decisions for the organization will be made. For example, the educational decisions that affect students logically are made by the experts nearest to the students: classroom teachers, paraprofessionals, and principals. At the district level, school administrators will continue to make decisions about overall district budgets, compliance with state and federal statutes, legal issues, school boundaries, school district policies, and many other organizational issues. The point is that the superintendent can have a positive impact on student learning by organizing the district to function so that the mission of the school is best facilitated. In this way, the superintendent utilizes executive leadership skills to empower those who work with the school district to benefit the students.

There are many ways to examine the school as an organization and to determine how it can better serve the needs of students. Resources should be organized so that they facilitate the mission: to produce young minds that are self-governing.

Staffing the School for Student Success

Knezevich[16] stated, "professional personnel stimulate pupil learning, translate instructional plans and strategies into reality, and influence the realization of predetermined educational objectives." The challenge facing the superintendent is to search for and retain teachers who possess the qualities of teaching that positively influence student learning. There are excellent research findings available to school administrators regarding the qualities of effective teachers, teaching, and classrooms. Additionally, there are tools available to assist school administrators with the selection process.

Walberg,[17] citing the work of Miller and Dollard, wrote about the psychological elements of teaching: cues, engagement, corrective feedback, and reinforcement.

> Teachers who provide cues show their students what is to be learned and provide explanations about how students can learn it.

> Engagement is a technique used by teachers to actively involve their students in the learning process; active learning and cooperative learning are examples.

> Teachers who provide corrective feedback rapidly detect student errors and provide on-the-spot strategies to help students correct them.

> Finally, reinforcement is a strategy used to recognize and reward student accomplishment. Teachers use a variety of strategies, such as written or verbal praise or allowance for contingent activities, to reinforce positive outcomes.

In their search for professional staff, superintendents should be aware of the psychological elements of teaching and try to discover if those characteristics are possessed by the candidates they interview. While information about these dimensions may not be included in credentials, they can be identified through the use of structured interviews or by requiring the candidate to participate in a microteaching exercise as part of the interview process.

Another strategy to assist superintendents in the identification of professional staff who are dedicated to student learning is to review the research findings about exemplary teachers and exemplary classrooms. Tobin and Fraser[18] studied science and mathematics teachers in an effort to identify the characteristics of exemplary teachers. They asserted that teachers in exemplary classrooms displayed the following characteristics:

1. Exemplary teachers used management strategies and practices that facilitated student engagement.

   These classroom were characterized by a high level of managerial efficiency; teachers moved around the classroom,

   spoke with students, and actively monitored student behavior.

2. Exemplary teachers used strategies that encouraged students to participate in the learning activities.

   Teachers provided a safe environment for students in the sense that students were never embarrassed when they provided incorrect responses, and student involvement was maximized.

3. Exemplary teachers used strategies to increase the understanding of student in the subject area (in this case, science and mathematics).

   Students were involved in activities that helped them construct an understanding of the subject matter.

4. Exemplary teachers maintained a favorable learning environment in the classroom.

Students perceived the classrooms of exemplary teachers to be environments where expectations were known, there was a clarity of rules, and the teacher was affiliated with the students.

There are a number of staff selection strategies available to school leaders. As mentioned, validated, structured interviews provide superintendents with a profile of a teaching characteristics as compared with an exemplary profile. The procedure for this type of interview involves asking the candidate a series of thematic questions and evaluating the responses by comparing them with the validated profile.

It was also mentioned that school administrators could observe a candidate's teaching expertise by having them participate in a microteaching exercise. Microteaching involves the candidate in the preparation and teaching of a simulated lesson. The lesson is usually videotaped and critiqued in accordance with the elements of effective teaching.

Regardless of the techniques used in the selection of faculty and staff, the superintendent must assign this activity a high priority. The acquisition and retention of exemplary teachers is one way the superintendent can ensure that the needs of students are being met.

Allocation of Resources

The superintendent is ultimately responsible for the proper allocation of resources within the district: materials, equipment, money, and personnel. This process is random, at best, if the district lacks a shared vision or mission to provide direction for such decisions. We have mentioned that the superintendent must provide visionary leadership for the district. This means that he or she promotes and shares goals or objectives that focus on potential outcomes for students. When the mission of the school is student-centered and the vision for the school assumes that students will graduate with knowledge, skills, and attitudes that enable them to perform in a variety of societal and work-related roles, resources can be allocated in a rational manner.

Focus is the key word in the process of resource allocation. When organizations, such as school districts, focus on their priorities, scarce resources will likely be properly distributed. A natural competition for scarce resources seems to develop during almost every budgeting cycle. Because most school districts do not have the resources to do everything they would like, the available resources must be distributed as equitably as possible. Without a focus, it is possible for the "squeaky wheel" syndrome to prevail: those who complain the loudest about the lack of resources for their programs can sway the allocation process in their direction. If this is the prevalent practice in a district, an uneven system is created.

On the other hand, when a superintendent is guided by a clear mission statement, the allocation process can be focused and fair. The concept is simple: the highest priorities of the school district should be the first to receive resources. Ideally, the highest priority for schools is the welfare of its students, and within that priority, the academic program must take precedence over all other wants and needs. While the idea may seem simple, many intervening variables complicate the distribution of scarce resources. State and federal mandates, necessary operations and maintenance items, a safe transportation system, and other appurtenant items compete for dollars that could be channeled toward materials, equipment, and staff to serve students.

The struggle over how to allocate scarce resources will remain a problem for superintendents. However, if he or she is focused on students and has developed a like sense of vision throughout the community, the process can be rational and beneficial for students.

Student Safety and Welfare

Johnson and Immerwahr[19] stated, "For most Americans, three images sum up their sense that the public schools are failing: metal detectors in high schools, students outside schools smoking during school hours, and supermarket checkout clerks who can't make change. People's fears and frustrations, and their strongest desires for progress, center on these three areas: safety, order, and the basics." This section will briefly address the problem of student safety and order in the schools.

The health and safety of students is a major concern of educators. For example, most states require students to be inoculated against major childhood diseases prior to their entry into school. School nurses and classroom teachers monitor the health of students throughout the year. Nearly every school has a well-articulated health education and physical education program to help instruct students about proper nutrition, the avoidance of harmful influences such as alcohol and other drugs, and the benefits of exercise and rest. In the past, student safety and welfare issues were confined to proper playground behavior, classroom courtesy, and the items just mentioned. More recently, however, these issues have been overshadowed by increased violence in and near the school and an increase in the number of children who are victims of physical, emotional, and sexual abuse. The schoolhouse, once a safe haven from much of the violence that existed in the larger society, has become a place where extraordinary measures have been implemented to ensure the safety of students. Another line has been added to the job description of school leaders: provide a safe environment for students where they can be protected from the violence that dominates American society.

Violence in Schools

In 1979 Feldhusen[20] reported the findings of The United States Senate Subcommittee to Investigate Juvenile Delinquency. It was the conclusion of the subcommittee that "there is abundant evidence that a significant and growing number of schools in urban, suburban, and rural areas are confronting serious levels of violence and vandalism." The report indicated that the number of assaults on teachers and students, seizure of weapons by school authorities, and the incidence of rape, robbery, and vandalism had increased dramatically between 1970 and 1973. This was yet another sign that acts of violence and vandalism had continued an upward spiral through the 1960s and into the early 1970s.

In 1994, Prothrow-Stith[21] stated, "many of our public schools, once considered safe, are devastated and destroyed by violence. According to the U.S. Department of Justice, almost 3 million crimes occur on or near school property each year. . . . Violence is the second leading cause of death for America's students." There is little doubt that violence has become an all too normal occurrence in contemporary society. The causes for violent behavior have been speculated about and researched for quite some time: drugs, civil unrest, poverty, the disintegration of the family, and homelessness, to name a few. It is a condition of the larger society that has come to rest in the schools. The job of the superintendent and staff is to define strategies for dealing with these phenomena.

School administrators play a key role in the implementation of school-based violence prevention programs. Prothrow-Stith provided a list of components of an effective violence prevention program. Some of her suggestions were "teaching social skills including problem solving [she also suggested a companion course for parents], a peer-mentoring program, conflict resolution programs; after-school activities, parenting courses for teens, gang and drug prevention programs, mentoring and job training programs, and peer leadership and peer-mediation programs."[22]

Hunter[23] addressed the dilemma that faces school administrators: "The trick for school administrators and politicals is to make schools significantly safer than the streets leading to the schoolhouse door while maintaining and open atmosphere that emphasizes learning and citizenship skills." Increased security and student control is not the panacea. The violence must be stopped, not merely controlled or maintained at its current level. Meanwhile, superintendents have committed scarce resources to violence prevention and security that could otherwise be allocated to academic areas. However, the commitment of the superintendent and other educators to the safety of students is vital.

While violence is a general, societal concern, it would be unwise to assume that all schools struggle with gangs, drugs, rape, robbery, and assault. While these may be all too prevalent, most schools continue to be safe places for children and teachers. The job of the superintendent, as he or she carries out a commitment to students, is to ensure students and their families that schools remain safe. Where they do not enjoy such status, the superintendent is responsible to enlist the support of parents, patrons, and the business and professional communities to help turn the problem around. The school cannot solve this problem alone—it is a community issue and a community response is required.

Other Student-related Issues

This chapter has centered on the superintendent's major responsibilities for students under such headings as the organization of the school, planning and implementing the educational program for students, the acquisition and retention of professional staff, the allocation of scarce resources for student programming, and student safety and welfare. While it is hoped those topics raise questions and stimulate dialogue, attention must also be paid to several other issues regarding the student personnel program. These issues include student accounting, ensuring student rights and responsibilities, and opportunities for the superintendent to have face-to-face involvement with students.

Accounting for Student Personnel

All potential school-age children who reside within a school district must be identified, registered, and prepared to be admitted to the public school. Even if students receive educational services from private schools or in home school settings, such an accounting must be made. Education statutes in most states require the public school to conduct a census of school-age children and maintain records of the same. Because of compulsory attendance laws, the census is a key record for school officials.

Second, students with special needs or those who require specialized learning environments must be identified and informed about programs designed to meet their needs. This process, generally referred to as "child find," requires school officials to survey households and families to ascertain whether they have children who might qualify for specialized services. Schools are responsible for the identification of children from birth through preschool age who qualify for specialized educational services.

Third, once students have been identified and have entered a school program, the school is responsible for the maintenance of records of membership and attendance. These records indicate the regularity with which students attend school and help alert school officials to potential problems faced by students. For example, when school officials observe irregular student attendance or sustained periods of student absence, they will investigate the situation to try to determine if the student is ill, in danger, has run away, or has moved to another school or community. This portion of the student accounting system is critical in helping to monitor the well-being of students.

In some states the amount of revenue received from state sources through the various state aid formulas may be based on average student membership and average daily attendance of students. Accurate records help ensure an adequate revenue flow.

Finally, excellent student accounting systems assist the superintendent and other school personnel in planning for program expansion, facilities improvements, and the hiring of faculty and staff. Because of the transient nature of many families, student accounting is a difficult task. It is, however, an integral part of the superintendent's database.

The Nature of Students, Their Rights, and Responsibilities

Superintendents should know that there is such a thing as a student culture. This is especially true for teenagers—junior high–middle school and high school students. Canaan[24] reported, "teenagers in our society have developed their own culture (usually referred to as a subculture) which includes a set of expectations about how to behave as students and how to behave as teenagers." This teenage subculture has developed a set of norms, which do not always agree with the norms of adults, and the subculture is not uniform; that is, there are multiple groupings within the subculture. Canaan pointed out that while adults invented the schools to help initiate the young into society, teenagers have learned how to manipulate the system and use it to their own ends.

Generally, the junior high–middle school subculture breaks down into several groups: those who are athletically or socially skilled, those who conform to both the teenage subculture and the adult subculture, and those who exhibit socially inappropriate behaviors. High school students tend to divide into two major groups. The first group is composed of those who excel in extracurricular activities and abide by adult rules inside the school but defy adult values outside of school. The second major group is made up of teenagers who typically defy adult values inside and outside of school. These subcultures and the actions of their members add yet another interesting perspective to the job of educators. As superintendents and other educators make plans for the enculturation of the young, they must be aware of these subcultures and deal with the reality of their actions.

Planning for the Consequences of Student Misbehavior

Related to the earlier discussion of student behavior, safety, and violence in school, administrators must define and establish rules and regulations for student conduct. School boards and superintendents establish board policies related to student conduct. Typically, the disciplinary actions taken against students are administered at the building level. However, in some circumstances students or their parents may appeal a discipline-related decision made at the principal's level. A hearing officer is then appointed to listen to the appeal and suggest a course of action. If the student or parent is not satisfied with the outcome from the hearing officer, the superintendent is asked to examine the case and provide a ruling. In these cases the superintendent must be conversant with the rights and responsibilities of students and the legal implications of disciplinary actions. A well-established set of school board policies related to student conduct is essential for the well-being of students and teachers.

Face-to-Face Involvement with Students

Cunningham expressed the work of the superintendent in terms of capacity building: developing a strong culture in the community.[25] One of the key elements of that culture was face-to-face involvement of appropriate stakeholders. We assume students are part of the group of appropriate stakeholders and as such must have access to policymakers at the local level. In truth, students may be best served by teachers, parents, and principals who represent their best interests in the policy-making arenas. However, superintendents likely will want and need more than passing contact with students if they are to be their advocates in board rooms and legislative chambers. Some of the strategies superintendents use to have face-to-face involvement with students follow:

- *Student Advisory Committees:*   Students selected by their teachers or by classmates can provide the superintendent with excellent information about school from the student perspective. Committees can meet once each month and rotate membership every six months to provide an opportunity for as many students as possible.
- *The Superintendent as Guest Teacher:*   Because most superintendents have had teaching experiences, they can lead a dialogue or teach a unit in a classroom and gain valuable information about the condition of students in the process.
- *Reading to Children:*   One of the most pleasant ways for the chief executive officer of the school to gain face-to-face contact with primary students is to read his or their favorite book to them in their classroom. This activity serves as a great reminder to superintendents of why they chose education as a profession.
- *Classroom Visitations:*   Regular, scheduled visits to school buildings, eating lunch with students and teachers, and visiting classrooms helps the superintendent keep his or her perspective about students and teaching and lets faculty and students know that the superintendent is interested in and supportive of them.
- *Attendance at Student Programs and Contests:*   Visibility at student events communicates the superintendent's belief in student activities and provides recognition for the efforts students expend beyond or in conjunction with classroom activities. Students pos-

sess a variety of talents and gifts that they display through the activity programs offered by the school. They appreciate the attention of the superintendent to their activities.

- *Include Students on District Committees:*   The superintendent should include students on district-level committees that deal with strategic planning or goal setting. The student perspective is crucial to planning efforts.

Each school superintendent must identify a system that enables him or her to engage in dialogue with students. While this activity may not be possible every day, it is possible to arrange some time to talk with or listen to students. The time invested with students will assist the superintendent focus on the importance of the role they serve.

Summary

The school superintendency is an executive position. In education, school executives are responsible to a variety of publics: parents, business, the community at large, and internal publics—including students. The work of the superintendent is focused on the safety and welfare of students, the programs created to ensure their success, and the allocation of scarce resources to meet the needs of students. The superintendent must be an expert on children and youth and in that role must understand the variety of environments from which the students come and the conditions they face.

School executives, like their counterparts in business and other professional arenas, are responsible for communicating vision and direction for the organization. To do that, they have to know how things work and what must be done to ensure the organization is in working order. Superintendents must be pupils of the organizations they lead. They have to know how to structure the organization to perform at peak levels for its clients—the students and families of the community. They also have to know when and how to make necessary changes in the structure of the organization.

If the superintendent began at the beginning, that is, developed a shared vision and direction so the school district could meet its obligations to students, the process of allocating resources can be based on those obligations. Usually, the goals and objectives of schools are framed in terms of student outcomes, so that the superintendent can justify requests for resources based on the mission of the district.

Safety for students and staff is a growing concern of school leaders. The superintendent must be prepared to address issues related to violence in the schools and student discipline. This issue has received widespread attention from the media and has raised major concerns among parents and citizens. Major strategies for resolving the issue will be forthcoming only if schools, communities, and other social agencies combine forces to address the situation.

Finally, the superintendent needs to see the faces and hear the voices of the youngsters for whose benefit he or she is working. Dialogue with students can be gained through classroom visitations, inviting students to participate on district-level committees, and forming a student advisory committee for the superintendent. Regardless of school district size or the complexity of the organization, superintendents must maintain contact with all clients of the school, and that emphatically includes students.

Discussion Questions

1. The superintendent's role requires expertise in a many areas. How does a person develop the necessary knowledge to be able to understand and deal with the conditions and subculture of youth?

2. What assistance does a superintendent need to organize schools so that they consistently meets the needs of children and youth, fulfill their obligation to the general society, and satisfy the tax-paying public?

3. Assume that the school district decided to combine efforts with other providers of social, health and welfare, and educational services. What would be the first steps you would take in organizing this effort?

4. Citizens have many occasions to read or listen to media reports about the failure of school and students. How does the superintendent provide citizens with access to the good news about schools and students?

5. What are some methodologies you, as a superintendent, would employ to involve yourself with elementary and secondary students?

6. To what extent do you believe that schools should be obligated to provide alternative settings or programs for students who cannot or will not conform to the traditional educational setting?

7. What is the purpose and function of schools? How would you design the school system to fulfill that purpose and function?

CASE 15.1   Whose Purpose and Function?

The College View School District has enlisted the assistance of community members, students, staff, and business and professional people to help design a school improvement plan. The team consists of 30 people, including 3 students and 3 retired citizens in the community.

The students, when asked to characterize their school day, stated that it involved a lot of sitting and listening to adults lecture about a particular subject with little or no time for them to become participants in the process. The students indicate that, for the most part, classes are boring, but school is a place to socialize with others of their age group. When classes were over, many of them engaged in athletics or participated in clubs, which they found fulfilling.

The retirees responded that they were disappointed by the attitudes of young people these days. They reminded the planning team, "we pay high taxes for an education that is apparently ignored by young people, and we are tired of seeing our money wasted."

Seeing an opening, two of the businesspeople on the planning team asked why schools were organized the way they were and asked for clarification about the education of students with special needs. "What do we hope to gain, as a society, by trying to educate people who may prove to be marginal in the productivity?" one of them asked. "Why aren't students and schools more like they were when I was in school?"

Questions

1.   Assume you are the superintendent of the College View School District. What would be your response to the commentary provided by each of the three groups: students, retired citizens, and businesspeople?

2. Because the purpose of the planning team was school improvement, what questions would you like to ask the team members?
3. How would you explain the role of the school and its obligation to students?
4. How would you propose to educate the retirees and businesspeople about students and their successes?

Inbasket Exercises

INBASKET 15.1

Opportunity Knocks?

The College View School District was informed that it has been nominated as the major demonstration site for a new "school-to-work" curriculum developed by the State University. The curriculum is designed to help students make a successful transition from school to the work place by teaching them about the skills needed in the job market and providing them with opportunities for internships prior to high school graduation. The university has obtained an implementation grant to pay for teacher training, curriculum material, equipment, and evaluation of the project.

The project involves a time commitment of six years on the part of the school district and the university. The results of the project will be published and could provide the district and the university with national recognition.

Response

As superintendent, prepare a list of questions you will need to answer before you can provide a response to the university. Your list should include, but not be limited to, the following:

a. Who will need to contacted about the project?
b. What are the likely impacts of this project? Who and what will affected by an affirmative or negative decision?
c. What are the implications of the project for staff and students?
d. Does the intent of the project match with the mission of the school?
e. Will students likely benefit from participation in this project? How many students might it affect? Will it enhance their opportunities after high school graduation?

INBASKET 15.2

Limitations

The College View Athletic Boosters have petitioned the board of education to buy new lights for the football field. The cost of the lighting package is estimated to be $85,000, not including modifications that will likely have to made to the site. The boosters have been successful in raising $35,000 from the community and will contribute that amount to the school district, but they want the board to pay the remainder of the expense.

There has been no allowance made in the current budget for football field lights; as a matter of fact, it was not even mentioned as a priority in the five-year budget planning document. The district desperately needs additional science and math equipment at the high school and lacks proper facilities for drama at the middle school level.

Response

Decide on the course of action you will take, and prepare a response to the athletic boosters. Provide a rationale for your decision.

Notes

1. Roald Campbell, Laverne Cunningham, Raphael Nystrand, and Michael Usdan, eds., *The Organization and Control of American Schools,* 6th ed. (Columbus, Ohio: Merrill, 1990), p. 22.

2. Committee for Economic Development, Research and Policy Committee, *Investing in Our Children: Business and the Public Schools* (New York: Committee for Economic Development, 1985), p. 1.

3. Thomas Glass, *The 1992 Study of the American School: America's Education Leaders in a Time of Reform* (Arlington, Va.: American Association of School Administrators, 1992).

4. Jonathan Kozol, *Savage Inequalities: Children in America's Schools* (New York: Crown, 1991).

5. Michael Kirst and Milbrey McLaughlin, in *Educational Leadership and the Changing Contexts of Families, Communities, and Schools,* ed. by Brad Mitchell and Laverne Cunningham (Chicago: National Society for the Study of Education, 1990), p. 87.

6. Harold Hodgkinson, "Reform versus Reality," *Phi Delta Kappan,* 73(1) (September 1991): p. 10.

7. Harold Hodgkinson, in *The Organization and Control of American Schools,* p. 23. (See n. 1.)

8. Harold Hodgkinson, "Reform versus Reality," p. 10.

9. American Association of School Administrators, *Professional Standards for the Superintendency* (Arlington, Va.: AASA, 1993), p. 3.

10. National School Boards Association, "NASB and AASA Sketch Your Roles," *American School Board Journal,* 181 (June 1993): p. 20.

11. Joseph Roth, "Of What Help Is He? A Review of *Focault and Education*," *American Educational Research Journal,* 29 (June 1992): p. 692.

12. U.S. Department of Labor, *What Work Requires of Schools: A SCANS Report for America 2000* (Washington, D.C.: U.S. DOL, 1991).

13. Ibid., p. v.

14. Fred Lunenburg and Allan Ornstein, *Educational Administration: Concepts and Practices* (Belmont, Calif.: Wadsworth, 1991), p. 37.

15. Fred M. Newman, "Beyond Common Sense in Educational Restructuring: The Issues of Content and Linkage," *Educational Researcher* 22 (March 1993): p. 5.

16. Stephen J. Knezevich, *Administration of Public Education: A Sourcebook for the Leadership and Management of Educational Institutions* (New York: Harper and Row, 1984), p. 377.

17. Herbert Walberg, in *Effective Teaching: Current Research,* ed. by Hersholt C. Waxman and Herbert Walberg (Berkeley, Calif.: McCutchan, 1991), pp. 33–62.

18. Kenneth Tobin and Barry Fraser, in *Effective Teaching: Current Research,* pp. 217–236.

19. Jean Johnson and John Immerwahr, *First Things First: What Americans Expect from the Public Schools* (New York: Public Agenda, 1994), p. 10.

20. John Feldhusen, "Problems of Student Behavior in Secondary Schools," in Seventy-eighth yearbook of the National Society for the Study of Education, *Classroom Management,* ed. by Daniel Duke (Chicago: National Society for the Study of Education, 1979), p. 218.

21. Deborah Prothrow-Stith, "Building Violence Prevention into the Curriculum: A Physician-Administrator Applies a Public Health Model to Schools," *School Administrator,* 4(51) (April 1994): pp. 8–9.

22. Ibid., p. 11.

23. Bruce Hunter, "Making Schools Safer than the Rest of Society," *School Administrator,* 4(51) (April 1994): p. 33.

24. J. Canaan, in *Educational Governance and Administration,* 3rd ed., ed by Thomas Sergiovanni, Martin Burlingame, Fred Coombs, and Paul Thurston (Boston: Allyn and Bacon, 1992), p. 300.

25. William G. Cunningham, "The Way We Do Things around Here," *School Administrator,* 11(51) (November 1994): p. 25.

Chapter *16*

The School Superintendent and School District Publics

Ralph Waldo Emerson said, "it is a luxury to be understood." While it may be a luxury, it is also essential, especially when the exchange of ideas centers on education. Schools want parents and patrons to understand the principles, processes, and intended outcomes of education. The community wants the school to understand its expectations for education. Effective school–community relations programs are specifically designed to build and maintain public confidence in schools. It is critical for key audiences to receive important messages at the proper time, from a reliable source, and that they receive the message in such a way they can understand it and respond to it.

People want desperately to believe in their public institutions, especially those charged with responsibility for the education of the young. American public education, one of the most exceptional experiments the world has ever observed, has consistently demonstrated that a nation can provide effective educational services for its youth by empowering local communities to build and maintain schools and establish courses of study. When the nation was young and eager to build a literate society, public school teachers taught boys and girls to read, write, and compute. Although it has been a challenge, the efforts of the local public schools positioned Americans eventually to become world economic leaders.

Certainly, times have changed since the inception of the American public school. The world has become smaller and more interdependent. American citizens continue to be among the best educated in the world, but they certainly are not alone in that category. Other nations have accepted the challenge of universal education and have experienced great success for their efforts. As educational levels of world citizens rose, especially among people in developing nations, the economic leadership gap between the United States and other countries narrowed. Perhaps as a result of the changing world conditions, the purpose and effectiveness of American public schools have come under intense scrutiny from national politicians and a wide assortment of special interest groups. "The over-riding challenge before tomorrow's school leaders," Culbertson stated, "is . . . to help articulate and implement an educational vision for a new society."[1] One aspect of the so-called new society most likely referred to the ease and speed with which people would be able to inform each other. Almost certainly true was that people around the world would be intimately connected via electronic telecommunications. Information from almost any location could be relayed instantaneously. This global orientation presumes a citizen who is aware of the happenings in his or her region and throughout the world, and one who will demand accurate and reliable communications from many sources. A valid source of constant information is the resource that contributes to the success of individuals and organizations.

George Bernard Shaw once noted, "the greatest problem of communication is the illusion that it has been accomplished." School leaders must be able to communicate a realistic, positive vision for public education to diverse constituencies inside and outside the formal structure of the school. To ensure that the illusion that Shaw described does not come to pass, the vision for education must be continuously proclaimed. The success of that proclamation depends on several things. First, school leaders must understand and articulate a clear sense of purpose and direction for schools. Second, they must continuously expand their capacity to understand and work with a variety of internal and external audiences. Each community is unique; each has certain protocols or ways of addressing important tasks. It is incumbent on the superintendent to discover how the culture of the community operates. Finally, the chief executive officer of the school district must present honest, reliable information about the impact of instruction on student success, raise the citizens' level of consciousness about the necessity to educate all children, and advocate for an educational system that focuses on the preparation of students to be adaptable, creative, lifelong learners. The superintendent must address educational issues from the perspective of researcher, citizen of the community, teacher, student, and articulate spokesperson.

This chapter provides information about the development of relationships between schools and the community at large *and* with those who work inside the schools. It is about leading schools as political organizations and communicating about student progress. It folds together several concepts that must work in equilibrium: to accept and work with the political nature of education, and to develop legitimate systems to inform all educational stakeholders about the successes and limitations of the system.

Some of the ideas presented in the following pages are based on the Dissatisfaction Theory of Democracy.[2] In reference to the governance of schools, the theory asserts that communities elect representatives to serve on the school board because they possess similar values to those held community-wide. The board then selects a superintendent with similar values who will administer an educational program that also reflects the values of the community. When a community changes, according to the theory, differences develop between the community and its schools. The differences may be manifest in how the administration and board view changes in the larger environment, the global work place, and future skills necessary for work and living compared with the way the local environment views the same transformations. Differences may result from the way in which special interests in a community view issues such as the necessity to teach about multiculturalism, ethnic diversity, religion, or competing economic systems. If the differences become too great, the board and superintendent are generally replaced. Thus, Lutz and Merz stated, "the purpose of school/community relations is to avoid extended dissatisfaction. . . . It is not necessary to 'satisfy' each group (active and potential) that makes demands for resources, it *is* necessary to prevent things from becoming dissatisfying enough to disrupt the normal functions of the school."[3] The Dissatisfaction Theory points to the need for an excellent system of communications between the school and the community and among and between those who work in the schools. This concept applies to internal and external audiences.

The second set of ideas woven into this chapter focuses on the absolute necessity for the superintendent of schools to observe and understand the community in which he or she practices. "Knowing the public and being able to keep abreast of the community's thinking are major requirements for today's successful administrators," according to Bagin, Gallagher, and Kindred.[4] The same rule applies to the superintendent's understanding of the community within the schools—the internal audience. All great organizations have one thing in common: they have excellent relationships with their clientele. Thus, the construction of relationships is an essential task of the superintendent. He or she must develop those relationships through open, honest, and regular communication. One of the objectives for the superintendent is to facilitate process (education) and clarify conflicts (build understanding). Well-organized school–community relations programs provide the avenue for this objective to be met. This chapter emphasizes the leadership role of the superintendent in accomplishing this objective.

Culture and Community

One can observe a customary pattern or way of doing things in all communities. These customs help define the culture of the community—the way it responds to the conditions it faces. One of the elements governing the success of a superintendency is the capacity to critically observe the cultural norms of the community and put those observations to use. While it is never too late to become a critical observer, the best time to begin this activity is during the initial stages of the superintendent's tenure. It is assumed that, prior to the acceptance of the position, the superintendent did some homework on the district and the community. School leaders cannot walk blindly into a position as important as the superintendency. The following resources will provide excellent information about a community for prospective superintendents:

- *The departing administrator*—to gain his or her perspective of the school district and community.
- *Board of education minutes* for the past three to five years—to gain an understanding of the issues faced by the board and to review how the situations were handled.
- *The State Department of Education*—to determine the standing of the district in financial and curricular areas.
- *Professional education associations*—to inquire about the professional reputations of teachers and administrators in the district.
- *The editor of the local newspaper*—to review the past three to five years of "press" about the educational system, and to gain the perspective of a professional observer.

After all of these avenues and others have been explored and the prospective superintendent is offered and accepts the position, the next step is to give attention to "how things work in the community." That process requires time, observation, and asking questions. The following sections focus on several aspects of this learning process.

Learning about the Community

During the first few weeks and months on the job, the superintendent will have opportunities to become active with numerous community service organizations such as the chamber of commerce, Rotary, Lions Club, and Kiwanis, to name only a few. These organizations are usually eager to become acquainted with the superintendent; assuredly, the superintendent will be invited to speak at one or more of their regular meetings. When the superintendent addresses the service organization membership, he or she has an opportunity to ask questions and form linkages with a variety of citizens in the community. It is an excellent way to learn about how and why the membership supports the community and how they perceive their schools. Such communications also provide the school leader a forum to explain current and future conditions necessary to support a sound educational system. At this point in their tenure the superintendent should concentrate on listening, observing, and looking for common themes that arise from the various community groups.

Establish a Professional Identity

The first few months of their tenure provides time for superintendents to build a professional identity with the community and the staff. Professional identity refers to the reputation the chief school officer constructs as a result of what he or she says and does about educational matters. A successful entry into a school district is critical. It is a time to listen to what citizens and employees value. Such information assists the school leader in the construction of a solid plan for communications. In a national study of beginning superintendents, Chapman et al.[5] reported that successful entry strategies included "knowing what you want to accomplish, ability to listen to all constituencies without becoming defensive, and willingness to keep my mouth shut and listen—being a very willing student." During these critical weeks and months the superintendent also has an opportunity to assess educational changes that are likely to occur and begin to build support for the school and educational programs. For example, there may be valid and reliable information that points to a need for facility improvement, expanded academic opportunities for students, or better discipline policies; this is the time to begin to address these issues and to build coalitions. The initial several months in a school district should be used to demonstrate to the community and staff that the superintendent is an excellent manager of attention, ideas, and self. It is a time to establish a strong foundation based on communication and trust. Covey[6] applied the phrase "seek first to understand then to be understood" to these capacity-building activities.

Power Structures

All communities have power structures—a group, an individual, or an organization that "runs things" or at least tries to do so. These power structures are not listed in the Yellow Pages so that the superintendent, faculty, and staff can gain access to them. In fact, in some cases, such influentials are well hidden from public view, but nonetheless, they are real and serve as centers of authority. Such influentials possess the capacity to assist in such actions as the passage of bond elections for schoolhouse construction, to support programs for children, and to influence the election of school board members.

During the 1970s, a study of community power structures was conducted by McCarty and Ramsey.[7] The study indicated that one way to classify communities was based on the power structures present within the community. McCarty and Ramsey indicated four community types: dominated, pluralistic, factional, and inert. The power in a particular community might reside in the business community via the chamber of commerce or it might rest with a wealthy, influential family or company (dominated). In some cases, the power structure is diverse, spread throughout the community: widely distributed among rational and reasonable community groups (pluralistic), or distributed among factions who continually vie for control (factional). In each case, the power structure can and does use its authority to influence public and private institutions within the community; public education is no exception. Chapter 5 discusses this issue in detail.

Superintendents must be aware of community power structures early in their tenure. Studies reveal that the type of power structure found in a community frequently is the same as that of the school board. It is important to know how school issues might be perceived by the power structure and who to talk with about issues requiring community support. While the reality of dealing with the power structure is essential, the superintendent must also become acquainted with all of the internal and external audiences who, in some form or other, influence decisions and require ongoing communications with school district personnel.

Recognize the Diversity of Publics

The board of education and the superintendent of schools are considered the initiators of the communications process. They share the responsibility for the implementation of communication processes designed to keep employees, students, and patrons well informed about the condition of education in the community.

Schools must have the support of the community they serve. Equally important is the level of support that is present from those who work for the school district. As organizations, schools are places where professional educators and other skilled employees apply their expertise, caring for and educating children. Schools are also the academic work places of students, the first-level client of the organization. Those who work inside the school system are considered the *internal audience* of the school. This audience is as complex and diverse as the larger community in which it resides. It deserves the same level of attention and information as the community at large.

The *external audience* of the school includes parents, taxpayers, business, professional community, and so on. External audiences can be subdivided in a number of ways; however, they are customarily viewed as the people or organizations that provide financial and emotional support for the school. They have a vital interest in the success of the school. Although such audiences may not be directly involved in day-to-day instruction, many of them contribute by serving as volunteers, boosters, and providers of student internships or work stations. Even if the external public is not involved with the school on a regular basis, it does contribute to the success of the school through its tax support. It is critical for them to hear and see evidence that its money has been well invested. Thus, a program of ongoing communication is of paramount importance.

Continual communication with internal and external audiences provides them with important information about the ordinary, routine workings of the school. A second important reason for a well-developed school–community relations program is to assist all publics to recognize and deal with change. At best, change is discomforting; at worst, it is highly disruptive. Communities and their schools constantly experience changes, some small, some very dramatic. Planned changes need to be communicated early so that the publics have information about how intended changes may affect them. The results of unplanned changes, such as crisis situations or natural disasters, must be dealt with in a timely fashion so that the community has information about how to adjust to the reality of the change. In each case, internal and external audiences need information, assurance, or direction.

It is also important that the information presented to one group should be consistent with the information presented to all other groups. Cantor,[8] writing about public relations for investors, stated, "it is important for any company, large or small, to speak to all of its audiences with one voice. Information that is provided to the general public . . . should never vary in any substantial way from that stream of information being delivered to investors, prospective investors, or lenders." School leaders are wise to adopt similar guidelines. While the details of the message may vary from audience to audience, the general message must be consistent.

Develop a Communications Plan

School leaders must develop and implement a school–community relations plan if they are serious about promoting learning and building confidence in the school system. The kind of plan that is developed will depend on the size of the district and the resources it can devote to such an effort. According to Kinder,[9] the plan should be founded on the concept that "schools are very interested in and responsive to public opinion and that education should be a partnership between the school, and the community." Certainly, parents also need to be included in that partnership. The following steps provide ideas for school districts to use when developing a school–community relations program.

The first step in the plan involves the board of education. The board can support a strong school-community relations effort by developing and approving a board policy that outlines the board's philosophy on the subject and delegates the responsibility for carrying it out to the superintendent.

Next, the district should develop a school–community relations committee to act as a coordinating agency for the district's efforts. It is recommended that this committee, composed of community and school district personnel, be headed by the superintendent. The committee should be large enough to represent a variety of views, yet small enough to manage: likely 12 to 25 people.

The committee, as its first duty, should conduct a public opinion poll to determine how schools are perceived. Students, teachers, school staff, and community members must be included in the audiences to be polled. Data can be collected via telephone polls, written surveys, or personal interviews. The committee can also access information about the schools from media sources. With information from the surveys and data collected from the media, the committee can form an image of the school as perceived by the community. The committee can then begin to develop a community relations plan. A comprehensive district plan should focus on, but not be limited to, the following purposes:

1. To enhance communications with internal and external publics.

   a. Teachers, administrators, staff, and students.
   b. Parents, business and professional people, senior citizens, civic and community organizations, special interest groups with an interest in education, and alumni and friends.

2. To stimulate the quality and quantity of involvement from members of the community.

   Encourage participation at school activities, board meetings, and other district programs.

3. To encourage open, two-way communications that have the potential to lead to productive changes.

   Just as the school has information that is important for the community to receive, the community has information needed by the school. Open exchanges assist all parties.

4. To make the community aware of the mission of the school and to illustrate how that mission is accomplished.

   The community must be aware of the mission (purpose and function) of the school district and how they can support that mission. Support for the school is much easier to gather when the patrons understand what the school is attempting to do.

Each piece of the plan can be developed and refined as needed. The important thing is for the district to develop a plan and then be certain to implement it. School–community relations is an "all the time" effort, not a part-time campaign to pass a bond issue or bail the district out of a crisis. An outline for a master communications plan is shown in Figure 16–1.

Internal Audiences

In educational organizations, internal audiences are generally identified as administrators; classroom teachers and other educators (guidance personnel, media personnel, etc.); classified staff, including paraprofessionals, secretaries, custodians, and food service and

Step I.	Develop a policy to address the necessity for a school–community relations plan. The board of education should officially adopt the policy.
Step II.	Form a School–Community Relations Committee. The committee of 12 to 20 people should represent a cross section of the school and community. The superintendent should chair the group.
Step III.	Conduct a survey of the school and community to gather information about how the school is perceived by faculty, students, staff, patrons, and community members.
Step IV.	Analyze the data from the public opinion survey. Categorize the information to ascertain where the school shows strengths and weaknesses in terms of its image.
Step V.	Develop a plan to address the issues discovered from the results of the public opinion poll. Implement the plan and continue periodically to survey school personnel and community members. Find out what people do not know or what they want to know—then provide them with accurate information that responds to their questions or concerns.

FIGURE 16–1   An Outline for a School–Community Relations Plan

transportation employees; and students. Each of these audiences has a definite need for information about the school district, its operation, plans, successes, and limitations. Too often, internal audiences are assumed to know everything that is going on in the school district or school building because they are a part of the organization. This is always an incorrect assumption. Internal audiences are primary and must receive constant and reliable information.

Bagin, Gallagher, and Kindred[10] identified three reasons that good internal communication is critical. First, good *external* communications are not possible without a good internal communications plan. Second, employees are likely to suggest innovative ideas when they know someone is informing and listening to them. Finally, a good internal communications program provides an avenue for employee recognition and helps establish a sense of belonging.

Good communications with internal audiences help build the trust so necessary to the positive functioning of a school district. The primary responsibility for this function rests with the superintendent of schools. Many school districts have public information officers on staff, but in most districts the task of communication rests with the superintendent and his or her office assistants.

Communicating about Board of Education Actions

The board of education is required by law to conduct its business in regular, open, public sessions. There is one exception: the board can meet in executive session to discuss matters pertaining to personnel, negotiations for the acquisition of property, or other matters as prescribed by state law. The public must know that nothing discussed in an executive session becomes binding until the board votes on the matter in an open, public meeting. While the board can establish its own set of policies and procedures for governing the local school district, many of the principles that guide board action are established in state statute.

Communication with the internal audiences of the school is carried out mainly by the superintendent. The superintendent must communicate the policies and operating procedures of the board through written guidelines that are readily available to all staff members and students. We suggest that policy handbooks be made available to the local education association and to all school staff. Further, the superintendent is responsible for the publication of the proceedings of school board meetings and should make them available in each building as soon after a board meeting as possible.

An increasing number of school boards record their board meetings on audio- or videotape. Many school districts provide live television coverage of their board meetings. This enables internal and external audiences alike to observe the board from the comfort of their homes if they cannot be present at the actual meeting. While such a provision does not allow for participation in the meetings, it provides access to the board room. Tapes of the proceedings can be made available through the office of the superintendent.

The Superintendent and Internal Audiences

The superintendent sets the pattern for relationships with the internal audiences of the school. Such relationships depend on several variables; one of the most important is the type of alliance enjoyed by the board and superintendent. When the superintendent and the board of education enjoy a good working association, those employed by the school district are likely to perceive the positive impact of that relationship. If, on the other hand, there is a weak alliance between the board and superintendent, school district personnel may become pessimistic about present and future conditions in the school district. An employee's perception of the relationship between the board and superintendent transfers to feelings about working conditions in the district, job security, planning for contract negotiations, and overall productivity. It is important, therefore, for the board and superintendent to maintain a professional public image at all times.

To Observe and Be Observed

One of the occupational hazards of the superintendency is to assume that teachers and staff members do not require regular communication with the superintendent; nothing could be further from reality. Everyone in the organization wants to see and talk to the superintendent; they want him or her to know who they are, what they do, and that what they do matters! One of the most effective internal communications strategies is for the superintendent to maintain a high level of visibility within the school organization. While much of superintendent's time is invested in gaining support from the larger community, his or her availability to meet with staff and be involved with staff is vital in building trust within the school organization. The following are ideas for methods to establish and maintain effective communications inside the school.

Advisory Committees
To assure there is a constant linkage with employee and student groups, the superintendent should maintain several advisory groups composed of internal audiences.

> *Teachers.*   Monthly meetings with representatives of the local education association serve to keep communications open between the administrative staff and the association.
>
> *Staff.*   The importance of meeting with classified staff cannot be overstated. An advisory committee with membership from each employee group can keep the superintendent aware of the needs and concerns of secretaries, custodians, food services personnel, paraprofessionals, transportation workers, and so forth. These groups are among the most important communicators about the school—the information they possess reaches almost every corner of the school community and the external community.
>
> *Students.*   Principals are the primary source of information about students, but students can provide the superintendent with information about curricular and instructional issues that are important for program planning. In organizations driven by attention to quality, feedback from internal customers is critical. Students make up the largest internal customer audience.

Visitations
Regular visits to school buildings and classrooms provide the superintendent with an opportunity to observe what is happening in the classrooms and to have meaningful dia-

logue with teachers and staff about their work. Visitations, like any other important event, should be scheduled so that teachers, principals, and staff can plan for them. Some variations of visitations are as follows:

Building-Level Breakfasts.   The superintendent can provide a light breakfast for staff prior to the opening of the school day. This informal setting is useful for staff to ask questions about district-level items or talk about their successes or needs.

Lunch in the Lounge.   Superintendents may want to consider scheduling brown bag lunches in the faculty lounge or have lunch with faculty and staff in the school cafeteria.

Walk Around.   Schedule a "walk-through tour" with the building principal. While a walk-through may not provide much personal time with teachers, staff, or students, it does demonstrate a commitment to the school and staff.

Meetings with Student Groups.   Most superintendents miss the opportunity to be in contact with students on a day-to-day basis. Among the most enjoyable moments a superintendent can have is to engage in activities such as reading his or her favorite children's book to primary students and carrying on a dialogue with them about their favorite stories. This activity serves to remind school administrators why they work so hard to gather community support for students and schools. Older students appreciate the chance to ask questions of the superintendent as well. Scheduled visits to classrooms at the middle school and senior high levels, as a speaker or listener, can provide insights about student concerns and establish linkages with students.

Celebrations and Recognitions

There should always be time to celebrate an achievement. When teachers, staff, or administrators reach milestones in their careers, celebrate that achievement by recognizing the accomplishment with a note, a visit, or recognition ceremony. A word to the wise: ask staff how they would like to be recognized for their achievements before the recognition is given. Some prefer to be recognized in public, while others are uncomfortable with recognition at teas or coffees given in their honor. Recognize the honorees as they wish to be recognized, but by all means recognize their accomplishments.

Electronic Mail

Many school districts are fortunate enough to have their central office and buildings networked via local area networks. While it is not face-to-face communication, electronic mail provides an excellent avenue to be electronically linked to staff and teachers. When it is impossible to meet or when the situation does not require a meeting, e-mail provides access to the superintendent. E-mail also eliminates "phone tag" and has the potential for much quicker response time.

Newsletters

The minutes of board meetings, announcements of general interest to all employees, job postings, announcements of employee recognition for length of service, and many other topics that are important but not urgent can be communicated in regular newsletters. A bimonthly or monthly newsletter from the office of the superintendent helps keep staff informed of district-level happenings and provides consistency in communication.

Surveys and Questionnaires

Communication is a many-faceted enterprise; it involves asking as well as telling. Staff surveys provide the superintendent with useful data about key issues facing the district. For example, opinions from the faculty and staff (also students and community) regarding an extended school year or alternative school calendar are important when a board engages in the study of such issues.

There are many ways in which the superintendent can remain in touch with internal audiences. The most efficient may be through regular newsletters, memorandums, or surveys; however, the most effective method is to be as visible as possible, as often as possible. The larger the district, the more difficult it becomes to maintain personal communication with every teacher or staff member, but it must remain a high priority. Effective organizations build relationships, and in schools, the superintendent is the front-line relationship builder. The foregoing ideas and practices are among those behaviors that help the school superintendent enhance such relationships.

External Audiences: They Need to Know

Nationwide, approximately 24 percent of the people who live in a community have children of school age. In most cases, these people receive regular information about educational performance from the school their child attends and periodic information from the school district office. However, the majority of citizens no longer have children or grandchildren in school and must rely on other sources for information about the performance of schools. These citizens also need to hear about active learning, innovative teaching methodologies, and successes of students. It is critical that they understand the problems faced by schools and the strategies schools apply to those problems. While it is possible for these citizens to obtain information about the schools through a variety of media sources, school leaders must communicate directly with this sizable audience.

Several issues have had a tremendous impact on American public education during the past two decades. First, there has been constant concern by parents, citizen groups, the business and corporate community, and the federal government about the capacity of public education to perform its academic functions. This condition results, in part, from the perceived weakness of American competitiveness with other industrialized nations and an increasing concern over the standards of public education.

Second, an increase in the number and type of educational opportunities has been extended by a competitive education marketplace. Private educational entrepreneurs are marketing a variety of alternatives to public schools, and home schooling has become a legal choice for many parents. Meanwhile, traditional private and parochial interests have continued to draw higher performing students away from public education.

Third, the explosion of information and access to it has given rise to the age of the informed citizen. Many public schools have not taken full advantage of the new information channels as tools for constructing relationships with communities.

Finally, real wages in the United States have risen slowly while taxes for working class citizens have steadily increased. All the while, the cost of educating America's youth has increased sharply. Part of the increase has stemmed from such new federal and state codes as those requiring asbestos removal, radon detection, testing for lead contamination in water, and educational programs to benefit handicapped individuals, and part comes from the cost of retooling from an industrial to an information society.

According to Cantor,[11] "most nonprofit organizations are mobilized around an issue or a set of issues. For them, communications activity often represents the continuum between ideas and achievement." Certainly, this is the case for public schools. As public education continues to occupy the media spotlight, public school leaders need to present information about the achievements of schools more aggressively rather than assume everyone is aware of them.

The Superintendent and External Audiences

In the past, public school districts have not needed to market their programs or successes to gain an advantage over their competition. Neither have they asked for or received valuable input from the mixed array of publics that make up the external audience. For the most part, programs planned with the purpose of communicating with external publics have been limited or nonexistent. Now, however, there is a necessity to inform and elicit information from those who are external to the schooling enterprise. The public is making choices about how it will spend its tax dollar. The legislative arena has been selected by special interest and pressure groups to lobby for or against concessions to public entities that use tax dollars. Public schools have found it necessary to inform internal and external publics about their plans and programs.

Communication with external audiences is a two-way street. Schools should utilize typical information channels such as newsletters, brochures, news releases, and radio or television programs. Additionally, Figure 16–2 lists several unique ways the school district can communicate with external audiences. School leaders must also invite external audiences to observe what the schools are doing and enlist their assistance in planning for the future. Worthwhile methods to involve external audiences include the strategic planning or school improvement process, the formation of advisory committees, and the use of public forum. These methods are effective for providing data and gathering information about important topics.

School Improvement Planning (Strategic Planning)

School districts have become much more sophisticated about planning for the future. One of the methodologies used to assist schools in the design of desirable futures is strategic planning, or school improvement planning. The concept underlying this type of planning is widespread involvement from internal and external audiences of the school. The process involves an examination of the mission (purpose and function) of the school, a study of the past performances of the school or school district, a look at strengths, weaknesses, opportunities, and threats, the development of objectives designed to enable the school to better accomplish its mission, and finally, the implementation of those objectives. One key to the success of strategic planning is the composition of the steering team, which usually has a membership of 25 to 30 people. Approximately one-half of this group should be made up of students, teachers, administrators, several board of education members (internal audiences), and one-half should be selected from the external audiences: representatives from business, the ministerial association, parents, senior citizens, non–public school parents, and other interested patrons. Strategic planning is discussed in detail in Chapter 7.

School improvement planning is a continuous process, but initially, the steering committee will be invited to work with the process for nine months to one year. During this

1. *Establish a Speakers' Bureau:* School staff members possess expertise in a variety of education-related and non-education related fields. The school can establish a speakers' bureau and furnish a list of names to community service groups, civic organizations, and public or private entities wishing to make use of the resource. School personnel can earn recognition for themselves and the school by demonstrating their talents and expertise in this manner.

2. *Participate in Community Activities:* School personnel can become isolated from the community by the very nature of their work. For example, teachers rarely have an opportunity to meet with members of the business community during the day. By participating in community-wide events or serving on special events committees, school staff members demonstrate their concern for community recognition or community betterment programs.

3. *Invite the Community to School:* When new programs are implemented at the school site level, invite the community to come to the school to view the program in operation. For example, when the school develops a new science or technology lab it should issue invitations to the primary employers (obtain a list through the local Industrial Development Foundation) in the community to visit the lab in action. Have students explain the operation of the lab to employers.

4. *Establish Partnerships:* Businesses and the professional community should be encouraged to form partnerships with schools to encourage academic achievement, provide training stations, or assist educators with the development of up to date programs of study. However, partnerships with parents are the most effective liaisons the school can provide. Parents must be encouraged to become partners with the school; to promote good study habits and positive attitudes toward learning on the part of students.

5. *Establish a School Foundation:* Public school foundations have been instrumental in raising funds for academics and activities. School foundations also can be extremely helpful in sponsoring recognition events. Schools are generally prohibited from expending tax dollars to recognize staff or students. Foundations can provide the funding for these important events and in the process promote the school and inform the community about student or staff achievements. Annual recognition banquets honoring student scholars, retiring faculty and staff, or the recognition of the accomplishment of various school goals can be handled through the school foundation. It is an excellent way to bring recognition to the school and involve the community in the process.

FIGURE 16–2   Strategies for Involvement with External Audiences

period school officials will provide vital information about the school, its operations and programs, and concerns for the future to the steering committee. The steering committee will be asked to examine future scenarios for the school and design objectives that will enable the school to be successful in the present and future. Once the steering committee has agreed on three to five high-priority objectives, another group of internal and external audiences will be invited to participate in the process by writing step-by-step plans for carrying out the objectives. Eventually, the process finds its way to the board of education for its approval. The utility of the process lies in its ability to capture ideas from diverse audiences while communicating the needs of the school. It provides for a voice by the community and enables the school to communicate its needs.

Key Communicators

As previously discussed, in every community there are people who other people talk to when they need to know something. Resource persons are often opinion leaders. The superintendent must identify and utilize these key communicators as an effective means of distributing information about the school. Business leaders, ministers, civic leaders, small business owners, and others who come into contact with many people during the course of the day should be considered key communicators. Key communicators must be honest, straightforward, and reliable. School officials must explain their role, invite them to serve in the capacity of key communicator, and meet with them regularly to keep them well informed. Such persons will serve as excellent sources of information for the superintendent in addition to their assistance in communicating about the school district.

Advisory Committees

An invitation can be a powerful motivator. When the invitation is in the form of a request to serve on a school advisory committee, most citizens welcome it as an opportunity. Advisory committees are designed to provide advice to the superintendent or the board of education. It should be made clear that the advice offered by the committee will be forwarded to the appropriate authorities but, for political, financial, or other reasons, may not always be accepted.

Advisory committees are an important means of gathering input about school boundary changes, facilities planning, bond elections, student discipline issues, program review, and other school matters. Many federal programs require input from citizen advisory committees; their scope should be extended to issues of state and local concern as well.

Public Forums

There are some issues that require immediate communication to the community or require input from a large number of people. Public forums are excellent strategies to do both. Public forums, which may be conducted as public hearings, require clear rules so the participants can proceed in an orderly, timely fashion. Prior to the opening of the public forum, guidelines for conducting the forum should be explained. These guidelines may include an introduction of the topic under discussion, a time for the school district to present facts about the topic or issue, limitations on the time of speakers and respondents, and so on. Each public forum should begin and end on time; if more time is needed to explain or address the issue, another forum can be scheduled. Public forums are used to explain and gain input about such matters as new policies, school district budgets, proposals for facility construction, or other issues that would best be discussed in an open, public arena.

The ideas just outlined are examples of methods to enhance communication with the public about important issues and receive its input as part of the process. Providing opportunities for two-way communications is critical to building trust with the community.

Crisis Communication

Communicating effectively during a crisis is crucial. School personnel cannot predict when a crisis may occur, but they can be ready if a crisis situation erupts. According to Linke,[12] "the consequences of miscommunicating in a crisis can be devastating to you, your employer, and others involved. Right after solving the crisis . . . communication is the most critical factor in determining how you and your organization will survive a crisis." Logically, schools are vulnerable to certain types of accidents and occurrences. Before a crisis situation arises, the superintendent, board, faculty, and staff should examine issues that have potential to develop into critical situations and examine ways to deal with them. The following examples are illustrations of potential crisis situations:

1. An accident involving a school bus carrying school children
2. A fire at a school building
3. The death or serious injury of a student, faculty, or staff member
4. Disagreements over school curriculum or textbooks that erupt into headline news
5. An alleged violation of a federal or state regulatory code
6. Reported drug use by students at a district event or in the school
7. An accusation that a faculty or staff member has mishandled school funds or was inappropriately involved with students

While it is not a pleasant task to outline the incidents that could lead to a crisis, it is inconceivable not to have done so. People are entitled to a rapid response from schools in the delivery of good and bad news. Once the areas of potential crises have been identified, school district personnel need to develop a plan of action to use if the worst-case scenario develops. In all cases the plan should include the following considerations:

1. Establish a predesignated site for a crisis control center. Usually, the site is the district office. Inform the board and all other key personnel of the crisis immediately.
2. The superintendent acts as the designated spokesperson in all crisis circumstances. He or she may refer media sources to other individuals if and when appropriate, but everyone should be made aware there will be only one designated spokesperson for the school district.
3. Address the situation immediately. Any delay in acknowledging the crisis or announcing probable courses of action will only complicate the issue.
4. Announce the procedure the district will follow to investigate and report developments in the matter.
5. Dispatch a crisis team to work with the situation. Most school districts have crisis teams of administrators, counselors, faculty, and staff members appointed and trained for emergency situations.
6. Be available to communicate about the crisis for as long as the situation exists or until it has been resolved.
7. Above all, be honest, open, and do not speculate. Act only on solid evidence.

Responding to Accusations and Criticism

Most organizations do not enjoy criticism, but it is a fact of life and must be accommodated. It is not unusual for various school publics to find fault with a school program, a teaching methodology, or student assessment plan. Some criticism results from misinformation or a lack of information. Regardless of the reason, the school leadership must respond in an appropriate manner. According to Arnsparger and Ledell,[13] it is important "to focus on communicating your message rather than on responding to accusations with point-to-point rebuttal. Accusations do not create an information base on which to conduct a debate." However, accusations and unfounded criticism can spark emotional statements and quickly escalate a situation to a conflict state. Under these circumstances, in addition to the steps mentioned for crisis communication, brief the staff, select a spokesperson, and invite the media to the school. We also suggest the following:

1. Be certain you are clear about the issue or issues that are the target of the criticism. Gather facts.
2. It is advisable to prepare a written statement about the situation and have it available for distribution. Avoid the use of educational jargon when preparing such statements.
3. Do not overreact or become defensive. Respond to all questions, and offer information to all who request it.
4. Do not personalize the situation. When insults or accusations are aimed at you, keep your emotions under control.

It is not uncommon for organized opponents of public education, poorly informed patrons, misguided citizens, or other groups and individuals to blame schools for many of the problems they see as rampant in the larger society. It may be difficult to remember when the school is being accused of malfeasance or misfeasance, but the public schools belong to the public. The superintendent and staff are employed to care for public education and create an understanding with the public about the mission of the schools. Superintendents and the staff must be prepared to deal with the situation in a rational manner, regardless of the nature of the attack.

The News Media

The news media are a primary source of assistance for schools and should be included in the communications plan of every school district. Schools are part of the mainstream of American life; people are naturally interested in them. Schools are a common topic of people gathered at work or at play. The role of the press is to help people stay informed about their world, and schools share the spotlight with other public entities. Ordovensky and Marx[14] put it this way: "When you decided to get involved in education, you also committed yourself to working with the news media." The news media provide people with access to the events of the day, week, month, and year. Many times those events involve the school.

News: what is it? Some describe it as occurrences or events that either fall short of or exceed commonly held expectations about organizations or people. For example, students are expected to perform at the national norm on standardized tests. It is news when they fall short or greatly exceed the norm. It is assumed that school are safe places for students. When violent outbreaks occur at a school site, that is news. News is the unusual. Ordovensky and Marx[15] stated, "Two times when educators must work with the media are: when the media want something from them and, conversely, when educators want something from the media." The relationship between the school and the media must accommodate both parties.

The definition of news as the unusual could lead school administrators to the conclusion that schools might not get much press. It is true that much of the activity in schools can be classified as information and not news. Superintendents and other educators must learn to recognize opportunities to invite the media to report stories that can enlighten readers about events in the school: the implementation of an advanced science program, a high technology lab, or the announcement of National Merit Scholarship recipients. By the same token, school administrators must be prepared to respond to media questions about staff reductions, budget proposals, or negotiations with employee groups. Communication is a two-way street.

Tips for Working with the Media

There are ground rules for working with the media. Many of the rules are universally accepted and should be understood and followed by every superintendent. Bagin, Gallagher, and Kindred[16] have provided excellent guidelines for school administrators and their working relationships with the press. Some of the guidelines are summarized as follows:

1. *Be honest!*   Above all else, tell the truth. If you do not know the answer to the question, say you do not know, but you will apprise the media when you have the information.
2. *Respond immediately.*   Reporters are on deadlines. They have a legitimate need for certain information. Build strong relationships by responding to the reporters' deadlines. It will pay dividends.
3. *Understand what kind of information is public.*   All surveys and reports conducted or issued by the district are public information. If they are preliminary, you do not have to release them, but if they are final copies, you must.
4. *Never say "no comment."*   It appears you have something to hide or are not willing to share information. Never, under any circumstance, resort to the "no comment" phrase!
5. *Stay away from educational jargon.*   All occupations have a certain jargon that may be commonly used by insiders. Educators have developed an extensive jargon, but it should be avoided when speaking with the media. Use common words and explanations if you want the public to understand and appreciate your story.
6. *Provide accurate information.*   Many stories about schools involve budget figures or staffing assignments. Be certain the information you provide is accurate. Your reputation and that of the reporter rests on the accuracy of your statements.
7. *Never go "off the record."*   When speaking with the media, the superintendent provides information for public consumption. There is no room for "off the record" comments; in actuality, there is no such thing. Anything the superintendent says is for the record. If there is something that should not be said or cannot be during an interview—do not say it.

These guidelines represent only a few of the important considerations the superintendent must consider when working with the media. It is critical that they be followed closely when the media are live television or radio. The opportunity to correct or clean up statements does not exist. Print media are more forgiving, but nonetheless, they rely on the accuracy of the statements made by the superintendent or district spokesperson.

The news media are an integral part of the school–community relations process. The best advice to superintendents is learn to understand and appreciate the role of the media. Its purpose is to provide citizens with vital information about their public schools. A good relationship with reporters and publishers creates the openness that is required for excellent school–community relations.

Summary

School restructuring and school reform are part of a common vocabulary shared by educators and policymakers. Restructuring implies change, and the prospect of change makes most people uncomfortable. Whether schools decide to change a little at a time, plan dramatic changes in their operations, or do not plan to change at all, the need for a well-designed school–community relations program is critical. People want and need to know about their schools, and school districts need to build and maintain a community awareness of the vision for education.

Every school district must implement a program designed to communicate with the internal and external audiences of the school. Teachers and staff, who are well informed about the mission and objectives of the school, serve as a strong foundation for communication with the larger community. Each community has a power structure, special interest groups, and people who pay the bills but may not ask many questions. Each of these audiences must have information about the purpose and function of the school and how the school performs in its mission. The visibility of the superintendent in community activities and his or her participation in service organizations and civic groups help build a strong professional identity, which is key to fruitful interaction with the community and culture surrounding the schools.

The school board, superintendent, and staff are responsible for the design and implementation of the school–community relations plan. The program must address routine and crisis situations in an active, responsive manner. Newly appointed superintendents should invest some of their time in observing the community and schools, asking questions about how things work, and becoming acquainted with the various sources of power within the education organization and the community at large. The job description of the superintendent usually includes the function of district spokesperson with the media and other audiences. This provision entails being honest and straightforward about the conditions facing the school and providing accurate information in all communications.

There are numerous ways to receive and distribute information. Advisory committees, strategic planning teams, key communicators, and regular visits to school buildings help the superintendent maintain a sense of perspective about the condition of the district. The news media are an important ally and a necessary part of the school–community relations plan. The superintendent has to develop the trust of the media and understand the important role they play in assisting the school to receive and disseminate information.

Schools often are convenient targets of criticism by special interest groups and concerned citizens. The schools belong to the public and are under constant scrutiny from internal and external constituencies. Superintendents must welcome the opportunity to serve as articulate spokespersons for education. The manner in which they communicate, the trust they build with audiences, and the way they build confidence in the system itself are measures of their success as school–community relations leaders. Information is the lifeblood of business and commerce; the schools are no exception. A well-planned program for communications aims to inform the public about the vision of education in the community and serves to build confidence in schools.

Discussion Questions

1. Why is it important for a school district to have a well-conceived, operational school–community relations program?

2. Make a list of the internal audiences in your school district. What kinds of information would be most helpful to each audience? How would you be certain they received timely, appropriate information?

3. What kinds of information would you prepare for a public hearing on the proposed school budget? When would the information be distributed and to whom?

4. Why is a crisis communication plan so important for a school district? List the elements of a well-designed crisis communications plan.

5. Why is it important to invest time and energy in communications with senior citizens? What other special interest groups would you identify as key audiences?

6. How does a school district know if its communications plan is working?

7. What kinds of information should school districts try to collect through written or telephone surveys?

CASE 16.1   Decisions about Decision Making

For the past two years the College View School District had studied the concept of site-based decision making, an idea that presumed the best decisions are made by those closest to the decision. For example, it is assumed that teachers can and should make decisions about the needs and wants of their students and classroom. By the same token, principals, with assistance from faculty and staff, make the best educational decisions at the building level. The concept had received favorable attention from the news media.

After discussions with faculty and staff, the board of education approved a plan, designed by Superintendent George Stephan, to implement site-based decision making in the College View schools. The plan included a description of the responsibility and authority held by each level of the organization. As an example, the superintendent's office had the primary responsibility for overall curriculum design, budget development, building operation and maintenance, and coordination of human services. Building levels were charged with such responsibilities as determination of instructional methodologies, selection and assignment of staff, and professional development.

As a first step the building principal, along with the faculty and staff, was empowered to decide how his or her building budget would be used. They were to assume the responsibility for developing a plan to use the money provided by the district. All funds that had previously been tightly categorized were now allocated as a lump sum with the instruction that the site level could best decide where to use its resources to affect education.

While Superintendent Stephan was confident that the plan would work, he anticipated a number of problems at the outset and was prepared to respond to questions and complaints as they surfaced.

Questions

1. Develop a list of questions that will most likely arise from faculty and staff as site-based decision making is implemented.

2. Recommend a plan to inform the public about the concept so that it is assured that tax funds continue to be well managed and spending is not out of control.

3. Recommend how Superintendent Stephan can keep administrators, faculty, and staff informed about their authority and responsibility.

4. Provide an assessment as to how long it might take for the site-based decision-making process to become an integral part of the district culture.

5. How would you answer critics in the community who accuse the board and superintendent of "giving up control of the district" to teachers and staff? How would you respond to teachers who complain that they are doing administrative work for teacher's pay?

Inbasket Exercise

INBASKET 16.1

School Bus Accident

One icy, winter morning a school bus with 40 elementary students on board was struck in the side by a truck that had failed to stop at an intersection. The impact caused the bus to tip over on its side and collide with a string of cars stopped at a red light. Several children and the bus driver were injured, although not seriously. A passerby called the school district office on her car phone to alert the superintendent of the accident. One of the local radio stations announced the accident within several minutes of its occurrence and had a crew on the scene almost immediately.

Phone calls poured into the superintendents office; parents, grandparents, reporters, and concerned citizens sought information.

Response

1. If you were the superintendent of schools, what would be your course of action in this situation?
2. How would you notify parents of the students who had been injured?
3. Make a list of the people you need to contact as a result of the accident. Who should be contacted first? How will the contacts be made and by whom?

Notes

1. Jack A. Culbertson, "A Century's Quest for a Knowledge Base, in *Handbook of Research in Educational Administration,* ed. by Norman J. Boyan (New York: Longman, 1988), p. 9.

2. Frank W. Lutz, and Carol Merz, *The Politics of School/Community Relations* (New York: Teachers College Press, 1992), pp. 4–11.

3. Ibid. p. 152.

4. Don Bagin, Donald Gallagher, and Leslie Kindred, *The School and Community Relations,* 5th ed. (Boston: Allyn and Bacon, 1994), p. 1.

5. Carolyn Hughes-Chapman (Research Team Coordinator), "A Study of Beginning Superintendents: Preliminary Implications for Leading and Learning," an unpublished paper presented at the annual convention of the University Council for Educational Administrators, Houston, Tex., 29 October 1993, p. 10.

6. Stephen Covey, *The Seven Habits of Highly Effective People* (New York: Simon and Schuster, 1989), pp. 235–260.

7. Donald McCarty and Charles E. Ramsey, *The School Managers: Power and Conflict in American Public Education* (Westport, Conn.: Greenwood, 1971), pp. 17–18.

8. Bill Cantor, *Experts in Action: Inside Public Relations* (ed. by Chester Burger) (New York: Longman, 1989), p. 154.

9. J. A. Kinder, *School Public Relations: Communicating to the Community* (Bloomington, Ind.: Phi Delta Kappa Educational Foundation, 1982), p. 11.

10. Bagin et al., *The School and Community Relations,* p. 91.

11. Bill Cantor, *Experts in Action: Inside Public Relations,* p. 106.

12. Ibid., p. 166.

13. Arlene Arnsparger and Marjorie Ledell, *How to Deal with Community Criticism of School Change* (Reston, Va.: Association for Supervision and Curriculum Development, 1993), p. 27.

14. Pat Ordovensky and Gary Marx, *Working with the News Media* (Arlington, Va.: American Association of School Administrators, 1993), p. 1.

15. Ibid., p. 2.

16. Bagin et al., *The School and Community Relations,* pp. 196–202.

Index

benefits of viable school policies, 159
chief executive officer/educational leader in district, 118–120
collective bargaining, 287, 289–291, 300
colonial America, 5, 6–7
culture articulation, 76
evaluations, 125–126
functions in 1923-1933, 12
issues and challenges of 1945-1982, 15-18
leadership in instructional planning, 256–259
maintenance and staffing of facilities, 244
newly employed and responsibilities of school boards, 115
organization climate, 302
privatization, 33–34
school board relationship, 120–125
understanding the community power structure, 95–96
Suppes, P., 147(15), *152, 153*
Support groups, 65–66
Support services, budget reductions, 207, 209
Surveys
school/community and facility planning, 229–232
superintendent communication with internal audience, 345
Swimming pools, 228. *See also* Facility planning
Sybouts, W., 137(12), 142(13), *152, 153*, 230(14), 232(14), *248,* 269(26), *273*
Sylvan Learning Systems, 32–33
Systems theory, educational planning, 133–134
Systems thinking, building strategies for leaders, 57

Taba, H., 251(6), 260(16), *273*
Talents, assignment process, 300. *See also* Human resources
Tannenbaum, A. S., 275(6), *293*
Task force, policy development, 170. *See also* Policies
Taxation
competing power bases, 97
school budgets, 27
Taylor, J., 211(42), 213(44), *220*
Teachers. *See also* Teaching
choosing in colonial America, 3
hiring and site-based budgeting, 204–205
needs and student enrollment, 39
role in charter schools, 32   student relationships, 316, 325–326
violence against, 42–43
Teachers' associations, 279–282

Teachers' unions
historical development and collective bargaining, 275–278
privatization, 33
Teaching. *See also* Teachers
colonial America and Boards of Education, 3
experience, 60
Team learning, building strategies for leaders, 56–57
Team Review process, 125–126
Technology
curriculum planning, 263
facility planning, 223–224
Teenagers, subculture, 329
Telephone banks, bond/budget campaigns, 217. *See also* Bonds
Television, cultural experiences, 89
Tenneman v. Town of Gorham, 193
Tensions, school boards and superintendents, 17–18, 21
Tenure, 66, 303. *See also* Human resources
Terms implied by law/customs, 181
Terms or acts prohibited by public policy, 180–181
Territory, new meaning, 89
Texas, 157
Textbook content, 255. *See also* Curriculum
Thefts, school property, 41. *See also* Crime; Violence
Thelen, H. A., 77(18), *85*
Theme, bond/budget campaigns, 214–215. *See also* Bonds
Thomas, S. B., 198(4), *219*
Thompson, D. C., 199(8, 10), 201(16), 204(23), *219*
Thompson, J. W., 80(28, 31), *86*
Time allocation, 258–259. *See also* Curriculum
Time demands, superintendents, 64–65
Timeliness, effective policies, 172. *See also* Policies
Tobin, K., 325(18), *334*
Toffler, A., 101(12), *107*, 131(2), *152, 153*
Tools, instruction, 262. *See also* Curriculum
Tort duty, 181
Tort of negligent hiring, 189
Tortious interference with employment relationship. *See* Employment expectancy
Total Quality Management (TQM)
curriculum planning, 259
performance link, 30
TQM, see Total quality management
Traditional school building, 227. *See also* Facility planning

Training
school board members and superintendent's role, 122–123
for workplace, curricular trends, 267
Transactional leadership, 30
Transformational leadership, 29–30
Trends
curriculum planning, 258
strategic planning, 138
Trust
building strategies for leaders, 53, 54
superintendent and school board members, 123
win-win bargaining, 284
Tucker, S., 29(17), 30(21), *48*
Twentieth century
public education, 88
school governance, 109
Tyack, D., 88(2, 3), *106*
Tyack, D. B., 9(28, 30), *24*
Tyler, R. W., 260(18), *273*
Ubben, G. C., 280(15), 286(23), *294*
Understanding of subject, exemplary teachers, 325. *See also* Students

Unionization, teachers, 15
United States Bureau of the Census, 113(9), *129*
United States Department of Education, 28, 39(63, 64), *49*, 253(12), *273*
United States Department of Labor, 321(12, 13), 323(12), *334*
University Council of Educational Administration, 14
Usdan, M., 315(1), *334*
Usdan, M. D., 111(5), *129*
User fees, 212. *See also* Nontax revenues

Values, politics relationship, 91–94
Van Zwoll, J., 300(13), *314*Vested interests, 284. *See also* Collective bargaining
Victims, students as, 41–42
Violations of Rehabilitation Act of 1973, 192
Violence. *See also* Crime
schools, 40–44, 327–328
tool for influencing policy/policymakers, 101
Visibility, superintendents, 63, 343–345
Vision
curriculum planning, 257
framework, building strategies for leaders, 54
implementation in school system culture, 82
as responsibility of superintendent, 120
strategic planning, 135, 136
Visioning leadership, characteristics, 79–80